Wen-lin *Studies in the Chinese Humanities*

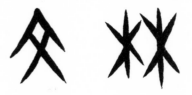

Wen-lin

Studies in the Chinese Humanities

Edited by
Chow Tse-tsung

PUBLISHED FOR
THE DEPARTMENT OF EAST ASIAN LANGUAGES AND LITERATURE OF
THE UNIVERSITY OF WISCONSIN
BY THE UNIVERSITY OF WISCONSIN PRESS
MADISON, MILWAUKEE, AND LONDON, 1968

Published for the
Department of East Asian Languages and Literature of
The University of Wisconsin
By the University of Wisconsin Press
Madison, Milwaukee, and London
U.S.A. : Box 1379, Madison, Wisconsin 53701
U.K. : 26-28 Hallam Street, London, W. 1

Printed in the United States of America
By Cushing-Malloy, Inc., Ann Arbor, Michigan

Library of Congress Catalog Card Number 67-20756

Preface

THIS publication has been inspired by the belief that the absence of a forum specifically for the study of the Chinese humanities can no longer be excused. In the last two decades, Chinese studies in America and Europe have experienced an unprecedented escalation as a result of political change. At present outside of China there are, by our estimate, over two hundred universities and colleges which offer facilities for Chinese studies; a great number of students and specialists are added to the field each year. In addition, the exodus of thousands of Chinese intellectuals and scholars from China and their indefinite residence in the West have brought Chinese and Western civilizations closer than ever before in the already shrinking, but still divided, world of the space age. Viewed in historical perspective, this situation should be recognized as an epochmaking phenomenon, a landmark of acculturation and of human progress. But this recognition comes slowly, and efforts to study Chinese civilization for its own sake and for its significance to mankind are often thwarted by short-range practical considerations. It is our feeling, then, that in the face of the present atmosphere of expediency, research towards a deeper understanding of Chinese civilization and in particular of the Chinese humanities is a most urgent need.

The editorial board of *Wen-lin* hopes that this may be the first of a series dedicated to critical scholarship in the Chinese humanities: language, literature, philosophy, logic, historiography, and the arts. It is our intention that each volume shall emphasize a single field. In this volume emphasis is on literature—especially poetry—although contributions on other subjects are included. The articles are arranged generally according to the time they were received. Against a trend to eliminate Chinese characters from publications in English, our policy is to include as many as necessary not only for the purpose of the identification of terms and for the control of translations but also to bring the subject matter closer to the reader. Unless otherwise credited, all translations in this volume are by the author of the article in which they occur.

The present volume reflects our desire to grant writers maximum freedom regarding both their views and the forms of expression they choose. Though in some cases we have disagreed with a translation, interpretation, or argument, we have not insisted on changes when an author has defended his stand against our editorial suggestions.

Chow Tse-tsung

Madison, Wisconsin
October, 1966

Contents

Wen-lin *Studies in the Chinese Humanities*

T'ao Ch'ien's "Drinking Wine" Poems

JAMES R. HIGHTOWER

T'AO CH'IEN provides a preface to the twenty poems that share the title "Drinking Wine" 飲 酒 二 十 首 :[1]

Living in retirement I have few pleasures, and now the nights are growing longer; so, as I happen to have some excellent wine, not an evening passes without a drink. All alone with my shadow I empty a bottle until suddenly I find myself drunk. And once I am drunk I write a few verses for my own amusement. In the course of time the pages have multiplied, but there is no particular order in what I have written. I have had a friend make a copy, with no more in mind than to provide a diversion.

> 余閒居寡歡 ，兼比夜已長 ，偶有名酒 ，無夕不飲 ；
> 顧影獨盡 ，忽焉復醉 。既醉之後 ，輒題數句自娛 。紙
> 墨遂多 ，辭無詮次 。聊命故人書之 ，以爲歡笑爾 。

This suggests that his title should be understood as "Twenty Poems Written after Drinking," not "Poems about Drinking" or "Poems in Praise of Drinking," which would be the alternate ways of taking it. None of the individual poems of the series has a title; in fact they could as well have been

---

[1] *Ching-chieh hsien-sheng chi*, 3:19b. This is T'ao Ch'u's 陶 澍 edition, 靖 節 先 生 集 , Chiang-su Shu-chü 江 蘇 書 局 wood-block print of 1883. References to T'ao Ch'ien's writings will be to this edition, identified as *Works*. Other editions referred to for their commentaries are Ku Chih 古 直 , 陶 靖 節 詩 箋 , Kuang-wen Shu-chü photographic reprint, Taipei, 1964 (*Yin-chiu* poems, 3:7b–14a, referred to as Ku Chih); Ting Fu-pao 丁 福 保 , *T'ao Yuan-ming shih chien-chu* 箋 注 , I-wen Yin-shu-kuan photographic reprint of original typeset edition of 1927, Taipei, 1964 (*Yin-chiu* poems, 3:12a–20b, referred to as Ting Fu-pao); Wang Yao 王 瑤 , *T'ao Yuan-ming chi*, Tso-chia Ch'u-pan she, Peking, 1956 (*Yin-chiu* poems, pp. 61–70, referred to as Wang Yao).

labeled "Untitled Poems," *tsa shih*,[2] a generic term for lyric poetry in Chinese,[3] or "Poems on the Feelings," *ch'ing shih*, or "Expressing the Feelings," *yung huai*. There is no precedent[4] for T'ao's title, and so it must be considered to be somehow significant, particularly since it is so easily subject to misunderstanding.

The preface further says explicitly that the poems were not written around a common theme,[5] nor on a single occasion, nor were they the product of that source of so much second-rate Chinese verse, social drinking. They are the reflection of the moods of a man with few friends, time on his hands, and wine to drink. T'ao Ch'ien did not always describe his situation in such terms.[6]

The preface is at some pains to warn us against taking the poems too seriously: they were written just for a laugh. The warning hardly seems necessary, given the title. We do not assume in advance that poems on drinking or poems written by someone who has been drinking are going to be serious.

So much for what the preface tells us. What it fails to tell is at least as important. The absence of a specific year is not in itself particularly significant, since only a few of T'ao's poems carry a date in the title.[7] In one poem of this series (XVI) he mentions his age as "nearing forty," but this does not automatically lead us to a date, for there is considerable doubt about when he was born.[8] In another (XIX) he says that a "cycle" has

---

2 Fang Tung-shu (方 東 樹 , 昭 昧 詹 言 , 4) remarked, "From the Preface it is also clear that these are untitled lyrics, in which he writes directly about his feelings or about events. He has just used 'Drinking Wine' as a title; the poems are not in celebration of drinking" (cited from *T'ao Yuan-ming shih-wen hui-p'ing* 彙 評 , Chung-hua Shu-chü, Peking, 1959, p. 158; subsequently referred to as *Hui-p'ing*).

3 Two poems of the series (V and VII) are included in *Wen hsüan* (*SPTK* ed., abbr. *WH*), 30:2a–3a, in the *tsa shih* 雜 詩 category, where they are given no other heading, although they are immediately followed by one of the "In Praise of Impoverished Gentlemen" 詠 貧 士 poems under that title.

4 The *Shu chiu* 述 酒 poem is almost certainly later (*Works*, 3:30a–32a); that it is grouped with this series and the "On Stopping Wine" 止 酒 is a piece of editorial whimsy (or stupidity).

5 Or so "no particular order" is to be understood. It suggests further that there is no meaningful order, that is, there is no hidden meaning beyond the immediate sense of each line.

6 In other poems he speaks of like-minded neighbors and describes visits and excursions with friends. Sometimes at least he had to work long hours in the fields, and one of his stock complaints is the lack of wine.

7 Nine, to be exact. They are all brought together in the beginning of *chüan* 3.

8 He died in 427, all sources are in agreement. The biographies in *Sung shu*, 93:15b, and *Chin shu*, 94:37b, both say he was 63 *sui* when he died. (These and subsequent references

elapsed since his retirement. The date of his final retirement is well established as A.D. 405, and so this gives us either 415 or 417 as the date of these poems, depending on whether you reckon a cycle as ten or twelve years.

The preface mentions "retirement" but does not say where. One is safe in inferring that he was on his farm near Hsün-yang, since in poem XIX he says that he came back to the farm on retiring ten (or twelve) years ago, and poem V says his house is in an inhabited area.

Where did the poet get the supply of wine that kept him going so long? At the rate of one poem per day, we should allow him at least twenty days—a month is not too much. When he could not afford a drink, he did not hesitate to say so. At one time it took the income of a magistrate to keep him in wine,[9] and this wine the preface describes as no ordinary brew. Surely this was a windfall, and one would like to know who the benefactor was. T'ao's biography (*Sung shu*, 93:13a–b) names two men who on occasion provided him with wine: his friend Yen Yen-chih (who, according to one anecdote gave him 20,000 cash, which he then deposited with a wine merchant) and Wang Hung, onetime governor of Chiang-chou, to whom he showed little gratitude for many favors. Yen Yen-chih was stationed in Hsün-yang in 415–416, and so is a possible source of T'ao's wine supply. Wang Hung, however, did not receive his appointment as governor of Chiang-chou until 418, and his reported acquaintance with T'ao must be after the latest probable date for these poems.

The preface does not say who the intended reader of the poems is, but the fact that the poet had someone make a clean copy strongly suggests that the poems were to be sent to someone, perhaps circulated among his acquaintances generally.

Perhaps it is best now to take a look at the poems themselves which are introduced so circumstantially and ambiguously. I have made the translations as close to the original as I could, compatible with a modicum of metrical regularity.[10] After each poem comes an interpretation, in which

---

to the Standard Histories are to the T'ung-wen ed. unless otherwise specified.) More recent guesses have been 56 (Liang Ch'i-ch'ao) and 52 (Ku Chih). The most recent, and exhaustive, treatment of this problem is by Yang Yung, 楊 勇, 陶 淵 明 年 譜 彙 考, 新 亞 學 報 7:1 (1965), 215–304, who argues persuasively for the traditional dates.

9 His biography (*Sung shu*, 93:12a) says that when he was given the post of Magistrate of P'eng-tse, he proposed to plant all the fields assigned him with glutinous rice, to brew wine with.

10 All twenty poems are in a regular 5-beat meter, with rhymes at the end of alternate lines. I have not tried to rhyme my translations, and for several poems have used a 4-beat meter to avoid the necessity of padding, something I have not altogether escaped in the others.

I try to make clear my own understanding—or lack of understanding—of the tenor of the poem. It is followed by a line-by-line commentary, dealing with alternate interpretations, significant variants,[11] deviations in my translation from the Chinese text, other translations,[12] allusions, and other passages in T'ao's poetry that seem relevant.

I

Decline and growth have no fixed time,	衰 榮 無 定 在
Everyone gets his share of both:	彼 此 更 共 之
Master Shao of the melon patch	邵 生 瓜 田 中
Used to be Lord of Tungling.	甯 似 東 陵 時
Cold weather alternates with hot	寒 暑 有 代 謝
And so it is with human lives —	人 道 每 如 茲
Intelligent men understand	達 人 解 其 會
And are beset no more with doubts.	逝 將 不 復 疑
When chance brings them a jug of wine	忽 與 一 觴 酒
They take it gladly as night comes on.	日 夕 歡 相 持

The first poem of the series begins with a statement of the vicissitudes of human life and ends by recommending a stoical acceptance of fate—tempered by recourse to the wine bottle — a theme T'ao Ch'ien has dealt with elsewhere, most dramatically in the "Substance, Shadow, Spirit" poems (*Works,* 2:1a–2b). All in all, this first poem accords well with what was promised in the preface.

In line 3, Master Shao is Shao P'ing, onetime Marquis of Tung-ling, who after the fall of the Ch'in, was reduced to raising melons for a living.[13]

The "human lives" of line 6 is literally "the Way of man," *jen tao,* i.e., good fortune and bad come in turn. The doubts (in line 8) of which intelligent men (*ta jen,* "men of understanding") are able to rid themselves are presumably those about the vagaries of fate and the course of action to pursue in

---

11 I have not listed the ones that are obvious corruptions or that cannot be treated meaningfully in translation. This is not to claim that there exists a satisfactory critical edition of T'ao Ch'ien's poetry. However, Ting Fu-pao's edition lists most of the textual variants.

12 I have not made any attempt to note every deviation in my version from other published translations. The only critical, scholarly translations of all twenty poems are: Anna Bernhardi, "Tau Jüan-ming," *Mitteilungen des Seminars für Orientalische Sprachen,* 15 (1912), 85–105; Anna Bernhardi and Erwin von Zach, "T'ao Yuan-ming," *MSOS,* 18 (1918), 189–228; Suzuki Torao, 鈴木虎雄, *Tō Emmei shi kai* 陶淵明詩解, Kōbundō, Tokyo, 1948; Shiba Rokuro, 斯波六郎, *Tō Emmei shi,* Tōmon Shohō, Kyoto, 1951; Ikkai Tomoyoshi, 一海知義, *Tō Emmei (Chūkoku Shijin Senshū),* Iwanami Shoten, Tokyo, 1958. My references to them are by author.

13 He is mentioned in Hsiao Ho's biography, *Shih chi,* 53:4a–b, for the advice he offered: to avoid future trouble by refusing an excessive reward.

a world of uncertainty. Line 8 is remarkable in consisting mostly of "empty" words, and it is reasonable to ask whether *fu* after the negative is no more than emphatic (as it often is in T'ao's poetry) rather than "again" ("no more" in the translation). But the force of *shih chiang*[14] is future time or intention, so it seems likely that the freedom from doubt is made contingent on grasping the principle.

"Chance" in line 9 is not really personified. The word is *hu*, "suddenly, unexpectedly," hence, "by chance." Line 10 "as night comes on" is literally "when the sun sets." There may be an echo of the same allusion that underlies line 10 of poem XIII, with the implied admonition "Prolong these uncertain joys."

II

Do good, they say, and your reward will come —	積 善 云 有 報
Po-i and Shu-ch'i found theirs on West Mountain.	夷 叔 在 西 山
Since good and evil go without reward,	善 惡 苟 不 應
What's the point of all the cant they talk?	何 事 立 空 言
Jung at ninety with his belt of rope	九 十 行 帶 索
Was cold and hungry as in youthful days.	飢 寒 況 當 年
A man must learn a firmness in adversity	不 賴 固 窮 節
For his name to live a thousand years.	百 世 當 誰 傳

There has been no preparation for the bitterness of this second poem. Po-i and Shu-ch'i are the favorite Confucian exemplars of unselfishness and loyalty: they left home so that their brother could inherit their father's fief, and they were loyal to the fallen Shang dynasty, refusing to eat the bread of Chou. Their reward was that they starved[15] on Shou-yang-shan (West Mountain). The conviction that there is a moral order in the world is basic to Confucian thinking, and a great deal is written about it in the classical texts, but such occurrences are enough to shake one's faith in the proposition. All that T'ao Ch'ien can salvage out of Confucian doctrine is the consolation Confucius offered his disciples when they found themselves in straits: "The gentleman is firm in adversity; the mean man in adversity goes all to pieces."[16]

Elsewhere T'ao Ch'ien expresses the hope that such "firmness in adversity"

---

14 *Shih-chiang* is an archaic formula from *Shih ching*, no. 113. Of the rest of the words in the line, only *i*, "to doubt," is technically a "full" word.

15 A variant reading of T'ao Ch'ien's line 2 has 飢 "starved" for 在 "were on."

16 *Lun yü*, 15/2, 君 子 固 窮 , 小 人 窮 斯 濫 矣 .

is as good a way to achieve lasting fame as is active participation in the affairs of the world:[17]

> In my poor hut I shall work out my salvation —   養 眞 衡 茅 下
> This too is perhaps a way to make myself a name.   庶 以 善 自 名

Here he only cites the examples of Po-i, Shu-ch'i, and Jung Ch'i-ch'i, without directly mentioning the word "fame," though the implication is clear. (Literally, the last couplet reads, "Had they not depended on firmness in adversity,/Who would have handed them down for a hundred generations?") T'ao would not have been surprised and might have been gratified to discover that his name was to be preserved in the histories among the recluses rather than the poets.[18]

The *I ching* is the immediate source for the *k'ung yen*, "empty words"[19] ("all the cant they talk") in line 4: "A family that accumulates good deeds will be sure to have abundant blessing."[20] T'ao Ch'ien challenged this idea in similar terms in his "Lament for Gentlemen Born out of Their Times,"[21] where he says of Po-i and of Confucius' disciple Yen-hui,

> Though the one loved learning and the other practiced   雖 好 學 與 行 義
>   righteousness
> Their lives were hard and their deaths bitter.   何 死 生 之 苦 辛
> I suspect that this is the way virtue is rewarded,   疑 報 德 之 若 茲
> I fear that this teaching is no more than empty words.   懼 斯 言 之 虛 陳

Jung Ch'i-ch'i is not mentioned by name in line 5, which reads "At ninety he was still[22] wearing a rope for a belt," a direct reference to *Lieh-tzu*, where Confucius meets Jung Ch'i-ch'i, "dressed in deerskin with a rope for a belt, plucking his lute and singing."[23] He occurs again in poem XI below, and in No. 3 of the series "In Praise of Impoverished Gentlemen" (*Works*, 4:10a): "Old man Jung wore a belt of rope/And

---

17 "Returning to Chiang-ling after Leave, Written at T'u-k'ou at Night during the Seventh Moon of the Year 401," lines 19–20, *Works*, 3:12b–13a.

18 His biography occurs in *Sung shu*, 93:11b–15b; *Nan shih*, 75:2a–5b, and *Chin shu*, 94:34b–37b, in the chapter devoted to Recluses 隱 逸 in each case.

19 A variant in line 4 is 空 立 言 "pointlessly establishes a principle." Though *k'ung yen* usually is contrasted with 行 事 "to carry out in practice" (e.g., the remark attributed to Confucius by Ssu-ma Ch'ien in his Postface to the *Shih chi*, 130:9b), T'ao Ch'ien elsewhere uses it as here; see below.

20 *I ching*, *k'un*, *wen yen*: 積 善 之 家 必 有 餘 慶 .

21 See J. R. Hightower, "The *fu* of T'ao Ch'ien," *HJAS*, 17 (1954), 207, where the second couplet is inadvertently telescoped into one line.

22 行 in the common Six Dynasties usage of "going on, still."

23 *Lieh-tzu* (*SPTK* ed.), 1:4b.

happily played his lute even so" — this right out of *Lieh-tzu*. However, the *Lieh-tzu* account does not make Jung Ch'i-ch'i an appropriate example of goodness unrewarded (the emphasis is rather on recognizing that the important things in life have nothing to do with poverty and low estate), and the second line of the couplet, "Cold and hunger all the worse[24] in the years of his prime,"[25] adds a detail for which we have no textual evidence. The reference in poem XI, "Old man Jung was said to be a sage,/ ... And he knew hunger all his life long," is in the same vein, and suggests that T'ao Ch'ien knew another anecdote about him.

The "thousand years" of line 8 is a metrical compromise with *po shih*, "a hundred generations."

III

The Way has declined almost a thousand years	道 喪 向 千 載
And all men now hold back their impulses.	人 人 惜 其 情
Give them wine, and they refuse to drink,	有 酒 不 肯 飲
Their only care is for their reputation.	但 顧 世 間 名
Whatever gives the body any value	所 以 貴 我 身
Is it not just this one single life?	豈 不 在 一 生
But how long is a lifetime after all?	一 生 復 能 幾
It is brief as the startling lightning bolt.	倏 如 流 電 驚
Staid and stolid through their hundred years	鼎 鼎 百 年 內
What do they ever hope to get from this?	持 此 欲 何 成

What is the Way that has been declining? A thousand is of course only a large, round number: counting back from A.D. 400 to the time of Confucius, for example, you get some nine hundred years — "almost a thousand."[26] But Confucius was no great advocate of yielding to impulse, and the statement about the Way's decline suggests, textually, *Chuang-tzu*: "The world has lost the Way, and the Way has lost the world. World and Way have lost contact with one another. How can a man committed to the Way prosper in the world, and how can the world prosper in the Way? ... A sage may not be a hermit in the hills, but [if he lives in the world], his virtue is hidden."[27] Kuo Hsiang's commentary on the passage brings in the word

---

24 This is perhaps taking 況 too literally. "Especially" or "one can be sure" is the force of the word here. There is a variant 抱 "he clung to (cold and hunger)."

25 For this meaning for 當 年 see the second of the two poems "In the Fifth Month of the Year 400 ... ," line 11: 當 年 詎 有 幾 "How many more years are left to me of youth" (*Works* 3:12a).

26 Exactly the same line occurs in the poem written to Chou Hsü-chih, *et al.* (*Works*, 2:10a), where it specifically refers to the Way of Confucius.

27 *Chuang-tzu* (*SPTK* ed.), 6:8a.

ch'ing, "feelings" (which I have translated "impulses"): "The reason [the sage] is not hidden today is because he has feelings and gives vent to them." It is not certain that T'ao Ch'ien had this passage in mind, but Ku Chih's guess may be right: "When the Way prospers, it is from having feelings; hence, if the Way is lost, it is from having no feelings."

That addiction to wine is incompatible with reputation is the burden of a remark attributed to Chang Han: "Rather than posthumous reputation I would choose a present cup of wine."[28] T'ao Ch'ien makes it stronger by preferring the wine to present reputation.

The fact that he is alive is what makes a man careful about his person, and by being careful he hopes to stay alive. But Yang Chu warns that no amount of care is going to prolong life indefinitely: "Meng-Sun Yang asked Yang Chu, 'Here is someone who values life and is careful of his body, hoping he will not die. What of him?' Yang Chu said, 'Fundamentally there is no such thing as not dying'" (*Lieh-tzu*, 7:7b). Since a lifetime is over in a flash (line 8), there is not much to gain by clinging to "this" — obsession with reputation (according to Shiba) or, possibly, this concern for one's health that keeps one from drinking or otherwise enjoying the little time at one's disposal. Ku Chih is certainly right in referring these lines to the Yang Chu chapter of *Lieh-tzu*.

A variant of line 8 reads 倏忽若沈星 "Evanescent as a falling star," but the violent image of the lightning is more effective in jolting the complacency of the circumspect men of the world against whom the poem is directed.

The word *ting-ting* in line 9, here rendered as "staid and stolid," is something of a puzzle. It occurs in the *Li chi* (*SPTK* ed., 2:14a) with the meaning "lax, slovenly," but the present context calls for the opposite, unless you take it as an admonition, as Ting Fu-pao does. He paraphrases, "The hundred years of a lifetime pass quickly, and so people should think of being free and easy." Another gloss on the term *ting-ting* rightly stigmatized by Ting as arbitrary, is "uninstructed, untaught," and the same applies to the more attractive "bustling," suggested by Ku Chih, which at least makes excellent sense and is followed by Wang Yao. Another solution is to take *ting-ting* as an attribute of "the hundred years (of a lifetime)," and invent an appropriate meaning for it, such as "inexorable" (Ikkai) or "abundant" (Suzuki). I can only agree with Shiba, who labels the term "unexplained," but it has long been standard practice among commentators to interpret

---

[28] Biography of Chang Han 張翰, *Chin shu*, 92:10a.

such reduplicative binomes arbitrarily to fit a context, and perhaps a translator may be allowed to do the same.

IV

Anxious, seeking, the bird lost from the flock —	栖 栖 失 羣 鳥
The sun declines, and still he flies alone,	日 暮 猶 獨 飛
Back and forth without a place to rest;	徘 徊 無 定 止
From night to night, his cry becomes more sad,	夜 夜 聲 轉 悲
A piercing sound of yearning for the dawn,	厲 響 思 清 遠
So far from home, with nothing for support	去 來 何 依 依
Until at last he finds the lonely pine	因 值 孤 生 松
And folds his wings at this his journey's end.	歛 翮 遙 來 歸
In that harsh wind no tree can keep its leaves.	勁 風 無 榮 木
This is the only shade that will not fail.	此 陰 獨 不 衰
The birds has refuge here and resting place,	託 身 已 得 所
And in a thousand years will never leave.	千 載 不 相 違

T'ao Ch'ien is fond of bird symbols; in particular he identifies himself with the homing bird that always comes back to its nest at the day's end after an excursion out into the world. In this poem the bird is lost from the flock; it stands for the man who is out of touch with his fellows or has lost his place in society. The frantic, uncertain flight through the dark is a search for a safe resting place in a world buffeted by harsh winds that lay bare the accustomed refuges of summer. It is the world T'ao Ch'ien had been living in, and the farm to which he retired is the unfailing refuge which he has resolved never to leave. It is appropriately symbolized by the pine tree which occurs frequently in his poems as a symbol both for constancy amidst uncertainty and for a refuge in times of hardship (see poem VIII of this series). It is something he always refers to with affection and admiration.

There are several variant readings in this poem. In lines 5 and 6 I have followed the one easier to English: 厲響思清晨 ，遠去何所依 in place of ｜ ｜ ｜ ｜ 遠 ，去來何依依 "A shrill sound, as it thinks of something pure and far-off,/Back and forth, so very yearningly." In line 8 I have chosen 終 "finally" in place of 遙 "from afar." For 勁風 "harsh wind" in line 9 there is a variant 動風 "moving wind"; and in line 10 the verb 交 "interlaces" in place of 獨 "alone."

No Chinese commentator glosses *pu hsiang wei*, "does not go away from it," in the last line. Ikkai translates *tagai ni somukiawanai* "do not play one another false." Both Suzuki and Shiba understand it as in my translation, but the other reading is quite possible.

V

I built my hut beside a traveled road	結 廬 在 人 境
Yet hear no noise of passing carts and horses.	而 無 車 馬 喧
You would like to know how it is done?	問 君 何 能 爾
With the mind detached, one's place becomes remote.	心 遠 地 自 偏
Picking chrysanthemums by the eastern hedge	采 菊 東 籬 下
I catch sight of the distant southern hills:	悠 然 見 南 山
The mountain air is lovely as the sun sets	山 氣 日 夕 佳
And flocks of flying birds return together.	飛 鳥 相 與 還
In these things is a fundamental truth	此 中 有 眞 意
I would like to tell, but lack the words.	欲 辯 已 忘 言

It is easy to understand why this is one of T'ao Ch'ien's most famous poems. It conveys admirably the detachment and repose of the Great Recluse[29] who makes his home among men yet remains uncontaminated by the world, whose communion with nature occurs as readily through the chrysanthemums by the eastern hedge as through the distant mountain scenery. A fundamental truth seems to have been communicated, even as the poet suggests, without having been formulated in words.

Some such reading of the poem seems to have inspired the seven pages of critical effusions in the *Collected Criticisms* (*Hui-p'ing*, pp. 167–173). That it is an inadequate understanding of a poem considerably more complex than that is best demonstrated by a detailed examination; essentially the clue is in the allusion that underlies lines 5–6.

The first line begins with an expression *chieh lu* which suggests "thatched hut,"[30] though the verb *chieh* is common enough in combination with words meaning "building" or "house."[31] Actually the line says nothing about a "traveled road"; a closer translation would be, "I built my hut in an inhabited area" (i.e., not off by itself in the wilds).

T'ao Ch'ien attributes his ability to ignore the world while living in it to a "mind that is far away," and the next couplet tells what his absent mind is concerned with. He is picking chrysanthemums, not to put in a vase for decoration, but to use as medicine, probably in a wine infusion (see discussion of poem VII, below). The purpose of such a concoction is to prolong life ("Chrysanthemum is tonic against growing old"),[32] and the

---

[29] For the types of recluse see Li Chi, "The Changing Concept of the Recluse in Chinese Literature," *HJAS*, 24 (1963), 243.

[30] Cf. the lines 潛 居 山 澤 , 結 草 爲 廬 "He hid away and dwelt amidst hills and marsh, and wove grass to make a hut," from the biography of Li Hsün 李 恂 in *Hou-Han shu*, 51:2a.

[31] See the entries 4, 12, and 20, *s.v.* 結, no. 27398 in Morohashi, *Dai Kanwa Jiten*.

[32] "Living in Retirement, on the Double Ninth Festival," *Works*, 2:4b.

Southern Mountain which catches his eye as he is picking the petals is not an irrelevant piece of scenery but a prime symbol of the thing he has in mind. "Longevity like the Southern Mountain"[33] is the irresistible associative link from the *Book of Songs*, one of T'ao Ch'ien's favorite texts. It provides a touch of irony as much as of reassurance, however, for even a confirmed believer in potions and exercises (which T'ao Ch'ien was not) could hardly hope for Long Life of such dimensions.

At the same time, this particular Southern Mountain (Lu shan?) had for T'ao Ch'ien another not unrelated meaning, which made the Mountain of Long Life the prospective site for his grave.[34] This appears quite clearly in No. 7 of the "Untitled Poems" (*Works*, 4:7b):

This house is an inn for travelers	家 爲 逆 旅 舍
And I am like the guest about to leave:	我 如 當 去 客
On and on, where should I wish to go?	去 去 欲 何 之
My old home is there on South Mountain.	南 山 有 舊 宅

All commentators agree that by "old home," *chiu chai*, he means his grave, a reading strengthened by the line from the "Elegy to be read at his own funeral" (*Works*, 7:6a): "Master T'ao is about to leave this inn for travelers and return for all time to his own home." This added association, if admissible here, reinforces the irony, for it is another reminder of the futility of picking chrysanthemums.

The line which introduces Southern Mountain is the one that has inspired the most critical appreciation; unfortunately it carries several variants. In place of 悠 然 "in the distance" some texts have 時 時 "from time to time." To Su Shih and those critics following him[35] the difference between 望 *wang*, "to gaze at from afar," and 見 *chien*, "to catch sight of," seemed of more importance than it will to a reader prepared to see another linkage than poetic caprice between this and line 5. (*Chien* of course remains the better reading, and for an analogous reason: it is the more dramatic.) The possibilities of *yu jan* are more interesting. Syntactically, "distant" modifies *chien*, and may be applied to the poet's state of mind (remote, detached, abstracted) as well as to the mountain he sees in the distance. It provides

---

33 *Shih ching*, 166/6, 如 南 山 之 壽 . Wang Yao is the only commentator to notice the allusion. [*Editor's note:* This question has probably been noticed by Chang Chiu-ch'eng 張 九 成 (1092–1159) and Chiang Hsün 蔣 薰 , of the seventeenth century, but with different interpretation.]

34 壽 "longevity" is frequently a euphemism for "death," as in the expressions ｜ 材 "coffin," and ｜ 穴 "grave."

35 They are quoted by Ting Fu-pao.

the usefully ambiguous bridge between preoccupation and perception, and introduces the mountain simultaneously as symbol and scenery.

Once it has engaged his attention, Southern Mountain off in the distance continues to carry him outside the world of men, and the symbol for long life comes into focus as an example of the enduring loveliness of nature into which the birds return at night and in which man is reabsorbed at the close of his life — this is part of the truth which the poet grasps and which he has no words to express, or rather, having grasped it, he can "forget words." [36]

VI

A thousand myriad ways to act	行 止 千 萬 端
And who can tell the right and wrong?	誰 知 非 與 是
Once wrong and right are given shape	是 非 苟 相 形
All will echo blame or praise.	雷 同 共 譽 毀
When times were bad this often happened,	三 季 多 此 事
But not with men of understanding:	達 士 似 不 爾
Contemptuous of the vulgar clods	咄 咄 俗 中 愚
They chose to follow Huang and Ch'i.	且 當 從 黃 綺

People generally have no standards of conduct and are content to call that right which is popular or convenient. This is particularly true in times of decadence (right now, for example), and it is only a man of real character who will deliberately retire, like the Four White Heads of the Han dynasty, rather than court the approval of the mob. (This poem should be read in connection with poem IX.)

The first couplet sounds very much like *Chuang-tzu* (1:26b, 28a): "And so there is the right and wrong of the Confucians and the Mohists, each asserting what the other denies and denying what he asserts. . . . The one has his right and wrong, the other has his own right and wrong." The second couplet implies the relativity of opposites; right and wrong define one another, so that standards of behavior are relative as well as arbitrary.

Do these generalities apply to any specific area of human action? Line 5 says this confusion between right and wrong was common "when times were bad," specifically during the last years of the Hsia, Shang, and Chou dynasties (*san chi*), and Wang T'ang thinks the poem was "probably directed against

---

[36] Commentators, beginning with Li Shan (*WH*, 30:2b), all quote *Chuang-tzu*, 9:11a, for the expression *wang yen*: "The point of words lies in their meaning. Once you have grasped the meaning, you may forget the words." But the other *Chuang-tzu* passage (1:36b) cited by Ku Chih is more relevant: "The Great Way applies no labels, the greatest explanation 辯 employs no words."

those who served the Sung dynasty."[37] Presumably T'ao Chien himself
was one of those "men of understanding" not misled by specious claims
to legitimacy offered by a would-be usurper, any more than Hsia Huang-
kung and Ch'i Li-chi.[38]

On the other hand, if the "man of understanding" is identified with the
"intelligent man" of the first poem of this series, he would be as little worried
by political vicissitudes as by the changes of fortune that plague the individual; he simply prefers to do his drinking in retirement, like others who left
the world, such as Huang and Ch'i. Against this is the indignation of line 7,
"Contemptuous of the vulgar clods," and the fact that the Four White
Heads were taking a moral-political stand.

For *yü*, "the stupid" (vulgar clods"), a variant is *wu*, "to dislike," giving
the sense "contemptuous of the dislikes of the vulgar" (cf. XI, line 11,
below).

VII

The fall chrysanthemums have lovely colors.	秋 菊 有 佳 色
I pluck the petals that are wet with dew	裛 露 掇 其 英
And float them in this Care Dispelling Thing	汎 此 忘 憂 物
To strengthen my resolve to leave the world.	遠 我 遺 世 情
I drink my solitary cup alone	一 觴 雖 獨 進
And when it's empty, pour myself another.	杯 盡 壺 自 傾
The sun goes down, and all of nature rests.	日 入 羣 動 息
Homing birds fly chirping toward the grove.	歸 鳥 趨 林 鳴
I sit complacent on the east veranda	嘯 傲 東 軒 下
Having somehow found my life again.	聊 復 得 此 生

Again the poet is picking chrysanthemums, and he begins with an aesthetic
appreciation of their beauty, though he has a use for the petals he collects.
The commentators are unanimous in referring the opening two lines to the
"Li sao":[39] "Evenings I ate the fallen petals of autumn chrysanthemums,"
where Ch'ü Yuan was clearly working on longevity. Drinking chrysanthe-

---

[37] 王 棠 , quoted by Ting Fu-pao. The anachronism in this statement could be avoided
by rephrasing.

[38] They are two of the Four White Heads 四 皓 , who retired to Mt. Shang in disapproval
of Ch'in's tyranny, but who, even after Han Kao-tsu had established a new dynasty, still
refused to come out and serve. Like Po-i and Shu-chi, they had high standards of legitimacy
for a dynasty.

[39] Line 34, *Ch'u tz'u* (*SPTK* ed.), 1:12b.

mum wine is mentioned elsewhere[40] as part of an Autumn Festival ritual for achieving Long Life, and the Care-Dispelling Thing in which T'ao is going to float the petals is of course wine. (This epithet for wine seems to be his own happy invention, based perhaps on Mao's *Shih ching* commentary.[41]) He had cares enough, but one that keeps turning up in his poetry, particularly when he mentions Long Life, is death.

He is drinking to prolong his life and also to forget death, suggesting a certain lack of confidence in the efficacy of his concoction. He is drinking alone, but the absence of a drinking companion does not keep him from filling his own cup until the sun goes down. As Wu Ch'i remarks,[42] the setting sun and the homing birds are not just an observation of the time of day, but a statement of a general principle: all nature rests at the close of day. He has left the world of activity and striving and, like the birds, he has come back home. Fortified by what he has drunk, he can afford a degree of complacency, for after all, by losing the world he has found himself.

There is no real doubt that it is the petals of line 2 which are dew-soaked, though grammatically it should be the poet himself. It comes to the same thing, actually. The dew is significant for the time of day, and possibly as enhancing the medicinal efficacy of the petals, for they will be wet too, whether or not any of it drops off on the picker.

Line 4 is ambiguous. There are a disconcerting number of possible readings, only one of which, and that perhaps the most obvious one, has to be excluded as contradictory to the sense of the poem as a whole. *Yüan wo i shih ch'ing*: *yüan* is a transitive verb, and hence causative, "to make distant," and this can mean either "to put away" or "to push to a distance, to intensify." *Wo* can be an indirect object, "put away from me," or it can modify the remaining three words, "put away my . . . " or, "intensify my . . . . " *I shih ch'ing*, "leave world feelings," may be put together in a variety of ways. *Shih ch'ing* occurs in T'ao's poetry with the meaning "worldly ambition."[43] Taking *i* as "leftover, remaining," the whole line could be read "Put from me any lingering worldly ambition," which makes sense.

---

40 Ikkai quotes *Hsi-ching tsa-chi* (*SPTK* ed.), 3:4a. The instructions given there for making chrysanthemum wine specify that it is brewed from the stalks and leaves and petals, along with a grain mash; it is not just an infusion of the petals in wine, of the sort T'ao refers to here (cf. V).

41 *Shih ching*, 26/1, "Not that I lack wine, / To dally, to joy." Mao paraphrases, "It's not that I lack wine, which may serve to forget care" 可以忘憂 .

42 *Hui-p'ing*, p. 177, 吳淇,六朝選詩定論 11.

43 "Returning to Chiang-ling . . . ," *Works*, 3:12b: "In grove and garden I had no worldly ambitions" 林園無世情 .

I-shih may be taken together, "leave the world" or, less likely, "an abandoned world." With *ch'ing*, then, it becomes "a wish to leave the world" or "feelings about the world I left,"[44] and either of these is something to be put away, out of mind, or pushed to an extreme, intensified. If he is drinking to "put away from me my feelings about leaving the world," then he is confessing to a regret that is never elsewhere expressed in this series, however implicit it may be in poem IX. In favor of keeping this reading somewhere in mind is the variant in the *Wen hsüan*, which has 達 "to succeed" in place of *i*, and here the only possible reading is "To put from me any desire to succeed in the world," a notable *lectio facilior*. It is to be rejected, not only as less interesting, but for conceding (even in denying) a wish that T'ao Ch'ien never brought himself to express, and though it may in some way underlie this whole series, it could come to the surface only in a Freudian sort of lapse. I hesitate to suggest seriously that it was the poet's own emendation of such an inadvertency that made this line a syntactic puzzle. The reading "To put away my feelings about the world I have left" is contaminated with the same ambivalence. He presumably would not want either "to intensify my feelings about leaving the world," or "to intensify my desire for a world I have left." The reading which I have used in my translation was suggested by Suzuki and adopted by both Shiba and Ikkai. It has in its favor the close parallelism of the preceding line, which helps eliminate the lexical combination *shih-ch'ing*, for example, but the most any translation can hope to do is present the reading that is likely to dominate and then call attention to the other possibilities that inevitably color it.

The trouble with solitary drinking (lines 5–6) is that there is no one to fill your cup for you when it is empty. The present solution is one that T'ao mentioned earlier.[45]

In line 9, following Lü Shang's *Wen hsüan* commentary,[46] I have treated *hsiao-ao* as a rhyming descriptive binome and let the "whistling" (*hsiao*) drop out of my translation. This requires supplying a verb ("sit") which is not in the text. Following immediately after *ming*, "chirping," *hsiao* is almost sure to be read "whistle" at first. Certainly the term *hsiao-ao* has overtones of "arrogance" (*ao*), and the two components appear separately

---

44 Some such reading must underlie von Zach's "Er macht, dass ich alle Erinnerung an die von mir aufgegebene Welt verliere" (*Die chinesische Anthologie*, p. 544).

45 "An Answer to Secretary Kuo," *Works*, 2:18a: "When the wine is brewed, I pour for myself." Also "The Return," *Works*, 5:9b: "I pull wine pot and cup toward me and pour it myself."

46 Ikkai makes the same suggestion.

in a similar context in "The Return,"[47] "I lean out the southern window and let my pride expand," and "Climbing the east hill and whistling."

Two commentators[48] remark on the complementary *te sheng*, "get life," of line 10 and *i-shih*, "leave the world," of line 4. The last line means "having found satisfaction in my life."

VIII

In the eastern garden grows a green pine	青 松 在 東 園
Its shape obscured behind surrounding growth,	衆 草 沒 其 姿
Until black frost destroys the other plants	凝 霜 殄 異 類
Leaving lofty branches there revealed.	卓 然 見 高 枝
Among the other trees it goes unmarked	連 林 人 不 覺
When isolated, everyone admires.	獨 樹 衆 乃 奇
I lift my jug to hang on a cold branch	提 壺 挂 寒 柯
From time to time I stare into the distance:	遠 望 時 復 爲
Born into the midst of dream-illusion	吾 生 夢 幻 間
Why should I submit to dusty bonds?	何 事 紲 塵 羈

This is one of T'ao Ch'ien's clearest uses of the pine tree symbol, here appropriate to his recurrent theme of firmness in adversity as a way to enduring fame. How completely he identifies himself with the tree appears in the gift of the wine jug: here is another who could use a drink, and who will know how to appreciate it. He is convinced that, like the pine tree, he will show to best advantage in isolation. Since life is both transitory and unreal, he has nothing to gain by submitting to the contamination of a worldly career. This last couplet, at first reading so incongruous with the rest of the poem, was perhaps prompted by the purely symbolic nature of the gesture of the wine-pot — no doubt empty — hung from a cold branch.

The first six lines are a versification of a line from the *Conversations* (*Lun yü*, 9/28): "It is only after the year turns cold that we notice that pine and cypress are the last to lose their leaves." The same text appears and is elaborated on in the "Po-i Shu-ch'i Biography" (see p. 42): "When all the world is befuddled, then the gentleman of pure morals stands out." The "east" of line 1 seems to have no more significance that it did in poem VII when applied to the veranda.

The "cold branch" of line 7 suggests winter;[49] there is a variant 撫 "to

---

[47] Lines 23 and 57, *Works*, 5:9b, 10b.

[48] *Hui-p'ing*, p. 176, Huang Wen-huan 黃 文 煥, 陶 詩 析 義 3; *ibid.* p. 177; Sun Jen-lung 孫 人 龍, 陶 公 詩 評 注 初 學 讀 本 2.

[49] Ting Fu-pao quotes a line from the Liang Emperor Yüan: 冬 木 曰 寒 枝 "A winter tree is called a cold branch."

caress, to stroke" for *kua*, "to hang"; compare the similar phrase in "The Return."[50] The syntax of line 8 is peculiar: "From afar I gaze and at times do again." It lays great stress on the repetition of the act of looking and insists on it as leading to the generalization of the last couplet.

The expression "dream illusion," *meng huan*, is probably not specifically Buddhist, though it occurs in the *Diamond Sutra*, and I can find no earlier secular use than this by T'ao Ch'ien.[51] However, the concept of life as dream or illusion, though not the term itself, occurs in both *Chuang-tzu* and *Lieh-tzu*, and in the fourth poem of the series "Returning to the Farm" T'ao also writes, "Human life is like a conjuror's trick."[52] The "dusty bonds" suggest "the world of affairs" as in the first poem of the same series, "by mischance I fell into the dusty net."[53]

IX

I heard a knock this morning at my door.	清 晨 聞 叩 門
In haste I pulled my gown on wrongside out	倒 裳 往 自 開
And went to ask the caller, Who is there?	問 子 爲 誰 與
It was a well-intentioned farmer, come	田 父 有 好 懷
With a jug of wine to pay a distant call,	壺 漿 遠 見 候
Suspecting me to be at odds with the times:	疑 我 與 時 乖
"Dressed in rags beneath a roof of thatch	襤 縷 茅 簷 下
Is not the way a gentleman should live.	未 足 爲 高 栖
All the world agrees on what to do —	一 世 皆 尚 同
I hope that you will join the muddy game."	願 君 汩 其 泥
"My sincere thanks for your advice, old man.	深 感 父 老 言
It's my nature keeps me out of tune	稟 氣 寡 所 諧
Though one can learn of course to pull the reins,	紆 轡 誠 可 學
To go against oneself is a real mistake.	違 己 詎 非 迷
So let's just have a drink of this together.	且 共 歡 此 飲
There's no turning back my carriage now."	吾 駕 不 可 回

Two specific allusions underlie this poem. The farmer, *t'ien fu*, presents the same appeal that the fisherman addressed to Ch'ü Yüan in the *Ch'u tz'u* piece (7:1b–2a): "If all the world is muddy, why not help them stir up the mud and beat up the waves, and if all men are drunk, why not sup their dregs and swill their lees? Why get yourself exiled because of your deep thoughts and your fine aspirations?" Though T'ao Ch'ien's answer is

---

50 *Works*, 5:10a, 撫 孤 松 而 盤 桓 "I walk around a lonely pine tree, stroking it."
51 See the examples in Morohashi, *Dai Kanwa Jiten*, 5802:48.
52 *Works*, 2:6b, 人 生 似 幻 化 .
53 *Ibid.*, 2:5a, 誤 落 塵 網 中 .

couched differently, we must remember Ch'ü Yüan's proud claim, "All the world is corrupt, I alone am pure."

However, the farmer here is more than just Mr. Worldly Wiseman. The early morning knock that got the poet out of bed was not likely someone paying a social call; note that the master of the household went in person to answer it, pulling on his clothes wrongside out in his haste. The *tao shang* is unmistakably a reference to the *Shih ching* poem (No. 100)

Before the east is bright
He pulls his clothes on upside down
Upside down and wrongside out —
From the court they call him.

東 方 未 明
顛 倒 衣 裳
顛 之 倒 之
自 公 召 之
（齊風："東方未明"）

Furthermore the poem specifies that the caller is not a neighbor; he is paying a distant call, and so has come from afar.

Ku Chih assumes that the poem was inspired by an actual summons from court and relates it to the entry in the *Sung shu* biography (93:13b): "Toward the end of the *i-hsi* period (405–418) he was offered the post of Adjutant, but he refused." This is not unlikely, and by reducing the expected court messenger to a lowly farmer, T'ao Ch'ien could make his refusal less seditious, even while giving his real reason. However, there remains a certain ambivalence of feeling. The eagerness with which he answered the knock at his door, the breathless expectancy of "Who's there?" seems inconsistent with the philosophical renunciation of a dirty world. Referred back to Ch'ü Yüan, his attitude becomes more consistent, for Ch'ü Yüan refused to serve only because he could not do so on his own terms. T'ao Ch'ien too would perhaps have been glad to serve if he could do so without compromising his integrity.

This poem is unique in the series for its use of dialog, a device which is common elsewhere in T'ao Ch'ien's poetry.

In line 2 the word *tzu*, "in person," has failed to appear in my translation, and "in haste," though implied, is not in the text.

Line 8 is literally "does not suffice to make a high perch," and Wang Yao glosses it as "to live in retirement," which hardly makes sense in context, though the term is often so used.

The variant 舉世 for *i shih* in line 9 is perhaps to be preferred for the alliterative echo with 皆 (*kiwo-kai*). T'ao Ch'ien consistently takes a jaundiced view of what "all the world agrees on" (see VI).

Ku in line 10 means both "to sully" and "to immerse in." The two meanings reinforce one another: "Plunge into the mud and get yourself dirty."

The carriage image of lines 13 and 16 is characteristic; T'ao Ch'ien often so symbolized the course of his life (cf. X, line 10).

The expression *wei chi*, "to oppose oneself, to go against oneself," in line 14 appears in the preface to "The Return" (*Works*, 5:8a): "Cold and hunger may be sharp, but this going against myself makes me sick."

X

Once I made a distant trip	在昔曾遠遊
Right to the shore of the Eastern Sea.	直至東海隅
The road I went was long and far,	道路迥且長
The way beset by wind and waves.	風波阻中塗
Who was it made me take this trip?	此行誰使然
It seems that I was forced by hunger.	似爲飢所驅
I gave my all to eat my fill	傾身營一飽
When just a bit was more than enough.	少許便有餘
Since this was not a famous plan	恐此非名計
I stopped my cart and came back home.	息駕歸閒居

All commentators agree that T'ao Ch'ien is referring to a specific trip in the past, the time (404) when he was in the service of General Liu Lao-chih 劉牢之 and went to Ch'ü-o 曲阿, a journey celebrated in one of his poems.[54] The geography of the poem is vague ("distant voyage," "Eastern Sea"), probably deliberately so, and it is better not to take Tung-hai as the name of the commandery in which Ch'ü-o was located, or to insist that it was the expedition against Sun En 孫恩 which he was remembering. It is, after all, his whole career that he has renounced (again the carriage image), and the voyage is properly a symbolic one.

The "wind and waves" of line 4 refer to the civil wars more than to the physical hazards of travel and are so used in the preface to "The Return,"[55] where there is a line[56] reflected in line 6.

The "famous plan" of line 9 may be nothing more than a good plan (and is so translated by Suzuki, Shiba, and Ikkai), but several commentators understand "a plan to become famous" and refer to his claim that firmness in adversity was the only way to achieve fame (see poem II). This accords with T'ao's use of the word *ming*.

The last line says specifically "I stopped my carriage and came back home to retire."

---

54 "Lines written on passing through Ch'ü-o, on first being made Secretary to the General," *Works*, 3:10a.

55 *Works*, 5:8a, 時風波未靜.

56 *Ibid.*, "I made myself my belly's slave."

XI

Master Yen they praised for being good	顏生稱爲仁
And Old Man Jung was said to be a sage:	榮公言有道
The one was often empty — he died young,	屢空不獲年
The other always hungry — he lived long.	長飢至于老
They may have left behind an honored name	雖留身後名
But was it worth a life of deprivation?	一生亦枯槁
What do they know now they are dead and gone?	死去何所知
Surely it is best to please oneself.	稱心固爲好
We indulge our thousand-precious bodies	客養千金軀
But as the change draws near the treasure melts.	臨化消其寶
No need to shy at naked burial —	裸葬何必惡
A man should get beyond accepted views.	人當解意表

This poem begins like II by casting doubt on the moral order of the world and then goes a step farther and removes the one prop left. There the conclusion was "A man must learn a firmness in adversity/For his name to live a thousand years." Here the value of posthumous fame is called into question: "They may have left behind an honored name . . . " but the price was a lifetime of hardship. It is essentially a development of Yang Chu's argument,[57] and the conclusion "Surely it is best to please oneself" is identical with Yang Chu's. But indulgence of the senses is no answer either, for the body we prize will dissolve at the end and may as well be thrust naked into the grave. It has ceased to be a treasure that needs to be treated carefully or with respect.

Master Yen is Yen Hui, Confucius' favorite disciple. The praise of him as a good man and the facts that he was "often empty" (i.e. hungry) (*Lun yü*, 11/8) and died young are combined into a single statement in the "Po-i Shu-ch'i Biography" (*Shih chi*, 61:8): "Of the seventy disciples, Confucius praised only Yen Hui for his love of learning, but 'Hui was often empty,' not having his fill even of coarse fare, and he died young; is this the way heaven rewards good men?" Jung Ch'i-ch'i has already appeared in poem II.

T'ao Ch'ien's ambivalent attitude toward posthumous fame is nicely summed up in lines 5–6, which grant that it is a good thing ("although they left a name behind . . . ") but manage to suggest that the price was too high ("still it was a whole lifetime of deprivation"). Contrast the poem "In Praise of Ching K'o" (*Works*, 4:15b):

---

[57] His strongest attacks are against the worth of reputation and posthumous fame; see chap. 7 of *Lieh-tzu*.

Alas that his swordsmanship was faulty	惜 哉 劍 術 疎
And left the unimaginable deed undone.	奇 功 遂 不 成
Although the man is dead and gone,	其 人 雖 已 沒
After a thousand years he inspires us still.	千 載 有 餘 情

In his "Bearers' Song" (*Works*, 4:22b-23a) he is wholly negative:

He no longer knows success or failure.	得 失 不 復 知
What has he to do with right and wrong?	是 非 安 能 覺
After a thousand or ten thousand years	千 秋 萬 歲 後
Who will know his fame or disgrace?	誰 知 榮 與 辱

The two conflicting attitudes keep cropping up with about equal frequency. It is when he is considering his own reputation that he is more inclined to question the value to him of something which in the nature of things he will not know about.

The translation of line 9 "we indulge our bodies" takes *k'o* as adverbial to *yang*: "we take care of them as one takes care of a guest." It is the reading suggested by Suzuki and followed by Shiba and Wang Yao, as well as Ikkai, who however remarks that it is an unusual combination. Ting Fu-pao (probably inspired by a comment by Wang T'ang),[58] takes *k'o* as a substantive and refers it to Yang Wang-sun, of whom his biography says he took his patrimony of "a thousand of gold" 千 金 and spent it on himself. This is an unlikely interpretation, but it is possible that T'ao Ch'ien's choice of words (*ch'ien chin ch'ü*) was influenced by the language of Yang Wang-sun's biography, since he is unmistakably referred to in the last couplet.

It was Yang Wang-sun[59] who insisted on the naked burial of line 11; it clearly held a sort of fascination for T'ao Ch'ien. It is mentioned in the Elegy he wrote for his own funeral (*Works*, 7:6b), where he rejects the idea as another extreme of behavior. It is well to recall that this was a shocking idea to the traditional Chinese reader, and that T'ao Ch'ien was not asking a rhetorical question (literally, "Why must one hate naked burial?").

For the last line Ku Chih quotes Kuo Hsiang's *Chuang-tzu* commentary as authority for an unlikely reading of *i piao* "one should understand its

---

58 *Hui-p'ing*, p. 183, as quoted by Wu Chan-t'ai 吳 瞻 泰 : "Wang T'ang says, 'Yen and Jung took fame as their treasure; the guest took his thousand-gold body as his treasure; but better than either is to make pleasing yourself your treasure.' "

59 *Han shu* (*HSPC*), 67:1a: "When Yang Wang-sun was ill and approaching his end, he ordered his son 'I wish to be buried naked so as to return to my true state; you are not to deviate from my will. When I am dead you are to make a cloth bag to cover the corpse. Lower it into the ground seven feet. When it has come to rest, pull the bag off, starting at the feet, so that my body may lie next the earth.' "

real significance," i.e., the acceptance of death and the ultimate dissolution of the body. This also yields sense, but taken at their face value, the words should mean "outside (ordinary) ideas," and are so understood by Shiba and Ikkai. This is more in line with T'ao's attitude in his Funeral Elegy: one must be able to have room in one's world view for even so bizarre a thing as naked burial — after all it doesn't much matter how the body is disposed of.

XII

Chang Chang-kung once served a term in office,	長 公 曾 一 仕
Still young he saw the times were out of joint.	壯 節 忽 失 時
He closed his gate and never more went forth,	杜 門 不 復 出
Renounced the world for his remaining days.	終 身 與 世 辭
When Yang Chung-li went back home to Great Marsh	仲 理 歸 大 澤
It was there his high renown began.	高 風 始 在 茲
You may go once, but then you ought to stop,	一 往 便 當 已
There is no place for any further doubts.	何 爲 復 狐 疑
Get out for good — what more is there to say?	去 去 當 奚 道
The world has long enough imposed on me.	世 俗 久 相 欺
Do away with all the far-fetched talk!	擺 落 悠 悠 談
	請 從 余 所 之

Like XI, this poem too begins with an appeal to precedent. The examples come from the history books this time, the first an obscure man whose name is preserved in two lines tacked on to the biography of his father, Chang Shih-chih, in the *Shih-chi*: "His son Chang Chih reached the rank of Great Officer in his official career before resigning. Because he was not able to adapt himself to the times, he did not again hold office for the rest of his life." [60] It is easy to see how T'ao Ch'ien could apply these lines to his own career. [61]

The second example is rather better known. Yang Lun had a more notable career than Chang Chih, but he suffered from the same inability to get along with his colleagues. On resigning his office he retired to Ta-tse (Great Marsh), where he taught, attracting over a thousand students. Subsequently he was thrice recalled and as often dismissed for his too frank remonstrances. He then went back home, closed his gate, and continued his teaching; for the rest of his life he had nothing more to do with the world of officialdom

---

60 *Shih chi* (Takigawa ed.), 102:11.

61 He also found occasion to eulogize Chang Chih in his "On Reading the *Shih chi*" 讀 史 述 (*Works*, 6:12a) and the "Inscription on a Fan" 扇 上 畫 贊 (*ibid.*, 6:13b).

(*Hou-Han Shu*, 79:21b–23b). This is also like T'ao's own experience in that he too vacillated between retirement and service before finally leaving the world.

Line 2 reads literally "In the period of his prime all at once he was out of tune with the times." *Hu* ("all at once") must be referred back to line one, "suddenly, one day when he was in office," suggesting a realization of the fact, not some sudden change in the times.

The words *i wang*, "once you leave," in line 7 could apply to either home or office; the second alternative would require the translation, "You may go once, but then you ought to stop." In context the sense is the same. Lines 7–8 together are at once a reference to Yang Lun and an admonition to himself. For the second time in this series he makes us aware that he has doubts or has had them by asserting that he does not or should not have them any more.[62]

Line 9 has the ambiguous word *tao* which can mean either "road" or "to say." My translation is based on the analogy of the similar line in the third of the "Bearers' Songs," 死去何所道 "What shall we say, we who are dead?" This is also Shiba's reading. Suzuki, Ikkai, and Wang Yao all take *tao* as "road," which yields the translation: "To keep on going, what road should I take?" This suggests that the poet is still considering alternatives to retirement, even as he rejects them. In either case, he ends by resolutely disposing of the wiles of the world and, as in XI, refuses to accept the duty insisted upon by convention: "Let me pursue the course which is my own," an allusion to Confucius' remark, "Let me do what I like" (*Lun yü*, 7/12).

XIII

I always have two guests who lodge with me	有客常同止
Whose inclinations keep them far apart;	取舍邈異境
One is always getting drunk alone,	一士常獨醉
One stays sober all the year around.	一夫終年醒
They laugh at one another, drunk and sober,	醒醉還相笑
And neither understands the other's words.	發言各不領
How very stupid is this hidebound fellow!	規規一何愚
The drunkard's scorn is more intelligent.	兀傲差若穎
A word of counsel to the drunken guest:	寄言酣中客
Light the candles when the sun goes down.	日沒燭當秉

---

62 See poem I, "Beset with no further doubts."

Of the commentators and translators only Ikkai calls attention to the parallel with the "Substance, Shadow, Spirit" poem (*Works*, 2:1a–2b), and draws the necessary conclusion, that here we have the same device of objectifying conflicting elements of the poet's own personality. To be sure this poem is in praise of drunkenness, while the other is weighted in favor of Spirit (who rejects it), but in both cases the alternatives exist in the poet himself. All through this series T'ao Ch'ien favors irresponsibility and duty to self over dedication and devotion to the public good, but only here does he speak with the abandon which one expects from a man who has been drinking and who has no patience with the stubbornly sober part of himself that looks on with uncomprehending disapproval.

The "scorn" of line 8 ("arrogance" might be better) is nearly the same word as the complacency in poem VII; it has also an implication of "independence" and is an index of his mood. The last line is a reflection of one of the famous "Nineteen Old Poems" (No. 15, *WH*, 29:9a):

The days are short and nights alas are long,	晝 短 苦 夜 長
Why not light a lamp to stretch the fun?	何 不 秉 燭 游

"Light the candles" amounts to saying, Keep on drinking.

It is perhaps too much to refer the setting sun to the decline of the dynasty or even to the general darkness of the times, though this is a common enough piece of symbolism in poetry of this period.

XIV

Sympathetic friends who know my tastes	故 人 賞 我 趣
Bring a wine jug when they come to visit.	挈 壺 相 與 至
Sitting on the ground beneath the pine tree	班 荊 坐 松 下
We keep on filling cups until we're drunk,	數 斟 已 復 醉
Venerable elders gabbing all at once	父 老 雜 亂 言
And pouring from the bottle out of turn.	觴 酌 失 行 次
Aware no more that our own "I" exists	不 覺 知 有 我
How are we to value other things?	安 知 物 爲 貴
So rapt we are not sure of where we are —	悠 悠 迷 所 留
In wine there is a taste of profundity.	酒 中 有 深 味

This poem really is about drinking, social drinking this time,[63] not the solitary communion with the wine bottle of the preface and poems VII

---

[63] In poem IX the old farmer was invited to share a drink with the poet, but the poem dealt with something else.

and XIII. And yet it is through this convivial drunkenness that T'ao experiences a rapture leading to a kind of mystical illumination.[64]

The informal drinking party with which the poem begins is reminiscent of the "Biography of the Gentleman of the Five Willows," where friends, knowing the poet's circumstances, would invite him to drink, and he would always end up drunk, indifferent to all around him (*Works*, 6:9b–10a).

Line 3 contains a literary expression *pan tso*, "sitting on the ground," derived from the *Tso chuan*. It appears in a similar context in the poem "An Outing on Hsieh Brook," where drinking with friends helped "forget those sorrows of a thousand years" (*Works*, 2:7b), but did not lead to the ecstatic state of the present poem.

Line 7 is a degree more complicated than it appears in my translation: "Unaware of knowing that 'I' exists," and it is a question whether to regard this circumlocution as a philosophical nicety or merely a convenience in filling out a five-word line, and so simply equivalent to "not knowing," as I have treated it. It hardly improves the force of the next line in any case, where *Chuang-tzu* is lurking in the background: "In perspective of the Tao, there is no noble or vile among creatures. From the point of view of creatures, each sees himself as noble and the others as vile" (*Chuang-tzu*, 17/29). So what T'ao Ch'ien is saying is that through wine he has achieved the higher perspective.

The commentators leave line 9 strictly alone, except to record the variants.[65] The difficulty is in the vague binome *yu-yu*, which T'ao Ch'ien uses frequently, but not always in the same sense. In poem XII it was *yu-yu t'an*, "far-fetched talk," and in V *yu-jan* occurs as "distant," its commonest meaning (the other meaning he uses is "yearningly," this twice). I take it here as "far away" — in thought, and though the rest of the line could mean "confused about the place to stay" (or "go," if you take the variant),[66] there is no need to break the chain of thought begun in the previous couplet. Drinking leads to forgetfulness of self and emancipation from false values, and in this state we are really uncertain about where we are, but not about where we should be; and this is precisely the profundity of drunkenness.

---

[64] T'ao records something similar in another poem written at about this same period, "Drinking Alone in the Rainy Season" (*Works*, 2:14b–15a), and the same concept underlies the "Hymn to Wine" of Liu Ling (*WH*, 47:11b).

[65] 咄咄 for 悠悠 and 之 for 留 .

[66] Shiba follows Suzuki, who applies the line to people generally and takes it in a bad sense: people are aimless and dilatory and do not know where they should take their stand.

XV

Through poverty I am short of hands	貧居乏人工
And bushes make my yard a wilderness.	灌木荒余宅
There in full view the soaring bird	班班有翔鳥
Lonely, silent, leaves no trace of passage.	寂寂無行迹
How endlessly vast is the universe	宇宙一何悠
And how few men will live to be a hundred!	人生少至百
The months and years jostle one another —	歲月相催逼
The hair at my temples long ago turned white.	鬢邊早已白
Unless we resign ourselves to whims of fate	若不委窮達
It's just too bad for what we started with.	素抱深可惜

Fang Tung-shu notes a discontinuity in this poem: "The first four lines are only setting, done from observation, and have no connection with what follows" (*Hui-p'ing*, p. 188). It no doubt does begin with observation, but the progression is not hard to follow through a chain of associations, first literary (from the bushes to the bird, through the *Book of Songs*), then from the flight of the bird which leaves no trace in the air, to man's life in the world which also leaves no trace and is so soon over. A man can come to terms with the shortness of life and its vicissitudes if he is prepared to accept what fate brings, and this is the only way he can preserve intact his true self.

In line 1 it is human labor, *jen kung*, he complains of lacking, surely implying hired help. Earlier he may have had one or more farm hands working for him,[67] but can no longer afford them.

Ikkai notes that the "soaring bird" in line 3 was probably suggested by the "thickly growing bushes," *kuan mu*, of the second line, by way of the *Shih ching* line[68] "The yellow birds fly/To rest in the dense bushes."

Line 4, which exactly parallels line 3, is understood by all the Japanese translators as applying to the house: "It is quiet (lonely, deserted), and there is no trace of men's passage" — i.e., no one comes to call. This is the obvious reading, but an inadequate one, being both banal ("Because of the undergrowth the bird takes the farm to be deserted, and there is no stream of visitors to disabuse it") and out of character: the poet does complain about his poverty in the first couplet, but the bird and the seclusion are not items he usually finds distasteful.

In line 5 "endlessly vast" is *yu* again, applied to time as well as to space. Shiba notes that line 7 is practically a condensation of a couplet from

---

67 The second of the two poems dated early spring 403, "In Praise of Ancient Worthies" (*Works*, 3:13b): "Holding the plow I rejoice in the season's duties, / With happy face I encourage the farmers."

68 *Shih ching*, 2/2, 黃鳥于飛，集于灌木 (quoted by Ku Chih).

No. 7 of the "Untitled Poems":[69] "Sun and moon are reluctant to go slow,/The four seasons jostle one another."

"Whims of fate" in line 9 is literally "failure and success." It gets its force from *Chuang-tzu* (5/43): "Failure and success, poverty and riches, these are vicissitudes of events, the operation of fate."

In line 10 "what we started with" is literally "what we clutched to our bosom from the start," that is, our inborn (good) qualities, or the ideals we cling to.

XVI

When young I had no taste for worldly things —	少 年 罕 人 事
My whole delight was in the Classic Books.	游 好 在 六 經
So it went and now I'm nearly forty	行 行 向 不 惑
With nothing done to show for all those years.	淹 留 遂 無 成
I clung to firmness in adversity —	竟 抱 固 窮 節
Of cold and hunger I have had my fill.	飢 寒 飽 所 更
A dismal wind blows round my wretched shack	弊 廬 交 悲 風
And a waste of weeds engulfs the courtyard.	荒 草 沒 前 庭
In coat of felt I sit the long nights out	被 褐 守 長 夜
When morning cocks refuse to start to crow.	晨 雞 不 肯 鳴
No Meng-kung here to aid the gifted poor,	孟 公 不 在 茲
And so I keep my feelings to myself.	終 以 翳 吾 情

This poem is first of all a confession of failure: "Though I had high ideals as a youth, I have wasted my life until now all I have is my capacity to endure hardship without compromising those ideals. It has not been easy, and recognition of some sort would be welcome, but I must accept the fact that I am alone."

Ch'iu Chia-sui[70] finds political allegory in the expressions "a dismal wind," "a waste of weeds," "the long night," and "morning cocks refuse to start to crow." The times are bad, Liu Yü has assassinated his ruler,[71] and the night is truly long. The lines are indeed reminiscent of Juan Chi's political-allegorical use of setting,[72] and — aside from chronological difficulties — such a reading is quite possible. On the other hand, the overgrown courtyard was mentioned in poem XV, and in any event the details must be taken literally as examples of the hardships T'ao has encountered.

---

69 *Works*, 4:7b, 日 月 不 肯 遲 ， 四 時 相 催 迫 .

70 *Hui-p'ing*, p. 190, 邱 嘉 穗 ， 東 山 草 堂 陶 詩 箋 3.

71 If these poems were written not later than 417, this is anticipating. It was only in 418 that Liu Yü had the Emperor An demoted and assassinated.

72 In fact, no. 15 of his 81 "Sorrowful Songs" (*WH*, 23:8a) could have served as a model for this whole poem. It begins, "Long ago when I was fourteen or fifteen" 昔 年 十 四 五 .

The first two lines closely parallel the opening lines of "Passing through Ch'ü-o..." (*Works*, 3:10b): "As a youth I stayed away from worldly things / All my love was for my lute and books." There is also a similarity, pointed out by Ting Fu-pao, to a line in the second of the "Returning to the Farm" series (*Works*, 2:5b): "In the country one has few worldly contacts."

I am not at all sure that the Six Classics of line 2 do not mean the Arts, as Ku Chih suggests. The terms *ching* 經 and *i* 藝 are interchangeable when six are specified, and the verb *yu* 遊 "to find diversion in" is in this context almost surely a reflection of *Conversations*, 7/6: "Put your mind on the Way, lay hold of virtue, rely on benevolence, find your diversion in the Arts." The Six Arts are (or were in Confucius' time) ritual, music, archery, charioteering, letters, and mathematics. On the other hand, T'ao Ch'ien does refer to the Six Books (*liu chi*), meaning the Classics, in poem XX, and he often mentions the *Songs* and the *Documents* as books in which he finds pleasure (see XX, l. 9).

Line 3 expresses age in terms of the famous *Conversations* passage (2/4) which T'ao so often quotes for the purpose: "At fifteen my mind was bent on study, by thirty I was established, at forty I had no doubts, at fifty I knew the Ordinances of Heaven and at sixty was obedient; by seventy I could follow my heart's desire without overstepping the bounds."

Line 4 is flatly contradicted by the last line in the poem "The Double Ninth, in Retirement," as Shiba and Ikkai point out: "There are really many joys in living here / To have stayed on is not to have failed altogether" (*Works*, 2:5a). The lines are actually closer than the translations suggest, since they differ only in the negative implied by the rhetorical *ch'i* 豈 in place of *sui*. In the present poem, coming right after the reference to his age, it strongly suggests Confucius' contempt for the man who at forty or fifty had done nothing with his life (*Lun yü*, 9/23).

The "firmness in adversity" theme in line 5 is repeated from poem II. The variant reading *ch'iung k'u* 窮苦 "in straits" for *ku ch'iung* is not appropriate in this context.

The verb *chiao* 交 used with "wind" in line 7 also occurs in line 7 of the second poem "Celebrating Ancient Worthies ..." (*Works*, 3:13b) (Ikkai).

Compare the following lines 12–14 from "A Lament in the Ch'u Mode" (*Works* 2:13a) with line 10:

Winter nights we slept without covers	寒夜無被眠
In the evening we would long for cockcrow	造夕思雞鳴
At dawn we prayed the crow would quickly cross.	及晨願烏遷

Line 12 says simply "Meng-kung is not alive today." There are two characters known under the polite name of Meng-kung. The older commentators seize upon Ch'en Tsun,[73] noted as a convivial drinker, and conclude that the poem is a lament that the wine has given out. Ku Chih[74] was certainly right in identifying Meng-kung as Liu Kung, who alone among his contemporaries recognized Chang Chung-wei, a poet living in poverty. T'ao Ch'ien celebrated the pair in No. 6 of his "Poems in Praise of Impoverished Gentlemen" (*Works*, 4:11a) and described Chang Chung-wei's circumstances in language very similar to that used in this poem:

Chung-wei was committed to poverty,	仲蔚愛窮居
Around his house the weeds grew tall.	繞宅生蒿蓬
Retired, he gave up social ties	翳然絕交遊
And wrote poems which were not bad.	賦詩頗能工
In all the world none knew his worth	舉世無知者
Save one man only, Liu Kung.	止有一劉龔

The account of Chang Chung-wei in the *Biographies of High-minded Men* also uses phrases which appear in this poem and which could have inspired the line "A waste of weeds engulfs the courtyard."[75] Presumably the point of line 12 is that he hides the feelings which he could properly express only to a sympathetic and appreciative friend. There may be a reflection here of poem III, "All men now hold back their impulses" — it is the same word *ch'ing*.

XVII

The hidden orchid growing in the courtyard	幽蘭生前庭
Holds back its perfume for the autumn breeze.	含薰待清風
The liberating autumn breeze arrives —	清風脫然至
Then one can tell the rare plant from the weeds.	見別蕭艾中
In going on I lost the old familiar road,	行行失故路
By sticking to the Way I might get through.	任道或能通
Awake at last, I thought of turning back:	覺悟當念還
The bow's discarded when the birds are killed.	鳥盡廢良弓

Of the whole series this poem is the most clearly political. It is also one of the least clear, and I have no hesitation in aligning myself with the unfortunate readers castigated by Wang Fu-chih, "Real sense! Real poetry! The shallow fellow who is always reading T'ao's words, when he gets to a poem like this, has no idea what it is about."[76] Wen Ju-neng is less enthu-

---

73 陳遵. His biography is in *Han shu*, 92:9a–12a.

74 He is echoed by Ting Fu-pao, without acknowledgment.

75 *Kao shih chuan* 高士傳 (*SPPY* ed.), B:10b–11a: 常居窮素，所處蓬蒿沒人 (cited by Ku Chih).

76 *Hui-p'ing*, p. 191, 王夫之, 古詩評選 4.

siastic; he also puts his finger on the awkward spot: "In this poem he is simply using the hidden orchid as a symbol for himself—it seems there is no other idea. But it is not especially clear what he is getting at in the concluding lines."[77]

There can be little doubt that the orchid in line 1 is such a symbol, if only from the contrast with the weeds of line 4 and the repeated use of this kind of floral symbolism in the "Li sao." The first four lines look to be closely analogous to the pine tree figure in poem VIII (as Ikkai points out). *Ch'ing feng* 清 風 is literally a "fresh breeze," but seasonally it belongs to autumn,[78] which season is also appropriate to the *lan* ("orchid") flower. The "weeds" are specifically *hsiao ai* "artemisia"; they occur as bad plants in the "Li sao," where they symbolize wicked, corrupt men and are contrasted with "fragrant grasses," standing for the poet himself.

The *hsing hsing*, "going on," of line 5 can be a literal trip (cf. "I kept on walking until I came to this town"[79]) as well as the figurative journey through life[80] which it must be here. The "old familiar road" presumably means the life of retirement, and some commentators[81] are sure it was by going to take office at P'eng-tse that he lost it.

Line 6 is perfectly straightforward, but hard to interpret. The *tao*, "way," seems to continue the traveling figure of line 5, but the commentators and Japanese translators are unanimous in understanding the abstract "Way of Nature." Perhaps it simply means "by sticking to my principles" — this could be a reflection of a sentiment expressed in similar language elsewhere.[82]

The thing he was enlightened about presumably is the truth of the proverbial saying quoted in the last line, and this raises a real problem. "When the flying birds are all gone, the good bow is laid aside; when the swift hare is dead, the running dog is cooked for dinner" — this was Han Hsin's remark as Han Kao-tsu disposed of his former colleagues who had helped him to power.[83] The same proverbial saying was also invoked by Fan

---

77 *Ibid.*, p. 192, 温 汝 能 ，陶 詩 彙 評 3.

78 Ku Chih quotes Wei Chao's commentary on *Kuo yü* to show that such a wind comes only after the frost has fallen, and so is a warning of cold weather.

79 "On Begging Food," *Works*, 2:10b: 行 行 至 斯 里 .

80 As in poem XVI: "So it went, and now I'm nearly forty."

81 T'ang Han refers to the preface to "The Return": "I was deeply ashamed for my lifelong principles" (*Hui-p'ing*, p.191, 湯 漢 ，陶 靖 節 先 生 詩).

82 "Drinking Alone in the Rainy Season," *Works*, 2:15a: "My outward form has long since changed, / What matter, while my heart stays constant?" (Compare 任 眞 and 任 道)

83 *Shih chi*, 92:36.

Li[84] as his reason for leaving Yüeh before Fu-ch'ai could show this charac-
teristically royal form of gratitude. The reference may well be to the political
assassinations practiced by the upstart Liu Yü, but it is not easy to see how
T'ao could identify himself with men who rendered important services to
an ingrate ruler.

The poem is still hard to read as a whole, though the theme of retirement
is implicit in both parts. In the first four lines the poet says "You can distinguish yourself even in retirement, though it takes something from the
outside to make your good qualities stand out." The last four could be
paraphrased "I made a mistake by entering public life, but fortunately
realized it and got out before suffering the consequences of having helped
someone to power." Not one of the more successful poems in the series, in
spite of Wang Fu-chih.

XVIII

Yang Hsiung had a natural taste for wine	子雲性嗜酒
But being poor he found it hard to come by.	家貧無由得
He had to wait for sympathetic friends	時賴好事人
Who brought him wine and had their doubts resolved.	載醪祛所惑
He would drink up as the bottle passed	觴來爲之盡
And let no question go without an answer.	是諮無不塞
The only time that he refused to speak	有時不肯言
Would be when someone asked about aggression.	豈不在伐國
The good man obeys the promptings of his heart	仁者用其心
And shows or is silent as the times require.	何嘗失顯默

The poem is ostensibly about the Han dynasty poet and philosopher Yang
Hsiung, with a conclusion about the behavior of a good man, as exemplified
by him. From its place in this series, one is prepared to infer that T'ao meant
the poem to apply in some measure to himself, and there is support for such
a view, as noted below.

The difficulty lies in Yang Hsiung's reputation as a turncoat and apologist
for the usurper Wang Mang. Wen Ju-neng's comment on the suggestion
that T'ao Ch'ien is comparing himself to Yang Hsiung is typical (*Hui-
p'ing*, p. 194): "It seems to me that in his unwillingness to speak about
aggression, Yüan-ming was far superior to Tzu-yün. How can they be
mentioned together on the same day?"

One way out, noted already by T'ang Han (*Hui-p'ing*, p. 192), is to apply
lines 7–8 to Liu-hsia Hui, who is the person in the anecdote that is alluded

---

84 *Ibid.*, 41:15.

to. This produces a violent wrench in the middle of the poem, and T'ao Chu (*Hui-p'ing*, p. 194) attempts to bridge the resulting gap in these terms: "For not refusing a drink when someone brings wine, he is ready to associate himself with Tzu-yün; for not replying when aggression is the subject he looks to Liu-hsia for a model. Now it was precisely because Tzu-yün did not know how to deal with a problem of aggression that he made his 'Critique of Ch'in and praise of Hsin.'[85] It is only someone like Liu-hsia who can serve as an example of a good man following the promptings of his heart and be a model for showing or being silent as the times require."

It seems unlikely that T'ao Ch'ien was making an oblique criticism of Yang Hsiung, whom he presents as congenial and from whose displeasure he had nothing to fear in any case, but there is no doubt that he meant the lines to be applied to the world he lived in. In any event, the business about aggression, *fa kuo*, meant specifically an attack on a foreign state, and was equally inappropriate applied to Wang Mang or to Liu Yü as a usurper (T'ao seems to have approved of his expeditions against Nan Yen and the Later Ch'in).

Lines 1–4 are a versification of a passage in Yang Hsiung's biography (*Han shu*, 87B:22b): "He was always poor, and he had a taste for wine. Few came to his door, but on occasion sympathetic friends would bring wine and goodies when they visited Hsiung for entertainment or study." If there were any question about T'ao Ch'ien's identifying himself with Yang Hsiung here, the very similar line in his autobiographical "Gentleman of the Five Willows" (*Works*, 6:9b) would settle the matter: "He had a natural taste for wine, but being poor could not always come by it."

Lines 7–8: It was Liu-hsia Hui (according to Tung Chung-shu) who said that you do not ask the good man (*jen jen*) about committing aggression (*Han shu*, 56:19b), but there is surely no need to change the person of reference abruptly at this point; it could as well apply to Yang Hsiung (as Ku Chih effectively argues).

Line 10: To be silent is to refuse to participate in the counsels of government. To show is to appear in court. Ting Fu-pao quotes Yüan Hung's "Eulogy of Famous Ministers of the Three Kingdoms": "When the times are topsy-turvy, it is better to hide away than to show. When all creation longs for order, then it is better to speak than to remain silent."[86]

---

85 This apology for Wang Mang is in *WH*, 48:9b–20a. Hsin is the name of Wang Mang's dynasty.

86 *WH*, 47:23a, 袁宏 , 三國名臣頌序贊 .

XIX

Some time ago, tired of constant hunger,	疇昔苦長飢
I left my plow behind and went to serve.	投耒去學仕
I failed in my duty to support my family,	將養不得節
Cold and hunger held us in their grip.	凍餒固纏己
I'd reached the age one should have made his start,	是時向立年
For lost ideals I was much ashamed.	志意多所恥
At last to carry out my lonely lot	遂盡介然分
I shook my robe and came back to the farm.	拂衣歸田里
The stars have flowed unceasing in their course	冉冉星氣流
Until a twelve-year cycle has gone by.	亭亭復一紀
The highways through the world are broad and long —	世路廓悠悠
This is what made Yang Chu stop and weep.	楊朱所以止
Although I have no royal gift to squander,	雖無揮金事
Cheap wine will serve my purpose just as well.	濁酒聊可恃

This is the third reference in this series to an indefinite past: "Long ago I made a distant voyage" (X), and "When young I had no taste for worldly things" (XV). This poem echoes the same themes as the other two, and like the others it attempts to explain how the poet got where he is. He was forced into a career[87] by the need to support his family; it was a distasteful venture which made him compromise his ideals, and after a time he gave it up, making a deliberate choice of farming and poverty. Wine will have to compensate for his hardships, since he received no pension from a grateful ruler when he retired.

In line 3, the term *chiang yang*[88] is applied more appropriately to the support of parents than to wife and children, and so probably refers primarily to the poet's mother.

In line 5, "the age one should have made his start," *li nien*, is thirty, from the same *Conversations* passage used in XVI. It is not clear from the context whether he was getting on toward thirty when he entered official life, or was thirty when he felt he was getting nowhere and could no longer stand the humiliation. Most commentators assume the former.

The reading of line 6 is clear from the similar sentiment in the preface to "The Return" (*Works*, 5:8a), "I was deeply ashamed that I had so compromised my lifelong principles."

---

[87] Underlying the term 學仕 is a *Lun yü* reference (19/13), "The student, having completed his learning, should apply himself to be an officer" (James Legge, *The Chinese Classics*, vol. 1, p. 344).

[88] 將養 is a pleonastic expression; cf. *Shih ching* no. 162/3, 4: 將父，｜母．

Line 7 could conceivably refer to his term of office, though the epithet *chieh jan* ("outstanding, egregious, uncompromising" — hence "lonely") does not fit so well. Such a reading does not affect the general tenor of the poem: either he is retiring after finishing his service, or he is retiring to finish his life in the role allotted him. The expression *fu i*,[89] "to shake out one's robe," means specifically to shake off the dust of office, preparatory to retiring.

Ku Chih refers the "flowing" of the stars in line 9 to the *Shih ching* line,[90] "In the seventh month there is the declining Fire-star." Probably the star in question is the Year Star, which follows a twelve-year progression. This makes it likely that the cycle in line 10 is twelve, not ten, years. These two lines are symmetrical in that each begins with a reduplicating binome, both adverbial and both referring to the passage of time.

In lines 11–12 the reference to Yang Chu is puzzling, for what bothered him was not that the roads were broad and long, but rather that they were multiple and led in different directions (*Lieh-tzu*, 8:6b); in other words, that it was so difficult to make a correct choice, and once you have taken a false step, you are irrevocably committed. For T'ao Ch'ien the roads are easily traveled (broad), but tedious (since they go on for a long way) and perhaps they lead nowhere (though this not an overtone of *yu-yu*). From poem X we learn that a long road is not a good one to travel, but there it was first of all a literal journey; here it is either a road through life or, more likely, the path to preferment, and his unwillingness to travel that particular road had of course nothing to do with its being broad or long. This makes the Yang Chu reference ironic, if indeed the line is not corrupt, as some of the variant readings[91] suggest.

Line 13 reads "Though there is no occasion for scattering gold," a reference, by way of a poem by Chang Hsieh,[92] to Shu Kuang, who was given a purse by the Han emperor Hsüan on his retirement as Chief Tutor to the Heir Apparent. Back home, he and his nephew Shu Shou, who had been Junior Tutor, spent the money lavishly on drink and entertainment of their fellow villagers (*Han shu*, 71:3b–5a). T'ao Ch'ien also wrote a poem "In Praise of the Two Tutors Shu (*Works*, 4:12a–b).

---

89 There is a variant 終死 "for the rest of my life."

90 *Shih ching*, no. 154, 七月流火.

91 Ting Fu-pao notes two: 揚歧何以止 , which makes no sense, and for 朱 an alternate 生 "Master" (Yang).

92 Chang Hsieh's 張協 poem, "Celebrating the Two Tutors Shu," is in *Wen hsüan*, 21:5b.

XX

The sages flourished long before my time,	羲農去我久
Few in the world today preserve their truth.	舉世少復真
Tirelessly he worked, the old man of Lu,	汲汲魯中叟
To fill and patch and make it pure again.	彌縫使其淳
Though while he lived no phoenix came to nest,	鳳鳥雖不至
Yet briefly rites and music were renewed.	禮樂暫得新
In Lu his subtle teaching came to an end,	洙泗輟微響
And the flood swelled to the time of reckless Ch'in.	漂流逮狂秦
The *Odes*, the *History* — what were their crimes	詩書復何罪
That they should be reduced one day to ashes?	一朝成灰塵
Careful and devoted, the old graybeards	區區諸老翁
Truly served the cause with all their strength.	爲事誠殷勤
Why is it now that in these later times	如何絕世下
The Six Classics have not a single friend?	六籍無一親
All day the hurried carriages dash by	終日馳車走
But no one comes to ask about the ford.	不見所問津
If I fail to drink to my heart's content	若復不快飲
I will be untrue to the cap I wear.	空負頭上巾
Still I regret the stupid things I've said	但恨多謬誤
And hope you will forgive a man in his cups.	君當恕醉人

This last poem of the series has been the delight of Confucian commentators, for here T'ao Ch'ien is celebrating the Confucian Classics, Confucian worthies, Confucian scholarship, and above all the Sage himself. If at the end he abandons himself to drink, it is clearly in despair at the bad times, not a rejection of the proprieties. And he concludes on a becoming note of modesty, begging his reader's indulgence for his mistakes. There is no undercurrent of irony: if he is repeating platitudes of Confucian history and hagiography, it is with a tone of seriousness and simple piety — the world has become a poorer place through the neglect of the Classics. This is hardly the language of a man in his cups; it has none of the drunken arrogance of the earlier poems, where the mistakes he asks to be excused are surely to be found.

The sages of line 1 are specifically [Fu-]hsi and [Shen-]nung, and their truth would be first of all the true principles embodied in the reigns of these mythical Good Rulers as well as the kind of values that prevailed in the world in their time. It would also be a man's true nature, which in the Golden Age was given free scope but which now is so abused and perverted it requires a real effort to get it back. "The old man of Lu" is of course Confucius, who worked to restore the purity of the Way of the Sages.

It was Confucius himself who complained, "The River puts forth no chart, the phoenix does not come — I am done for" (*Lun yü*, 9/9). These omens occur only in a time of perfect rule, which of course Confucius never experienced. But he made his contribution by preserving cultural traditions already suffering neglect.[93]

A closer translation of line 7 would be "The faint echo stopped by the Chu and the Ssu." The excuse for rendering *wei hsiang* as "subtle teaching" comes from the passage, "Confucius died and his subtle words (*wei yen*) came to an end" (*Han shu*, 30:1a). The Chu and the Ssu are two rivers in Lu where Confucius taught.[94]

In lines 9–10 the reference is to the famous Burning of the Books under the Ch'in Emperor Shih-huang-ti. The Confucian Classics, including the *Shih* and the *Shu*, were among those proscribed. Lines 11–12 recall the work of old men like Master Fu who in the early years of the Han dynasty, after the fall of the Ch'in, wrote down from memory the texts of the Classics.

The Six Books in line 14 are certainly the Six Classics. The commentators believe that T'ao Ch'ien is deploring their neglect by his contemporaries, who favored the writings of the Taoists, but surely it is not too far-fetched to apply his remark to the ethical contents of the Classics. There was no question, in his time, of the texts of the Classics being lost — there were, after all, officially appointed scholars responsible for their study and preservation — but men in official positions who practiced Confucian principles were notably a minority.

Line 16 contains another *Conversations* allusion (*Lun yü*, 18/6): "Ch'ang-chü and Chieh-ni were pulling the plow together when Confucius came along and sent Tzu-lu to ask them about the ford. Ch'ang-chü said, 'Who is it you are driving for?' Tzu-lu said, 'For K'ung Ch'iu.' 'K'ung Ch'iu of Lu?' 'Yes.' 'He already knows the ford.'" T'ao Ch'ien says in effect that he, become a recluse like Ch'ang-chü, sees no followers of Confucius, a complaint he has made in an earlier poem,[95] "Plowing and planting are over for the time,/But no one comes to ask for the ford."

Ho Meng-ch'un, one of the old commentators, refers lines 17–18 to the episode related in Hsiao T'ung's biographical sketch, "When the wine was brewed, he took the cloth turban from his head and strained the wine through it. When he had finished, he put it back on again." Wang Yao suggests that it is rather his Confucian cap, and this would be the obvious meaning

---

[93] *Shih chi*, 130:18: "By Confucius' time the Chou house had declined, and rites and music were neglected."

[94] *Li chi*, 3/36: "Tseng tzu said to Tzu-hsia, 'You and I served the Master in the region of the Chu and the Ssu'" (Ku Chih).

[95] "Remembering Ancient Worthies ... " *Works*, 3:13b.

if the anecdote had not been preserved. The line "I would be wearing the cap on my head to no purpose," is open to either interpretation, but the irony in claiming it to be his Confucian duty to get drunk, conditions being what they are, is preferable.

The term *miu-wu* in line 19 is not limited to verbal errors, but Ku Chih is surely right in saying that he is pleading drunkenness in extenuation of the many offensive things he has said in these poems.

In these twenty poems T'ao Ch'ien reflects on the world, on his lot, on his place in the world. They touch on a variety of his concerns, and he is not altogether consistent in his attitude; but in nearly every poem there is some reminder of what he has already said in his preface, that he is living in retirement. Sometimes he presents his unemployment in terms of success and failure; and if he has failed he can console himself with the thought that this is the way the world goes (I), a man of understanding should be able to accept his lot (I, XV), and anyhow, with wine to drink one can be content (VII). Another time his retirement appears to have been deliberate choice, a better way of living: it is quiet (V), one has peace of mind (VII), one has friends who come to share their wine (XIV, XVIII). It is a place of refuge (IV, VII) in a dangerous (X, XVII) and unsympathetic (III, IV, XVIII) world. But not always a comfortable refuge. The house is inadequate (IX, XVI), the surroundings wild (XV, XVI), there is real hardship — cold and hunger (XVI), and a lack of understanding friends (XIX, XX). But there are other reasons than escape for coming here: this is a way of preserving one's integrity, of fulfilling one's ideals (XIX). It is also an alternative way of making a name for oneself (XII); it is only through trials that a man's moral fiber shows (II, VIII, XI, XVI).

The one constant underlying all these conflicting attitudes toward retirement is the view of the world from which he retires as an essentially bad place. It is not only deceitful (XII), dreary (VIII), and unpredictable (I), it has no bias in favor of morality (II, XI, XIX), and moreover it has been getting worse (III, XX). It has nothing to offer an honest man, whose very character disqualifies him for playing an effective role in affairs. Now these observations are not original with T'ao Ch'ien, though he expressed them often enough in his writings both before and after the "Drinking Wine" poems. There is no doubt that his suspicion of the world was based on his own experience, but he was not unaware of literary and historical precedents to which he could appeal. In particular he was familiar with the biography of Po-i and Shu-ch'i in the *Shih chi*, a text which I have already mentioned in commenting on II and VIII. A longer excerpt is called for here (*Shih chi*, 61:8a–10b):

It has been said that "it is the Way of Heaven to have no favorites; it always sides with good men" [*Tao te ching*, 79]. Then is it wrong to say that Po-i and Shu-ch'i were good men? — To accumulate virtue and pure conduct as they did, and then to die of starvation!

Of the seventy disciples, Confucius praised only Yen Hui for his love of learning.[96] But "Hui was often empty" [*Lun yü* 11/18], not having his fill even of coarse fare, and he died young; is this the way Heaven rewards good men? The Robber Chih killed innocent people every day and ate their flesh. Perverse and violent, he assembled his several thousand followers and hacked a way through the empire [*Chuang-tzu*, 29]. But he lived to a ripe old age in consequence of what virtue? These are the greatest and most flagrant examples.

In recent times there have been those whose conduct was improper, who made a point of violating taboos, and yet who lived happily to the end of their lives and whose descendants have enjoyed unbroken prosperity through generations. And on the other hand, there are any number of people who are particular about what ground they walk on, who speak only at the proper time, who will not follow bypaths and who are enthusiastic about nothing that is not right and proper — and who come to grief. I find this very confusing. Is this thing they call Heaven's Way real or illusory?

The Master said, "If his is another Way, I will undertake nothing with him; let each do as he likes."[97] That is why he also said, "If riches and honor were anything to be had for the seeking, I would do it, even if I had to be a groom with whip in hand. But since they are not to be got that way, I shall do what I like" [*Lun yü*, 7/12]. When the weather turns chill, then you notice that it's the pine tree endures cold [*Lun yü*, 9/28]. When all the world is befuddled, then the gentleman of pure morals stands out.[98] How can Heaven treat those others so generously and these so contemptuously?[99] The gentleman hates it that he dies without making his name known [*Lun yü*, 15/20]. Chia Yi said,[100] "The miser will do anything for his hoard, the hero for his repute,/The vainglorious is ready to die for power, the common man clings to life."

Brightness finds its reflection, congeners seek one another out: "clouds follow the dragon, wind follows the tiger; the sage acts and all creation is displayed."[101] Po-i and Shu-ch'i were worthy in their own right, but their fame was made manifest through Confucius. Though Yen Yuan was devoted to learning, his conduct was made famous through his clinging to the race-horse's tail.[102] Gentlemen who live in retirement, whose activity is

---

96 *Lun yü*, 6/3: "There was Yen Hui who loved learning. . . . Now that he is no more, I know of no one who loves learning."

97 *Lun yü*, 15/40. The concluding words 亦 各 從 其 志 are not in the *Lun yü* passage.

98 *Tao te ching*, p. 118: "It is when the state is in disorder that you have loyal subjects." The point of view is different here.

99 A very uncertain line. Literally, "How so heavy as the former, so light as the latter?" The commentators provide a wide range of interpretative guesses. I have followed the second one provided by Ssu-ma Chen.

100 In his "Owl fu," *WH*, 13:14a–b.

101 *I ching*, 1: 文 言 .

102 Ssu-ma Chen notes that it is a fly that goes a thousand *li* by clinging to the race horse's tail.

timely — alas, that the names of such should perish and be heard of no more! How can a man who lives in an out-of-the-way place, who wants to cultivate his conduct so as to make a name for himself, ever get to be known to later generations without the help of a well-placed patron![103]

The general tenor of the passage is clear enough, though the links between paragraphs are not always obvious. Ssu-ma Ch'ien says in effect that history provides examples of good men who went unrewarded and of wicked men who lived out their lives unpunished. Heaven clearly does not do anything to promote morality among men, so why be moral? Well, as Confucius pointed out, there is no sure way, dishonorable or otherwise, to riches and honor — the things ordinarily taken as signs of Heaven's approval. So Heaven does not actively encourage unscrupulous behavior either, and one might as well stick to one's own standards. After all, adversity does try a man, and it is because the world is wicked that the good man stands out. Still, it is not enough to be egregiously good to be famous, particularly famous after death, and a gentleman is concerned about his reputation. But because likes attract one another, there is always a chance that a good man will be made known to the world through the praise of another good man, as Yen Yuan was through Confucius. It is really too bad that obscure men of high ideals are not better known. What they need is an appreciative and well-placed friend or patron — or the services of a good historian.

This piece could easily serve as a general introduction to the whole "Drinking Wine" series. Like Ssu-ma Ch'ien,[104] T'ao Ch'ien was very much concerned with the name he was going to leave behind him, and he was just as ready to leave a written record of his life,[105] though his medium was poetry rather than history.

The theme of the "Drinking Wine" poems, then, is the situation of a man of principle who voluntarily retires from an unprincipled world, renouncing the chance for a distinguished career. In the ten-odd years since he gave up his last official position, T'ao Ch'ien had written — and continued to write — similar poems, alternately complaining about and celebrating his life in

---

103 A "blue-cloud gentleman" 青 雲 之 士 can be a recluse in the hills, a person of high ideals, or someone high up in court, as Murao Genyū (quoted by Takigawa) pointed out. I have followed Chang Shou-chieh in choosing the one that makes best sense.

104 See his "Letter to Jen An," WH, 41:23b, "I hated it that . . . I might perish and my literary work be unknown to later ages."

105 For example, the concluding lines of the preface to the poem "Inspired by Events" (Works, 3:37a), "As the year draws near its end, I am burdened with care. I should write about it, if posterity is to know."

retirement. Why then did he provide this particular series with a misleading title, a disclaimer for a preface, and a conclusion begging pardon and pleading drunkenness as an excuse? It looks as though he felt that here he had written something subversive and was afraid of getting into trouble.

In these poems T'ao Ch'ien most often presents himself as a Confucian recluse in the classical tradition, whose models are Po-i and Shu-ch'i, the Four White Heads, Chang Chih, and Yang Lun. Although pleased with the quiet and leisure provided by retirement, he does not claim to have retired for purposes of religious contemplation, either Buddhist or Taoist, nor to be engaged in any Taoist alchemical practices that would justify abandoning other pursuits. Actually he does not seem to have gained much leisure by being unemployed, since he still has to make a living. His retirement is essentially Confucian,[106] the gesture of a man who, on ethical grounds, cannot come to terms with the world, and so becomes a recluse who renounces all further dealings with officialdom.

Such a recluse is not just a harmless eccentric with unconventional manners and tastes. His very existence, if not actually a threat, is a rebuke to those in power. Here is a man, qualified by education and training to hold a place among the elite of his society, who refuses to accept such a post because he feels himself to be morally superior to those who do, so much so in fact that his superior virtue would be sullied by contact with them. This holier-than-thou attitude is not one calculated to endear, and those against whom it was directed were accustomed to make the professional recluse uncomfortable by offering him a chance to show how much better he could do the job himself. The recluse could and usually did refuse to accept such offers, but if it were often enough repeated, or if it came from a dignitary too august to ignore, or if it were accompanied by marks of favor too loaded with prestige, he had no choice but to accept. He might make his escape on the way to the capital and disappear into the mountains,[107] he might beg off after his arrival,[108] or he might so embarrass his

---

106 See F. W. Mote, "Confucian Eremitism in the Yüan Period," *in* Arthur Wright, ed., *The Confucian Persuasion* (Stanford University Press, 1960), pp. 203–212, and the works cited there in notes 2 and 5.

107 Like Han K'ang 韓康 , who refused repeated summonses until the Emperor sent presents and a comfort carriage, which he would not ride in, choosing instead a wood wagon. It was taken away from him by a local sheriff who mistook him for a nonentity. After interceding for the man, Han K'ang went on toward the capital, but never arrived there, and lived out the rest of his life in seclusion (*Hou-Han shu chi-chieh*, 83:11a–b).

108 Like Chou Tang 周黨 , who very nearly got into trouble by neglecting the proper etiquette when he finally deigned to appear at the Emperor Kuang-wu's court. Fan Sheng

would-be patron that he was gladly let go.[109] The important thing is that he was not always free to refuse, because refusal was a positive act of criticism that placed the recluse in a precarious position.

T'ao Ch'ien, in resigning after his brief tenure as magistrate of P'eng-tse, was giving up on recognized, valid grounds a post he had actually solicited.[110] In the years after 405 he was always in a position to petition for another appointment, but his retirement presumably did not attract attention until sometime around 415, when he was offered a new office. His refusal marked him for the first time[111] as a Recluse, a man who felt himself too good to serve, even when asked to. (Most men did not wait to be asked.)

The temptation to read into poem IX a record of the offer and his refusal is irresistible. It makes all the coy ambiguity with which T'ao has surrounded the poems meaningful. It also gives us some idea of the drama and inner conflict hidden behind the innocent entry in his (and so many other) biographies,[112] "Toward the end of the i-hsi period (405–418) he was offered the post of Adjutant, but he refused." If T'ao Ch'ien is more ready to tell us the hardships such a decision exposed him to than the sort of rewards that he surrendered by not accepting, it is no doubt because these latter were obvious to any reader he could imagine having. It was more than just being better off, enjoying status and prestige. He was very likely wholly sincere in dismissing these as not attractive to him. The thing harder to renounce was the chance to play an active role in society, to make a name that would be worthy of his distinguished ancestor.[113] No wonder, when the offer came, he (figuratively) rushed to the door, pulling his gown on wrongside

---

范升 , in a memorial, challenged his motives as well as his behavior, accusing him of arrogance and hypocrisy. The Emperor let him off with a reference to Po-i and Shu-ch'i (*Hou-Han shu chi-chieh,* 83:4b–5a).

109 Ching Tan 井丹 refused offers by five princes. When a sixth, one with powerful court connections, made a special effort, he was forced to accept. He sneered at the coarse food offered him ("I came because I thought I could get a decent meal"), and remarked of a sedan chair brought for his use, "This must be the sort of 'human cart' used by the Tyrant Chieh." They were glad to let him go (*Hou-Han shu chi-chieh,* 83:7a–b).

110 Both his biography and the preface to "The Return" say as much.

111 The offer of a post as Secretary 主簿 mentioned in all versions of his biography came before his term as P'eng-tse magistrate.

112 義熙末徵著作佐郎不就 . *Nan shih,* 75:3b; *Sung shu,* 93:13a. The *Chin shu* version does not give a date for the offer.

113 He claimed as his great-grandfather T'ao K'an 侃 , who was enfeoffed Lord of Ch'ang-sha 長沙郡公 for his services under the Chin Emperor Ming (323–325).

out in his haste, only to decline politely when it turned out to be nothing but the same old chance to "join the muddy game."

It is the intrusion of these brief moments of weakness, of regret, of dissatisfaction with the life he deliberately chose, that introduces the ambiguity and complexity into these poems, keeping them from monotony in spite of his compulsive worrying the same theme over and over.

I believe that practically the whole body of T'ao Ch'ien's poetry can profitably be regarded in this light. Certainly it is the work of a man who, if he found a solution to his problems, did not find it an easy one to live with.

The Double Ninth Festival in Chinese Poetry:
A Study of Variations upon a Theme

A. R. DAVIS

BY the last century of the Six Dynasties period the Double Ninth Festival had been given a precise origin. The *Hsü Ch'i-hsieh chi*[1] 續齊諧記 of Wu Chün 吳均 (469–520) has the following account, widely accepted in popular tradition:

Huan Ching 桓景 of Ju-nan 汝南 was a companion of Fei Chang-fang[2] 費長房 in his studies for many years. Chang-fang once said to him: "On the ninth day of the ninth month there will be a great disaster on your household. You should hurry and order the persons of your household each to make red bags, fill them with dogwood and hang them on their arms. If you climb a hill and drink chrysanthemum wine, this disaster can be dispelled." Ching did as he said, and with all his household climbed a hill. In the evening they returned home and saw that the fowls and dogs, the oxen and sheep had died violently, all at once. Chang-fang said: "They took your place." This is why men of the present day always on the Ninth Day climb a hill and drink chrysanthemum wine, and the women carry dogwood bags.

Wu Chün's account which thus places the origin of the festival in the later Han period is no doubt apocryphal,[3] but it brings in all the basic associations of the Double Ninth — dogwood, the climbing of a height, the drinking of chrysanthemum wine, and the idea of the preservation of life.

---

[1] Translated from the quotation in *I-wen lei-chü* 藝文類聚 (photolith. reprint in series *Ssu-pu chi-yao*, Taipei, 1960), 4:17b.

[2] Biographical notice among the practitioners of "medical arts" in *Hou-Han shu* 後漢書, 112B.

[3] I am concerned here only with the literary aspect of the Double Ninth; for a sociological discussion see Wolfram Eberhard, *Lokalkulturen im alten China* II, *Monumenta Serica* Monograph 3 (1942), 376–378.

A description of the festival in more abstract, symbolic terms is found in a letter by Ts'ao P'ei 曹丕 (Emperor Wen of Wei) (186–226) to Chung Yu 鍾繇 (151–230):[4]

The year goes, the months come. Suddenly it is again the ninth day of the ninth month. Nine is the number of the Light Force (Yang) 陽 , and day and month correspond with one another. Common people delight in its name and believe it appropriate to long life. Therefore on it they give banquets and meet together on heights. This month is in the pitch-pipes Wu-i[5] 無射 ; that is to say, of the mass of trees and many plants there are none which shoot from the ground and grow. Yet the fragrant chrysanthemums abundantly bloom by themselves. If they did not contain the pure harmony of Heaven and Earth and embody the clear essence of fragrance, how could they do so? Therefore Ch'ü P'ing grieved at his steadily growing old and thought of eating the fallen blossoms of the autumn chrysanthemums.[6] For supporting the body and prolonging life nothing is as valuable as these. I respectfully offer a bunch to aid in the art of P'eng-tsu.[7]

Chung Hui 鍾會 (225–264), the youngest son of the recipient of Ts'ao P'ei's letter, expressed similar ideas in a *fu* 賦 on the chrysanthemum, of which fragments have survived;[8] and T'ao Yüan-ming (365-427), from whose hand we have the first extant Ninth Day poems, clearly shows knowledge of Ts'ao P'ei's letter in his "Living in Retirement on the Ninth Day" 九日閒居 . This poem begins with a short preface in prose.

When I was living in retirement, I delighted in the name of the Double Ninth. The autumn chrysanthemums filled my garden but I had no means of taking wine. So in want for it, I partook of the Ninth Day flowers and put my feelings into words.

> 余閒居 ， 愛重九之名 ， 秋菊盈園 ， 而持醪靡由 ， 空服
> 九華 ， 寄懷於言 。

Life is short but desires are always many;	世短意常多
We men delight in living long.	斯人樂永生
The day and month come at due time;	日月依辰至
Every common man delights in the day's name.	舉俗愛其名
The dews are chill, the genial breezes cease;	露淒喧風息
In the clear air the heavenly signs are bright.	氣澈天象明
Of the departed swallows not a shadow remains,	往燕無遺影
From the arriving geese there is abundance of noise.	來鴈有餘聲
Wine can drive out manifold cares,	酒能祛百慮
Chrysanthemums may arrest declining years.	菊解制頹齡
How is it with the rustic hut scholar?	如何蓬廬士

4 From quotation in *I-wen lei-chü*. 4:19b–20a.
5 *Li-chi* 禮記 (*Yüeh-ling* 月令 , *SPPY* ed., 5:20a–b).
6 "Li-sao" 離騷 , *Ch'u-tz'u* 楚辭 (*SPPY* ed.), 1:10a.
7 I.e., of living long.
8 Collected by Yen K'o-chün 嚴可均 in *Ch'üan San-kuo wen* 全三國文 , 25:1b.

In want, he watches the season passing.	空 覰 時 運 傾
The dusty cup shames the empty wine-jar;	塵 爵 恥 虛 罍
The cold flowers vainly display themselves.	寒 華 徒 自 榮
Adjusting my robe, alone I sing a song at leisure;	斂 襟 獨 閒 謠
In my brooding arise deep feelings.	緬 焉 起 深 情
At rest, truly there are many joys:	棲 遲 固 多 娛
My lingering is surely not without achievement?9	淹 留 豈 無 成

This poem might stand at the beginning of an anthology[10] which one might compile of Chinese Ninth Day poems. For the Double Ninth was especially beloved of Chinese poets, and one or more poems written for this day of the year are to be found in the collected works of great numbers of major and minor poets. Since this theme has thus attracted such a wealth of exposition, we are afforded in Ninth Day poems a great depth of material for the consideration of the problem of "imitation" in Chinese poetry. The examination of a fairly large number of poems from different periods on a common theme may give insight into how later poets succeeded or failed to accommodate what one might call the burden of memory, the heritage of famous lines, bequeathed them by eminent predecessors. We shall see that, apart from the deliberate imitation or quotation of famous lines, there is a certain furniture which seems to become established for the poem upon the recurrent theme. It is not of course necessary that each piece should invariably find its place, but rather it stood ready for use.

One such piece for Ninth Day poems may be introduced immediately. Since T'ao Yüan-ming became especially associated with the chrysanthemum, he came very readily first to mind, when a Double Ninth poem was to be written, and it was very often T'ao as he appeared in a particular anecdote, found in the Sung-shu 宋 書 (chüan 93) and Nan-shih 南 史 (chüan 75) biographies and also in the biography of him by Hsiao T'ung 蕭 統 (510-531). This anecdote was quite likely taken from T'an Tao-luan's 檀道鸞 Hsü Chin yang-ch'iu 續 晉 陽 秋 into the Sung-shu and thence into the other two biographies. At any rate the anecdote was quoted from Hsü Chin yang-ch'iu in the early encyclopedias, and since this article will in part attempt to

---

9 *T'ao Ching-chieh chi* 陶 靖 節 集 (Basic Sinological Series), 2:15. [*Editor's note*: For the last line, cf. no. 16 (line 4) of T'ao's "Drinking Wine" poems translated by James Hightower in this volume.]

10 A considerable sample of poems on the Double Ninth up to the Ming period, both *shih* 詩 and *tz'u* 詞 , may be found in the encyclopedia *Ku-chin t'u-shu chi-ch'eng* 古 今 圖 書 集 成 , *chüan* 77–78. Many but not all of the *shih* poems I have translated in this article are included there.

show that these encyclopedias contributed to the source material for poetry,
I shall translate from the version in *Pei-t'ang shu-ch'ao*:[11] "T'ao Yüan-ming
on the ninth day of the ninth month had no wine. Among the chrysanthemum
clumps by the side of his house he plucked handfuls and for a long while
sat by them. He saw in the distance a man in a white robe coming: it was
in fact [Wang] Hung[12] 王弘 bringing wine. They at once poured out the
wine and not until they were drunk, did Hung go home."

Many commentators have made a factual connection between this
anecdote and T'ao Yüan-ming's poem, cited above. A little serious reflection
will suffice to show that this connection is to be suspected rather than enter-
tained, but this is a question which need not detain us here. We shall find,
however, that the anecdote becomes perhaps more important in the tradition
of the Double Ninth than the poem from which it probably grew. There
is another poem by T'ao Yüan-ming, which may be usefully set with the
first to show this poet's variation on his own theme, the urgent but hopeless
desire to arrest the passing of time.

The Ninth Day of the Ninth Month
of the Year Chi-yu [Oct. 3, A.D. 409]

己 酉 歲 九 月 九 日

Slowly the autumn has come to its close;	靡 靡 秋 已 夕
Chilly the wind and dew mingle.	淒 淒 風 露 交
The creeping plants no longer flower,	蔓 草 不 復 榮
The garden trees, bare, have lost their leaves.	園 木 空 自 凋
The clear air is cleansed of the last murkiness,	清 氣 澄 餘 滓
Dimly seen, the bounds of heaven are high.	杳 然 天 界 高
Of the sad cicada there is no lingering sound,	哀 蟬 無 留 響
But flocking geese cry among the clouds.	叢 鴈 鳴 雲 霄
Ten thousand transformations follow on one another:	萬 化 相 尋 繹
Man's life, how should it not be laborious?	人 生 豈 不 勞
From of old all have had to die:	從 古 皆 有 沒
When I think of it, my heart within me burns.	念 之 中 心 焦
How shall I accord with my feelings?	何 以 稱 我 情
With cloudy wine let me gladden myself.	濁 酒 且 自 陶
A thousand years I shall not know;	千 載 非 所 知
Let me with it prolong this morning.[13]	聊 以 永 今 朝

Before passing on from T'ao Yüan-ming one further anecdote may be
added, in this case one which the poet himself published. He wrote a

---

11 (Photolith. reprint, Taipei, 1962), 155:12a.
12 Governor of Chiang-chou. 418–425.
13 *T'ao Ching-chieh chi*, 3:39.

biography of his maternal grandfather Meng Chia 孟 嘉 , in which the following account appears:

Chia's manner was affable and correct: [Huan] Wen14 桓 温 greatly esteemed him. On
the ninth day of the ninth month Wen made an excursion to Lung-shan15 龍 山 . His aides
and assistant officials were all in the company, and his four younger brothers and two sons-
in-law were present. On this occasion his subordinates were all in military dress. There was
a wind which blew Chia's hat to the ground. Wen gave a look to his staff and his guests to
say nothing, so that he might observe how he would behave. Chia at first did not notice,
but after some while, he went to relieve himself. Wen then ordered the hat to be picked up
and returned to him. The Regulator in the Commandery of Justice, Sun Sheng 孫 盛 of
T'ai-yüan 太 原 , who was Counsellor-aide, was present at the time. Wen called for paper
and brush and requested him to satirize Chia. When it was completed, he showed what he
had written to Wen. Wen put it on Chia's seat. When Chia returned and found that he had
been satirized, he asked for a brush and composed a reply, completing it in a moment. The
diction was superlative; the whole company admired it.16

I have quoted this anecdote in full and it is fair to describe it as producing
one of the most commonly introduced pieces in the "furniture" of Ninth
Day poems. Yet it will be seen from my subsequent examples that, whereas
T'ao Yüan-ming used the whole of this story as an illustration of his grandfather's Confucian quality of a genial correctness, it gave to the Ninth Day
tradition two details, in the original only incidental — first, a place-name,
Lung-shan, which could immediately suggest enjoyment of the Ninth Day
in company; and, second, the simple fact of the blown-off hat. This simple
fact, taken from its context, is surely trivial, and yet its continual recurrence,
if not the result of the most sterile repetition, should indicate some potent
association. Let us look at some examples. First a whole poem, a five-
character *chüeh-chü* 絕 句 by Li Po 李 白 (701–762):

The Ninth Day's Drinking on Lung-shan	九 日 龍 山 飲
At the Ninth Day's Lung-shan drinking	九 日 龍 山 飲
The yellow flowers smile at the banished subject.	黃 花 笑 逐 臣
Drunk, he sees the wind blow down his hat;	醉 看 風 落 帽
Dancing, he loves the moon for making him stay.17	舞 愛 月 留 人

---

14 312–373, leader of one of the most powerful families of his period.

15 By the time of the compilation of the *Yüan-ho chün-hsien t'u-chih* 元 和 郡 縣 圖 志
(*ca.* 815) the hill in question had been identified as that southeast of modern Tang-t'u 當 塗 ,
Anhui (see *chüan* 28). The rival identification as the Lung-shan 龍 山 northwest of Chiang-
ling 江 陵 , Hupei, seems more probable. See also nn. 18 and 50.

16 "Biography of the Former Chief of Staff to the Chin Generalissimo for Subduing the
West, His Excellency Meng," *T'ao Ching-chieh chi*, 6:84.

17 *Li T'ai-po ch'üan-chi* 李 太 白 全 集 (*SPPY* ed.), 20:22b.

Although the location of the Lung-shan of the Meng Chia incident is in dispute and the dispute may be continued in the case of Li Po's poem,[18] we might argue that Li Po, at any rate believing himself to be passing the feast on Meng Chia's mountain, is moved by the association of place, which is strong for all poets, not Chinese poets alone. Nevertheless the blown-off hat occurs in two other of his Ninth Day poems:

> My hat falls and I am drunk in the mountain moonlight;　　　落 帽 醉 山 月
> Singing in vain, I think of my friends.[19]　　　　　　　　空 歌 懷 友 生

and:

> The guests are scattered with the falling leaves;　　　　　賓 隨 落 葉 散
> My hat is blown away by the autumn wind.[20]　　　　　　　帽 逐 秋 風 吹

One, if not both,[21] of these poems is certainly unconnected with either Lung-shan to which the Meng Chia story has been related, and thus here one cannot speak of any association of place. In both of these poems the blown-off hat is no more than a glancing reference: it seems to have no major part in them. If one took up any of the examples separately, one might simply speak of a "literary allusion" and commentators would generally dutifully cite the passage from which it comes. Yet when one puts together three occurrences in three poems on the same theme by a poet acknowledged as one of China's greatest, is it sufficient to talk of "literary allusions"? Was Li Po wanting in the imagination or the energy to vary his allusion or had he become obsessed with blown-off hats? I have emphasized the triviality of the reference, for I think that its very triviality should compel us to think the more seriously about its significance. But perhaps I may remove any particularity of connection with Li Po by adding a further example, taken more or less at random. We find the same reference in a poem by Yang Wan-li 楊 萬 里 (1124–1206), entitled "On the Double Ninth, Rain and the Chrysanthemums also Unopened, Written in the 'Windlass' Style":[22]

---

18 See Wang Ch'i's 王 琦 commentary, *Li T'ai-po ch'üan-chi*, 20:22b, and Chan Ying 詹 鍈, *Li Po shih-wen hsi-nien* 李 白 詩 文 繫 年 (Peking, 1958), p. 153. Both accept the Tang-t'u Lung-shan identification: Chan thus dates the poem 762. But see n. 50, below.

19 "The Ninth Day" 九 日, *Li T'ai-po ch'üan-chi*, 20:22a. Because of the similarity of language with "The Ninth Day's Drinking on Lung-shan" (a very dubious criterion), Chan Ying, p. 153, provisionally dates this poem also 762.

20 "Climbing a Hill on the Ninth Day" 九 日 登 山, *Li T'ai-po ch'üan-chi*, 20:21a.

21 "Climbing a Hill on the Ninth Day" was written in 754 at Hsüan-ch'eng 宣 城, Anhui.

22 Chou Ju-ch'ang 周 汝 昌, *Yang Wan-li hsüan-chi* 楊 萬 里 選 集 (Shanghai, 1962), p. 113. "Windlass" style is the use of rhymes from different classes in the 1st and 2nd four lines of a *lü-shih*.

I have shut my door, so luckily I shall avoid
　　my black hat blowing off;

I have wine, so why need I look out for the
　　white-robed man?

閉 門 幸 免 吹 烏 帽

有 酒 何 須 望 白 衣

Yang Wan-li's lines, added to Li Po's, make it clear that the hat blown off by the autumn wind is not an association of place, but rather a permanent association of the Double Ninth in the poetry written for that festival day. I have called it part of the furniture of the tradition which formed around the writing of Ninth Day poems, and in each of the poems cited the poet must have been introducing it for some purpose, even if only dimly formulated. I would suggest that that purpose was to link his particular poem to the general stream of Chinese poetry. In few countries can poetry have been so emphatically a shared and corporate activity as in China. Thus I think that in this matter of permanent associations in Ninth Day poems we are face to face with one particular aspect of the Chinese sense of the community of poets and poetry and of their abiding desire to affirm it.

After sounding this high note of conclusion from the consideration of a very slight piece of evidence, it is necessary to descend bathetically to examine the question of the manner in which the Lung-shan where Meng Chia's hat blew off became a permanent association of the Double Ninth. I believe that it came about through the arrangement of literary extracts under topical headings in the *lei-shu* 類 書 or encyclopedias. If we examine the entries under our particular topic, the Double Ninth festival, we shall find a great similarity of citation from the *Pei-t'ang shu-ch'ao* 北 堂 書 鈔 of Yü Shih-nan 虞 世 南 (558–638) through *I wen lei-chü* 藝 文 類 聚 and *Ch'u-hsüeh chi* 初 學 記 to the *T'ai-p'ing yü-lan* 太 平 御 覽 at the beginning of the Sung period, and, if one likes to go further, to the sixteenth-century *T'ien-chung chi* 天 中 記. The first three works named appeared in the period of the development of the Sui-T'ang civil service examination system and there is obviously a causal relationship between the two. We may describe them as works of academic study and reference, and they had the effect, which such works always have, of creating a common fund of knowledge among their users. In case I should seem here to be in danger of modifying what I said above about the Chinese poet's desire to establish a connection with the general tradition, I would stress that I do not think that Li Po made this particular reference three times because the encyclopedias had made the incident so familiar to him. What I am suggesting at this point is only that the existence of the encyclopedias could have been the reason why he knew of the incident *at all*. I believe that these encyclopedias worked directly and indirectly to create what I have called the permanent associations of a particular topic, but how and when a writer used these permanent associations we may leave to the credit of his creative choice.*

A rather nice piece of evidence for this assertion may be seen, if we turn back to the second reference in the couplet quoted from Yang Wan-li's poem. The "white-robed man" here is Wang Hung, governor of Chiang-chou 江州 in the anecdote about T'ao Yüan-ming, cited above from the quotation of *Hsü Chin yang-ch'iu* in *Pei-t'ang shu-ch'ao*. Now, we must particularly notice that the one phrase which is picked up to make reference to this story is "white-robed." The same means of reference is used also in Li Po's poem "Climbing a Hill on the Ninth Day," previously mentioned, viz.:

When Yüan-ming returned home,	淵明歸去來
He had no intercourse with the world.	不與世相逐
Yet because he was without "the thing within the cup,"	爲無杯中物
When he chanced to meet his prefecture's governor,	遂偶本州牧
He accordingly beckoned the white-robed man,	因招白衣人
And, smiling, he poured the yellow-flowered chrysanthemum.	笑酌黃花菊

The phrase "white-robed" does not in fact occur in the version of the story in the *Sung-shu* or *Nan-shih* or in Hsiao T'ung's biography. It occurs only in the encyclopedia quotations of the *Hsü Chin yang-ch'iu*, of which Li Po is not likely to have seen the original text. A strong probability is indicated that this particular permanent association of the Double Ninth came to Li Po through the agency of one or other of the early encyclopedias.

Like the basic associations of the Double Ninth, some of the most enduring of the secondary associations — the poet T'ao Yüan-ming's lack of wine to celebrate the festival, his grandfather's blown-off hat — were established by the great period of T'ang poetry in the first half of the eighth century probably through the medium of the encyclopedias. After the initial establishment in poems of famous writers, these poems would themselves have exerted an influence. Not all of the encyclopedia associations of the Double Ninth seem to have gained an equal prominence in the tradition.

On the Double Ninth of A.D. 418, Liu Yü 劉裕, who was on the verge of overthrowing the Chin dynasty and becoming the first emperor of the [Liu-]Sung dynasty (420–478), held a banquet on the Racing Horse Terrace (*Hsi-ma T'ai* 戲馬台) at P'eng-ch'eng 彭城 (Kiangsu) to send

---

* [*Editor's note*: For a discussion of the influence of *lei-shu* upon poetry, see Wen I-to's 聞一多 "Lei-shu yü shih" 類書與詩, in his *T'ang shih tsa-lun* 唐詩雜論 (1945), *Wen I-to ch'üan-chi*, vol. 3, *ping*, pp. 3–10.]

off K'ung Ching 孔靖, who had declined a high personal appointment. On this occasion Hsieh Chan (387–421) and his cousin Hsieh Ling-yün (385–433) both wrote poems, which have been preserved through inclusion in Hsiao T'ung's anthology *Wen-hsüan*.[23] Since these closely rival T'ao Yüan-ming's work for the honor of being the earliest Ninth Day poems to be preserved, and since they are certainly the earliest examples by two poets on the same Double Ninth, I translate them in full. Both appear also in the encyclopedias.

Hsieh Chan's poem reads:

When the wind comes, winter clothes are given out:	風 至 授 寒 服
When the frost descends, all crafts are stopped.	霜 降 休 百 工
From the luxuriant wood are taken its summer colors;	繁 林 收 陽 彩
In the close-growing garden thinned are the flower clumps.	密 苑 解 華 叢
Nesting in the tent, there remain no swallows;	巢 幕 無 留 燕
Flying along the islets, there are arriving geese.	遵 渚 有 來 鴻
Light clouds cover the autumn sun,	輕 霞 冠 秋 日
A rushing autumn wind reaches the blue sky.	迅 商 薄 清 穹
The Saintly Man's[24] heart delights in the fair season;	聖 心 眷 嘉 節
Setting in motion his carriage bells, he comes to the traveling palace.	揚 鑾 戾 行 宮
The mats on every side are wet with fragrant wine;	四 筵 霑 芳 醴
In the central hall there arises the sound of the lute.	中 堂 起 絲 桐
The sun's light hurries to its western limit;	扶 光 迫 西 汜
While joy abounds, the banquet has its end.	歡 餘 宴 有 窮
He must go, the guest who is returning home!	逝 矣 將 歸 客
Nourishing his original nature, he will achieve a proper end.	養 素 克 有 終
At the water's edge I grieve not to follow;	臨 流 怨 莫 從
My festive heart sighs for the flying down.[25]	歡 心 歎 飛 蓬

Hsieh Ling-yün's poem is even more heavily laden with reminiscence of and reference to earlier works of literature:

In the last month of autumn the frontier north is harsh;	季 秋 邊 朔 苦
The migrating geese avoid the frost and snow.	旅 鴈 違 霜 雪
Chilly the summer plants decay,	淒 淒 陽 卉 腓
Brightly the wintry pool shines clear.	皎 皎 寒 潭 潔
This auspicious day has moved our Saintly Man's heart;[26]	良 辰 感 聖 心
The cloud banners are raised for the year's late festival.	雲 旗 興 暮 節
Sounding flutes come to the Red Palace;	鳴 笳 戾 朱 宮

---

23 *SPTK* ed., *chüan* 20:26a–27b and 28b–29b.
24 I.e., Liu Yü's.
25 "Flying down" symbolizes the traveler, here the departing K'ung Ching.
26 Again refers to Liu Yü.

Orchid cups are offered to the wise man of the age.[27]
At the farewell feast conspicuously there is trust;
Harmonious pleasure abounds where it was lacking.[28]
By "letting be and indulgence" the world is ordered;
By "being blown on in ten thousand ways" all regions
    are joyful.[29]
The returning guest goes to a corner of the sea;
He doffs his cap and takes leave of the court ranks.
Staying the oar, he comes to the curved islet;
Pointing to the sun, he waits for the music's end.
In the river's flow there are swift waves;
For the flying team there is no slow course.
Surely it is not the thought of the journey by water and land,
But my former feelings make me ashamed as we part.
His fair way of hills and gardens
Makes me, sighing, lament my inferiority.

蘭卮献時哲
餞宴光有孚
和樂隆所缺
在宥天下理
吹萬羣方悅
歸客逐海隅
脫冠謝朝列
弭棹薄枉渚
指景待樂関
河流有急瀾
浮驂無綏轍
豈伊川途念
宿心愧將別
彼美丘園道
喟焉傷薄劣

Though the *Ch'u-hsüeh chi* specifically lists the Racing Horse Terrace as an association of the Double Ninth festival, it does not seem to have come to the minds of T'ang and post-T'ang poets nearly so frequently as Meng Chia's Lung-shan. There is a reference in the second of the two poems which Li Po wrote to his friend Ts'ui Tsung-chih 崔宗之 from Hsüan-ch'eng 宣城 (modern Ning-kuo 寧國, Anhui) on the Double Ninth of A.D. 753:

From a distance I admire your Double Ninth writing,   遙羨重陽作
Which should surpass that of the Racing Horse Terrace.[30]   應過戲馬臺

Here Li Po in an elegant compliment to his friend suggests that his Ninth Day poem will be superior to those of the two Hsiehs. The poetry of Hsieh Ling-yün was widely admired during the T'ang, but his Double Ninth poem and that of his cousin Chan, in spite of their inclusion in the encyclopedias, do not seem to have won for their writers the same degree of continuing association with the festival as was enjoyed by their older contemporary T'ao Yüan-ming. One can guess at reasons for this. Among

---

[27] K'ung Ching.

[28] Line 9 appears to be founded on *I*, Hexagram 64, top line, "There is trust in drinking wine; no blame." Li Shan 李善 in his commentary to line 10 cites as from the *Mao Shih Preface*: "When the *Lu-ming* (title of *Song* 161) was abandoned, harmonious pleasure was lacking." This seems a very probable source for Hsieh's line, but it does not appear in the transmitted *Great* or *Small Prefaces*.

[29] "Letting be and indulgence" derives from the opening words of *Chuang-tzu, chüan* 11: "I have heard of letting the empire be and being indulgent to it, but I have not heard of ruling the empire." "Being blown on in ten thousand ways" is adapted from *Chuang-tzu, chüan* 2's description of the "pipes of Heaven."

[30] *Li T'ai-po ch'üan-chi*, 14:9a.

them pure chance might rank high, but there is also some justification for arguing that the personality of the poet, both as expressed through his own work and as defined by anecdotes which might cluster round him, was of great importance to his continuing appeal to the affection of his successors. As a man, T'ao Yüan-ming obviously attracted the sympathy of later poets in a way which Hsieh Ling-yün did not. Yet of more significance for our present topic is the fact that, when a comparison is made between T'ao's "Living in Retirement on the Ninth Day" and the Hsiehs' poems, the former, alone of the three, would, in the absence of a title, appear certainly to be a Ninth Day poem. In other words, although generally similar techniques are employed in the three poems to establish the general season of the year, the Hsiehs' poems do not introduce the basic associations of the particular day, and thus remain undifferentiated from "parting-feast" poems. For this reason especially they were less likely to come into the thoughts of a later poet who was concerned with the day in any symbolic aspect rather than as a red-letter day in the calendar.

Thus far our emphasis has been on the common and collective features of Ninth Day poems and we may now turn to examine and compare individual responses. For this purpose we may distinguish particular conditions under which the poet passed the Double Ninth. First, since T'ao Yüan-ming's "Living in Retirement on the Ninth Day" may again be included, we may consider examples where the poet passed the day in solitude, a condition contrary to the essential character of the festival, which called for the company of friends or colleagues. Here is Li Po alone in his "Ninth Day," a poem of which I have already quoted the last couplet:[31]

Today the clouded scene is fair,	今日雲景好
The water green amid autumn hills' brightness.	水綠秋山明
I clasp the wine-pot and pour "Drifting Clouds,"	攜壺酌流霞
Pluck chrysanthemums and float on it cold petals.	搴菊泛寒榮
The place is remote, the pines and rocks are old;	地遠松石古
The wind rises with strings and pipes' shrillness.	風揚弦管清
As I peer into the cup, it reflects my happy features:	窺觴照歡顏
Alone I laugh and still tilt the jar myself.	獨笑還自傾
My hat falls and I am drunk in the mountain moonlight;	落帽醉山月
Singing in vain, I think of my friends.	空歌懷友生

Li Po in this poem does not refer to T'ao Yüan-ming by name as he does elsewhere, nor does he introduce any reminiscence of T'ao's Ninth Day

---

31 *Ibid.*, 20:22a.

poems, yet he has subtly conjured the spirit of the old poet by faint suggestions of two of his "Drinking Wine"[32] poems, the famous fifth ("I have built my hut within men's borders") and the seventh ("The autumn chrysanthemums have beautiful colors"). This is a very interesting feature of a poem which in sum displays a decidedly more extrovert attitude and gives a much stronger sense of having captured the immediate moment than is felt in T'ao Yüan-ming's poems.

From Li Po's great contemporary, Tu Fu (712–770), we have two "Ninth Day in solitude" poems, written at different periods of his life and in different poetical forms. The first, in the five-word "old-style" form, was written for the Double Ninth of 754, a year of which the autumn brought sixty days of continuous rain to the area of the capital Ch'ang-an 長 安 and ruined the harvest. Tu Fu, living on the outskirts of the city at this time, addressed the poem to his great friend Ts'en Shen (715–770), who would seem to have returned to Central Asia on the staff of the An-hsi Governor-General Feng Ch'ang-ch'ing 封 常 清 :[33]

I go out of the gate, again come in at the gate;	出 門 復 入 門
The rain-clouds are still just as before.	雨 脚 但 如 舊
Wherever one goes, mud splashes;	所 向 泥 活 活
Thinking of you makes me thin.	思 君 令 人 瘦
Humming low, I sit in the western side-room;	沈 吟 坐 西 軒
Eating and drinking become confused between night and day.	飲 食 錯 昏 晝
A tiny step to the Curving Stream's side,[34]	寸 步 曲 江 頭
Yet hard it is to pay a single visit.	難 爲 一 相 就
Oh! Alas! for the common folk!	吁 嗟 乎 蒼 生
Their harvest cannot be saved.	稼 穡 不 可 救
How can we subdue the Rain Master?	安 得 誅 雲 師
Who can stop up the sky's leak?	疇 能 補 天 漏
The great brightness is hidden, of sun and moon;	大 明 韜 日 月
In the deserted wild cry birds and beasts.	曠 野 號 禽 獸
The gentleman may force his winding way,	君 子 强 逶 迤
But the little man is restrained from hurry.	小 人 困 馳 驟
In the south are the revered hills;	維 南 有 崇 山
I fear they will be drowned in the rivers.	恐 與 川 浸 溜
This season's eastern fence chrysanthemums	是 節 東 籬 菊
Abundantly open for whom their beauty?	紛 披 爲 誰 秀

[32] *T'ao Ching-chieh chi*, 3:41–42.

[33] See Wen I-to, "Ts'en Chia-chou hsi-nien k'ao-cheng" 岑 嘉 州 繫 年 考 證 in *Wen I-to ch'üan-chi* 聞 一 多 全 集 (1948), vol. 3, *ping* 丙 , pp. 121–122.

[34] The Curving Stream (*Ch'ü-chiang* 曲 江), an artificial waterway, was one of the chief pleasure-resorts of Ch'ang-an.

You, Master Ts'en, write many new poems,　　　　岑 生 多 新 詩
And by nature too are fond of good wine.　　　　性 亦 嗜 醞 酎
Numerous are the golden flowers,　　　　　　　　采 采 黃 金 花
But how can I fill my arms with them?[35]　　　　何 由 滿 衣 袖

From Tu Fu, as from Li Po, in his solitariness, the remembrance of T'ao Yüan-ming was not absent. There is a reference in the "eastern fence chrysanthemums" to the same fifth poem of the "Drinking Wine" series, and, when he writes of his friend as "by nature too, fond of wine" he is probably putting him in the company of the "Gentleman of the Five Willows." Very frequently in Tu Fu's thoughts at this time of continuous rains was T'ao's poem "Hanging Clouds" of which the first stanza reads:

Dense the hanging clouds,　　　　　　　　　　　　靉 靉 停 雲
Misty the seasonal rains,　　　　　　　　　　　　濛 濛 時 雨
Beyond the Eight Directions the same murk;　　　　八 表 同 昏
The level road now is difficult.　　　　　　　　　平 路 伊 阻
Quietly I stay in the eastern room;　　　　　　　靜 寄 東 軒
The spring wine I, solitary, cherish.　　　　　　　春 醪 獨 撫
My good friend is far away;　　　　　　　　　　　良 朋 悠 邈
I scratch my head and linger.[36]　　　　　　　　搔 首 延 佇

(With this the second line of the second of Tu Fu's "Sighing in the Autumn Rain,"[37] a three-poem series of the same period, may be compared: "Over the Four Seas and the Eight Wilds lies the same one cloud." 四 海 八 荒 同 一 雲) Nevertheless, although the situation of separation from his friend on this day of friendship is treated within a consciousness of the fellowship of Chinese poets, the middle eight lines of the poem are individual to Tu Fu, for they show one of his characteristic flashes of sincere and spontaneous sympathy for the common people, directly and simply expressed.

The second of Tu Fu's solitary Double Ninth poems — actually it is a series of five poems[38] — was written a dozen or so years later in 767. Now the aging and ailing poet was living near K'uei-chou 夔 州 , above the Yangtze gorges. I quote the first three poems as a sufficient sample.

---

35 Ch'ou Chao-ao 仇 兆 鰲 , *Tu Shao-ling chi hsiang-chu* 杜 少 陵 集 詳 註 , *chüan* 3 (Basic Sinological Series, 2:114–115).

36 *T'ao Ching-chieh chi*, 1:1.

37 *Tu Shao-ling chi hsiang-chu, chüan* 3 (2:119), 秋 雨 歎 .

38 *Ibid., chüan* 20 (8:69–70).

I

On Double Brightness, alone, I pour the wine within the cup;   重陽獨酌杯中酒
Sick, I get up and climb the terrace by the River.   抱病起登江上臺
Since of "Bamboo Leaves"[39] for me there is no share,   竹葉於人既無分
The chrysanthemum flowers from now need not open.   菊花從此不須開
In a strange place at sunset the black gibbons howl;   殊方日落玄猿哭
From my old country before the frost the white geese come.   舊國霜前白雁來
My brothers and my sister, lonely, each in what place?   弟妹蕭條各何在
While war and age both press on me.   干戈衰謝兩相催

II

In former days on Double Brightness Day,   舊日重陽日
When the cup passed, I never rejected the cup.   傳杯不放杯
Now when my tangled hair has changed,   即今蓬鬢改
I am only shamed by chrysanthemum flowers' opening.   但媿菊花開
Towards the northern palace-gate my heart long has yearned;   北闕心長戀
From the western river my head in solitude is turned.   西江首獨回
The dogwood is presented to the court officers,   茱萸賜朝士
But it is very hard for a single branch to come here.   難得一枝來

III

In the past I went with Vice-Rector Su;   舊與蘇司業
Together we accompanied Professor Cheng.[40]   兼隨鄭廣文
The plucked flowers' fragrance drifted,   采花香泛泛
The guests' drunkenness was disorderly.   坐客醉紛紛
On the wild tree, reclining, one still might lean;   野樹歌還倚
The autumn washing-stone, sobering, one still might hear.   秋砧醒却聞
But the joys for both are sunk in darkness;   歡娛兩冥漠
In the northwest there is a lonely cloud.[41]   西北有孤雲

In these poems of intense personal emotion Tu Fu laments his physical decline, his separation from home and kin, the death of his old friends, but also expresses the desire which continued with him almost to the end of his life to serve his country in an official post. All this personal and very real feeling, it must be agreed, is set within the proper context of Ninth Day poetry. These are poems which by their use of the basic associations of the Double Ninth are true Ninth Day poems. It must be remembered that even

---

39 The name of a wine.

40 Su Yü 蘇預 (Su Yüan-ming 蘇源明), Vice-Rector of the Imperial University (Kuo-tzu ssu-yeh 國 子 司 業), and Cheng Ch'ien, Professor of the College for the Extension of Literature (Kuang-wen kuan po-shih 廣 文 館 博 士), close friends of Tu Fu in Ch'ang-an, both died in 764.

41 The lonely cloud in the northwest symbolizes Tu Fu, the survivor, returning in imagination to the scene of former celebrations in Ch'ang-an.

by Tu Fu's time very great numbers of poems for this day had been written, as year followed year, and scores of admired examples had been preserved. Thus the pressure not merely towards stereotyped expression, but also towards conventionality of thought had intensified so that the ability to convey the *individuality* of sincere emotion within the accepted terms of reference and also, as in these present "regulated" poems of Tu Fu, within comparatively stringent limitations of the poetical form must emerge as an important criterion for the judging of such poetry.

The consideration of the great gifts of Tu Fu should, however, not prevent our appreciation of achievement at a lower degree of intensity, and as an illustration I shall cite a poem by an admittedly minor poet, which at first glance seems highly conventional, but yet has its individuality.

I laugh at myself for being unable to pass the Ninth Day alone,	自笑不能孤九日
With a single jar of cloudy wine facing the western hills.	一壺濁酒對西山
From afar I pity the jade tree in the autumn wind;	遙憐玉樹秋風裏
Quietly I gaze at the dark geese in the setting sun.	靜看冥鴻落日間
Plants and trees sigh, clouds turn bluer;	草木蕭蕭雲更碧
Hills and streams are silent, birds fly home.	山川漠漠鳥飛還
On a long journey who is a T'ao P'eng-tse[42]	長途誰是陶彭澤
In rough clothes to walk singing, his thoughts at ease?[43]	被褐行吟意自閒

This "Ninth Day" by the famous Yüan landscape painter Ni Tsan (1301–1374) is a gentle but effective expression of the loneliness of the traveler.

Nostalgia is a prime theme of Chinese poetry, for the poet in his alternate role of official so often passed many years of his life away from home and might travel from one end of China to the other. The many wars and rebellions of China's history were also a frequent cause of enforced separation from one's native place. The Double Ninth was an occasion which naturally evoked feelings of homesickness and separation, and many of its poems can be classified under this theme. Here are three four-line *chüeh-chü* by prominent T'ang poets:

Alone in a strange district I am a stranger;	獨在異鄉爲異客
At every auspicious season I doubly think of my kin.	每逢佳節倍思親
Far off, I know my brothers will climb a high place;	遙知兄弟登高處
All will put on their dogwood, with one man missing.[44]	遍挿茱萸少一人

---

[42] I.e., T'ao Yüan-ming who was for some eighty days in 405 Magistrate of P'eng-tse 彭澤 (Kiangsi).

[43] Translated from the text in *Ku-chin t'u-shu chi-ch'eng, chüan* 78 (22:12a).

[44] Wang Wei, "On the Ninth Day of the Ninth Month, Remembering My Brothers East of the Mountains," *Wang Mo-chieh ch'üan-chi chien-chu* 王摩詰全集箋注 , 14 (World Book Co. ed., 1936), 203.

This morning, as I take up the wine, I am again sad, 今朝把酒復惆悵
Thinking of the time upon the farm at Tu-ling. 憶在杜陵田舍時
Next year on the Ninth where shall I be? 明年九日知何處
In the times' troubles going home has no date.[45] 世難還家未有期

I would like to climb up high, 强欲登高去
But there is none to bring wine. 無人送酒來
From afar I pity my old garden's chrysanthemums, 遙憐故園菊
Which must on a battlefield flower.[46] 應傍戰塲開

Yet homecoming after too long an absence has an equal sadness, as this first poem of a ten-poem series for the Double Ninth by Yüan Hao-wen (1190–1257) shows:

The army's tents now move southwards; 行帳適南下
The people are confined within their homes.[47] 居人跼庭戶
In the city I gaze at the green hills: 城中望青山
A single river is not easy to cross. 一水不易渡
This morning the river and road are quiet, 今朝川涂靜
And I have the chance to stretch my feeble legs. 偶得展衰步
Free have I escaped of bonds; 蕩如脱囚拘
Widely opens the prospect every way. 廣漠開四顧
For half my life I have had no roots; 半生無根著
My strength is worn by the world's affairs. 筋力疲世故
Greatly I resemble Ting Ling-wei,[48] 大似丁令威
Returning to sigh over mounds and tombs. 歸來嘆壚墓
My village has long been ruined; 鄉閭喪亂久
What meets my eye is other than it was. 觸目異平素
Although the elms still yet remain, 枌榆雖尚存
In the year's lateness are many frosts and dews.[49] 歲晏多霜露

---

45 Wei Ying-wu, "Ninth Day," *Ch'üan T'ang-shih* 全唐詩, *chüan* 193 (Chung-hua Book Co., Shanghai, 1960, vol. 3, p. 1991).

46 Ts'en Shen, "In Camp on the Ninth Day Thinking of My Old Garden at Ch'ang-an," *ibid.*, *chüan* 201 (vol. 3, pp. 2102–2103). Wen I-to, p. 124, dates 757.

47 Shih Kuo-ch'i 施國祁 in his *nien-p'u* 年譜 of Yüan Hao-wen included in his *Yuan I-shan shih-chi chien-chu* 元遺山詩集箋註 , (Peking, 1958), p. 54, dates this poem in Yüan's 50th year, 1239. The first two lines refer to the movement of the Mongol armies against Southern Sung.

48 For Ting Ling-wei 丁令威 see *Sou-shen hou-chi* 搜神後記 (1st story in version in one *chüan* in *Lung-wei pi-shu* 龍威秘書 , 4th collection). Ting Ling-wei, a man of Liao-tung 遼東 through Taoist studies turned into a crane. After a thousand years he returned home and said (this is Yüan Hao-wen's particular reference): "The city walls are as of old, but the people are not. How continuous are the graves of those who did not study to be immortals!"

49 Shih Kuo-ch'i, *Yüan I-shan shih-chi chien-chu*, p. 132.

Since we have been citing poems for the Ninth Day spent in solitude or away from home, it is not perhaps surprising that most of the examples have sounded a strong note of sadness. Yet when one turns to poems for the day passed in agreeable company and desired surroundings, the note of melancholy frequently persists. There is the earliest of Tu Fu's surviving Double Ninth poems, written at one of the capital's favorite pleasure resorts, the "Ch'ü-chiang" (The Curving Stream), probably in the year 753.

We put together our mats, while the dogwood is fair;	綴 席 茱 萸 好
We set drifting our boats, while the lotus withers.	浮 舟 菡 萏 衰
Of my hundred years' autumns half are already past;	百 年 秋 已 半
The Ninth Day's thoughts are doubly sad.	九 日 意 兼 悲
The River's waters in this clear spring's curving,	江 水 清 源 曲
Ching-men on this road I seem to see.[50]	荊 門 此 路 疑
Of late my high spirits have failed,	晚 來 高 興 盡
And I am troubled by chrysanthemum time.[51]	搖 蕩 菊 花 期

Again, in one of the most admired of his poems, written for the Double Ninth of 758, "At Tso's Estate in Lan-t'ien on the Ninth Day," in spite of his apparent intentions to be gay, the sadness of age and its attendant loss of friends creep into Tu Fu's lines, and the symbol of the dogwood turns from the preservation of life into the reality of death:

Although, aging, I grieve at autumn, I forced myself to be easy,	老去悲秋强自寬
And gladly came this day to taste your pleasures to the full.	興來今日盡君歡
I should be ashamed, with my short hair, if still my hat should blow away,	羞將短髮還吹帽
And laughingly I trouble a companion to set it straight for me.	笑倩旁人爲正冠
Lan River from afar through a thousand gullies falls;	藍水遠從千澗落
Yü-shan, rising as high as the twin peaks, is cold.	玉山高並兩峯寒
Next year for this gathering who will be hale?	明年此會知誰健
Drunk, I take the dogwood and peer at it closely.[52]	醉把茱萸仔細看

In his poem for 763's Double Ninth (this time he was at Tzu-chou, the modern San-t'ai hsien, Szechwan) Tu Fu struck a contrast between his

---

[50] Ching-men 荊 門 probably refers to a stretch of the Yangtze above I-tu 宜 都. It seems likely that Tu Fu is making an oblique reference to the Meng Chia story and, if so, he must have placed Meng Chia's Lung-shan in the Chiang-ling area. Cf. n. 15, above.

[51] *Tu Shao-ling chi hsiang-chu, chüan* 2 (2:90–91). Lan-t'ien 藍 田 was southeast of Ch'ang-an.

[52] *Ibid., chüan* 6 (3:123–124).

white hair and the yellow chrysanthemum flowers, which Po Chü-i (772–846), who also left a long series of poems for the Double Ninth, was to take up and repeat in self-imitation.

Last year I climbed the heights to the north of
  Ch'i-hsien,[53]
Today I am again on the banks of the Fu River.[54]
Sadly I face my white hairs' inevitability,
With shame I see the yellow flowers' unlimited
  renewal.
In the disorder of the times I am troubled to be
  so long a guest,
Amid the difficulties of the road I am sad always
  to depend on others.
When the feast is ended I still think on the events
  of these ten years,
Heartbroken at the dust on the pure road to Li-shan.[55]

去年登高鄧縣北
今日重在涪江濱
苦遭白髮不相放
羞見黃花無數新
世亂鬱鬱久爲客
路難悠悠常傍人
酒闌卻憶十年事
腸斷驪山清路塵

Po Chü-i at Chiang-chou 江州 (modern Kiukiang 九江, Kiangsi) in 818 (he had arrived there in the tenth month of 815) wrote in the opening lines of "Drunken Song on the Ninth Day":

My grieving head is still white,
The unfeeling chrysanthemums naturally yellow.
Since once I became Marshal of a prefecture,
Three times I have seen the annual Double Brightness.[56]

有恨頭還白
無情菊自黃
一爲州司馬
三見歲重陽

Seven years later (825) he reflected on another three years, of which he had spent part in Hangchow, part in Loyang, and part in Soochow:

Two years ago on the Ninth Day I was at Yü-hang,
And invited my guests and ordered the banquet
  in the Hall of Empty Purity.
Last year on the Ninth Day I had reached eastern Lo,
This year on the Ninth Day I have come to Wu-chün.
The tangled hair on both my temples all the time was white,
In the three places the chrysanthemums were the
  same yellow. . . .[57]

前年九日在餘杭
呼賓命宴虛白堂
去年九日到東洛
今年九日來吳鄉
兩邊蓬鬢一時白
三處菊花同色黃

---

53 Ch'i-hsien 鄧縣 lay to the south of Tzu-chou 梓州.

54 The Fu 涪 River flows past San-t'ai hsien 三台縣 (the former Tzu-chou).

55 *Tu Shao-ling chi hsiang-chu*, *chüan* 12 (5:125). Li-shan 驪山 is the name of the mountain east of Ch'ang-an, on which Hsüan-tsung 玄宗 built the Hua-ch'ing Palace 華清宮. Here he went often with Yang Kuei-fei 楊貴妃. Tu Fu is wistfully recalling the time before An Lu-shan's 安祿山 rebellion.

56 *Po Hsiang-shan shih-chi, Ch'ang-ch'ing chi* 白香山詩集, 長慶集 (*SPPY* ed.), 17:10b.

57 *Ibid., hou-chi*, 1:7a.

Finally he was to identify chrysanthemums and himself in a neat epigram.

The blooming chrysanthemums which fill the
   garden are a mass of golden yellow;
In their midst is a solitary clump whose color is like frost.
It is just like this morning's feast of song and wine,
Where a white-headed old man enters a place of youth.[58]

滿園花菊鬱金黃
中有孤叢色似霜
還似今朝歌酒席
白頭翁入少年場

All of Tu Fu's Double Ninth poems were written after the onset of middle age, as were those of Po Chü-i, just quoted. The same is true of the two poems of T'ao Yüan-ming with which we began and which I have suggested were to have a considerable influence over later treatments of the theme. It is of course likely that a great part of a poet's surviving work will come from his later years, after his reputation has been firmly established: comparatively few of Tu Fu's more than 1400 poems date from before his fortieth year. One might argue that this fact makes for some distortion of the picture. Obviously a young man could not and would not have responded to the Double Ninth in the manner of these poems of T'ao Yüan-ming, Tu Fu, and Po Chü-i. In spite of the possibility of some slight distortion of our evidence, I believe it can be said that for these three major poets the poignancy of the symbolism of the Double Ninth, which they, as it were, inverted, became increasingly moving and evocative of poetry, whether they responded with passion or gentle, ironic humor. I believe that this is why their poems for the day were admired and each in turn molded the tradition. It is perhaps interesting to note that among the fairly extensive collection of Li Ho 李賀 (791–817), a poet who made a reputation early, since he died at the age of twenty-six, there is no Double Ninth poem. Clearer evidence, however, for the tradition of tender melancholy, which by the late T'ang period had invested the Double Ninth, is the famous "Climbing the Heights of Ch'i-shan on the Ninth Day" by Tu Mu (803–852). For this poem seems only fully meaningful in terms of a tradition against which it is a protest.

The River drowns the autumn shadows, the geese begin to fly;
With my guests, wine-pots in hand, I ascend the green slope.
In the dusty world it's hard to find open-mouthed laughter;
The chrysanthemums require us to submit our
   whole heads to their flowers.
Only by becoming drunk shall we match the
   auspicious time;

江涵秋影雁初飛
與客攜壺上翠微
塵世難逢開口笑
菊花須插滿頭歸
但將酩酊酬佳節

58 *Ibid.*, *hou-chi* 11:1b.

There is no need to climb up and down to grieve
  at the setting rays.
From of old till now it was only like this;
On the Bull Mountain why must we simply
  weep upon our gowns.[59]

不用登臨恨落暉
古往今來只如此
牛山何必獨霑衣

What I have written here is in no way exhaustive of the theme of the
Double Ninth in Chinese poetry, and I am conscious of omitting some
famous poems. Sometimes there was a reason, as in the case of Su Shih's
Yellow-Crane Tower poem, written in 1078 to mark the opening of that
tower in commemoration of the saving of Soochow from flood disaster.[60]
This was clearly too special for my purpose, which has been to trace the
main tradition in its formative and early developmental stages. To follow
out that tradition which certainly endured through successive centuries and
properly to evaluate individual responses to it would require studies of
individual authors, such as I have leaned on here for the early period.
Unfortunately these in few cases exist. Yet perhaps even what has been said
may induce some slight caution in the too facile dismissal of so much later
Chinese poetry as purely imitative. The study of a recurrent theme can
show us that the greatest of the T'ang poets were imitative of each other
and of themselves. Without qualification, "imitation" has little meaning as
a critical term.

---

59 Feng Chi-wu 馮 集 梧 , *Fan-ch'uan shih chi-chu* 樊 川 詩 集 注 , 3 (Chung-hua Book
Co., Shanghai, 1962), pp. 209–210.
  60 See Lin Yutang, *The Gay Genius* (New York, 1947), pp. 180–183.

Ambiguities in Li Shang-yin's Poetry[*]

JAMES J. Y. LIU

THE title of this article will probably remind some readers of William Empson's famous book, *Seven Types of Ambiguity*, so that it seems desirable to make clear at the outset in what sense I am using the word and how far my use corresponds to Empson's. Generally speaking, I use the word "ambiguous" to describe a word, a line, an image, or a whole poem, that allows for more than one interpretation. This is largely similar to Empson's revised definition of ambiguity as "any verbal nuance, however slight, which gives room for alternative reactions to the same piece of language."[1] However, I do not propose to follow his scheme for the analysis of ambiguity in poetry, for it would obviously be unwise to expect to find exactly the same types of ambiguity in a language as different from English as Chinese, let alone the fact that I cannot hope to emulate the subtlety and ingenuity of Professor Empson's mind. Furthermore, Empson's classification of ambiguity, according to himself, is based on degrees of logical disorder, conscious apprehension, and psychological complexity,[2] all of which seem to me rather tricky and intractable, so that the distinctions between any two of the seven types are by no means always easy to see.[3] To avoid this

---

[*] This article is a revised version of a lecture delivered at Cornell University, December 8, 1964.

[1] William Empson, *Seven Types of Ambiguity* (2d ed., London, 1947), p. 1.

[2] *Ibid.*, p. 48.

[3] Cf. Elder Olson, "William Empson, Contemporary Criticism, and Poetic Diction," *in* R. S. Crane, ed., *Critics and Criticism* (University of Chicago Press, 1952), pp. 45–82, esp. p. 52.

difficulty, I shall deal with ambiguities simply according to the different sources from which they may arise, as I hope to show below.

As for the choice of Li Shang-yin as an exponent of ambiguity in Chinese poetry, I hardly need any justification, since he is one of the most ambiguous, if not *the* most ambiguous, of all Chinese poets. Yet my interest in him is not one based on mere curiosity or a taste for the abstruse for its own sake, but one that has grown with admiration and love. Nor am I alone in this: some of Li's most ambiguous poems are also among the most admired and best loved in the language. Indeed, some readers would even claim that they enjoy reading Li Shang-yin's poetry without knowing what it means. For instance, the famous scholar Liang Ch'i-ch'ao (1873–1929) remarked of Li's ambiguous poems: "What they are about I can't figure out. I can't even explain the literal meaning line by line. Yet I feel they are beautiful, and when I read them, they give me a new kind of pleasure in my mind."[4] This attitude I do not share, for it is one of my simple critical tenets that poems consist of words, and words have meanings. On the other hand, I do not wish to follow the examples of previous Chinese commentators on Li's poetry, most of whom seem to have fallen under the "intentional fallacy,"[5] in that they are bent on discovering the poet's intention in writing a particular poem and the actual person or event he had in mind while writing it. These commentators may be divided into three schools: first, those who believe that many of Li's ambiguous poems refer to various clandestine love affairs with court entertainers and Taoist nuns;[6] second, those who see in these same poems veiled expressions of frustrated ambition and oblique references to the poet's relation with one of his patrons;[7] third, those who take these poems as political satire against the court.[8] Now, short of resurrecting the poet, we can never be absolutely sure which of

---

[4] Liang Ch'i-ch'ao 梁 啓 超 , "Chung-kuo yün-wen li-t'ou so piao-hsien ti ch'ing-kan" 中 國 韻 文 裡 頭 所 表 現 的 情 感 , in *Yin-ping-shih wen-chi* 飲 冰 室 文 集 (Shanghai, 1926), *chüan* 71, p. 38.

[5] W. K. Wimsatt, Jr., with Monroe C. Beardsley, *The Verbal Icon* (University of Kentucky Press, 1954), pp. 3–18.

[6] Su Hsüeh-lin 蘇 雪 林 , *Li Yi-shan lüan-ai shih-chi k'ao* 李 義 山 戀 愛 事 蹟 考 (Shanghai, 1927); Chu Hsieh 朱 偰 , "Li Shang-yin shih hsin-ch'üan" 李 商 隱 詩 新 詮 in *Wen-che chi-k'an* 文 哲 季 刊 , 6:3/4 (1937), 589–624, 775–841.

[7] Feng Hao 馮 浩 in his edition of Li Shang-yin's poems, *Yü-ch'i-sheng shih chien-chu* 玉 溪 生 詩 箋 注 (1780, reprinted in the *SPPY*); Chang Ts'ai-t'ien 張 采 田 , *Yü-ch'i-sheng nien-p'u hui-chien* 玉 溪 生 年 譜 會 箋 (Peking, 1917; reprinted Shanghai, 1963).

[8] Ku Yi-ch'ün 顧 翊 羣 , *Li Shang-yin p'ing-lun* 李 商 隱 評 論 (Taipei, 1958); Sun Chen-t'ao 孫 甄 陶 , "Li Shang-yin shih t'an-wei" 李 商 隱 詩 探 微 in *New Asia Journal* 新 亞 學 報 , 4:2 (1960), 159–241.

these schools of interpretation is right. But, the poet's external intention or motive in writing a poem is not necessarily the same as the artistic intention of the poem; the former is what caused him to write, the latter is the guiding principle which has shaped the poem. My purpose, therefore, is not to establish beyond doubt what caused Li to write his poems, but to examine some of his ambiguous poems and see whether ambiguities add to or detract from the total poetic effect of these poems.

In order to consider the possible meanings of Li's poems, and also to understand how the different schools of interpretation arose, it is necessary to keep in mind a few simple facts about the poet's life and times. Li Shang-yin was born in A.D. 812 or 813,[9] and died in 858. During his lifetime, the T'ang dynasty was disintegrating. At court, the eunuchs had usurped much of the power of the throne, so much so that two of the six emperors whose reigns covered the poet's life span were murdered by eunuchs, and three of the others owed their accession to the throne to their support. The emperors were little more than puppets, who either tried unsuccessfully to get rid of the eunuchs, or gave up all attempt to rule and indulged in sensual pleasure. Some of them believed in popular Taoism and vainly and foolishly sought to prolong their lives with drugs. The cult of pseudo-Taoism at court also led some imperial princesses to leave the palace and live in Taoist nunneries, nominally to devote themselves to religion but actually to free themselves from the restrictions at court and lead a life of luxury and licentiousness. Such was court life in the late T'ang period. At the same time, the traditional ruling class consisting of scholar-officials was torn by a bitter strife between two political factions, one led by Li Tê-yü and the other by Niu Seng-ju, who engaged in mutual incriminations and retaliations and were not above seeking the help of the eunuchs in their struggles against each other. The empire was further weakened by the presence of powerful military governors, who owed only nominal allegiance to the crown and sometimes openly defied the imperial government. All these disruptive forces — the eunuchs, the political factions, and the military governors — eventually combined to bring the fall of the dynasty in 906, some fifty years after Li Shang-yin's death.

Li's own life was inevitably influenced by the political situation of his day. He was the son of a junior provincial official and was orphaned as a boy. In his late teens, he already showed unusual literary ability and was

---

9 The year of Li's birth is not known for certain. Feng Hao argues for 813 and Chang Ts'ai-t'ien for 812. I am inclined to accept the former.

patronized by Ling-hu Ch'u, who belonged to the "Niu faction." After the death of Ling-hu Ch'u, Li Shang-yin married the daughter of Wang Mao-yüan, who belonged to the "Li faction." This did not greatly help the poet's official career, while it incurred the resentment of Ling-hu Ch'u's son, Ling-hu T'ao, who eventually rose to be prime minister and who refused to promote the poet's interests. For the rest of his life, Li Shang-yin never attained high rank, and most of the time he served various provincial officials, largely as a ghost writer, drafting memorials to the throne and such-like documents on their behalf. He died before he was fifty, a sad, disappointed man, his wife having preceded him in death by several years.

From this brief sketch of Li's life, it may be seen that the various inter-pretations of his poetry are not entirely groundless. Since many of his poems are at least superficially concerned with love, and in one case the poet has added an explicit preface to a group of love poems to explain for whom they were written,[10] no serious objection can be raised to reading these as love poems. However, when Miss Su Hsüeh-lin finds clues in these poems to the poet's secret love affairs with two court entertainers and a Taoist nun, we may have reason to hesitate to follow her, since her reconstruction of the poet's love life is largely based on ingenious reading between the lines of the poems themselves and not supported by independent external evidence. Even if it could be proved that Li did have love affairs with these ladies, it still would not mean that all his ambiguous poems referred to them. Indeed, the same poems can, with equal plausibility, be taken as satirical descriptions of the licentious and decadent life led by some of the imperial princesses who ostensibly took Taoist vows. Thus, we can only say that some of Li's poems appear to be concerned with clandestine love affairs involving court ladies and Taoist nuns, but we cannot say to what extent these were based on personal experience. At the same time, since it was a well-established convention in Chinese poetry to compare oneself to a deserted wife and the ruler to the husband or lover, a convention that goes back to the poet Ch'ü Yüan (ca. 340–277 B.C.), it is possible to take some of these love poems as indirect expressions of the poet's frustration in his official career. But here again we would do well to pause before accepting the interpretations of the commentators Feng Hao (1710–1801) and Chang Ts'ai-t'ien (1862–1945), who tend to see hidden references to Ling-hu T'ao in the most unlikely places.

---

10 The poems addressed to a girl named Liu-chih 柳枝 ("Willow-branch"), in Chu Ho-ling's 朱鶴齡 edition of Li Shang-yin's poems, *Li Yi-shan shih-chi* 李義山詩集 (1659, reprinted 1870), *chüan hsia* 卷下, pp. 20a–b.

In short, I am not trying to discredit any of the previous interpretations of Li's poems, but only to show that it is possible to make sense of a poem without committing ourselves to a definite theory as to for whom or for what it was written. To do this, we may have to read a poem "dramatically," by which I mean we would have to reconstruct, from hints in the poem itself, a situation in the context of which the poem makes sense in one way or another, or in more than one way, without trying to identify the prototypes of the *dramatis personae* involved. In this way, we may hope to free ourselves from irrelevant biographical detective work and concentrate on the poems themselves. To draw an analogy with English poetry, those interminable attempts to identify the Dark Lady and "Mr. W. H." are no doubt fascinating in themselves, but are hardly relevant to our understanding and evaluation of Shakespeare's sonnets: all we need is the dramatic situation implicit in the sonnets themselves.

So far I have touched on one source of ambiguity: uncertainty as to what the poem is about, or in other words, what its referent is. This kind of ambiguity may be dubbed "ambiguity in reference." There are of course other kinds of ambiguity, such as ambiguities in attitude, in grammar, in imagery and symbolism, and in allusions. Ambiguity in attitude is present when the referent of a poem is not in doubt, but we are not sure what the poet's attitude is towards his subject and how we are meant to take it. More specifically, there may be room for doubt as to whether the poet is being serious or ironic, whether we are supposed to feel sympathy or scorn. As for ambiguity in grammar, this is far more common in Chinese than in English, since the Chinese language has no inflexions and is extremely fluid with regard to the so-called parts of speech. I have discussed elsewhere how the freedom from restrictions of number, gender, case, tense, etc., enables Chinese poets to present the essence of a scene or a mood while disregarding irrelevant accidental details, and how the frequent omission of the subject of a verb gives much Chinese poetry a feeling of impersonality and universality.[11] Now, while this grammatical fluidity is admirably suited to certain kinds of poetry, notably the kind of Nature poetry which seeks to convey a sense of Nature as she is, not as observed by man, its advantages may be questioned when it comes to intimate personal poetry, as in the case of many of Li Shang-yin's poems. It is a measure of his achievement as a poet that he overcame such inherent difficulties in his medium and managed to express complicated and often conflicting emotions in his poetry, generally

---

[11] *The Art of Chinese Poetry* (London and Chicago, 1962), pp. 39–41.

without using pronouns or identifying the subject of a verb. Such a feat would have scarcely been possible in English: just try to imagine what Shakespeare's sonnets would have been like if he had had to write them without using pronouns! Thus, partly by the flexibility of the Chinese language and partly by his own poetic skill, Li Shang-yin succeeded in writing some intensely personal poems while leaving open such questions as who the "speaker" of a poem is or whether the poem concerns the present or the past.

Next, let us consider ambiguity in imagery and symbolism. In Li Shang-yin's poetry, the individual images and symbols are generally clear and precise, but there may be ambiguity in their application; in other words, whereas there is no difficulty in identifying the vehicle of an image or symbol (that is, the thing that represents something else), we are often not sure about the tenor (or what is represented). Similarly, in his use of allusions, it is usually their application rather than their origin which is in doubt. We know what stories he is alluding to, but we are not always sure what the implications of the allusions are. All these different kinds of ambiguities may be present at the same time, though of course each may also occur by itself. That is why I have refrained from giving examples of each kind separately. Now we may proceed to examine some actual instances of ambiguity in Li Shang-yin's poetry. However, I must first point out the great dilemma I have had to face in translating these poems: on the one hand, if I gave a strictly literal translation, the result would be a sort of pidgin English which would hardly make any sense, let alone convey any poetic quality; on the other hand, if I gave a free paraphrase, the very ambiguities I am hoping to illustrate would largely disappear. I have tried to solve this dilemma by following a middle course, and have translated the poems line for line, sticking as closely as possible to the original, while making such concessions to the demands of English grammar and idiom as seemed necessary. In addition, I shall point out sources of ambiguity in my discussions even if they do not appear in the translations.

Let us begin with a simple case: a poem that involves no verbal ambiguity but only ambiguity in reference.

Without Title	無　題
At eight, she stole a look at herself in the mirror,	八 歲 偷 照 鏡
Already able to paint her eyebrows long.	長 眉 已 能 畫
At ten, she went out to tread on the green,	十 歲 去 踏 青
Her skirt made of red lotus flowers.	芙 蓉 作 裙 衩
At twelve, she learnt to play the small zither,	十 二 學 彈 箏
The silver plectrums she never took off.	銀 甲 不 曾 卸

At fourteen, she was hid from her six relations,	十 四 藏 六 親
And, one imagined, not married yet.	懸 知 猶 未 嫁
At fifteen, she weeps in the wind of spring,	十 五 泣 春 風
Turning her face away from the swing.[12]	背 面 鞦 韆 下

This, on the face of it, is a straightforward poem. The original of course contains no pronouns, but the context makes it clear that the subject is a girl, so that we may feel quite safe in using the pronoun "she" in the translation. Only a few more points require any explanation. In line 3, the expression "to tread on the green" refers to a custom in T'ang times to go out into the country or to the Meandering Stream (Ch'ü-chiang) in the capital on the third day of the third Moon, known as *T'a-ch'ing*, 踏 靑 or "treading on the green grass." In line 5, the small zither is the *cheng* 箏 which originally had twelve strings but in its modern version has sixteen strings. It is the prototype of the Japanese *koto*. In line 7, the expression "six relations" has been explained in several ways, none of which is particularly relevant, since the poet is using the term loosely for relatives in general and not any special group of relatives. It is enough to know that a girl of marriageable age was kept away from her male relatives.

So much for the literal meaning of the poem. What about its deeper meaning, if any? Feng Hao takes this as an allegorical expression of the poet's disappointment at his lack of success in his official career despite his precocious talents, and cites a passage from a piece of Li's prose which contains verbal similarities: "I began to study the classics at five, toyed with the writing brush and ink-slab at seven, and wrote essays at sixteen."[13] This interpretation is plausible but not strictly necessary, since the poem is moving enough taken at its face value. Moreover, the phraseology of the poem can be regarded as a conscious imitation or an unconscious echo of some lines from the anonymous earlier ballad known as "The Peacock Flies to the Southeast" 孔 雀 東 南 飛 , which tells how a young man was forced by his mother to divorce his wife and how the young couple both committed suicide. In this ballad the young wife complains:

At thirteen I could weave plain silk,	十 三 能 織 素
At fourteen I learnt to make clothes,	十 四 學 裁 衣
At fifteen I began to play the harp,	十 五 彈 箜 篌
At sixteen I knew the *Books of Poetry* and *History*,	十 六 誦 詩 書
At seventeen I became your wife,	十 七 爲 君 婦
My heart has often been filled with grief.	心 中 常 苦 悲

---

[12] Chu Ho-ling, *chüan shang* 卷 上 , p. 46a.

[13] Feng Hao, *chüan* 1, p. 8a–b.

The resemblance of Li's poem to these lines makes it possible to take it as a description of an unhappily married girl, without any allegorical significance. Another interpretation is offered by Miss Su Hsüeh-lin, the critic who sees evidence of secret love affairs in almost all Li's poems: that this poem too alludes to the two court entertainers with whom the poet was allegedly in love.[14] Thus, the poem can be taken on three different levels — as a description of an unhappy girl, as an allegorical self-lament, and as an oblique reference to a secret love. But its total significance transcends all three. Whatever the poet may have had in mind, the effect of the poem is to make us feel the sadness of wasted youth, beauty, and talent, no matter where or how incurred. We may compare this poem with Keats's "La Belle Dame Sans Merci," which may be taken at its face value as a fairy tale, or as an expression of the poet's unhappy infatuation for Fanny Brawne, or as an allegory of the poet's intoxication with Beauty, or all three at once, for the total meaning of the poem transcends them all, though none of them need be excluded.

In our next example, the referent of the poem is even more ambiguous:

High Noon   日　高

The doorknockers with old-brocade tags can be
   lightly pulled;   鍍鐶故錦縻輕拖
The jade key does not turn, the side door is locked.   玉筦不動便門鎖
Who is it lying asleep inside the crystal curtain,   水精眠夢是何人
Her hair piled up like red peonies at high noon?   欄藥日高紅鬖鬖
The floating fragrance ascends the clouds to   飛香上雲春訴天
   complain to heaven in spring,   雲梯十二門九關
But Oh, the twelve cloud-stairs and the ninefold gates!   輕身滅影何可望
What hope is there for one who takes life lightly?   粉蛾帖死屏風上
The white moth dies stiff upon the folding screen.[15]

It should be explained that doors in the palace had tags made of old brocade tied to the knockers to make it easier to pull them open, and that there are supposed to be twelve jade towers (which presumably have stairs of clouds) in the palace of the Queen Mother of the Western Heavens (Hsi Wang Mu) and ninefold gates leading to the palace of Heaven. Feng Hao takes this poem to be a veiled reference to the emperor, who is as hard to approach as Heaven, and the moth to represent a loyal official risking death in his attempt to admonish the sovereign.[16] This seems too far-fetched

14 Su Hsüeh-lin, p. 114.
15 Chu Ho-ling, *chüan chung* 卷 中 , p. 64a.
16 Feng Hao, *chüan* 1, pp. 4b–5a.

and does not fit all the details of the poem. Chang Ts'ai-t'ien takes it as
an allegory about the poet's longing for the favor of Ling-hu T'ao and the
latter's inaccessibility.[17] This also seems forced. A more likely interpretation
is that the poem describes a hopeless passion for some palace lady, whether
felt by the poet himself or imaginary. The door looks inviting enough; it
could be pulled open easily, yet the key does not turn and the door remains
locked. The beauty lies tantalizingly within the transparent curtain: one
can see her but cannot come near. One would like to complain to Heaven
(or perhaps she would like to complain to Heaven), but Heaven is inaccessible with its manifold stairs and gates. Even if one takes life lightly and does
not mind risking death, what hope is there? One can only despair and die
like the moth that courts its own destruction by throwing itself against the
screen. This image of the moth in the last line reminds one of Shelley's
well-known lines:

> The worship the heart lifts above
> And the Heavens reject not;
> The desire of the moth for the star,
> Of the night for the morrow;
> The devotion to something afar
> From the sphere of our sorrow.

Thus, the whole poem may be regarded as a symbol of a kind of romantic
désir de l'impossible, of universal human aspirations for the unattainable, not
merely as the expression of a personal longing for a particular woman or
for the favor of a particular patron.

Ambiguity in attitude may be illustrated by the next poem.

Self-congratulation	自　喜
I congratulate myself on my snail-cottage,	自 喜 蝸 牛 舍
Which also accommodates a swallow's nest.	兼 容 燕 子 巢
The green bamboos shed their powdery leaves,	綠 筠 遺 粉 籜
The red peonies burst their fragrant buds.	紅 藥 綻 香 苞
A tiger passes: aware of the distant trap;	虎 過 遙 知 穽
A fish comes: let it enrich my meal!	魚 來 且 佐 庖
Walking slowly, I gradually get drunk;	慢 行 成 酩 酊
My next-door neighbor has a pine brew.[18]	鄰 壁 有 松 醪

Taken at its face value, the poem is a description of the poet's modest
and simple pleasures: his small but cosy cottage like a snail's shell, the

---

17 Chang Ts'ai-t'ien, p. 199.
18 Chu Ho-ling, *chüan shang*, pp. 3b–4a.

pleasant surroundings with their flora and fauna, the casual walk, the
convivial drink with a neighbor. Yet, as the commentator Chu Ho-ling
(1606–1683) suggested, the poem may be ironic: perhaps it is really not
self-congratulation but self-lament.[19] The snail-cottage in the first line may
suggest the humble conditions in which the poet is living. The swallow's
nest in the second line may contain further irony: since in Chinese poetry
swallows' nests are often associated with noble mansions, the presence of
one here could either mean that the poet is comparing himself to the bird
forced to live in modest circumstances, or that he is contrasting his own
hospitality to the swallow with some high official's refusal to shelter him.[20]
The next two lines can be taken simply as descriptions of the actual scenery,
but they may also indicate the passing of spring, which symbolizes the
passing of youth. Line 5 in the original contains a grammatical ambiguity
which leads to an ambiguity in imagery: the subject of the verb "to be
aware" (*chih* 知) is not stated, so that it could be identified with the tiger
or with the poet. If it is the tiger that is aware of the distant trap, it would
seem that the poet is comparing himself to the tiger to show that he is aware
of the dangers of political life and is glad to be out of it. If it is the poet who
is aware of the trap lying in wait for the tiger, then he would seem to be
expressing concern over some high official who may be in danger. The
remaining lines could be regarded either as an expression of self-content
or as self-mockery at the cold comforts he has as compensation for lack of
official honor and position. We are left in some doubt whether the poet is
congratulating himself for being able to lead a simple but pleasant life or
voicing his discontent in an ironic manner. Should we then condemn the
poem as a failure in communication? No, on the contrary, its very ambiguity
seems to reflect accurately a complex state of mind, for is it not possible that
the poet is feeling two opposite urges at the same time? On the one hand he
wishes to be free from the disadvantages of high office and enjoy the simple
pleasures of life, on the other hand he cannot quite reconcile himself to
a life of obscurity. This mental conflict is conveyed by the ambiguity of the
poem.

We have just seen how ambiguities in grammar and imagery affect the
final effect of a poem. As for ambiguities in allusions, they often occur
together with imagery, since allusions, especially those to myths and legends,

---

19 *Ibid.*

20 This is suggested by Ho Cho 何 焯 (1661–1722) in a marginal comment printed in
Chu Ho-ling, *chüan shang*, pp. 3b–4a.

naturally involve the use of concrete imagery. Li Shang-yin is very fond
of using such allusions, and some of them recur in many of his poems.
While allusions to the same stories in different poems need not carry the same
implications in all cases, sometimes they do seem to contain cross references.
I shall now consider together four quatrains which contain allusions to the
goddess of the moon in Chinese mythology, Ch'ang-O, also known as
Heng-O, or the White Lady (Su-O). In the first of these poems the poet
also alludes to the goddess of frost, called the Blue Maid (Ch'ing-nü):

Frosty Moon   霜　月

As soon as the migratory wild geese are heard,   初聞征雁已無蟬
   the cicadas are silent;   百尺樓高水接天
The hundred-foot tower overlooks the water that   青女素娥俱耐冷
   touches the sky.   月中霜裏鬬嬋娟
The Blue Maid and the White Lady both can
   endure the cold:
The one in the moon, the other in the frost, they
   compete in beauty.[21]

This can be taken simply as a description. The first line indicates the
coming of autumn and the end of summer. The second line, which in the
original reads literally, "The hundred-foot tower is tall; water touches sky,"
seems to describe the tower above the moonlit water which stretches as far
as the horizon, but it is possible that "water" is a metaphor for the moonlit
frost. Perhaps in the poet's mind three images — that of the water reaching
the sky, that of the tower touching the sky, and that of the moonlit frost
like water — were fused in one. The last two lines can be regarded merely
as a fanciful way of saying that the moonlight and the frost are vying with
each other in beauty. But they may also be taken as an oblique reference to
two Taoists nuns, for in another poem entitled "Again to the Sung sisters
of Hua-yang Nunnery, Written on a Moonlit Night,"[22] the poet also alludes
to the goddess of the moon. Though the relation between the poet and these
two nuns is not clear, it is certainly not too far-fetched to see a reference to
them in the present poem.

In the next poem, the poet alludes to the legend that Ch'ang-O fled to
the moon after having stolen the elixir of life from her husband, King Yi:

---

21 *Ibid.*, *chüan shang*, pp. 4b–5a. Another version has 南 for 高 in the second line.
22 *Ibid.*, *chüan chung*, p. 45b. "月 夜 重 寄 宋 華 陽 姊 妹"

Ch'ang-O   常　娥

Against the mica screen, the candle throws its deep shadow;　　雲母屛風燭影深
The Long River gradually sinks, the morning star sets;　　　　長河漸落曉星沈
Ch'ang-O should regret having stolen the elixir:　　　　　　　常娥應悔偷靈藥
The green sea, the blue sky, her heart every night![23]　　　　碧海青天夜夜心

In this poem, the goddess may represent a nun who, the poet imagines, must feel regret at having taken the vows of chastity as she faces the moon alone every night, though Chang Ts'ai-t'ien suggested that the poet is comparing himself to the goddess and is expressing his regret at having left the Ling-hu family and gone to serve Wang Mao-yüan.[24] Be that as it may, even at its literal level the poem shows considerable power of imagination: the mythological scene is imagined in concrete detail — the screen made of mica (which in Chinese is called *yün-mu* or "cloud-mother" and therefore may contain a pun), the candle, the Milky Way (which in Chinese is called the Heavenly River), and the morning star setting at the approach of dawn, the solitary figure of the goddess, or nun, or both, facing the immensities of the sea and the sky. The theme is reiterated in another poem:

Moonlit Night   月　夕

The autumn insects under the grass, the frost on the leaves;　　草下陰蟲葉上霜
The vermilion balustrade presses down the light on the lake.　　朱欄迢遞壓湖光
The hare is chilly, the toad cold, the cassia flower white:　　　兔寒蟾冷桂花白
In such a night, Heng-O would surely break her heart![25]　　此夜姮娥應斷腸

Here, in addition to the goddess of the moon, the poet refers to legends that in the moon there are a white hare preparing the elixir of life with a mortar and pestle, a three-legged toad who is the spirit of the moon, and a cassia tree. Since even these are feeling the cold, the goddess, or the nun, herself must be heartbroken in the cold night.

The last poem I shall consider in connection with the goddess of the moon is the following quatrain:

Stockings   韈

I have heard that Princess Fu's stockings　　　　　　　　嘗　聞　宓　妃　韈
Enabled her to cross the water like land.　　　　　　　　渡　水　欲　生　塵
Why not lend them to Ch'ang-O, that she　　　　　　　　好　借　嫦　娥　著
Could tread on the moon's wheel in the autumn air?[26]　　淸　秋　踏　月　輪

---

23 *Ibid.*, *chüan chung*, p. 33a.
24 Chang Ts'ai-t'ien, pp. 206, 398.
25 Chu Ho-ling, *chüan shang*, p. 71b.
26 *Ibid.*, *chüan shang*, p. 73a.

Princess Fu is another name for the goddess of the river Lo, made famous
by the poet Ts'ao Chih (A.D. 192–232), who describes her as treading on the
water in her stockings. The point of this allusion seems to be: the speaker
wishes that the nun could find some miraculous means to come out and meet
him in a moonlit night. In all the poems I have just considered, we may see
at least two levels of meaning: on one level, they describe the beauty of
moonlight by means of imagery derived from mythology: on another level,
they express the imagined loneliness and regret of nuns, whether the poet
was personally involved or not.

Let us now examine some poems in which ambiguities in grammar,
imagery, and allusions are all interrelated.

Peonies Damaged by Rain at Hui-chung   回中牡丹爲雨所敗
(Second of two poems under this title)   （第二首）

Laugh as you may at the pomegranate that
    blooms too late for spring;   浪笑榴花不及春
To fall before your time is even greater cause for grief.   先期零落更愁人
Tears sprinkled on jade plates repeatedly hurt one's heart; 玉盤迸淚傷心數
Surprised strings on the ornamental zither   錦瑟驚絃破夢頻
    frequently break one's dreams.   萬里重陰非舊圃
Ten thousand miles of gloom — unlike the old garden;   一年生意屬流塵
A whole year's life — gone with the floating dust!   前溪舞罷君迴顧
After the Dance of the Brook when you turn back to look, 併覺今朝粉態新
You'll feel the powdery beauty of today to be fresh still.[27]

The place Hui-chung mentioned in the title is near Ching-chou, where the
poet's father-in-law Wang Mao-yüan was living as military governor of
Ching and Yüan, and the poem was probably written in 838, when Li
Shang-yin had recently married and was on Wang's staff. The first line is
grammatically ambiguous: the words which I have translated as "Laugh
as you may," in the original read literally "Recklessly laugh" (lang hsiao
浪笑), and the subject of the verb is not identified. We may take the line
as addressed to the peonies, or the poet himself, or the reader, and paraphrase
the first two lines together as follows: "You may laugh (or, one may laugh)
at the pomegranate that blooms after spring is over and misses the best
part of the year, but you, the peony, who blossom early and wither early,
and what is more, are so damaged by the rain that you will fall before your
time, are even more to be pitied." Further, the first line may contain an

---

27 *Ibid.*, *chüan hsia*, pp. 67a–b.

allusion to the following episode.* When the first Emperor of the T'ang dynasty, Kao-tsu, ascended the throne, K'ung Shao-an 孔 紹 安, an official who had served the previous Sui dynasty, came to offer his services, but since he had been anticipated by another man, he was only given a post of secondary importance. Later, at a court banquet, when he was ordered by the Emperor to write a poem on pomegranate blossoms, K'ung took this as an opportunity to show his discontent by writing these lines:

It is only because it came too late   祗 爲 時 來 晚
That its blossoms were not in time for spring.   開 花 不 見 春

How this allusion would affect the interpretation of the poem we will consider later. Meanwhile let us go on to the next two lines. Here, the imagery is both complicated and striking. The raindrops on the peonies are compared to tears on jade plates, while the sound of the rain beating on the flowers is compared to zither (*sê* 瑟) strings being abruptly plucked. Moreover, these two images may be associated with two allusions. The image of tears on jade plates reminds one of the story about a mermaid (or merman, since there is no gender in Chinese!) who stayed with a human being, and who, on leaving, asked for a jade plate. On this she shed tears which turned into pearls. Thus, through this literary association, the raindrops are compared implicitly to pearls as well as tears. The image of the zither strings may be associated with the spirit of the river Hsiang, who is supposed to play this instrument. According to legend, the two daughters of the sage Emperor Yao were both married to the Emperor Shun, and when their husband died, the two sisters drowned themselves in the river Hsiang and became the goddesses of this river. The "spirit of River Hsiang," therefore, could refer to either of the two goddesses, or both. In another poem, Li Shang-yin writes, "The rain beats on the fifty strings of the spirit of River Hsiang,"[28] so that we are certainly not being too fanciful in seeing an association between the comparison of the sound of the rain to the zither and this legend. Line 5 contrasts the gloomy surroundings of the present with the old garden from which the peony has presumably been transplanted, and line 6 laments the passing away of time. In line 7, the "Dance of the Brook"

---

* [*Editor's note*: See Yu Mou (attrib.) 尤 袤 (1127–1194), *Ch'üan T'ang shih-hua* 全 唐 詩 話 , 1. The *Ch'u-hsüeh chi* 初 學 記 by Hsü Chien 徐 堅 (659–729) and others has "只 謂 來 時 晚, 開 花 不 及 春 ." This version of the *Ch'u-hsüeh chi* is quoted by *Shuo-fu* 說 郛 as "只 爲 生 來 晚, 花 開 不 及 春 ." The *T'ang shih chi-shih* 唐 詩 紀 事 by Chi Yu-kung 計 有 功 (fl. 1121) gives the text similar to Yu Mou's but also has 及 for 見 .]

28 Chu Ho-ling, *chüan shang*, p. 27a.

refers to an ancient dance tune, the words of which run to the effect that a flower by the brook will fall and float away on the water, and that even if it could ever come back it would no longer be fresh. Our poet has developed the idea in the ancient song in a different direction by saying that after the peony has finished its dance in the wind and withered away completely, one will realize in retrospect that its beauty now, though damaged, is still fresh and worth watching. The word which I have translated as "you" is in fact ambiguous: in the original the word is *chün* 君 , which can be used as a polite form of the second person pronoun or as a noun meaning "lord" or "sovereign." If we take it as a pronoun, it is still ambiguous, for it could be identified with the peony, or the poet himself, or some would-be inter-locutor, though in each case the meaning would remain largely the same: "In the future, when you recall the present, you will realize that the peony's beauty (or, your beauty, if the words are addressed to the flower) is still fresh." If we take the word *chün* to mean "sovereign," then the peony would seem to be compared to a court lady, with a pun on the words "powdery beauty," which in Chinese do not differ from "powdered beauty," and the poet would seem to be pleading on behalf of this metaphorical lady to the Emperor: "Favor her while her beauty still remains, otherwise in retrospect, you may regret what you have missed."

So far, we have considered the poem on the literal level, as a poem about peonies. On another level, we could take it as a poem about a beautiful lady, or beautiful ladies in general, as suggested by the ambiguity in the last two lines. However, it is doubtful if the jade plate and the zither allude to actual gifts the poet exchanged with two court ladies, as Miss Su Hsüeh-lin believes.[29] On yet another level, the poem may be taken as an expression of the poet's disappointment in life and the peony as a symbol of his frustrated genius, though here again we need not go so far as Chang Ts'ai-t'ien, who thinks the poem shows Li Shang-yin's anticipation of Ling-hu T'ao's resent-ment at the poet's marriage with Wang Mao-yüan's daughter.[30] Taken on this third level, the first couplet may be roughly paraphrased thus: "You may laugh at someone else who arrived too late on the scene and missed the boat, but what about yourself, who showed early promise but are now aging before your time?" The next two lines could either allude to unhappy love through associations with tearful mermaids and tragic goddesses, or express sadness at the poet's own failure in life. Lines 5 and 6

---

29 Su Hsüeh-lin, pp. 110–118.
30 Chang Ts'ai-t'ien, p. 56.

bring out the contrast between the poet's present environment far from the
capital and the good old days in the imperial city, while lamenting the
passing away of another wasted year. The concluding couplet pathetically
expresses the wish that the Emperor, or the poet's patron, may yet relent
and show some appreciation of his talents before it is too late.

To sum up: it is not necessary to say dogmatically which of the three
interpretations of the poem is the correct one; all three are possible meanings
of the poem, of varying degrees of consciousness in the poet's mind, perhaps.
He may have been genuinely moved by the sight of actual peonies damaged
by rain (otherwise there would have been no need to mention the place-name
in the title), and then he could have been reminded by this of his own
unhappy life, and possibly also of some ill-fated beautiful lady or ladies.
Whatever made him write the poem, its effect is to make us sense the tragic
waste of something precious and to feel the pity of it all. The peony becomes
for us a fused symbol of ravaged beauty (natural or human), wasted youth,
and frustrated genius, just as in Apollinaire's lines,

> O ma jeunesse abandonnée
> Comme une guirlande fanée,

the faded garland becomes a symbol of all wasted youth, not merely the
poet's own.

Finally, I would like to discuss two of a group of four untitled poems 無題
which are given together in Li's collected works.

I

Coming is an empty word; going, you leave no trace.	來是空言去絕踪
The moonlight slants over the roof, the bells strike the fifth watch.	月斜樓上五更鐘
Separated far from you in a dream, I cry and can hardly be aroused;	夢爲遠別啼難喚
Hurried to write a letter, I cannot wait for the ink to thicken.	書被催成墨未濃
The candlelight half encircles the golden kingfishers;	蠟照半籠金翡翠
The musk perfume subtly penetrates the embroidered lotuses.	麝熏微度繡芙蓉
Young Liu already resented the distance of the P'eng Mountain;	劉郎已恨蓬山遠
Now ten thousand more mountain ranges rise!	更隔蓬山一萬重

II

The east wind soughs and sighs as a fine drizzle falls;	颯颯東風細雨來
Beyond the lotus pond there is the noise of a light thunder.	芙蓉塘外有輕雷
The golden toad bites the lock through which the burnt incense enters;	金蟾齧鏁燒香入

The jade tiger pulls the silk rope while turning
    above the well.
Lady Chia peeped through the curtain at young
    Secretary Han;
Princess Fu left a pillow to the gifted Prince of Wei.
Do not let the amorous heart vie with the flowers
    in burgeoning:
Every inch of longing will turn an inch of heart to ashes![31]

玉虎牽絲汲井迴
賈氏窺簾韓掾少
宓妃留枕魏王才
春心莫共花爭發
一寸相思一寸灰

These poems might well be called the translator's nightmare as well as
the ambiguity-hunter's paradise: they involve ambiguities of all kinds.
First, there is ambiguity in reference. Some critics take these as passionate
love poems, while others prefer to see in them the ubiquitous shadow of the
heartless patron who refuses to take the poet back into his favor. And since
the referent is ambiguous, naturally there is also some ambiguity in attitude.
Is the poet asking for sympathy or is he laughing at his own helpless situation?
At the end of the second poem, is he seriously telling himself to stop all
longing, or is this merely a self-consciously futile gesture (that is, assuming
the injunction is addressed to himself)? Then, there are grammatical
ambiguities. In the original poems, the speaker is not identified, nor are
the subjects of some of the verbs. For instance, who is "going and leaving
no trace," and who is crying in his dream? Finally, there are ambiguities
in imagery and allusions. What, for example, is the significance of the
golden toad biting the lock or the jade tiger pulling the strings above the
well? And what is the point of the allusion to Emperor Wu of Han as
"young Liu" (Liu *lang* 劉 郎) and his complaint against the distance of the
fairy mountain P'eng? Most of these ambiguities I have tried to preserve
in the translations, though it has not been possible to keep them all, such
as when I had to use the first person pronoun or add a subject to a verb.
However, I hope sufficient ambiguity remains to justify the laborious
exegesis below!

In order to make sense of these poems on at least one level, it seems best to
take them as love poems, whether based on personal experience or not.
Further, we have to assume the speaker to be either the man or the woman;
on the whole, it seems to make better sense to assume the former. Next,
let us reconstruct a dramatic situation and try to read the poems in the light
of this situation. In the first poem, let us imagine that the lover has waited
all night in vain for his beloved. He now complains: "You said you would

---

[31] Chu Ho-ling, *chüan shang*, pp. 43a–b.

come, but this proved an empty word; and once you are gone, you leave no trace behind." He sees the fading moonlight slanting over the roof, and hears the bells strike the fifth watch, announcing the coming of dawn, since a night is divided into five watches. The third line in the original literally reads, "Dream of distant parting, crying hard to call." Two ambiguities are involved here. First, who is dreaming of parting? This I have tried to solve by assuming it is the speaker. Secondly the word "call" (*huan* 喚) could be taken either in the sense of "to summon" or in the sense of "to call up" or "wake up." I have chosen the second meaning and taken the whole line to mean, "While waiting for you, I dozed off and fell into a dream, and even in my dream we seemed to be facing a distant separation. So I began to cry in my dream, and now can hardly be called up." Now the question is, who is trying to wake him up? Of course, not the woman he loves, since she has failed to come. I would suggest that it is a messenger from her. This would also make it easier to understand the next line, which literally says, "letter finished by hurrying, ink not yet thickened." Taken together, the two lines could be interpreted this way: "your messenger arrived to find me crying in my sleep, and had some difficulty in waking me up. He (or she) then gave me your message, and hurried me to write a letter in reply to take back, not allowing me time to wait for the ink to thicken." (One should remember that the traditional way of preparing ink in China is to rub an ink-stick with water on an ink-stone, so that normally it takes some time for the ink to reach the required degree of thickness.) After the messenger is gone, the speaker looks wistfully at the candlelight that half encompasses the kingfishers threaded in gold on the bed coverlets and smells the musk perfume which has gradually penetrated the bed-curtains embroidered with lotus flowers: all these elaborate preparations have been in vain! In the final couplet, the speaker compares himself to the Emperor Wu of Han, Liu Ch'ê, who wished to become an immortal and resented the distance of Mount P'eng, the Taoist fairyland. Moreover, it seems that new obstacles have arisen, for the lover complains: "I already resented your being so inaccessible, like the fairy mountain P'eng, but now ten thousand more mountains seem to lie between us!" This suggests that perhaps the messenger brought the news that the beloved is leaving for some distant place, so that any future meeting would be even more unlikely than before. If this is so, we can turn back to the first line and see more meaning in the words "going leaves no trace," which would now seem to mean, "not only have you failed to come as you promised, but you are going away and I will not be able to trace your movements."

To go on to the second poem: the opening couplet describes the scene of a secret rendezvous: "amidst wind and rain, we met by the lotus pond, from beyond which came the noise of thunder." There is a possible allusion here: the poet Ssŭ-ma Hsiang-ju (179–117 B.C.) in his *The Long Gate Palace (Ch'ang-men Fu)*, written on behalf of the Empress Ch'en when she was living at the Palace of Long Gate after having lost the favor of the Emperor Wu of Han, compared the sound of the imperial carriage to thunder. Our poet Li Shang-yin in another poem alludes to this in the line, "His carriage, rolling past like thunder, allowed no time to talk."[32] Thus, we may take the thunder as an indirect way of referring to the imperial carriage, in which case the scene would seem to be set in the palace and the beloved woman would be a court lady risking great danger in coming to meet her lover. Even if we take the thunder literally, it would still add to the already threatening atmosphere created by the wind and rain, and emphasize the desperate passion of the lovers by contrasting it with the harsh natural environment.

The imagery in the next couplet requires careful consideration. The toad was supposed to be good at holding its breath and was therefore used as decoration on locks to signify secrecy. Here the image probably suggests that the woman is closely guarded, behind locked doors, in an inner chamber where incense burns. Or perhaps the incense represents messages from the lover, which have managed to get in despite the locked doors. In the next line, the jade tiger, which decorates the pulley above the well, possibly represents a messenger who commutes between the lovers: just as the pulley pulls the strings to fetch up water from the deep well, so does a secret messenger bring news of her from the deep recesses of her abode. The allusions in lines 5 and 6 may be briefly explained. Lady Chia, the daughter of Chia Ch'ung, peeped through the curtain at her father's handsome young secretary named Han Shou, and had a love affair with him. The affair was discovered by Chia Ch'ung when he smelt on the young man's clothes a rare imported perfume which he himself had given to his daughter. Thereupon the young lovers were allowed to be married. Princess Fu, as mentioned above, is the goddess of the river Lo, and the Prince of Wei refers to the poet Ts'ao Chih, with whom the goddess is supposed to have had a romantic encounter. By alluding to these two stories, the poet is either drawing an analogy or pointing at a contrast: either he is saying, "You have shown your favor to me, as Lady Chia did to Han Shou and the goddess

---

[32] *Ibid., chüan chung*, p. 41b.

of River Lo did to the poet Ts'ao Chih," or he is saying, "I am not a handsome young man like Han, nor am I a genius like Ts'ao, how can I hope to win your love?" In the final couplet, the poet apparently warns himself not to let his heart blossom forth with love, for he knows only too well the suffering this will bring, but we get the feeling that he cannot really help it. Such is the intensity of his passion that he cannot stop his longings and can only watch his heart being gradually consumed by his desires until it turns to the ashes of despair.

These poems may be ambiguous in reference but not so in emotional import. Whatever caused the poet to write them, he has succeeded in bodying forth an intense, hopeless passion, through an integration of ambiguous words, images, and allusions. Those who wish to find out the name of the lady who inspired such passion are welcome to do so; those who think that it was the poet's desire for the favor of his former patron that reduced him to such despair are likewise entitled to their opinion. But our appreciation of these poems is not affected by such considerations, any more than our appreciation of Emily Brontë's passionate poem, "Cold in the earth, and the deep snow piled above thee," is affected by the knowledge that it was based not on real experience but childhood fantasy.[33]

From the examples of Li Shang-yin's poetry given above, I hope one can gain some idea how rich and subtle Chinese poetry can be in feeling and expression, and how, in Li's poetry, as in the works of many another poet Chinese or Western, ambiguity is not merely an affectation or mannerism but just another name for complexity of verbal structure and multiplicity of meaning. Naturally, not all Li's poems are ambiguous, nor can they all be treated in the same way. Some of his poems on historical and contemporary events cannot be understood without reference to the particular persons and affairs concerned, and these poems, of course, should not be interpreted in the way I have interpreted some of the ambiguous poems above.[34] Finally, lest there be any misunderstanding, let me state that I am not trying to impose the "New Criticism" on Chinese poetry, but only using the method of verbal analysis (which is generally associated with the "New Criticism") when this promises to be fruitful, as in the case of some of Li Shang-yin's ambiguous poems.

---

[33] The poem is addressed by "R. Alcona" to "J. Brenzaida," two of the characters who inhabit Gondal, the imaginary island invented by Emily and Anne Brontë in their childhood. See C. W. Hatfield, ed., *The Complete Poems of Emily Jane Brontë* (New York, 1941), pp. 222–223.

[34] See, for example, my article, "Li Shang-yin's Poem *The Memorial Inscription by Han Yü*," in *East-West Center Review*, 1:1 (Honolulu, 1964), 13–20.

Metrics in Yüan *San-ch'ü*

WAYNE SCHLEPP

THE songs that were popular in the northern cities of China under Mongol rule are what we now call Yüan *san-ch'ü* 散 曲 . Ta-tu 大 都 (near modern Peking), the Mongol capital in the thirteenth and fourteenth centuries, was one of the major points at which foreign culture came into direct contact with Chinese literary art; the Mongols had brought with them a new language as well as a different kind of music, and it was in such an atmosphere that *san-ch'ü* was able to flourish. Being popular literature unrestricted by classical rules of form, *san-ch'ü* easily assimilated the foreign music and the new trends of language, and was able to develop in a manner sufficiently unique to earn a separate place in Chinese literature.

During the Southern Sung (1127–1279) *tz'u* 詞 had begun its development as a literary form separate from music. Even though phonetic changes in the language began to show in late *tz'u* it was in the less conservative North under the Liao (937–1125) and Chin (1115–1234) that they were most rapid. It was there also that a more colloquial style of *tz'u* came to be written both to the old tunes and to new tunes as well. Its language was the changing language of the North. By the middle of the thirteenth century when the Mongol empire was at its height, the influences of the North became more widespread. Its colloquial form of *tz'u* is what we now call *san-ch'ü*.

In the Yüan dynasty, songs were basically of two classes: there were the *san-ch'ü* (separate songs) written for the enjoyment of the poet's friends, or for singing girls at banquets or simply to satisfy the poet's own particular desire for expression. There were also songs written in narrative sequence specifically for performance on the stage. The latter are distinguished from *san-ch'ü* by the term *hsi-ch'ü* 戲 曲 (songs of the drama).

85

The *san-ch'ü* fall into two further classes: the *hsiao-ling* 小令 (single lyrics) on the one hand and the sets of songs which combined two or more *hsiao-ling* to make up a complete song. The simplest of these song groups is the *tai-kuo* 帶過 (the carry-over) in which most frequently two songs only are used. A group consisting of more than two songs is called a *t'ao-shu* 套數 (a song set). These often have at the end a special "tail-song" whose purpose is to bring the poem to a proper conclusion. In form the *t'ao-shu* are virtually the same as the song sets used in the drama but they are not used with dialogue, as the custom is with drama, nor are they intended for dramatic performance.[1]

As they were pieces of music intended for performance, the *t'ao-shu* had to be composed of lyrics in the same mode. There were eleven such modes in traditional Chinese music. Even when in later times the music was no longer current it was felt that these model distinctions should be maintained and writers religiously kept to established precedents. For Yüan writers, however, a choice of songs need never be so mechanical as this because they were able to base their development of a *t'ao-shu* on an understanding and appreciation of the music itself.

II

The formal structure imposed on the language of poetry is usually based upon one of the three fundamental aspects of syllable enunciation, i.e. stress, duration, or pitch. Since a system of pitch variations is most decisive in understanding Chinese utterance, it is only natural that the language of Chinese poetry be analyzed and described in terms of pitch, as in fact it has been for the past several centuries.[2] In a line of Chinese verse the patterns which stress and duration form do not so easily allow arrangement into a fixed metric structure.[3] For the same reason, it would be as difficult to

---

[1] For a more detailed discussion of the forms, see Lo Chin-t'ang 羅錦堂 , *Chung-kuo san-ch'ü shih* 中國散曲史 , (Taipei, 1956), vol. 1, pp. 20–30; and A. Hoffmann, "Kurze Einführung in die Technik der San-ch'ü," *Chung Te Hsüeh-chih* 中德學誌 , 5:1/2 (Peking, 1943), 119–135.

[2] We are speaking here of the pitches themselves, which, though they differ considerably in contour from one dialect to another, are the basis for a system of tones that is standard throughout the language.

[3] This is an extremely complex problem; duration is closely bound up with pitch in Chinese poetry but not so simply as to say merely that the *p'ing* 平 tone is long and the *tse* 仄 tone is short. For discussions of this problem, see Chou Fa-kao 周法高 , "Shuo P'ing-tse 說平仄 ," *Chung-yang yen-chiu-yüan, li-shih yü-yen yen-chiu-suo chi-k'an* 中央研究院 ,

develop a metric system for English verse on the pitch of a syllable, or even the general intonation of a line, because it is so likely to vary among speakers of English.[4]

As in other Chinese verse, the metric patterns of *san-ch'ü* are given in terms of the pitches of individual syllables. In a study of *san-ch'ü* it is perhaps easier than with other verse to distinguish attitudes of the "artistic" writer from those of the "scholarly" writer. The former clearly had a far greater feeling for the music of the song; the latter, if he knew the music at all, was generally inclined to put elegance of language first. Since the Yüan *san-ch'ü* writer's choice of tones was governed by the melody of the song to which he was writing, he had considerably more flexibility than the poet writing to an abstract metric pattern. To appreciate this, it is necessary to know something of the melody and tempo of *san-ch'ü* and to understand the contours of the pitches in the Yüan dialect.

In earlier metric systems there were only two contrasting elements, the *p'ing* 平 and *tse* 仄 tones, which, before the Southern Sung, distinguished a level tone having an unchanging pitch from clipped tones and the oblique tones that were either rising or falling. Although the best *shih* 詩 and *tz'u*[5] poets may have been more meticulous about the use of tones than the *p'ing-tse* system required, it was only in *san-ch'ü* that the *p'ing*, *shang* 上 , and *ch'ü* 去 tones were distinguished strictly enough to have an effect upon the metric description of the verse forms.

Because of developments in the tone system of the spoken language, the *p'ing* tone in the Yüan Dynasty split into two types: the *yin-p'ing* 陰 平 which approximated a level tone in the middle register and the *yang-p'ing* 陽 平 which was a rising tone in the middle register. The *shang* tone was still

---

歷 史 語 言 研 究 所 集 刊 13 (1948), 153–162; and Chou Ts'e-tsung 周 策 縱 , "Ting-hsing hsin-shih-t'i de t'i-yi 定 形 新 詩 體 的 提 議 ," *World Forum* 海 外 論 壇 , 3:9 (September, 1962), 2–14, but see especially pp. 5–6. It can be seen that certain tone patterns yield a fairly definite tendency in a normal reading of traditional poetry to elongate some of the *p'ing* tones in the line, but not much has yet been done to ascertain whether it is a particular pattern of durations that determines the pitch pattern or whether it is a certain pitch pattern that dermines the durations. It is perhaps safest to assume the latter, especially in poetry written under the influence of traditional concepts of meter.

4 For a discussion of this see J. H. Levis' *Chinese Musical Art* (Peiping, 1936), Part 1. In his introduction, p. 4, he refers to the surd-sonant scale of initial consonants as a type of "stress." I prefer at present to look on it as alliteration, though it may be at a point such as this that the relationship between pitch, stress, and perhaps duration as well is to be found.

5 For a full discussion of strict patterns in *tz'u*, see Wang Ch'in-hsi 王 琴 希 , "Sung-tz'u shang-ch'ü-sheng tzu yü hsi-ch'ü kuan-hsi ji ssu-sheng-t'i k'ao-cheng 宋 詞 上 去 聲 字 與 戲 曲 關 係 及 四 聲 體 考 證 ," *Wen shih* 文 史 , 2 (1963), 139–162.

in the high register; whether it was level or rising during this period is a matter of conjecture. The *ch'ü* was a descending tone probably in the lower register.[6]

The relative pitch and perhaps contour of the *yang-p'ing* and *shang* tones are similar; therefore it is natural that they were often used interchangeably. On the other hand, there were times when the *yin-* and *yang-p'ing* tones were best kept separate. In his postface to the *Chung-yüan yin-yün*, 中 原 音 韻 , Chou Te-ch'ing 周 德 清 recounts the following incident:

... Fu-ch'u 復 初 raised his cup; the singer was singing the popular song *Ssu-k'uai yü* 四 塊 玉 and when he reached the lines

彩 扇 歌 青 樓 飲
cai shàn gō, qīng loú yǐm[7]

(Lo) Tsung-hsin (羅) 宗 信 stopped the song and said to me, "When you sing *cai* parallel to *qīng*, *qīng* becomes *qíng* 晴 . In my estimation of the melody, if in this positon a *p'ing* tone is to be used, its pitch must be raised, but with *qīng* 青 its pitch is held down; that makes it incorrect. . . .[8]

In the same way there were positions in which the *shang* and *ch'ü* tones, though traditionally in one category, were no longer compatible. Again Chou Te-ch'ing writes:

---

6 Wang Li 王 力 , *Han-yü shih-lü-hsüeh* 漢 語 詩 律 學 (Shanghai, 1962), p. 787.

7 I have found it necessary to use two different romanizations: for names of people or places, for the names of song forms, or for other technical terms in Chinese, the Wade-Giles system is used; for the texts of the songs and for words or lines from the songs a system is used which was based on the decisions of the February 1958 language reform committee of the Ch'üan-kuo jen-min tai-piao ta-huei 全 國 人 民 代 表 大 會 with the exception of the final *-uon*, which does not occur in modern Mandarin, and of *-r* as a vowel instead of *-i* after the initials *zh-*, *ch-*, or *sh-*, and *-z* as a vowel instead of *-i* after *z-*, *c-*, or *s-*. Vowels spelled with *-r* or *-z* fall into the same rhyme group, i.e. 支 思 , and so are not confused with 齊 微 *-i*, *-ei* rhymes. For words in the 先 天 rhyme group I prefer *-ien* rather than *-ian* because there are times when medial *i* is required for words in the 寒 山 *-an* rhyme group. Similarly, I retain the *o* in *-iou* finals in the 尤 候 *-ou* group so they are not confused with 魚 莫 *-yu*, *-u* rhymes. All finals spelled *-ong* come under rhyme group 東 鍾 and all spelled *-ung* under 庚 青 . After *l* and *n*, *ü* is spelled *-yu*. For the values both of initials and of finals Chao Yin-t'ang's 趙 蔭 棠 reconstructions in his *Chung-yüan yin-yün yen-chiu* 中 原 音 韻 研 究 (Shanghai, 1956) were most helpful. The tones, *yin-p'ing*, *yang-p'ing*, *shang*, and *ch'ü*, are indicated with diacritical marks, e.g., *diēm, diém, diěm, dièm,* respectively. For unstressed syllables no tone mark is used. Extra-metric syllables, discussed in detail later, are indicated in the romanized text with parentheses. Readings or tones differing from modern standard Mandarin are italicized.

8 Chou Te-ch'ing, *Chung-yüan yin-yün* (1926 photo-reprint; calligraphy on the title page by Ch'en Nai-ch'ien 陳 乃 乾), vol. 1, Hou-hsü 後 序 , p. 1a.

... *mì* 蜜 [in the verse form *Hsi ch'un lai*, 喜 春 來 line 1, last syllable], being a *ch'ü* tone, is a good choice; in this position there definitely cannot be a *shang* tone. It is important that *huòn* 喚 is a *ch'ü* tone but *qǐ* 起 [i.e. the position in which *qǐ* occurs] can be either *p'ing* or *shang* [*huòn* and *qǐ* are the second and last syllables of the fourth line, which is three syllables in length].[9]

It is not possible to say whether this separation of the *shang* and *ch'ü* tones arose from developemnts in the spoken language or from changes in music. It is important to remember, however, that not in all positions of the line were tones so strictly governed, and we shall see later that in many positions, even occasionally the rhyme positions, any tone was allowed.

The way in which Wu Mei 吳 梅 in his *Ku ch'ü chu t'an* 顧 曲 塵 談 [10] describes the vocal delivery of tones in singing is useful here because it shows the musical characteristics that the tone of a syllable takes when translated into song. He states that a *p'ing* tone is longest in duration; its point of most stress is at the beginning, from which it tapers off gradually. In a *yin-p'ing* the note is continuous and clear and must be sung in one breath, but a *yang-p'ing* is in two notes, the first of which is short and clearly separate from the second; this second note "is sung continuously in one breath until the tone is completed."[11] The *shang* tone begins in the same manner as a *p'ing* tone but briskly rises and does not return to the original pitch. The *ch'ü* tone has an "elliptical" shape when sung; from the initial note the pitch gradually rises and then returns to the same pitch.

This is not to suggest that every syllable in a song is sung in the above manner, but at the positions in an established metric pattern where a particular tone seems to be preferred, it is safe to assume that the technique of delivery Wu Mei describes is generally characteristic of the melody in that position and that it dominated the metric form of the line. If we see it is only at such points that the melody was distinctive enough to require the use of certain tones in the metric pattern, it becomes easier to understand why there was the relative strictness in some positions and laxness in others. When songs became recited poetry, however, the metric pattern, being

---

9 *Ibid.*, vol. 2, p. 53b; cf. also Jen Chung-min 任 中 敏 , *Tso tz'u shih fa shu cheng* 作 詞 十 法 疏 證 , *San-ch'ü ts'ung k'an* 散 曲 叢 刊 (Shanghai, 1931), pp. 58b–59a. But see also Chao Ching-shen 趙 景 深 , "Chou Te-ch'ing te hsiao-ling ting-ko 周 德 清 的 小 令 定 格 ," *Tu-ch'ü hsiao chi* 讀 曲 小 記 (Shanghai, 1959), pp. 137–140, in which Chao applies to Chou Te-ch'ing's own songs these critical standards of tones.

10 (Shanghai, 1926), vol. 2, pp. 36–39; although it is the *k'un-ch'ü* 崑 曲 style that he discusses, its vocal delivery is perhaps the closest to that in the Yüan Dynasty of any we now know.

11 *Ibid.*, p. 37.

the only "music" left, dominated the line, and choice of tones became much stricter throughout.

Before examining the tone patterns of *san-ch'ü*, it would be helpful to look at Wang Li's system (pp. 75–76) of measuring *chieh-tsou* 節奏 (units of rhythm). He divides all lines into groups of bisyllables; thus a six syllable line has three rhythm units, e.g.

$$\text{pp tt pp} \ ^{12}$$

which are designated from right to left as the ultimate, the penultimate, and the antepenultimate rhythm units. The extra syllable in a normal line with an odd number of syllables (five or seven) stands alone as the ultimate rhythm unit of the line; thus a five syllable line is divided:

$$\text{pp tt p}$$

Normally a seven syllable line is merely five syllables with a "head" rhythm unit added *at the front*. In the same manner the six syllable line can be thought of as four syllables with another rhythm unit added also at the front. The fundamental difference between the odd and even lines, therefore, is that the caesura in an odd line will always be followed by an odd number of syllables, usually three, and in an even line by an even number, most often four.

In regular poetry this would be a somewhat useless observation, but because syllables may be added quite freely to a line in *san-ch'ü*, the position of the caesura can at times become a problem. If, as is often the case, a line of seven syllables is actually only a six syllable line with one syllable added at the beginning, it would be incorrect to place the caesura after the fourth syllable as in the normal seven syllable line; instead it would be:

$$\text{t pp tt pp} \quad or \quad \text{tpp ttpp}$$

but never:

$$\text{tppt tpp}$$

In this type of seven syllable line the caesura corresponds with a natural break in the six syllable line; therefore, although it has seven syllables, it has the rhythmic characteristics of a line with six syllables. Because these rhythm patterns were determined by obvious patterns in the music, it is natural that they were always observed by poets.

---

12 The letters *p* and *t* stand for the *p'ing* and *tse* tones respectively.

To illustrate briefly the freedom with which tones might be used in practice I have set out below the tone patterns of the first two lines from ten poems in the verse form *Hung hsiu hsieh* 紅繡鞋 [13]

1. *a)*　老夫人寬洪海量
　　　(laŏ) fū rén kuān hóng haĭ liàng　　　　　pq pq sc[14]

　 b)　去筵席留下梅香
　　　(qù) yén xī lioú xià meí xiāng　　　　　qp qc qp

2. *a)*　掐掐拈拈寒賤
　　　taō taō niĕn niĕn hán jièn　　　　　pp ss qc

　 b)　偷偷抹抹姻緣
　　　toū toū muŏ muŏ yĭn *yén*　　　　　pp ss pq

3. *a)*　背地裏些兒歡笑
　　　bei dì (lĭ) xiē eŕ huān xiaò　　　　　cc pq pc

　 b)　手指兒何曾湯著
　　　shoŭ zhĭ (eŕ) hó céng táng zhaó　　　　　ss qq qq

4. *a)*　不付能尋得個題目
　　　(bŭ) fù néng *xīm deĭ* (gè) tí mù　　　　　cq ps qc

　 b)　點銀燈推看文書
　　　(diĕm) yīn dēng *chuī* kàn wén shū　　　　　pp pc qp

5. *a)*　手約開紅羅帳
　　　shoŭ yò kaī hóng luó zhàng　　　　　sc pq qc

　 b)　欵擡身擦下牙牀
　　　(kuŏn) tái *shīn că* xià yá chuáng　　　　　qp sc qq

6. *a)*　欵欵的分開羅帳
　　　kuŏn kuŏn (di) fēn kaī luó zhàng　　　　　ss pp qc

　 b)　輕輕的擦下牙牀
　　　qīng qīng (de) *că* xià yá chuáng　　　　　pp sc qq

7. *a)*　雖是間阻了咱十朝五夜
　　　(suī shŕ) jiàn zŭ (le zā) shŕ zhaō wŭ yè　　　　　cs qp sc

　 b)　你根前沒半米兒心別
　　　(nĭ) gēn qién (méi) *buòn* mĭ (eŕ) *xīm* bié　　　　　pq cs pq

8. *a)*　結些裏焦天撇地
　　　jiĕ xié (lĭ) zhaō tiēn piĕ dì　　　　　sq pp sc

　 b)　橫枝兒苦眼鋪眉
　　　héng zhī (eŕ) *shēm ăn* pū meí　　　　　qp ps pq

9. *a)*　背地裏些兒歡愛
　　　bei dì (lĭ) xié eŕ huān ai　　　　　cc qq pc

13 See the ten anonymous *Hung hsiu hsieh* in the *Hsin chiao chiu chüan pen yang ch'un pai hsüeh* 新校九卷本陽春白雪 (Peking, 1957) annotated by Sui Shu-shen 隋樹森, 1, *chüan* iv, pp. 81–83.

14 As earlier in the article, the letter *p* stands here for the *p'ing* tone. For the analysis of these ten examples the *yang-p'ing* is indicated with *q* to distinguish it from the *yin-p'ing*. The *shang* and *ch'ü* tones are *s* and *c*.

  b) 對 人 前 怎 敢 明 白
      (duì) rén qién zěm gǎm míng baí   qq ss qq
10. a) 小 妮 子 頑 涎 不 退
      (xiaǒ) ní zž wán xién bǔ tuì   qs qq sc
  b) 老 敲 才 飽 病 莫 醫
      (laǒ) qiaō caí baǒ bìng muǒ yī   pq sc cp

It is possible, ignoring exceptions and the poet's liberties, to reduce these
lines to a pair of highly regular patterns:

$$a) \text{ tt pp tt} \quad b) \text{ pp tt pp}$$

A writer skilled in *shih* composition might fill in these patterns quite
easily but the result would hardly be in a true *ch'ü* style. If we look more
closely at the tones, simply by noting which ones occur most frequently
in a position we can formulate a pattern that reveals the manner in which
the writers of these twenty lines coped with the metrical restrictions. Such
a pattern can be represented:

$$a) \text{ xx pq } sc \quad b) \text{ pp xt qq}^{15}$$

Only the last syllable, or rhyme position, in either line is fully consistent;
in the *a*-lines it is a *ch'ü* tone and in the *b*-lines a *p'ing* tone. Moving toward
the head of the line, the first syllable of the ultimate foot in the *a*-lines is
definitely a position in which the *shang* and the *yang-p'ing* are interchangeable;
a *yin-p'ing* sometimes is substituted as well. In the *b*-lines this position is
clearly a *p'ing* tone. The *ch'ü* tone in 10*b* is exceptional; presumably the
author felt that *muò*, parallel with another negative and in an obvious
context, would be recognizable even if sung as a *p'ing* tone. For both syllables
of the penultimate foot in the *a*-lines a *p'ing* tone is preferred but a *shang*
may fit in a pinch, even though it would appear from our examples that
a *shang* tone is exceptional all three times it occurs in this foot, lines 2*a*
and 4*a*. It is interesting also that when the final syllable of this foot is a
shang tone the initial syllable of the ultimate foot is, at least in these examples,
always a *p'ing* rather than a *shang*. In the *b*-lines the final syllable of the
penultimate foot falls easily into the *tse* category; the *p'ing* tone in 3*b* is
exceptional. The initial syllable, however, seems to allow any tone. Both
syllables of the antepenultimate foot in the *a*-lines are quite free but in the
b-lines they are *p'ing* tones, line 3*b* again being an exception. There are no
cases in these examples in which the *yin-* and *yang-p'ing* are incompatible.

---

15 Here *x* allows any tone and italic *s* allows either a *p'ing* or a *shang* tone.

As Yüan music is no longer extant, this is perhaps the best way in which to judge a poet's use of tones in a verse form. The patterns given in most registers of *ch'ü* verse forms are usually too regular to show what tendencies there were among writers to alter tones or what latitudes they allowed themselves with certain lines. One can see quite quickly what criteria the editors of *ch'ü* registers used by comparing, somewhat as we did above, several songs in the same verse form and matching results.[16] To illustrate, three registers give metric patterns for our examples as follows:

Li Yü[17]	Wang Li[18]	Lo K'ang-lieh[19]
1. *a)* ttt pppc	1. *a) pp*t tppc *or p*t tp pc	1. *a)* xt xp xt
b) ptt ptpp	*b)* tpp ttpp *or p*p tt pp	*b)* xp xt pp

Judging only on the basis of our ten examples, it would appear that Lo K'ang-lieh's analysis is closest to normal practice, though he should probably have specified a *ch'ü* tone in the rhyme position in the *a*-line as the other two registers did. It is understandable that his pattern more closely approximates ours, because he concerns himself only with *hsiao-ling*, as we necessarily did, whereas both Wang Li and Li Yü consider in their analysis examples from the drama, which are always much looser in form. It was Li Yü's practice to base his description of the metric form on only a single example. In this case it is not incompatible with the general metric structure of the lines, but it would be quite incorrect to take it as an absolute standard — nor indeed was this Li Yü's intention. None of the registers shows the nature of the initial syllable in the ultimate foot of the *a*-line. It is not a *p'ing* tone, as Li Yü and Wang Li both suggest, nor is it so free as Lo K'ang-lieh implies. However, the freedom of the initial syllables in the penult and antepenult of either line as Lo K'ang-lieh sees it probably represents actual practice better than our analysis, based as it is only on limited material.

Yet these twenty lines are sufficient to show that not all the tones in a line are governed with the same strictness. Whether this has to do with the melody, the tempo, the rhyme, or all three, is difficult to say. From these particular lines, however, we have seen that only in the rhyme positions are

---

[16] For this purpose I found Ch'en Nai-ch'ien's 陳乃乾 *Yüan-jen hsiao-ling chi* 元人小令集 (Shanghai, 1962) most useful.

[17] Li Yü 李玉 , *I-li-an pei-tz'u kuang cheng p'u* 一笠庵北詞廣正譜 (Ch'ing-lien shu-wu 青蓮書屋 , no date); cf. *Chung-lu* 中呂 mode, 15th verse form, p. 11b.

[18] Wang Li, p. 810. Italics mean either *p'ing* or *tse* may be used.

[19] Lo K'ang-lieh 羅慷烈 , *Pei-hsiao-ling wen-tzu p'u* 北小令文字譜 (Hongkong, 1962), p. 47.

the tones fixed; following that in order of strictness is the final syllable in all rhythm units. Looser still are syllables in the initial positions of rhythm units and syllables generally nearer the beginning of the line.

It is not always possible to know whether a strict metric pattern in the texts of *san-ch'ü* was owing entirely to the melody and tempo or whether there only appears to have been a strict pattern because the words of most surviving songs were composed as a sequel to an original set of words. Undoubtedly in many cases both music and previous texts influenced the poet's feeling for what a good tone pattern should be.

There is one point in every song where a good writer allegedly paid strict attention to tones; that was the *wu-t'ou* 務頭. From all accounts this was a form of musical climax or point of melodic beauty that a writer with a good feeling for the song would reflect in his text. Chou Te-ch'ing said that if one knew the position of the *wu-t'ou* in a particular tune, elegant language could be used with it to achieve effects of special beauty.[20] Except where Chou Te-ch'ing points it out in his critical notes, the positions of the *wu-t'ou* are no longer clear. For purposes of analysis, where tone combinations like *ch'ü-shang, ch'ü-p'ing, shang-p'ing, ch'ü-shang-p'ing*, etc., are considered fixed in the metric patterns and allow no substitution, we can assume that the melody of the song was most attractive and that it was at such places the "elegant language" was to have been used.[21]

In the opposite extreme, we might wonder how an author could allow himself the freedom that we see in example 3 above. Comparing it with the standard pattern,

Standard: *a)* xx pq *s*c   *b)* pp xt qq
Example 3 :   *a)* cc pq pc   *b)* ss qq qq

the first line we find acceptable, but in the second line the tones of the penult and antepenult are reversed. If in the other examples the second line had indicated a particularly free use of tones, this line in example 3 might have been judged acceptable as well. This disregard for tonal pattern may be owing to the fact that *shoŭ zhř* 手指 and *hó céng* 何曾 , being colloquial

---

20 Chou Te-ch'ing, vol. 2, p. 47b. Jen Chung-min, pp. 23a–32b, gives a most useful resume of previous critical discussion on this point, to which he adds: "It is obvious that *wu-t'ou* was at first purely a matter of the music and not the text. . . . It is also clear that from being an aspect of music, *wu-t'ou* gradually became a literary feature. Chou Te-ch'ing's statement about 'using elegant language' means that beauty of melody and beauty of language must, being brought together, produce the most brilliant effect; they must not be used separately for it would detract from the effect of both" (pp. 23a–b).

21 Jen Chung-min, pp. 24a–b.

expressions, can stand a certain amount of tonal manipulation before being rendered unrecognizable. Considering that these are not words that attract attention because of their weightiness or special beauty, it is easier to see how the author could use them in spite of a conflict between their tones and the melody. Naturally this would not be accepted by traditional critics as the best of form, but without hearing the song as it was sung originally, it would be difficult merely on the basis of the abstract form to call these lines poor song verse.

San-ch'ü is noted for the freedom with which its lines can be expanded. The syllables added to a line beyond those required in the metric pattern are most frequently referred to as *ch'en-tzu* 襯字 ("extra-metric" syllables) and, as the translation implies, they are not counted as part of the metric pattern. Usually they are grammatical particles or colloquial expressions whose omission from the line affects the sense only very little. They may occur in almost any position but are generally found at the beginning of a line.[22] The ten examples above illustrate the general distribution of extra-metric syllables. The most common type appears in example 6:

6. *a)* 欵 欵 的 分 開 羅 帳
    kuǒn kuǒn (di) *fēn kaī luó zhǎng*   ss pp qc

  b) 輕 輕 的 擦 下 牙 牀
    qīng qīng (di) *cǎ xià yá chuáng*   pp sc qq

The syllable *di* in either line is not counted in the metric scheme and when sung it was most likely given no stress and very little duration. It is for this reason that the question of tone does not arise so clearly for extra-metric syllables. Here we can be fairly certain that a reading of *di* in a normal recitation is similar to the manner in which it was originally sung.

There are cases in which it becomes necessary to compare the line with a standard metric pattern before the extra-metric syllables are revealed. In the third example, for instance,

3. *a)* 背 地 裏 些 兒 歡 笑
    beì dì (lǐ) *xiē er huān xiaò*   cc pq pc

the syllable *er*, although a noun suffix with no meaning, has a position in the metric pattern and must have been sung in the manner of a word with full meaning. A natural recitation of this line emphasizes *huān* and *xiaò*, but if we read the line to scan as a regular six syllable line, *er* gets much more of the emphasis. The only alternative would be to have sung *xiē* with the

---

22 For a useful discussion of extra-metric syllables see Wang Li, pp. 715–729.

duration, i.e. the portion of melody, allowed for both the third and fourth syllables, in which case *er* would have been like *di* in example 6. This, however, is unlikely; the syllable *er* has the function here of filling out the line.

It would appear also that an extra-metric syllable may sometimes have been used to make a word fit better into the tune of a song. If the melody in a certain beat of the line were *mi sol*, for example, it is likely that in such a position a *yang-p'ing* syllable would sound most natural; in other words, a syllable of any other tone would tend to sound like *yang-p'ing* tone and might result in some confusion. If, therefore, a poet found that the word he wanted to use was in the *ch'ü* tone, he might, if it were a noun, add the suffix *er* 兒 ; he could then sing the *ch'ü* tone syllable on the lower pitch and let the suffix occupy the higher pitch; thus the *ch'ü* tone noun in the song would remain nearer its normal tonal characteristics. In the last line of Kuan Han-ch'ing's 關漢卿 *Huang chung wei* 黃鐘尾, quoted below, the noun *lù*, "path," appears to be helped by its suffix in this way.

不 向 烟 花 路 兒 上 走
bŭ xiàng yēn huā lù (er) shàng zoŭ   *ttpp pcs*

Without the suffix, the syllable *lù* might sound like 驢 *lú* (or *lyú*); when *er* is added, however, if *lù* 路 were sung on the pitch *mi* and *er* 兒 followed on the pitch *sol*, the tones would more truly approximate spoken tones and therefore produce a much more normal effect. Obviously not many extra-metric syllables function in this manner nor indeed do most extra-metric *er*.

In the case of a line expanded to extremes through the use of extra-metric syllables, it might appear that all relationship to the normal rhythm would be lost. Usually, however, the rhythmic breaks fall in the correct places and the line scans either with the original or a similar rhythm pattern, depending on the extent of the expansion. Line 7 is a less extreme example:

7. *a*)   雖 是 間 阻 了 咱 十 朝 五 夜
         (suī shì) jiàn zŭ (le zā) shí zhaō wŭ yè   cs qp sc

Without the extra-metric syllables, the line reads:

7. *a*)   間 阻 十 朝 五 夜
         jiàn zŭ shí zhaō wŭ yè   cs qp sc

The extra-metric syllables, all concentrated in the antepenult, were undoubtedly sung very briskly. If the rhythm units were strictly observed, the four final syllables in the line were probably delivered in the normal manner. This is not necessarily how the line is recited now but the example shows the rhythmic effects that may have accounted for novelty in the original presentation of the song.

The effects to be achieved through the use of extra-metric syllables were many and in general appreciated by the writers adept in the colloquial style. It was usually true that writers who closely observed the line patterns of a verse form used a language that tended to be closer to the poetic tradition. On the other hand, when a poem was written with less conscious attention to form and when the writer took greater advantage of the vocabulary and rhythms of the colloquial language, there was often a natural increase in the number of extra-metric syllables. The two following poems are in the same verse form, *P'u t'ien lo,* 普 天 樂 , but treatment of the meter is entirely different, each achieving its proper effect. Chao Shan-ch'ing's poem has a poetic dignity and a certain serenity about it that comes not only from the meanings of its words but from the rather static syntax and the smooth way in which it fits the verse form. In the prostitute's song, however, it is the torrent of words and the abundant colloquialisms that strike us first and these are what make her anger vivid and her disappointment believable.

Chao Shan-ch'ing 趙 善 慶 (fl. 1320); (*Chung-lü*): 中 呂 *P'u t'ien lo*: Chiang-t'ou ch'iu hsing 江 頭 秋 行 :[23]

1. *a)*   稻 粱 肥
          daò liáng feī   tpp *r*[24]
          The corn is fat,

   b)   兼 葭 秀
          jiēm jiā xioù   ppt r
          The rushes tall;

2. *a)*   黃 添 籬 落
          huáng *tiēm* lǐ luò   xpxt *r*
          More yellow is on the hedge[25]

   b)   綠 淡 汀 洲
          lyù *dàm* tīng zhoū   xtxp r
          Fainter green on the sandbar.

3. *a)*   木 葉 空
          mù yè kōng   xtp *r*
          Tree leaves are gone,

---

23 *Yüeh-fu ch'ün yü* 樂 府 羣 玉 , Hu Ts'un-shan 胡 存 善 , editor, *San-ch'ü ts'ung k'an* ed., p. 20a. See also Ch'en Nai-ch'ien, p. 78.

24 The letter *r* marks the lines that are usually rhymed; when italicized, rhyme is optional.

25 The yellow flower here is the chrysanthemum.

    b) 山 容 瘦
        shān róng shǒu   ppt r
        The mountain's face looks thin;

4. *a*) 沙 鳥 翻 風 知 潮 候
        shā niǎo fān fōng *zhī* chaó hoù   xtpp ppt r
        The wind rising, sand birds know the tides,

    b) 望 烟 江 萬 頃 沈 秋
        wàng yēn jiāng wàn qǐng chén qioū   tpp xtpp r
        Before one's eyes, the misty river, ten thousand
           acres of heavy autumn.

5. *a*) 半 竿 落 日
        buòn gān luò *rì*   xptx *r*
        But half a rod more and the sun will be down,

    b) 一 聲 過 雁
        yǐ shēng guò *àn*   xptx *r*
        With a single cry the wild goose is gone,

    c) 幾 處 危 樓
        jǐ chù weí loú   xtpp r
        Here and there a tall house rises steep in the air.

Anonymous: (*Chung-lü*): *P'u t'ien lo*: no title:[26]

1. *a*) 兩 三 日 不 來 家
        (liǎng *sām rì*) *bǔ* laí jiā   tpp r
        (I thought when) he hadn't been here for three
           or four days,

    b) 入 門 來 猶 咱 罵
        (*rì* mén laí) yoú zá mà[27]   ppt r
        When he walks in the door I'll still be cursing him.

2. *a*) 走 將 來 便 口 兒 裏 哩 哩 喇 喇
        (zoǔ jiāng laí biàn koǔ eř lǐ) lǐ lǐ là là   xpxt *r*
        He'll come over to me, full of excuses

    b) 吃 的 來 無 上 下 稷 稷 答 答
        (jí *dǐ* laí wú shàng xià) *jǐ jǐ* dā dā   xtxp *r*
        Spluttering, making no sense, stuttering;

3. *a*) 劣 性 子 用 心 機 怎 捉 拿
        (liè xìng zž yòng *xīm* jǐ) *zěm* zhaǒ ná   xtp *r*
        The slippery devil will try to worm out of it, how
           can anyone trap him!

    b) 涎 眼 腦 巧 待 詔 也 難 描 畫
        (xién *ǎn* naǒ qiaǒ daì zhaò *yě*) nám miaó huà   ppt r

---

26 *Yüeh-fu ch'ün chu* 樂 府 羣 珠 (Shanghai, 1955), annotated by Lu Ch'ien 盧 前 , *chüan* iv, p. 274. See also *Tz'u-lin chai yen* 詞 林 摘 艷 (1525, photo-reprinted, Peking, 1955), Chang Lu 張 祿 , ed., vol. 1: *Nan pei hsiao-ling* 南 北 小 令 , pp. 17b–18a. Also Ch'en Nai-ch'ien, pp. 83–84.

27 *Yoú zá* probably used here for *yoú zž* 猶 自 .

I can't describe how I long for him to ask for my
favors;

4. *a)* 割捨了我咬着牙狠一會兒和他罷

gǒ shě (le, ngǒ) *jiaō* (zhe) yá (hěn yi huì er)

huó tā bà   xtpp ppt *r*

But I'll put him out of mind, and when I've got
over it, I'll tell him we're through.[28]

b) 罷則罷他害羞也顛倒做了眞假

(bà *zaí* bà, tā) haì xiou yě diēn daǒ (*zù* le) zhēn jiǎ   tpp xtpp *r*

If we're through, we're through, but even if he's
sorry I won't be able to tell whether he really
means it.[29]

5. *a)* 他猛可裏便走將來問一聲我好麼

(tā mǒng kǒ lǐ bièn zoǔ jiaī laí wèn) *yi* shēng

(*ngǒ*) haǒ mā   xptx *r*

(But then) he boldly came up and asked me how
I've been,

b) 我只索陪着笑忍着氣怕他怒發

(ngǒ zhǐ suǒ peí zhe xiaò rěn zhe qì) pà tā nù *fā*   xptx *r*

And all I could do was smile back, keep in my
temper for fear he'd get angry,

c) 一兩日不來家覓一箇人去尋他

(*yi* liǎng *ri* *bǔ* laí jiā *mǐ* *yi* gò) rěn qù *xim* tā[30]   xtpp *r*

So when he (leaves and) doesn't come back again
for a couple of days, I'll be looking for someone
to go and hunt him up.

The attitude toward subject matter and the manner of setting it to words
is at two opposite extremes in these poems. We can be quite certain that the
second song was clearly understood and enjoyed by the illiterate, but to
appreciate Chao's song fully a listener would undoubtedly have needed
a certain literary background. It was considered bad form to use too many
extra-metric syllables,[31] but obviously this was a judgment made with a
rather limited view of verse in mind which did not condone use of the
colloquial language or metric roughness. It is perhaps unfortunate that critics,
even down to the present day, find it difficult to recognize properly used

---

[28] *Jiaō zhe yá hèn yi huì er*, "clenching my teeth in resentment."

[29] *Diēn daǒ zhēn jiǎ*, to turn truth and falsehood upsidedown, "pull the wool over"
someone's eyes.

[30] *Tā*: this reading is not given in the *Chung-yüan yin-yün*; the character is listed under the
-*o* rhymes and read *tuǒ*. It is obviously read *tā* here and must commonly have been so read
in certain areas of China in the Yüan dynasty.

[31] Chou Te-ch'ing, vol. 2, pp. 46b–47a. For similar comment by later critics see Jen
Chung-min, pp. 15b–20b.

harshness of sound or roughness of meter as an important part of poetic beauty and to understand that it takes as much skill to make a good poem in the colloquial style as it does in the traditional.

Certain *san-ch'ü* writers were able to make use of contrasting free and strict meters to develop particular effects. A group of four *Tao ch'ing* 道情 poems by Teng Yü-pin 鄧玉賓 make an excellent illustration of this. The first three all show the responsibilities of life in a bad light, insisting cynically that no matter how hard one strives, one's efforts are bound to come to nothing. The rhythm of the lines is irregular and the language fresh and vigorous. Because this gives the poems a kind of spontaneity, one cannot help feeling that the poet was writing with sincerity about matters close to him. In the last poem, however, Teng Yü-pin, with quite regular meters, brings in all the clichés of the *Tao ch'ing* style expressing idealistic escape from society and the ideal contentment that it provides. This is no less sincere than the first three poems, but it is clear that the focus is on an ideal and not necessarily on the writer's own experience. The poetic effect is very successful. Real life in the first three poems is expressed in rougher rhythms; the last poem with its more flowing regularity strongly contrasts the ideal life against the troubles of society. To illustrate, I quote the second and last poems below:

Teng Yü-pin (fl. 1294); (*Cheng-kung* 正宮): *Tao-tao ling* 叨叨令 : Tao ch'ing.[32]

The second poem:

1. *a)* 一個空皮囊包裹着千重氣

     (*yǐ* gò kōng) pí náng baō guǒ (zhe) qién chōng qì   xpxt ppc r

     An empty skin sack filled with ambitions,

  b) 一個乾骷髏頂戴着十分罪

     (*yǐ* gò gān) kū loú dǐng daì (zhe) shŕ fēn zuì   xpxt ppc r

     A dried skull heaped up with blame;

  c) 為兒女使盡些抾刀計

     (weì) eŕ nyǔ shŕ jìn (xiē) tuō daō jì   xpxt ppc r

     For daughters and sons I've schemed all I can

  d) 為家私費盡些擔山力

     (weì) jiā sz̄ feì jìn (xiē) dān shān lì   xpxt ppc r

     And used up my strength for the family's fortune

2. *a)* 你省的也麼哥

     (nì) xǐng *dǐ* yě mā gō   xttpp

     Do you understand this?

---

[32] *T'ai-p'ing yüeh-fu* 太平樂府 , Yang Chao-ying 楊朝英 editor (*SPTK* ed.), *chüan* i, pp. 6a–b. See also Ch'en Nai-ch'ien, pp. 7–8.

b) 你省的也麼哥
(nǐ) xǐng dǐ yě mā gō   xttpp
Do you see it at all?

3.   這一個長生道理何人會
(zhè yǐ gò) cháng shēng daò lǐ hó rén huì   xpxt ppc r
Who really knows how to become immortal?

The fourth poem:

1. a) 白雲深處青山下
bai yún shīm chù qīng shān xià   xpxt ppc r
Deep among white clouds in green mountains,

b) 茅菴草舍無冬夏
maó ām caǒ shè wú dōng xià   xpxt ppc r
A thatched and humble dwelling with neither
winter nor summer;

c) 閑來幾句漁樵話
xián laí jǐ jù yú qiaó huà   xpxt ppc r
In leisure I can talk with simple folk,

d) 困來一枕胡盧架
kùn laí yǐ zhǐm hú lú jià   xpxt ppc r
When tired, sleep under the gourd-vine trellis;

2. a) 你省的也麼哥
(nǐ) xǐng dǐ yě mā gō   xttpp
Do you understand this?

b) 你省的也麼哥
(nǐ) xǐng dǐ yě mā gō   xttpp
Do you see it at all?

3.   煞强如風波千丈擔驚怕
(shaì qiáng rú) fōng bō qiēn zhàng dān jīng pà   xpxt ppc r
It's better than bearing fear in a world of strife.

One's attention is drawn here also to the contrast in syntax of the fourth
poem. The second poem's lines are characterized by firm subject-verb-object
relationships while in the fourth poem the verbs are merely implied, as is
often the case in more "poetic" style, by the juxtaposition of certain nouns
or noun phrases. Only in the last line is there a verb clearly expressed.

It is not always the grammatical particle or parenthetical expression
that falls into the extra-metric positions; there was no rule stating that
an extra-metric syllable could not be a noun, verb, or similar word that
had a basic function in the syntax of the line. A writer of the Yüan dynasty
would not have given this much thought; it was only after *san-ch'ü* was no
longer sung that the "sense-stress" given in recitation set this syntactically
functional type of extra-metric syllable apart from the weaker type and it
became impossible in some cases to distinguish these words from the basic
text; so they often came to be taken as part of the original metric pattern.

This perhaps accounts for the many variant forms in the song registers of later times. The syllables that were found to be in excess of a "normal" verse form were called *tseng-tzu* 增字 (added words). We have already seen that Wang Li (p. 810) described the lines in our ten examples above as basically seven syllables with the note that they "can be six syllables." In the *Pei-tz'u kuang cheng p'u* a seven syllable line only was given. Clearly this is a case of simply adding a syllable to the basic six syllable line and the preference in a song register for the seven syllable line merely indicated the frequency with which it occurred in practice. The reason for such common use obviously means that one syllable, whether grammatically forceful or not, made little difference in the rhythm so long as the caesura was observed. Therefore, as far as the musical structure was concerned, this type of variant verse form is a fiction because such minor changes in text did not constitute a change in the music. Not all variant forms are fictions, however. Unfortunately we have no way of explaining them unless early music can be recovered or until more thorough comparative studies of the *san-ch'ü* can be made.

A case in point is the verse form *Che-kuei ling* 折桂令. Wang Li lists the five more common variant forms, which may be arranged as five "sentences" in nine to twelve lines:

		I		II		III		IV		V
1.		*pptt*pp	*or*	tpp ttpp	–			–		–
2.	*a)*	*t*tpp		–		–		–		–
	b)	*t*tpp		–		–		–		–
3.	*a)*	*t*tpp	*or*	*t*tpp	*or*	*t*tpp	*or*	ttp	*or*	*t*tpp
	b)	*t*tpp	*or*	*pptt*pp	*or*	tpp *t*tpp	*or*	tpp	*or*	*t*tpp
	c)	–		–		–		*t*tpp	*or*	*t*tpp
4.	*a)*	*t*tpptt	*or*	*p*tt pptt	–		–		–
	b)	*pptt*pp	*or*	tpp *t*tpp	*or*	tpp *t*ttpp	–		–
5.	*a)*	*t*tpp	*or*	*t*tpp	*or*	*t*tpp	–		–
	b)	*t*tpp	*or*	*t*tpp	*or*	*t*tpp	–		–
	c)	–		*t*tpp	*or*	*t*tpp	–		–
	d)	–		–		*t*tpp	–		–

Although not the most popular version of this song, its most condensed form is given first to show how the lines develop. Writers most often used versions III and IV of the third sentence; in the fourth and fifth sentences version II is most frequently seen.

The variant lines in lines 1 and 4a are again only a case of adding a syllable at the beginning of the basic line; even line 4b of version III simply has a syllable added before the antepenultimate and penultimate rhythm units. The third sentence, becoming three lines in some versions, is slightly more complicated, but it is still easy to see how line 3b in version III, tpp ttpp, develops into the two lines 3b and 3c of the version IV, tpp and ttpp, which would have been a simple matter of syntax. It is somewhat more difficult to see how the fifth sentence was expanded to twice its normal length. It may have been possible for a Chinese singer to slow down the tempo so that the time between beats was much longer; he then would be able to add several extra words and still not alter the speed of delivery beyond practicability. On the other hand, as appears to be the case here since the rhyme seems often to be repeated, the music of lines 5a and 5b may merely have been repeated for the extra lines 5c and 5d.

It is also interesting that rhymes occur in this song only at the ends of sentences, the fifth excepted, no matter how expanded they may be. This seems to give vague indications, at least in this particular case, of regulating influences in the melody on the metric system, which brings us to certain basic questions on metrics. Why is it, in a song like the *Che-kuei ling*, most of whose lines can be doubled in length, that there are lines like 2a and 2b which are rarely if ever anything but the basic four syllables? This leads us in turn to the broader question: what exactly is the nature of the influence melody can exert upon the metric structure of a whole piece? If unanswerable specifically, these questions at least force us to consider the song behind the verse form which, in a sense, allows a somewhat broader critical view of meter because it makes us realize that the writer who knew the music could successfully take liberties with the verse form that others who worked only with an abstract pattern could hardly be expected to understand. The melody is a freely flowing pattern. It is intricate in the demands it makes on the line, yet it is easily remembered and can be followed with hardly a thought to its complexities. It is a complete entity that can be comprehended all at once in the writer's mind, and so its artistic structure is constantly before the author as he writes. In the hands of a skillful versifier the balance and climax of the melodic structure develop naturally in the text. It is this that accounts in part for the success of certain pieces less elegant in diction and line and also for the failure of certain others in which there may be isolated masterful lines.

The variations we have seen in the *Che-kuei ling* are typical of those appearing in other verse forms. There are, however, those that can be even more radically changed as, for example, the 100-word *Che-kuei ling*. It is basically the same as the twelve line version except that it is greatly expanded with extra-metric syllables. How this is achieved in relation to the music is again only a matter of conjecture, but it may be useful to examine one such expanded song, a good illustration of which is the final song of Kuan Han-ch'ing's *t'ao-shu*, "The Refusal to Get Old." For the sake of continuity I have included the first of the four songs as well.

Kuan Han-ch'ing (*ca.* 1220–*ca.* 1300); (*Nan-lü* 南 呂): *Yi-chih hua* 一 枝 花: Han-ch'ing bu fu lao 漢 卿 不 伏 老.[33]

Yi-chih hua:

1. *a)* 攀 出 牆 朶 朶 花
   (pān) qǔ qiáng duǒ duǒ huā   *p*p ttp
   I've plucked every flower that grows over the wall,

   b) 折 臨 路 枝 枝 柳
   (zhě) lím lù zhī zhī liǒu   *t*t ppt r
   and gathered every willow overhanging the road[34]

2. *a)* 花 攀 紅 蕊 嫩
   huā pān hóng ruǐ nùn   pp ptt
   The tenderest buds were the flowers I picked;

   b) 柳 折 翠 條 柔
   liǒu zhě cuì tiaó róu   tt tpp r
   And the willows I gathered, of the supplest green
      fronds;

3. *a)* 浪 子 風 流
   làng zǐ fōng liǒu   ttpp r
   A wastrel, gay and dashing

   b) 憑 着 我 折 柳 攀 花 手
   (píng zhe ngǒ) zhě liǒu pān huā shǒu   tt ppt r
   Trusting to my willow gathering, flower plucking
      hand,

   c) 直 熬 得 花 殘 柳 敗 休
   (zhí aó dei) huā cán liǒu bai xioū   ppttp r
   I kept at it till the flowers fell and the willows
      withered;

4. *a)* 半 生 來 折 柳 攀 花
   buòn shēng lai zhě liǒu pān huā   tpp ttpp
   Half my life I've been willow gathering and flower
      plucking

---

33 *Yung-hsi yüeh-fu* 雍 熙 樂 府 (*SPTK* ed.), *chüan* x, pp. 20a–21a.

34 Flowers and willows refer throughout the poem to courtesans. In the two songs not quoted here Kuan Han-ch'ing lists his talents in defense of his feeling that, though old, he still has qualities the young cannot emulate.

b) 一世裏眠花臥柳
　　yǐ shr̀ lǐ mién huā wò lioǔ　　　　　　　　　ttt ppts r
　　And for a whole generation slept with flowers and
　　lay among the willows.

Huang chung wei:

1.　我却是
　　(ngǒ què shr̀)
　　But I am an

　　蒸不爛煮不熟
　　(zhēng *bǔ* làn, zhǔ *bǔ* shǔ)
　　un-steam-soft-able, un-boil-through-able

　　搥不匾炒不爆
　　(chuí *bǔ* biěn, chaō *bǔ* baò)
　　un-pound-flat-able, un-bake-dry-able

　　響噹噹一粒銅豌豆
　　xiǎng dāng (dāng) *yǐ* lì tóng wān doù　　　　*ppt*t ppt r
　　rattling plunkety-plung coppery old bean[35]

2.　您子弟誰教鑽入他
　　(nǐm zz̀ dì shuí jiaò *zuōn* rì tuǒ)
　　Who said you young gentlemen could intrude
　　　upon her

　　鋤不斷斫不下
　　(chú *bǔ* duòn, zhaǒ *bǔ* xià)
　　un-hoe-up-able, un-cut-down-able

　　解不開頓不脫
　　(*jiaǐ* *bǔ* kaī, dùn *bǔ* tuǒ)
　　un-disentwine-able, un-cast-off-able

　　慢騰騰千層錦套頭
　　màn tēng (tēng) qiēn céng *jǐm* taó toú　　　*t*tpp ttp r
　　Intricate, thousand-fold brocade snare?[36]

3. *a)* 我頑的是梁園月
　　(ngǒ *wòn di* shr̀) liǎng yuén yuè　　　　　　ppt
　　As for me, I can take pleasure in the Liang-yüan
　　　moon,[37]

　　飲的是東京酒
　　(*yǐm di* shr̀) dōng jǐng jioǔ　　　　　　　　　*pp*t r
　　Drink no less than East Capital wine,

---

35 *Tong wan dou*, copper garden pea, Yüan slang for a libertine who is somewhat past his prime.

36 *Jǐm taó toú*, the brocade snare, i.e. a courtesan's methods of getting a man into her clutches.

37 Liang-yüan was a vast park made in Han times by Prince Hsiao of Liang, 梁孝王.

b) 賞 的 是 洛 陽 花
(shǎng *di* shr̀) luò yáng huā   tpp
enjoy the flowers of Lo Yang

扳 的 是 章 臺 柳
(pān *di* shr̀) zhāng taí lioǔ   ppt r
and pluck the willow of Chang-t'ai.[38]

4. *a)* 我 也 會 吟 詩 會 篆 籀
(ngǒ yě) huì *yím* shr̄, huì *juàn* zhoù   tpp ttt r
Besides, I can compose poems, write ancient
   script[39]

b) 會 彈 絲 會 品 竹
huì tán sz̄, hui pin *zhoǔ*   t*p*p *tt*t r
play the lute and play the flute;

c) 我 也 會 唱 鷓 鴣 舞 垂 手
(ngǒ yě huì) chàng zhē gū, wǔ chuí shoǔ   ttp t*p*t r
I know how to sing the *Che-ku*, dance the
   Ch'ui-shou,[40]

d) 會 打 圍 會 蹴 踘
huì dǎ wei, huì cù *jiǔ*[41]   ttp ttt r
drive game for the hunt, kick the football

e) 會 圍 棋 會 雙 陸
huì wei qí, huì shuāng lioǔ   t*p*p t*p*t r
play chess and roll dice;

f) 你 便 是 落 了 我 牙 歪 了 我 口
(nǐ bièn shr̀) luò (le) ngǒ yá, waī (le) ngǒ koǔ   tt*p* *p*tt r
Even if you knock out my teeth, stretch my mouth
   out of shape,

g) 瘸 了 我 腿 折 了 我 手
qué (le) ngǒ tuǐ, *zhě* (le) ngǒ shoǔ   p*t*t *tt*t r
lame my legs, break my arms,

h) 天 與 我 這 幾 般 兒 歹 症 候
(tiēn yǔ ngǒ zhè jǐ bàn er) daǐ zhèng hoù   *tt*t r
Even if heaven afflicted me with these several ills
   and disabilities,

---

38 The Eastern Capital, i.e. Lo Yang, was noted for its luxuriance and beauty, but see also the note on flowers and willows in the first song above. Chang-t'ai was a district of Ch'ang-an 長 安 where lived a famous T'ang courtesan named Liu, i.e. willow; Chang-t'ai liu is often used in reference to courtesans generally.

39 Refers to pre-Ch'in script or its imitations.

40 *Che-ku* or *Che-ku t'ien* 鷓 鴣 天 is the name of a *tz'u* verse form; *Ch'ui-shou* is the name of a song to which one danced, hands hanging down the while.

41 The last syllable in this line is not in the *Chung-yüan yin-yün* as *jioǔ*; this reading is according to earlier rhymes.

尚兀自不肯休
(shàng wǔ zź) *bǔ* kěn xiōu   ttp r
I'd still not give up;[42]

5. *a)* 除是閻王親令喚
(chú shŕ) *yèm* wáng qĭn lìng *huòn*   *p*p ptt
Not unless Yama himself gives the order

神鬼自來勾
shén guĭ zź laí gōu   *t*t tpp r
and the evil spirits themselves come to hook out

b) 三魂歸地府
sām hún guĭ dì fŭ   *p*p ptt
my three souls and return them to Hell,

七魄喪冥幽
qĭ *paĭ* sàng míng yōu   *t*t tpp r
my seven shades and consign them to oblivion[43]

6. 那其間纔
(nà qí jiān caí)
Only then

不向烟花路兒上走
bǔ xiàng yēn huā lù (eŕ) shàng zǒu   tt*p*p pts r
will I retire from the path of mist and flowers.[44]

---

42 In the *Pei-tz'u kuang cheng p'u*, cf. *Nan-lü* 南 呂 , pp. 15b and 16a–b, Li Yü quotes this song as two shorter songs, dividing them at this point, i.e. the end of the sentence four. The first part he calls a *Shou-wei* 收 尾 , the second a *Wei-sheng* 尾 聲 . In both cases, however, his texts differ widely from other versions. He changed the final line of the poem to fit the *Wei-sheng* metric pattern ttppcps, whereas the normal *Huang chung wei*, being ttpppcs, is much nearer the last line of the text quoted above. In view of this I prefer to take the song as a *Huang chung wei* expanded in the manner of, for example, a 100-word *Che-kuei ling*. This is further justified in that the basic structure of all the lines in sentences 3 and 4 of this version of the poem is trisyllabic like that in lines 3 and 4 of the standard *Huang chung wei*. (Cf. also the discussion below.) Wu Hsiao-ling 吳 曉 鈴 , *Kuan Han-ch'ing hsi-ch'ü chi* 關 漢 卿 戲 曲 集 (Peking, 1958), pp. 949–953, divides the song on the basis of Li Yü's analysis but calls the first part *Huang chung wei*, as the song form is called in the *Yung-hsi yüeh-fu* version, which he uses. By so dividing this version he ignores the fact that his last lines fit the metric patterns of neither the *Huang chung wei* nor the *Wei-sheng*. For this reason alone, to say nothing of the fact that the lines readily fall into the *Huang chung wei* verse form, it would seem that such a division is questionable.

43 The belief being that one dies only after the evil spirits have hooked out of one's body all ten of its souls.

44 Mist and flowers, i.e. the gay life, life among the courtesans. The text of the *Huang chung wei* is according to the *Ts'ai pi ch'ing tz'u* 彩 筆 情 辭 , *chüan* v, as quoted by Cheng Chen-to, 鄭 振 鐸 *Chung-kuo su wen-hsüeh shih* 中 國 俗 文 學 史 (Peking, 1959), pp. 168–169; and Lo Chin-t'ang, vol. 1, p. 42; see Wu Hsiao-ling, p. 952, nn. 20–22, and Sui Shu-shen, *Ch'üan-Yüan san-ch'ü* 全 元 散 曲 (Peking, 1964), notes p. 173. The *Ts'ai pi ch'ing tz'u* is not available to me.

The metric patterns I give at the right of these two songs are based
generally on Wang Li's description of the verse forms *Yi-chih hua* and *Huang
chung wei*.[45] As we can see, Kuan Han-ch'ing's *Yi-chih hua* is fairly regular
but the *Huang chung wei* is about four times as long as it would ordinarily be.
Wang Li gives the verse form as follows:

1. *pp*t*t* ppt r
2. *tt*p*p* ttp r
3. ttp ttp r
4. ttp ttp r
5. tpp ttpp r
6. *tt*p*p* pcs r

In his note on the *Huang chung wei*, Li Yü points out that the number of
lines and words in this song is not fixed.[46] He also says that the final line
must be tppcs,[47] though there are no cases of its being less than seven
syllables. He mentions that there can be a great many trisyllabic phrases
used one after another (i.e., as in lines 3 and 4 above) and that sometimes
four syllables may be added after a trisyllabic phrase (as in line 5).[48]

If we examine the groups of syllables Kuan Han-ch'ing added to the first
two lines of this song we can see that they bear little metric similarity to
the regular lines; they are added as elements extraneous to the line, and build
a rhythmic pattern of their own. In lines 3, 4, and 5, however, whole line
patterns similar to those in the standard form are repeated over and over,
or sometimes are matched with a line in an inverse tone pattern. He uses
many three syllable phrases to expand the third and fourth lines, but they
never keep strictly to the pattern ttp ttp as suggested by Wang Li. A syntax
pattern of three-four, similar to line 5 in the standard form, is often used
by writers to conclude the series of trisyllabic phrases that make up lines
3 and 4; rarely, however, do they have such extended series as sentence 5
in Kuan Han-ch'ing's *Huang chung wei*.

Without more information about the music, it remains difficult to state
exactly how in this particular case the song was made to cover all the lines.
The most likely explanation is that certain musical phrases were repeated
or improvised to accommodate the extra length of the poem.

---

[45] Wang Li, pp. 808 and 809; he follows, however, the *Pei-tz'u kuang cheng p'u* verse forms
very closely.

[46] Cf. *Nan-lü, Huang chung wei*, p. 16b.

[47] He is following Chou Te-ch'ing, vol. 2, p. 49b.

[48] This is quickly seen to be true by a glance at the many examples of *Huang chung wei*
in the *Yüan-ch'ü hsüan* 元 曲 選 .

The Yüan *san-ch'ü*, therefore, can be seen to have its own distinctive metric structure which, because of special characteristics, could not always be described properly in traditional terminology. Although it may appear to be free in form at times or even without form, we have seen that in all but the extreme cases consistent meter and verse forms can be traced. Inconsistencies that do arise are easier for us to understand if we keep in mind that music was the basis of *san-ch'ü* form. With but an elementary appreciation of these matters it becomes possible to gain greater insight into the Yüan writer's use of meter to express his themes.

A Note on Chung Hung and His *Shih-p'in*

HELLMUT WILHELM

THE official biography of the fifth-century literary critic, Chung Hung 鍾嶸,
reads as follows:[1]

> Chung Hung's *tzu* was Chung-wei 仲偉; he hailed from Ch'ang-she in Yin-ch'uan
> 潁川長社.[2] He was the descendant in the seventh generation of Chung Ya 鍾雅,[3]
> Imperial Secretary of Chin 晉 times. His father Chung T'ao 鍾蹈 was on the Staff of the
> Central Army of Ch'i 齊. Chung Hung, his older brother Chung Yüan 鍾岏,[4] and his
> younger brother Chung Yü 鍾嶼 all loved learning; [their production] had a central theme
> and was well reasoned.[5]

---

[1] *Liang-shu* 梁書, 49:110–160; *Nan-shih* 南史 (*Po-na* ed. 百衲本), 72:140–160.
My translation follows the *Liang-shu* version; additions from the *Nan-shih* are indicated.

[2] In southern Honan 河南.

[3] *Tzu*: Yen-chou 彥冑. He was killed in the rebellion of Su Chün 蘇峻 under Emperor
Ch'eng 成帝 (326–342). Biography: *Chin-shu* 晉書, 70.

[4] Yen K'o-chün's *Ch'üan Liang wen* 嚴可均: 全梁文, *chüan* 55, p. 1a, lists one item of
Chung Yüan 鍾岏: *Shih sheng wu i* 食生物議.

[5] *Yu ssu-li* 有思理. On the concept of *ssu* 思 see Liu Hsieh 劉勰, *Wen-hsin tiao-lung*
文心雕龍, chapter *Shen-ssu* 神思. Liu occasionally also uses the term *wen-ssu* 文思.
Liu's conception of *ssu* seems to be that of a central idea of a piece of writing formed by the
meeting of a receptive mind with phenomenal impressions. See Lo Ken-tse 羅根澤,
Wei, Chin, Liu-ch'ao wen-hsüeh p'i-p'ing shih 魏晉六朝文學批評史 (Chungking 重慶
1943), pp. 98–99, and Vincent Shih 施友忠, trans. *The Literary Mind and the Carving of
Dragons* (New York, 1959), pp. 154–158. A paternal uncle of Chung Hung 鍾嶸, Chung
Hsien 鍾憲, was a poet of some renown. Chung Hung mentions him in his *Hsia-p'in* 下品
section: "The poetry of . . . the Imperial Secretary of Ch'i, Chung Hsien (and others) all
follows in the lineage of Yen Yen-chih 顏延之. It is joyful without getting wearisome, and
achieves the elegant attainment of scholar-official poetry. My paternal uncle, the Imperial
Secretary, once told me that in the periods Ta-ming 大明 and T'ai-shih 泰始 (457–464
and 465–471, respectively) the style of Pao Chao 鮑照 in polite literature was the one to

Chung Hung was an Imperial Student in the Yung-ming 永 明 period (483–493) of Ch'i and specialized in the *Book of Changes.* When General of the Guard Wang Chien 王 儉 6 became concurrently the Libationer [of the Imperial College] he had frequent intercourse with him. [At that period] he passed the *hsiu-ts'ai* 秀 才 examination of his home district and raised the position of his house. ‡ In the beginning of the Chien-wu 建 武 period (494–497), he was secretary of the Nan-k'ang Prince 南 康 王 . At that time, Emperor Ming of Ch'i 齊 明 帝 personally handled the details of official business, and the regulations also became more and more confining. Thereupon the local as well as the central officials, transacting their official duties, all vied with each other to conform to precedents and to follow directions; in their memorials on civilian and military affairs they observed the old usage, and nobody dared to revert to selecting his own position. Furthermore they utilized their influence to promote each other, and the duties of the Prince became cluttered with annoying details. At that time Chung Hung submitted a memorial, saying:

"The illustrious princes of antiquity considered talent and on the strength of it distributed political position, they weighed ability and on the strength of it appointed officials. The Three Dukes sat in conclave and discussed the principles, the Nine Ministers acted and accomplished all duties. Thus the Son of Heaven would receive reverence by simply facing South."

When the memorial was submitted, the Emperor was not pleased; he said to the Grand Secretary Ku Hao 顧 昌 : "What kind of man is Chung Hung, wanting to decide on my prerogatives and meddling in affairs which my ministers are not competent to respond to?"

Ku answered: "Chung Hung's position may be low and his reputation not above the ordinary, but his words might contain something that is worth considering. In particular: for all the manifold details of official business responsible positions have been established. If now the Lord of Men in one sweep personally seizes all this, that means that the Lord of Men accumulates toil and his officials accumulate leisure. This is like doing the butchering for the cook and like splitting wood for the woodworker."

The Emperor did not take notice and talked about other things.7

Toward the end of the Yung-yüan 永 元 period (A.D. 500) Chung was removed from civilian office and served on the staff of the army. At the beginning of the T'ien-chien 天 監 period (of Liang) (502–519), even though the political order had changed, the flaws of the preceding dynasty had not been completely removed.8 At that time Chung Hung submitted a memorial, saying: [The memorial, on the position of military officials, is not translated here.]

---

distinguish oneself and to make an impact on the world. Only these few authors maintained the style of Yen and Lu Chi 陸 機 . Even though they are not as self-possessed as Yen, they all succeeded in carrying a sound of intimacy." Ting Fu-pao's *Ch'üanCh'i shih* 丁 福 保 , 全 齊 詩 , *chüan* 4 has one poem of Chung Hsien.

6 *Tzu*: Chung-pao 仲 寶 , staunch Confucianists, strong in the Ritual Classics and the *Ch'un-ch'iu* 春 秋 . Biography: *Nan-ch'i shu* 南 齊 書 , 23, and *Nan-shih*, 22.

7 The passage beginning at ‡ is not in the *Liang-shu*, where the text reads instead: "As the secretary of an Imperial Prince he was transferred to the staff of the army and then promoted to the position of Prefect of An Kuo 安 國 ." This could only have been an appointment *in partibus infidelium* as An-kuo was a northern prefecture.

8 The *Liang-shu* differs slightly.

[The memorial] was passed to the Imperial Secretariat and acted upon. He was again transferred to the military and acted on the staff of the Lin-ch'uan Prince 臨川王 .[9]

When the Heng-yang Prince 衡陽王 Yüan-chien 元簡 [10] was sent out to the defense of K'uai-chi 會稽 , he appointed Chung Hung secretary[11] of Ning-shuo 寧朔 [12], and Chung concentrated his literary abilities on his work. At that time, the recluse Ho Yin 何胤 [13] had built a house in the Jo-yeh Mountain 若邪山 .[14] When a great flood occurred on the mountain, uprooting trees and boulders, this house alone had remained untouched. Then Yüan-chien ordered Chung Hung to compose a eulogy of the *jui* mansion 瑞室 as a testimonial of merit. Its text is of classical beauty. Then he was transferred to serve in the Western Secretariat and as a secretary of the Chin-an Prince 晉安王 .

[Chung Hung had once sought acknowledgment from Shen Yüeh 沈約 , but Shen had repudiated him. After Shen's death][15] Chung Hung classified former and contemporary five word poems, discussing their strong and weak points, calling his book *Criticism of Poetry*.[16] In its preface, he says: [The *Shih-p'in* 詩品 preface, omitted here, follows.[17]]

A short time later, he died in office.

(Chung Hung's) older brother Chung Yüan's *tzu* was Chang-yüeh 長岳 ;[18] he died holding the position of a Prefect of Chien-k'ang 建康 . He wrote a collection of *Biographies of Good Officials* (*Liang li chuan* 良吏傳) in ten *chüan*. ⟨His younger brother⟩ Chung Yü's *tzu* was Chi-wang 季望 . He was administrator of Yung-chia 永嘉 . When in 514 a list of Imperial Academicians was composed, Chung Yü was also included. All three brothers left literary collections.

---

9 I.e., Hsiao Hung 蕭宏 .

10 Hsiao Tao-tu 蕭道度 .

11 Chi-shih 記室 , an official position in the local administration with lower secretarial functions.

12 Present-day Ning-Hsia 寧夏 , again out of reach of Liang rule.

13 *Tzu*: Tzu-chi 子季 , Grand Protector of Chien-an 建安 , later retired, did not accept office under the Liang. Specialist in the *Book of Changes* and the *Songs*, he died in 531, aged eighty-six. Ting's *Ch'üan Liang shih* 全梁詩 , *chüan* 12, has one series of poems.

14 Near Shao-hsing 紹興 in Chekiang 浙江 .

15 The bracketed passage is added from the *Nan-shih*. Shen Yüeh died in 513.

16 The book is, of course, now known by the name *Categorization of Poetry, Shih-p'in* 詩品 . The *Sui-shu* 隋書 catalogue lists it as *Shih-p'ing* 詩評 with the additional remark: also called *Shih-p'in*. I have used the edition of Cha Chu-whan 車柱環 , "*Chung Hung Shih-p'in chiao-cheng kao* 鍾嶸詩品校正稿," *Journal of Asian Studies* (Seoul), 3:2 (1960), 117–158, and 4:1 (1961), 203–237; addenda, 6:1 (1963), 299–330 (cited hereafter as Cha). There are several other useful commentated editions of the *Shih-p'in*, among them Hsü Wen-yü 許文雨 in *Wen-lun chiang-su* 文論講疏 (Nanking, 1937), pp. 153–320, and Tu T'ien-mi 杜天縻 , *Shih-p'in hsin-chu* 詩品新註 , Shih-chieh 世界 (Taipei, 1956). See Cha 3:2 for additional references to the book by the name *Shih-p'ing*. Cha argues that Chung's original title was *Shih-p'in* and the *Shih-p'ing* was an adaptation to a genre name widely used in contemporary and later literature.

17 In the *Nan-shih* only a short summary, which stresses the point that it was written to get even with Shen Yüeh. See Cha on the question of the preface.

18 *Yüeh* is the reading of the *Liang-shu* version in the T'ung-wen 同文 and the *Po-na* editions. Both editions read *ch'iu* 丘 in the *Nan-shih* version.

Except for the *Shih-p'in* and the two memorials quoted in his biography, no writings of Chung survive.[19] No poem of his has been handed down.

The claim of the *Nan-shih* biography that Chung composed the *Shih-p'in* in order to get even with Shen Yüeh seems hardly justified. It could of course be argued that in the time of Emperor Wu of Liang, who was not convinced by Shen's intonational postulates, it was sagacious to take a stand against them. However, Chung's rebuttal of Shen's rules, contained in the intro-duction of the *hsia-p'in* section, represents a well-sustained position within this discussion and does not have to be explained as engendered simply by ill will.[20]

Chung's fight against the rigid tonal requirements of Shen does not make Chung deaf to the acoustic values of the language. His reference to "pure and turbid sounds" does not necessarily embody the distinct meanings ascribed to these terms by contemporary Chinese linguistics. It is, however, clear that he meant a poem to be read and that he emphasized sound qualities as a specific, even determinant, aspect of poetry.

Nor has the insertion of Shen's poetry at the end of the *chung-p'in* section necessarily been dictated by malice.[21] This passage reads:

From among the poems of Shen Yüeh, Kuang-lu to the Left 左 光 祿 of Liang times, when his entire production in the field of polite literature is considered, the five word poems are the most outstanding. An investigation into their structure and into their overtones will reveal beyond doubt that he followed the model of Pao Chao; this is why he is not encum-bered by classical learning and excels in genuine emotions. The Hsiang Prince of Yung-ming 永 明 相 王 times[22] loved literature. Wang Jung, Shen Yüeh, and others all attached themselves to him respectfully.[23] At that time, Hsieh T'iao's 謝 朓 reputation had not yet been consolidated, Chiang Yen's 江 淹 talent had run dry, and Fan Yün's 范 雲 fame was still[24] small; and thus Shen Yüeh was considered the "lone pacer."[25] Even though his literary production was not of the highest quality, its refinement was still the choice of the times. [His poems] were repeated in all quarters; they were recited and set to music. In my

---

19 See Yen, *Chüan-Liang wen*, *chüan* 55, pp. 1a–12a.

20 The passage is translated in Ch'en Shou-Yi 陳 受 頤 , *Chinese Literature* (1961), pp. 228–229. The Wang Yüan-chang mentioned in the passage is Wang Yung 王 融 .

21 The *Ssu-k'u t'i-Yao* 四 庫 提 要 takes Shen Yüeh's place within Chung's categories as perfectly justified; see Cha for further quotes agreeing with this position. See also Chu Tung-jun 朱 東 潤 , *Chung-kuo wen-hsüeh p'i-p'ing shih ta kang* 中 國 文 學 批 評 史 大 綱 (Chungking, 1944), p. 62. However, even though Chung's position can be justified, it does not seem to have come hard to Chung to phrase his evaluation just the way he did.

22 I.e., Hsiao Tzu-liang.

23 Text amended following Cha's suggestion.

24 Text corrected following Cha.

25 That is to say, the only outstanding person. The reference comes from the Tai Liang 戴 良 biography in the *Hou-Han shu* 後 漢 書 .

opinion, Shen Yüeh has just written too much. If the lascivious and the miscellaneous are removed and only the essential and the important are selected, then he can justifiably be ranked in the Chung-p'in category. The texture of his texts might be more compact than that of Fan Yün; what he conveys however is more shallow than Chiang Yen.

Even though Chung's evaluation of Shen Yüeh is now, as a rule, taken as justified, that does not mean to say that Chung's categorizations have been generally or even widely accepted. Later literary criticism contests the sanity of his judgment in many individual instances. Particularly, the fact that T'ao Ch'ien is rated in the *chung-p'in* has aroused a storm of indignation.[26] Chung's passage on T'ao reads:

The poems of T'ao Ch'ien, Court Scholar of Sung,[27] can be traced back to Ying Chü 應 璩 and an additional influence came from Tso Ssu 左 思 . His style is sparing [or intro-verted?] and quiet, but he does not excel in apt formulations. He sincerely strove to convey genuine archaism, his wording arouses contentment and cheer. Whenever one peruses his writings, he is reminded of his [T'ao's] human virtues, and the world delighted in his upright disposition. When it comes to lines like "Happily talking, we drink the spring wine,"[28] or "At the day's end there are no clouds in the sky,"[29] then their mood is luxuriant and their clarity is lavish. How should they just be the words of a rustic? He is the ancestor of poets of all times who were given to retirement and abandon.

Faced with ratings like these and the subsequent criticism they aroused, it might be wise to recall the remark of the *Ssu-k'u t'i-yao* that Chung's evaluations were judgments arrived at in his own period, the tradition of which has in great part been lost, a period necessarily unfamiliar with later predilections and evaluations. The *Wen-hsin tiao-lung* does not mention T'ao Ch'ien at all.

Another point on which Chung's *Shih-p'in* has been frequently attacked is its emphasis on literary influences, which, it has been felt, does not do justice to individual creativity. Without exception, Chung would trace a poet back to one (or several) predecessors, and eventually all poetry is in this way derived from either the *Kuo-feng* 國風 or the *Ch'u-tz'u* 楚辭

---

26 On this, see Wang Shu-min 王 叔 岷 , "Lun Chung Hung p'ing T'ao Yüan-ming shih" 論 鍾 嶸 評 陶 淵 明 詩 in *Hsüeh-yüan* 學 原 , 2:4 (1948), 68–69. The thesis has been proposed that Chung had T'ao originally ranked *shang-p'in* 上 品 and that his appearance in the *chung-p'in* section is a later corruption. Cha argues with good reasons against this thesis.

27 Cheng-shih 徵 士 ; this was a current epithet of T'ao.

28 From the *Tu Shan-hai-ching* 讀 山 海 經 ; Chang-Sinclair, *The Poems of T'ao-Ch'ien* (Honolulu, 1953), p. 92. The line is closely modeled after one of Ying Chü quoted in the *Pei-t'ang shu-ch'ao* 北 堂 書 鈔 , *chüan* 48.

29 From the *Ni ku-shih* 擬 古 詩 ; Chang-Sinclair, p. 78.

tradition.[30] Among the more stringent critics of this emphasis were Yeh Meng-te 葉夢得 of Sung and Mao Chin 毛晉 of Ming.[31] The most objectionable application of this principle of influence seems to have been the tracing back of T'ao Ch'ien to Ying Chü. This emphasis of Chung certainly throws light on his position on the problem of tradition versus creativity. His image of the literary tradition as an uninterrupted flow is as such very appealing and does give cohesion to the body of literature he is dealing with. No literary historian or literary critic can dispense with synoptic assays of this kind. Furthermore, his emphasis on affiliations within the tradition at no place obstructs his judgment on individual creativity. In his evaluations the specific contributions and the personal spirit of his authors are always treated discriminately and judiciously.

On what points Chung establishes this indebtedness to a literary predecessor is not quite clear. In most cases this indebtedness is expressed by the term *yüan-ch'u* 源出. Quite frequent also is the expression: "he follows the lineage of," *tsu-hsi* 祖襲; occasionally he uses the term *hsien-chang* 憲章, or *mu* (*mou-mou*) *chih feng* 慕 (某 某) 之風. The word *feng* in the last statement might involve some concrete point of reference. In one other case (T'ao Ch'ien) the term *feng-li* 風力 is used. Now, the connotations of the term *feng* in other parts of Chung's writings and in contemporary usage can be at least tentatively determined, one connotation being "mood," and this might also be the point of reference here. In very few other cases these bare terms are qualified. The *Ku-shih* 古詩 are said to emanate, as far as their *t'i* 體 is concerned, from the *Kuo-feng t'i* meaning something like style or structure. Also Shen-Yüeh is said to be indebted for his *wen-t'i* 文體 to Emperor Wen of Wei 魏文帝. The same indebtedness is traced here to a similarity of *yü-lun* 餘論 (overtones?). Thus, in the few cases in which the similarity is made concrete, its character seems to be quite different.

At times, the evaluations of a poet and his predecessor furnish a clue. For instance, both T'ao Ch'ien and Ying Chü, on whom T'ao is said to depend, are praised for their archaism. In both cases their luxuriance and lavishness are mentioned. These cases are, however, rare, and it is much more common to find vastly differing evaluations of a poet and his predecessor. An investigation into these relationships reveals, however, that Chung

---

[30] The only exception is Juan Chi 阮籍 who is traced back to the *Hsiao-ya* 小雅 tradition. Lo Ken-tse, p. 118; Chu Tung-jun, p. 58; and Tu, pp. 5–6, tabulate these lines of influence.

[31] See Lo Ken-tse and Cha for quotes from these and other critics.

might have had yet another point in mind, which is direct borrowing. This can be shown in the case of T'ao Ch'ien and Ying Chü and in other cases.

Chung Hung's *Shih-p'in* categorizes and evaluates five word poetry only. In his introduction Chung develops an argument in favor of the five word poem, which starts out with a historical survey of this genre. This survey is not convincing throughout, as it takes the "Song of the Five Sons" as the ancestor of the genre and accepts other examples which are now generally taken to be late. Chung does, however, go on to say that the five word poem was definitely a creation of the Han dynasty and that it achieved its first peak in the Chien-an period, particularly in the hands of Ts'ao Chih 曹植 . The later part of his argument reads:

... These are the crowning examples of the five word poem, the verses of which rule the [literary] world.

As for the four word poem, its verses are too restricted for a broad meaning. As long as it took its direction from the *feng* and the *sao* 騷 , it could have some achievements, but still it always labored under the affliction that the verse length could adapt only a limited meaning. That is why it was rarely practiced through the generations. The five word poem on the other hand accommodates the essentials of a verse, and thus all who practice it achieve a certain flavor; therefore it can be said to befit the [poetic] trend. Indeed, it is the form most apposite to point out events, to create shapes, to express emotions, and to describe reality.

This argument, interesting as it is with reference to the flavor of a poem as created by form, justifies as a matter of fact a genre which was predominant in Chung's time anyway. He did not have to make room for the five word line next to the four word line any more, and it was not yet necessary to make room next to the seven word line.

Chung Hung's basic position on problems of poetics does not appear indebted to any spiritual or doctrinal tradition. Whereas Liu Hsieh borrows from Buddhism and feels committed to Confucianism,[32] Chung is surprisingly free of any such bonds. His interest is in poetics which he does not expound in religious or philosophical terms. For him poetry can stand on its own feet; it is justified on its own terms and does not have to appropriate an argument extraneous to its own sphere. Even when he quotes from the *Lun-yü* or the "Great Preface," he does not do so in order to put himself within the Confucian tradition, but to say something meaningful about poetics.

---

[32] See Vincent Shih, "Classicism in Liu Hsieh's Wen-hsin tiao-lung," *Asiatische Studien* (1953), pp. 122–134.

On some of the problems of poetics, Chung's position comes close to that of Liu Hsieh. This is, for instance, true with regard to his emphasis on spontaneity. That for Chung this spontaneity is not equivalent to (Taoist) simplicity is borne out by his constant references to craftsmanship, artistic skill, and to the luxuriant, the elegant, and the marvelous aspects of poetry. Another instance is the role of impressions on the creation of a poem. Impressions from nature, history, and human fate are rated highly in the creative process; he has, however, much less to say than Liu on the question of natural endowment and on the problem of creativity in general. He is more interested in modes of expression and in evaluating poets. In his preface he says:

The spirit (*ch'i* 氣) sets the phenomena in motion, the phenomena influence man, hence human nature and emotions are agitated and seek expression in dancing and singing; the three forces are illuminated and all existence is beautified. The divine action of the spirits depends on this to derive nourishment, the dark and the sublime need it to become communicable. Of what moves Heaven and Earth, what influences the outgoing and returning spirits, nothing comes close to the poem.

Poetry includes three modes of expression, the evocative image (*hsing* 興), the association (*pi* 比), and the description (*fu* 賦).[33] When, after the verse has come to an end, what it expresses still lingers on this is due to an evocative image. To adduce phenomena in order to illustrate one's aspirations, this is an association. Straight writing about affairs and parabolic depiction of phenomena, this is description. Vast, indeed, are these three modes of expression. When they are used judiciously, when they are given body by the power of mood, when they are given grace by the color of cinnabar, so that their flavor becomes boundless and their sound moves the heart, then the poem is at its acme. . . .

Now there are spring wind and spring birds, autumn moon and autumn cicadas, summer clouds and rain during the hot season, winter moon and abundant cold, four seasons of the year which all have their influence on the poem. . . . [Here follows an enumeration of grievous historical events and tragic human fates, dealt with in poetry] all these agitated the human soul. Except for the poems of Ts'ao Chih,[34] who was able to develop this mode of expression? Except for the Long Song,[35] what could give reign to these emotions?* That is why it is

---

[33] This is, of course, from the "Great Preface." I reverted to Legge's term "description" for *fu* as it seems to fit Chung's definition below.

[34] I take Ch'en-shih 陳 詩 to refer to the poetry of the Ch'en-ssu Wang 陳 思 王 , i.e., Ts'ao Chih. Otherwise *ch'en-shih* would mean: to state in poetic language.

[35] I take this to refer to the *yüeh-fu* song of this name.

* [*Editor's note*: The original text for the two sentences concerned in the last two notes reads, " 非 陳 詩 何 以 展 其 義?非 長 歌 何 以 騁 其 情 ?" We intend to suggest that it may be translated as: "Except by presenting them in poetry, how could they [i.e., the poets mentioned in the preceding passage which has been omitted in the quotation] explain sufficiently their ideas? Except by singing in prolonged sounds, how could they express freely their emotions?" To interpret 陳 詩 as 陳 (思 王) 詩 or 陳 思 is very unusual, as we have no other textual support for this interpretation. The term 陳 詩 in the meaning

said: "Poetry will lead you to associate with people, it will lead you to grieve."[36] To make the poor and lowly accept their lot peacefully, to make those who dwell in darkness cease to mourn, there is nothing superior to poetry.

On one point, however, Liu and Chung differ decidedly: Chung argued extensively against the use in poetry of borrowings and quotes,[37] a usage which appears commendable to Liu. This diatribe seems puzzling in view of Chung's implicit and explicit reference to such borrowings, which, when occurring, are not stated to be objectionable as such. Apparently what he warns against here is an excess rather of this usage, which when applied formally and studiedly would do damage to the immediacy of the poem.

It does not seem to be an accident that no poem of Chung is preserved. He might not have written any or, if he has, none which was worth preserv-

---

"to present a poem" is actually quite well known. In the *Book of Poetry* (no. 252, "卷 阿 ") there are the lines " 以 矢 其 音 " and " 矢 詩 不 多 ." Cheng Hsüan 鄭 玄 notes: " 矢，陳 也 ." " 獻 詩 以 陳 其 志 ." The *Li Chi* 禮 記 (" 王 制 第 五 ") says, " 命 大 師 陳 詩，以 觀 民 風 ." Cheng's commentary here also says, " 陳 詩，謂 采 其 詩 而 視 之 ." Yen Yen-chih 顏 延 之 wrote in A.D. 433 in a poem: " 觀 風 久 有 作，陳 詩 愧 未 妍 ." In a eulogy written on October 1, 498 (齊 敬 皇 后 哀 策 文), Hsieh T'iao 謝 朓 says, " 顧 史 弘 式，陳 詩 展 義 ." The *yüeh-fu* song title 長 歌 行 is probably based on a common term " 長 歌 " (sing in prolonged sounds). The "Hsi-ching fu" 西 京 賦 by Chang Heng 張 衡 has the line: " 女 娥 坐 而 長 歌 ." Hsieh Chuang 謝 莊 in his "Yüeh-fu" 月 賦 says, " 情 紓 軫 其 何 託 ？ 愬 皓 月 而 長 歌 ." The *Yüeh-fu ku t'i yao-chieh* 樂 府 古 題 要 解 based on Lu Chi's poem, explains the meaning of the title as " 言 人 運 短 促，當 乘 間 長 歌 ." The *Yüeh-fu shih chi* 樂 府 詩 集 quoting from a *ku-shih* 古 詩 (attributed to Su Wu 蘇 武) " 長 歌 正 激 烈，" from Ts'ao Ts'ao's 曹 操 song 燕 歌 行 ： " 短 歌 微 吟 不 能 長，" and from Fu Hsüan's 傅 玄 (A.D. 217–278) song 豔 歌 行 ： " 咄 來 長 歌 續 短 歌，" also explains, " 歌 聲 有 長 短 ." The term might be derived from " 歌 永 言 " in the *Book of History*. At least scholars of the Han dynasty interpret it this way. Cheng Hsüan's commentary to the latter says, " 永，長 也， 歌 又 所 以 長 言 詩 之 意 ." Wang Su 王 肅 also notes, " 歌 詠 其 義，以 長 其 言 ." We may notice that Chung Hung's two sentences are verbally similar to the lines by Hsieh T'iao and Hsieh Chuang as quoted above. It also seems unlikely for Chung Hung in the context to exalt merely Ts'ao Chih and the particular *yüeh-fu* tune.

In a letter to the editor concerning the above suggestion, Hellmut Wilhelm says, "I am well aware of the fact that my interpretation is daring. I arrived at it by looking at the second sentence first. The Long Song of the *Yüeh-fu* fits perfectly into the context of this sentence and so I assume that here a specific piece of writing is referrred to. Looking for a parallel piece of writing in the first sentence, I could not think of anybody but Ts'ao Chih. As I indicate in my footnote that another reading is possible, I would like to suggest that you leave my text as it is." The author seems to have good reasons; so we keep his translation intact. And it may be pointed out further that, if 陳 should be interpreted as a proper name, we may also cite Pao Chao's 鮑 照 " 芙 蓉 賦 "： " 感 衣 裳 於 楚 賦，詠 憂 思 於 陳 詩 ." Here 陳 詩 means the poem " 澤 陂 " from the state of Ch'en 陳 風 in the *Book of Poetry* (no. 145).]

36 *Lun-yü*, 17:9.

37 The pertinent passage is translated in Ch'en Shou-yi, p. 229.

ing. His essay is thus basically a critic's criticism and not a poet's criticism. He does not seem to be particularly interested in or sensitive to those aspects of poetry which are exclusively the poet's domain. What he has to say about poetic creativity rarely goes beyond the commonplace, and he seems to have been tone-deaf to some of the particular issues of the poet's craftsmanship, such as Shen Yüeh's musical underpinning of poetic prosody.

As a critic, however, he stands out as an innovator with daring and taste. Categorization of literature was one of the issues with which contemporary and earlier criticism was very much concerned. The principle of categorization has, however, usually been genre.[38] That he categorizes according to quality rather than genre is a step which has advanced this issue of Chinese criticism from the pedestrian to the imaginative. His determination of quality is not and cannot possibly be systematic. All poetic appreciation will become dull once it is systematized. The systematizing urge is on the other hand taken care of by his construction of a developing body of Chinese poetry, flowing from generation to generation and from poet to poet. His familiarity with the *Book of Changes* might have trained him to conceive of an image like this.

---

[38] See James R. Hightower, "The *Wen-hsüan* and Genre Theory," *HJAS*, 20 (1957), 512–533.

A Geometry of the *Shr̄ Pǐn**

E BRUCE BROOKS

Il y a trois sortes de critiques: ceux qui ont de l'importance; ceux qui en ont moins; ceux qui n'en ont pas du tout. Les deux dernières sortes n'existent pas: tous les critiques ont de l'importance.

ERIK SATIE, *Eloge des Critiques*

AN understanding of the *Shr̄ Pǐn*[1] is subtly difficult to achieve, not because the work itself is notably obscure, but simply because the burning issues with which it attempts to deal have long since been resolved. The history of taste (as distinct from that of poetry itself) has blurred the *Shr̄ Pǐn*'s radicalism by coming to agree with many of its strictures, to the extent that modern taste takes any account of pre-Táng poetry at all. No statement in the work, with the important exception of its disapproval of Táu Chyén (B12),[2] is capable of raising the average modern eyebrow. Most of us,

---

* The author wishes to express his thanks to Oberlin College for the research grant under which most of the work on the study presented here was done. Copyright is not claimed for any part of this article.

Romanization used here is the Yale (IFEL) system modified by the use of the colon (:) for the vowel of "bug," and the digraph *ae* for the vowel of "bag," permitting less ambiguous use of the remaining vowel symbols. Thus *a*, "father"; *e*, "get"; *o*, "gonna"; *i*, "seat/sit"; *u*, "suit/soot"; *yw* instead of *yu* for the first vowel-sound in "über."

[*Editor's note:* There was considerable disagreement between the author and the editor on many points that are made in this article, such as Jūng Húng's general viewpoint; his evaluation of Táu Chyén and Shǐn Ywē, his alleged knowledge of the *WSDL*, the style/substance ratio of Tsáu Pǐ's poems, and certain translations; but because of space the discussions of these differences are not included here.]

[1] Translations in this paper are based chiefly on the Takamatsu text 高 松 亨 明 , 詩 品 詳 解 (弘 前 : 弘 前 大 學 文 理 學 部 內 , 中 國 文 學 部 , 1959, itself based on a Míng woodprint of 1561, which is appended in facsimile), with some variant readings adopted from the standard text, i.e., Ch:n 陳 延 傑 , 詩 品 注 (香 港 : 商 務 印 書 館 , 1959).

[2] Parenthesized formulas refer to the placing of a poet in the *Shr̄ Pǐn*. The arrangement of the first two ranks is given in the third column of Chart 1, where characters are available

if we dip into it at all, are content to take it passively, picking out the tidbits of philosophy in it, noting the "progressiveness" (materialistic or psychological, according to geography) of some of its features, and letting the rest go.

It is extremely unlikely that the work was written or received with any such comfortable detachment. The late Six Dynasties were not a placid age, politically or intellectually, and poetry was fought over no less hotly than politics, religion, or the hills and streams themselves. The literary scene was polarized, in Jūng Húng's time, by the battle over tonal prosody, championed by Shĕn Ywē (B21) and his group. This was, in context, merely the final phase of an increasing post-Hàn concern with poetic technique as such. Prosody was closely associated[3] with an even more widespread vogue for the poetry of feminine psychology. Emperor Wŭ of Lyáng 梁武帝 (during whose reign the Shr̄ Pĭn was written[4]), though cold to prosody as such, was himself a love-poet of some note. A random sample of his pieces in the courtesan-song genre,[5] arranged by myself in seasonal order, will suggest the typical range of this poetry.

Spring Song   春　歌

across the ice, the glare of crimson sun   朱 日 光 素 冰
against the snow, the sheen of yellow flowers   黃 花 映 白 雪

to my love I send a spray of plum —   折 梅 寄 佳 人
it and I in hopes of warmer hours   共 待 陽 春 月

Summer Song   夏　歌

about the room stand flowers in bright array   閨 中 花 如 繡
upon the screen lies dew in pearly drops   簾 上 露 如 珠

---

for readers initially puzzled by the romanization. I follow Takamatsu for the arrangement of poets in the third (C) rank, which differs somewhat from that of the usual text.

[3] Shĕn Ywē's prosodic rules, so far as they can be reliably recovered, are followed more closely in his "light" poetry than in his more "personal" poetry. Love-poetry, the bulk of which was written for the sake of writing poetry rather than out of an intense autobiographical urge, had a natural affinity for the more objective trends in literature. Opposition to love-poetry was based perhaps more on this emotional "artificiality" than on the (usually quite mild) impropriety of its content.

[4] I follow Takamatsu (pp. 134–136, quoting Wáng Dá-jĭn, 1957) in accepting ca. 468–518 as Jūng Húng's dates. From internal evidence, the Shr̄ Pĭn cannot have been written later than 517. Internal and anecdotal evidence suggests terminal dates of 507 for the Wĕn-syĭn Dyāu-lúng, 527 for the Wĕn Sywǎen, and 537 for the Yẁ-tái Syĭn-yŭng.

[5] From Yẁ-tái (YT) 吳兆宜 ， 玉臺新詠箋注 (1879), 10, modeled on the "Songs of Wú," which may be inferentially dated from the Yẁ-tái at about 450. I have restricted myself to poems not otherwise attributed in different anthologies.

can't you tell she's thinking of her love? —	欲 知 有 所 思
her movements falter, and her weaving stops	停 織 復 竚 嶇

Autumn Song 秋 歌

a lover's knot her silken sash holds firm	繡 帶 合 歡 結
linked designs her broidered coat adorn	錦 衣 連 理 文
her love is poured into the moon of night —	懷 情 入 月 夜
her smile is hidden in the clouds of morn	含 笑 出 朝 雲

Winter Song 冬 歌

the clepsydra has dripped a year away	一 年 漏 將 盡
a thousand miles he went, and has not come	萬 里 人 未 歸
milord must surely have a place to go —	君 志 固 有 在
and I, no lover to be hearing from	妾 軀 乃 無 依

The leader of the avant-garde, however, was not the Emperor himself but his son Syāu Gāng 蕭 綱 , who became Heir Apparent in A.D. 531 on the death of his older brother Syāu Tüng 蕭 統 , and succeeded briefly to the throne in 550. Syāu Gāng is a much smoother poet, more at home with Shǐn Ywē's prosodics than his father. We may include a specimen of his boudoir poetry, also in quatrain form.

the quilts are empty; frequently she wakes	被 空 眠 數 覺
the cold is heavy and the night winds blow	寒 重 夜 風 吹
the hangings of the bed are not an ocean —	羅 帷 非 海 水
across her fears, what way is there to go?	那 得 度 前 知

This type of poetry came to be known as "palace poetry" after its intense cultivation at the Heir Apparent's palace during Syāu Gāng's tenure. Beside the avant-garde poets who grouped themselves around him, there were two principal opposing factions, identified in a letter written by Syāu Gāng to his younger brother Syāu Yì 蕭 繹 (then King of Syāng-dūng 湘東王 ; Emperor in 552–554).

Further, there are in our times the imitators of Syè Líng-yẁn (A12) and Péi Dž-yě 裴 子 野 , who are quite deluded in their efforts. Why? because Syè spews forth words like a man possessed; he is natural, but sometimes unrestrained. Such is his roughness. Péi is a good orthodox historian, and totally devoid of poetic beauty. So if you cultivate Syè's style, you will be unable to compass his brilliance, and only get his prolixity; if you make Péi your master, you will miss all his virtues, and only get his faults. Syè is thus too skillful to be equaled, and Péi too heavy to be advisedly emulated.

Péi Dž-yě (469–530) and his followers are represented in the histories as votaries of the plain old style, with no use for the new; they may fairly be called conservatives. Though some of the school (including Péi himself, a great favorite with Emperor Wŭ) held high office, they do not seem to have wielded much poetic influence.[6] The leader of the Syè Líng-ywn group, however, appears to have been Syāu Tŭng (Heir Apparent from 506 until his death in 531), a much more significant figure.

Syāu Tŭng was a serious-minded boy, fond of the poetry of Táu Chyén, which he edited, though primly disapproving of the mildly erotic "Rhapsody to Calm the Passions" 閑情賦, which he stigmatized as "the flaw in the jade." The W:n Sywǎen, compiled under his patronage, contains no love-poetry genre in the poetry section (though a few have crept in under other rubrics). The Lyáng History remarks that he "loved nature, and liked to roam among the lookouts and pavilions of his park with court scholars both high and low. Once while boating on the back pond, someone observed what a splendid place it would be for performances by female musicians. The Heir Apparent did not reply, except to sing part of Dzwŏ Sž's (A11) 'Summons to the Hermit' 招隱詩,

> what need is there for sounds of pipe and string?   非必絲與竹
> the hills and streams are music in themselves   山水有清音

whereupon the man was ashamed, and desisted." Syāu Tŭng wrote a letter of his own to Syāu Yì, stating his program as against that of the avant-garde and the conservatives:

> Now, if poetry is simple, it becomes too crude; if lovely, it tends toward superficiality. If it could be lovely but not superficial, simple but not crude, then style and substance would be in harmonious balance, and the gentlemanly ideal would be realized. I have always wanted to do this, but to my sorrow I have not yet succeeded.

Inasmuch as Syāu Tŭng's ideal was the combining of the good features of both extreme factions, it will be convenient to call his group the eclectics.

The Shř Pĭn (SP), on its own account, is a controversialist work. The preface states its central motive as follows:

> I have observed that kings, princes, gentlemen, and scholars, in the appendages to their multifarious discourses, never fail to busy themselves with the topic of poetry, each following his own inclination, with no uniformity of principle. The muddy Dž and the clear Sh:ng

---

6 On the conservatives, and to some extent on the other groups, see Jōu Sywn-chū 周勛初, "梁代文論三派述要," 中華文史論叢 (上海：中華書局, 1962). Jōu's article is very suggestive, but overtidy; Emperor Wŭ, for instance, is far too complex a figure to be contained in a single faction, let alone the conservative one, which can scarcely have monopolized imperial sponsorship.

flow together, crimson and scarlet infringe on each other, tumult and controversy arise, and there is no basis for standards of taste. The late Lyóu Hwèi (C22b) of Pǐng-Chǐng, a discriminating scholar, was concerned about this confused state of things, and intended to do an Evaluation of Contemporary Poetry. He had set forth the arrangement orally, but the work itself was never finished. I have, accordingly, been moved to supply the lack.

This normative intent is effected chiefly by evaluating (*pǐn*) poets in one of three ranks, which we shall call A, B, and C. The format is unique as such in its time, for poetry at least, but as a means of discovering where the *SP* fits into Lyáng literary factionalism, its arrangement can be compared with the implicit preference profiles of two definitive anthologies. These are the avant-garde *Yù-tái Syīn-yǔng* (*YT*), compiled under the patronage of Syāu Gāng during his years as Heir Apparent, and the eclectic *Wǐn Sywǎen* (*WS*), which has an exactly similar relation to Syāu Tǔng. (Even allowing for the fact that Péi Dz̄-yě never became Heir Apparent, there seems to be no parallel conservative anthology.) Excluding from these works all poets outside the time-span of the earlier *SP*, and ranking the rest by the number of pentameter poems (the *SP* is limited to pentameter) by which they are represented, we obtain a rough index of their relative popularity with the two schools in question. The result, for all poets represented by three or more poems, is compared in Chart 1 with the A and B ranks of the *SP* itself.[7]

The *YT* and the *WS*, not surprisingly, differ a great deal from each other. It is also obvious from the chart that the *SP*, while not identical with either, corresponds much more closely to the *WS*. The *WS* list can in fact be rearranged so as not to conflict with the *SP* A and B groupings by drawing the dividing line at *WS* no. 16 (8 or more poems), promoting Lǐ Líng (A2), and demoting the following poets — Syè Tyàu (B17), Bàu Jàu (B16), Shǐn Ywē (B21), Yén Yén-jr̄ (B13), Jyāng Yēn (B18), and Táu Chyén (B12). To evaluate the credentials of the *SP* as an eclectic work, we must determine whether these divergences are trivial, or constitute disagreement on major principles. Reserving Lǐ Líng for the subsequent discussion of the positive program, we shall first consider the five aspects of the negative one.

Syè Tyàu and Bàu Jàu evidently stand, in the *SP*, for the light-poetry writers. The preface, surveying the contemporary literary scene with patent disapproval, comments on them in the following terms:

Then there are the shallow frivolous sort, who laugh at Tsáu Jŕ (A4) and Lyóu Jǐn (A5) as old-fashioned, and think Bàu Jàu (B16) to be His Majesty Fú-syǐ, and Syè Tyàu

---

7 Within each of these ranks, the order is, in the author's words, "approximately chronological."

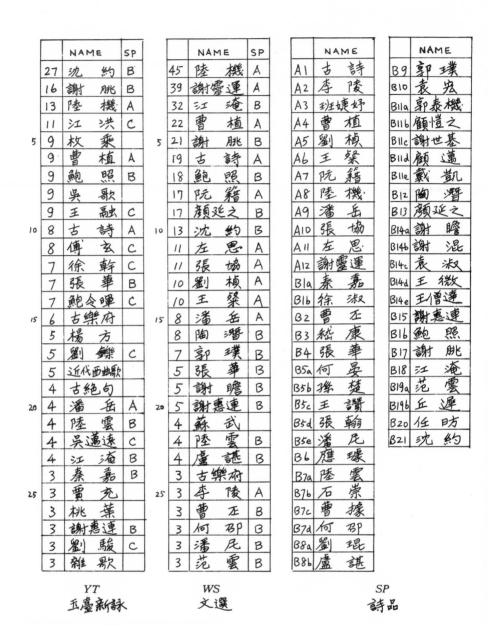

		NAME	SP
	27	沈　約	B
	16	謝　朓	B
	13	陸　機	A
	11	江　洪	C
5	9	枚　乘	
	9	曹　植	A
	9	鮑　照	B
	9	吳　歌	
	9	王　融	C
10	8	古　詩	A
	8	傅　玄	C
	7	徐　幹	C
	7	張　華	B
	7	鮑令暉	C
15	6	古樂府	
	5	楊　方	
	5	劉　鑠	C
	5	近代西曲歌	
	4	古絕句	
20	4	潘　岳	A
	4	陸　雲	B
	4	吳邁遠	C
	4	江　淹	B
	3	秦　嘉	B
25	3	賈　充	
	3	桃　葉	
	3	謝惠連	B
	3	劉　駿	C
	3	雜　歌	

		NAME	SP
	45	陸　機	A
	39	謝靈運	A
	32	江　淹	B
	22	曹　植	A
5	21	謝　朓	B
	19	古　詩	A
	18	鮑　照	B
	17	阮　籍	A
	17	顏延之	B
10	13	沈　約	B
	11	左　思	A
	11	張　協	A
	10	劉　楨	A
	10	王　粲	A
15	8	潘　岳	A
	8	陶　潛	B
	7	郭　璞	B
	5	張　華	B
	5	謝　瞻	B
20	5	謝惠連	B
	4	蘇　武	
	4	陸　雲	B
	4	盧　諶	B
	3	古樂府	
25	3	李　陵	A
	3	曹　丕	B
	3	何　劭	B
	3	潘　尼	B
	3	范　雲	B

	NAME
A1	古　詩
A2	李　陵
A3	班婕妤
A4	曹　植
A5	劉　楨
A6	王　粲
A7	阮　籍
A8	陸　機
A9	潘　岳
A10	張　協
A11	左　思
A12	謝靈運
B1a	秦　嘉
B1b	徐　淑
B2	曹　丕
B3	嵇　康
B4	張　華
B5a	何　晏
B5b	孫　楚
B5c	王　讚
B5d	張　翰
B5e	潘　尼
B6	應　璩
B7a	陸　雲
B7b	石　崇
B7c	曹　攄
B7d	何　劭
B8a	劉　琨
B8b	盧　諶

	NAME
B9	郭　璞
B10	袁　宏
B11a	郭泰機
B11b	顧愷之
B11c	謝世基
B11d	顧　邁
B11e	戴　凱
B12	陶　潛
B13	顏延之
B14a	謝　瞻
B14b	謝　混
B14c	袁　淑
B14d	王　微
B14e	王僧達
B15	謝惠連
B16	鮑　照
B17	謝　朓
B18	江　淹
B19a	范　雲
B19b	丘　遲
B20	任　昉
B21	沈　約

YT
玉臺新詠

WS
文選

SP
詩品

Chart 1. — Shī Pǐn External Geometry.

(B17) to be the best of poets old and new. But those who go to school to Bàu Jàu never get as far as "the sun is high, the market place is full," and those who study Syè Tyàu have all they can do to manage "a yellow bird skims past a leafy bough." They foolishly turn away from all that is lofty or wise, and never get into the mainstream of literature.

Inasmuch as this paragraph directly precedes the one quoted above, setting forth the motive of the *SP*, it would seem that light poetry bulked rather large in the author's antagonisms. In the evaluative notices in the body of the work, the note of "frivolity" is expanded in various ways. Syè emerges as a fragile figure, "a trifle overly exquisite," and "good at starting out on a poem, though he usually stumbles at the end. This is because his ideas are ingenious, but his talent is weak. As to his being the darling of latter-day scholars, Tyàu often used to discuss the art with me, and his enthusiasm and capriciousness were too much for his poetry." Bàu's notice is not at first glance unflattering, but concludes, "Yet, in his emphasis on skillful description he did not altogether avoid the perilously oblique, greatly violating the pure, courtly mode. Thus those whose language is dangerously vulgar mostly follow in his footsteps."

Both these comments refer more or less obliquely to Shĭn Ywē, the next figure on the list. Ywē was, without doubt, the most prominent figure on the late Chí and early Lyáng literary scene, and he haunts the *SP* pervasively, an evil omnipresence brooding around many a corner. He was a close friend of Syè Tyàu, and once observed of Tyàu's works, "There has been no poetry like this for two hundred years." Syè Tyàu died in 499, but Ywē continued to bestow his praises on the brighter poets of the next generation. To Hǐ Sywn (d. 527, and, like Syè Tyàu, represented by sixteen poems in the *YT*), for instance, he remarked, "Whenever I read one of your poems I go back to it three times the same day, and still I can't put it down." It may have been to counteract the influence of such statements that Syè Tyàu's notice closes on its caustic note. The close of Bàu Jàu's notice, similarly, sets up the beginning of Ywē's — "If we consider all of Ywē's numerous compositions, the pentameter ones emerge as the best. If we analyze his style and examine his appended discourses, we can see clearly that he models himself on Bàu Jàu." Ywē is the only poet, in the *SP*, who is derived from Bàu Jàu.

These statements of filiation, which always bulk large in discussions of the modernity of the *SP*'s method, normally appear as the first line of notices (39 per cent) that have them at all. In this case, uniquely in the work, the filiation-statement is preceded by a justification, suggesting that the author felt a bit defensive about his statement. His proof reads strangely, to say the least. The "appended discourse" (echoing the same phrase in the section on diverging standards of taste, quoted above) can only refer to the concluding essay appended to the memoir on Syè Líng-ywn (A12) in the *Sùng History* (which Ywē wrote). This essay presents the platform of the prosody movement, which claimed to have discovered the secret of euphony — in effect, of beauty — in poetry, of which all the great writers of the past, culminating in Syè Líng-ywn, had been ignorant. Attaching this manifesto to Syè's notice is Ywē's way of claiming to be continuing (albeit perfecting) his tradition. To Bàu Jàu he gave no such token recognition, omitting him altogether from the *Sùng History*. This might well be mere propagandistic window-dressing on Ywē's part. Of his own poetry, however, the early Chīng critic Chín Dzwò-míng states that "Shín Ywē's poetic style derives entirely from Syè Líng-ywn," and that the *SP* derivation is "a misrepresentation."

The filiation is not the only defensive note in the evaluation. The remainder of it is devoted to defending Ywē's B rank. Three other notices in the work specifically defend the assigned rank (all of them in B); none this extensively. It concludes, "I would comment that Ywē's works are very numerous, but if we prune away the devious and the miscellaneous, and admit only the essential, we can allow him a place in B."

The two groups of poems intended here are remarkably easy to determine. Ywē is represented in the original layers of the *YT* by twenty-seven pentameter poems; in the *WS*, by thirteen. With the exception of one poem common to both groups, these are completely separate areas of his work. As a sample of the *YT* type of poem, we may take the (not quite pentameter) "Six Memories" 六憶詩, of which *YT*,5, tantalizingly preserves only four.

remember how she came —	憶來時
up the terrace like a glowing flame	灼灼上階墀
earnest in the saying of farewell	勤勤叙離別
promising her love would stay the same	慊慊道相思
all too short, the times we were together	相看常不足
but sorrow vanished, when we met again	相見乃忘飢
remember how she sat —	憶坐時
timidly, before the drapery	黠黠羅帳前
first she sang some ballads, four or five	或歌四五曲
then she played some pieces, two or three	或弄兩三弦
smiling in a way that had no equal	笑時應無比
frowning even more adorably	嗔時更可憐

remember how she ate —	憶 食 時
above the dish, her color came and went	臨 盤 動 容 色
wanting to sit, too modest to give in	欲 坐 復 羞 坐
wanting to eat, too modest to consent	欲 食 復 羞 食
nibbling bites as though she were not hungry	含 哺 如 不 飢
raising her cup as if her strength were spent	擎 甌 似 無 力
remember how she slept —	憶 眠 時
keeping wide awake with all her might	人 眠 強 未 眠
she loosed her robe, not waiting to be coaxed	解 羅 不 待 勸
but once in bed she pulled it round her tight	就 枕 更 須 牽
the thought that he would see had got her frightened	復 恐 傍 人 見
shy and winsome, in the candlelight ...	嬌 羞 在 燭 前

In the *WS*, on the other hand, Ywē is represented by poems like "An Overnight Stay at East Manor" 宿 東 園 , written in 507 (at the age of sixty-six) at his estate outside the capital, and less expressive of the joys of life than of the pathos of mortality.

where Tsáu Jŕ had his cockfights once before	陳 王 鬥 雞 道
and Pān Ywè gathered kindling long ago —	安 仁 采 樵 路
has the Eastern Suburb changed since then?	東 郊 豈 異 昔
here I walk, both leisurely and slow	聊 可 閑 余 步
moorland paths go winding back and forth	野 徑 既 盤 紆
lonely trails run crisscross to and fro	荒 阡 亦 交 互
dense by sparse, the Rose-of-Sharon hedge	槿 籬 疏 復 密
here and there, a rustic bungalow	荊 扉 新 且 故
in the treetops, crying breezes whirl	樹 頂 鳴 風 飆
by the grassroots, hoarfrost patches show	草 根 積 霜 露
startled deer run off without a check	驚 麏 去 不 息
birds of passage sometimes glance below	征 鳥 時 相 顧
from roofs of thatch the mournful screech-owl wails	茅 棟 嘯 愁 鴟
o'er meadow hummocks winter rabbits go	平 崗 走 寒 兔
evening dark enfolds the terraced hills	夕 陰 帶 層 阜
strands of mist draw forth their pale white glow	長 煙 引 輕 素
fleeting Time has suddenly made me old	飛 光 忽 我 遒
it is not just the season that is so	寧 止 歲 云 暮
could I find the Western Mountain herbs	若 蒙 西 山 藥
longer years of life they might bestow	頹 齡 儻 能 度

It is understandable enough that, for Jūng Húng, "The pentameter works emerge as the best." In the *WS*, however, which in its own way "prunes away the devious and miscellaneous," he still ranks fairly high on the basis of his serious works alone.

Ywē is not, however, merely another votary of light poetry; his prosody movement was evidently something that Jūng Húng held in special detestation. A lengthy section of the preface is devoted to proving that the movement had neither historical foundation nor contemporary significance. The argument concludes on an unmistakably indignant note.

> Wáng Yúng (C22a) started it, and Syè Tyàu and Shǐn Ywē spread it. These three worthies chanced to be sons of noble families, known in literary circles even as youths; thus the scholarly world emulated them, concentrating on exquisitudes, and footling trivialities proliferated endlessly. They hedge literature round with taboos, violating its essential beauty. I would comment that a piece of poetry is basically something to be read aloud, and ought not to be hobbled and hindered; it is sufficient if the tessitura flows smoothly, and the sounds are easy to pronounce. As to "level, high, going, and entering," I am sorry to say I am incapable of them, and "wasp-waists and crane-knees" can be had in any hamlet.

The imputation of peasant vulgarity at the end of this is a normal feature of *SP* style, as an epithet of people and ideas distasteful to its author; it is not stylistic description in the usual sense. The trouble with prosody was, indeed, its too obvious urbanity. It, and the bookishness mentioned next, were both "vulgar" in the sense that they contravened the Confucian gentlemanly ideal, with its emphasis on general moral excellence rather than on the narrow skills of the specialist, literary or otherwise.

Like Shǐn Ywē, Yén Yén-jr̄ receives extended consideration in the preface; he is faulted for his densely allusive texture. It will suffice to quote this section, omitting the lines of poetry mentioned as examples.

> Now, it is the prevalent opinion that "the choice of words is a subtle comment on the thing described." In state papers, no doubt, erudition is in order, and in exhortatory memorials the paragons of the past all find their proper place, but when it comes to singing forth one's inward emotions, what value is there in topical allusions? ... So we see that the best lines of poetry, old and new, are virtually never patched together from borrowed matter; all of them come from being directly sought after.
>
> Yén Yén-jr̄ and Syè Jwāng (C13) were especially intricate and influential; hence in the 460's literature became to all intents and purposes indistinguishable from document-copying. More recently, Rǐn Fǎng (B20), Wáng Yúng (C22a), and others, despising the unhackneyed, vied with each other in devising novel references, and writers since then have become increasingly vulgar, until there is not an empty phrase in a line, or an empty word in a phrase; crabbed and patchy bookworm-poetry is now the order of the day.

Shǐn Ywē and Yén Yén-jr̄ (both "vulgar") bring us to the end of the major villains. Jyāng Yēn, by contrast, does not merit a denunciation of his own in the preface; even his own notice (B18) consists solely of an anecdote, preceded by the following: "Jyāng Yēn's poetic style is heterogeneous; he is good at imitations. He is more forceful than Wáng Wēi (B14d); more proficient than Syè Tyàu (B17)."*

Jyāng is represented in the *WS* by thirty-two poems, thirty of which are imitations of the styles of earlier poets. His facility at this sort of thing is the only attribute mentioned in the notice. Are we to conclude that he is merely a grade-B talent, pure and simple? I believe that, on the contrary, he is demoted for this very versatility. The term "heterogeneous" (dzŭng-dzá 總雜) is used at one other point in the text (A1), definitely in a pejorative sense. In Jūng Húng's literary program (somewhat to anticipate the following discussion), this portability of style is a kind of personal insincerity — an attitude toward style as something exterior and alienable, rather than the direct and inevitable imprint of the personality itself. The anecdote which concludes Yēn's notice makes precisely this point.

Once, when Yēn had finished his assignment at Sywāen-chíng Commandery, and was passing the night at Yĕ Pavilion, he dreamed that a handsome man who called himself Gwō Pŭ (B9) said to him, "You have had that brush of mine for many years now; it is time it was returned." Yēn reached into his bosom and drew forth a five-colored brush, which he gave the man. Thereafter, he could never recapture his former facility. Hence the popular saying, "Jyāng Yēn's talent is played out."

His fault, then, lay in possessing a style that was *not* the man. The case of Táu Chyén, aside from its far greater notoriety down through the ages, is quite similar. Chyén's evaluation (B12) reads:

---

* [*Editor's note*: The text is 筋力于王微，成就于謝朓 and might also be translated: "His strength derived from Wang Wei, his achievement (performance?) from Syè Tyàu."]

Author's comment: The suggested translation is closer to what we expect the *SP* to say, and is certainly an improvement on my own version. There is a difficulty with the oblique preposition 于, which cannot by itself mean "derives from" (always 出 于 in this text); it may be best to follow Takamatsu in taking 筋力 and 成就 as verbal, thus perhaps "Jyāng Yēn's poetic style is heterogeneous, and he is good at imitations — he exerts his strength thanks to Wáng Wēi, and realizes his intention courtesy of Syè Tyàu." I think this is intended to sound sarcastic (commenting on the total derivativeness of Jyāng's style), the more so when we notice that Wáng Wēi (B14), and Jāng Hwá (B4) before him, and Wáng Tsàn (A6) before *him*, are described as increasingly hollow stylists. There is thus no question here of genuine forcefulness of style. So also with "realization of intention" in Syè Tyàu, stemming from the same feeble sources. The ultimate force of the comment is thus to allow Jyāng no poetic qualities in his own right, and only attenuated ones by secondhand borrowing. This point is wittily reinforced by the anecdote which follows in the *SP*.

Jyāng is omitted from chart 2 by the principle given in the legend. It would be better to amend both the chart and the principle.

He derives from Yǐng Chyẃ (B6), and also has some of the forcefulness of Dzwǒ Sz̄ (A11). His style is spare, never obtrusive; his sincerity is authentically antique, and his language is pleasant. Whenever we look at his poetry, we are reminded of the character of the man. The world admires his simple straightforwardness. But how can lines like "Happily, I pour the wines of spring," or "The sun goes down; no cloud is in the sky," frivolous and idle as they are, be the simple language of a mere farmer? He is the ancestor of the hermit poets, old and new.

Up to the word "but," this reads like a description of a poet who has avoided all the faults so far catalogued. So favorable has it seemed to Chyén's less critical partisans that they have claimed (based on a disputed[8] quote in *Tài-píng Yẁ-lǎn*, 586) that he must originally have been in A, and that his present rank is in the nature of a textual corruption. The indictment is muted, perhaps, but not unrecoverable. The first of the two objectionable lines is from the well-known poem "Reading the *Classic of Hills and Seas*," in which Chyén takes an unfarmerly delight in retiring to his study for an afternoon's leisure over cup and book. The second, seemingly so innocent, turns out to be more citified yet. It is from one of his "Imitations of Old Poems" 擬古詩 ·

the sun goes down; no cloud is in the sky	日 暮 天 無 雲
the spring wind fans us in delightful style	春 風 扇 微 和
a lovely lady and a crystal night	佳 人 美 清 夜
with wine and song, our leisure to beguile	達 曙 酬 且 歌
when the song is done, I heave a sigh	歌 竟 長 歎 息
these things are for man a bitter trial	持 此 感 人 多
bright, so bright, the cloudwrapped moonbeams glow	明 明 雲 間 月
fair, so fair, the leafgirt flowers smile	灼 灼 葉 中 花
not that they aren't splendid for a time,	豈 無 一 時 好
but what will happen in a little while?	不 久 當 如 何

The bad thing about this modicum of wine, women, song, and literacy in Chyén's verse is not any inherent impropriety, as such, but rather that such things involve him* in inconsistencies with his persona — they are not,

---

8 See Takamatsu, pp. 176–180, for a review of the controversy.

* [*Editor's note*: In line 5 of the above poem, "she heaves a sigh" probably would be a more accurate translation than "I heave a sigh." Therefore, Táu Chyén (T'ao Ch'ien) himself might be less involved than the author suggests here.]

Author's comment: The poem as a whole is modeled on something like no. 4 of the "Nineteen Old Poems" (*WS* 29:4), where beauty and conviviality (and the words of the banquet-song) move the company to reflections on the impermanence of things, issuing either in resolution (prototype) or in melancholy (Táu). I doubt that it can be read (unlike 仲春遘時雨 in the same group) as focusing on the lovely lady, mourning an absent lover or something of

in the words of the text, "the simple language of a mere farmer." Jyāng Yēn's difficulty was his lack of a consistent personal style; Táu Chyén is criticized here for having one and being unfaithful to it. The quality of personal deviousness is the same in both cases.

The last line continues the same charge. To modern readers, well steeped in the Táu Chyén cult, it is both obvious and admirable that their hero is "the ancestor of the hermit poets, old and new." In the *SP*, this statement has a slightly different nuance. Jūng Húng's view of the desirability of hermit poets can best be instanced from C16, where three of them are considered together. The first of them, in particular, was one of the better-known love poets of Chí-Lyáng times, who renounced his vows at the behest of Emperor Wǔ and ended his career as governor of Yángjōu.

Tāng Hwèi-syōu is licentious; his emotions overpower his talent. The world accordingly pairs him with Bàu Jàu, for whom I fear he is no match. Yáng Yàu-fán (C10b) said, "It was Yén Yén-jī's jealousy of Bàu's poetry that moved him to set up this theory of Tāng and Bàu." Kāng Dàu-yóu and Bwó Bǎu-ywè, both foreigners, have some fine lines. "The Hardships of Travel," however, is actually the work of Chái Kwò of Dūngyáng. Bǎu-ywè happened to be staying with the family when Kwò died, whereupon he made off with the piece and kept it as his own. Kwò's son set out for the capital with the original MS, intending to go to law over it, but was bought off with heavy bribes.

Of Tāng, we are told elsewhere (C19b) that the younger poet Wú Mài-ywǎen was once told by him, "My poetry is the father of your poetry." Wú asked Syè Jwāng (C13) about it, and Syè replied, "No, Tāng is not your father — he is your illegitimate brother."

Juicy as this is, the case of Táu Chyén's fellow-clansman Táu Húng-jǐng 陶弘景 (*ca.* 452–536), a prominent contemporary of Jūng Húng's, is even more instructive. Húng-jǐng was a devotee of the occult sciences, and a past master of the fine art of public relations. He began with a modest official post, but soon thought better of that and retired to the mountains. Emperor Wǔ of Chí, fascinated, tried to coax him out again with the query, "What

---

the kind. So also Acker (*T'ao the Hermit,* London, 1952, p. 80) and Chang/Sinclair (*The Poems of T'ao Ch'ien,* University of Hawaii Press, 1953, pp. 79–80). In any case, my point (and, I think, Jūng Húng's) is that Táu is indeed not particularly involved here; the imitations belong to those works (see also Hightower, "The *Fu* of T'ao Ch'ien," *HJAS,* 17 [1954], 169–230) in which Táu serves out his literary apprenticeship to earlier masters. We have, then, not his usual "mere farmer" persona, but the would-be poet practicing his craft. It is this element of craft (hence crafty, hence personally and politically devious, of Húng's indictment of the hermit-poets) that Jūng Húng seems to dislike; it is instructive to regard him as an early defender of the "amateur ideal" (on which see Cahill, "Confucian Elements in the Theory of Painting," *in* Arthur Wright, ed., *The Confucian Persuasion,* Stanford University Press, 1960) which dominated later art and literary criticism.

is there so special, in the mountains?" Húng-jǐng responded with a poem —

what is there so special, in the mountains?	山 中 何 所 有
fleecy clouds the mountaintops afford	嶺 上 多 白 雲
good for nothing more than private pleasure —	只 可 自 怡 悅
not a thing to offer to milord	不 堪 持 寄 君

— the deftness of which marks the true courtier. Coupled with the usual carefree idling in a mysterious otherworld of eddying clouds, there is the subtly flattering suggestion that the Emperor, of course, is a man of wholly public sentiments, with no use for mere "private pleasure." Talent of this order easily weathers dynastic transitions, and we find Emperor Wǔ of Lyáng, in Jūng Húng's time, going over the heads of his duly constituted ministers to submit virtually every policy to Húng-jǐng's consideration, until he became popularly known as the "Prime Minister in the Mountains." Notwithstanding the press of these worldly duties, he still managed to keep up his poetry, which is very suave, very polished, very much along "palace poetry" lines. The lyric piece "A Winter's Night" 寒 夜 怨 is typical.

clouds of night go by	夜 雲 生
swans of night do fly	夜 鴻 驚
with their heart-afflicting notes,	悽 切 嘹 唳
all the night they cry	傷 夜 情
empty hills are white with frost,	空 山 霜 滿
level mists are high	高 煙 平
leaden flowers gleam and fade,	鉛 華 沈 照
lonely dawn is nigh	帳 孤 明
sun of winter weak	寒 月 微
wind of winter strong	寒 風 緊
heart of sorrow deep	愁 心 絕
tears of sorrow long	愁 淚 盡
full of love, and cannot bear the wrong	情 人 不 勝 怨
should she think, what memories would throng!	思 來 誰 能 忍

We note in the *History of the South* (*Nán-Shř*) that Jūng Húng once memorialized Emperor Wǔ in protest against his arrogating the ministers' proper functions. Even apart from the poetry, Táu Húng-jǐng does not seem calculated to endear him to the hermit tribe. We may assume, then, that when Húng described Táu Chyén as their ancestor he meant it as something less than a compliment.

We find, in sum, that the five groups of "demotions" represent strongly held positions of the *SP*. Of the five (light poetry, prosody, allusions, imitations, insincerity), only the first is also opposed by the *WS* which, though it has no love-poetry genre, does have one for imitations, and freely includes the works of Yén Yén-jř and Táu Chyén (including the one quoted), and the more serious ones of Shřn Ywē and the light poets. The eclecticism of the *WS* is precisely its receptivity to the poetry of its own time, while still excluding the one trend it felt to be improper. Jūng Húng's attitude toward contemporary poetry, on the other hand, is one of fairly thoroughgoing rejection. When we have deducted him from the *WS*, we find that the most recent poet who remains is Syè Líng-yẅn, who died in 433, more than eighty years previous to the *SP*. Eighty years, especially Chinese years from the fifth and sixth centuries, may not seem like much. If someone undertook an Evaluation of American Poetry in 1968, however, in which top rank was granted to no poet later than Longfellow (d. 1882), the general impression would be somewhat less than progressive.

That leaves the conservatives. Péi Dž-yě himself (one year younger than Jūng Húng) wrote a *Discourse on the Carving of Insects*, in which he inveighs against the frivolity of the younger generation and the unclassicality of tonal prosody. There is, however, no evidence (as far as I know) of a strictly personal connection between him and Jūng Húng, such as exists between Syāu Tǔng and the *WS*. Not to prejudice this point, which later historical research may be expected to elucidate, I shall withhold from the *SP* the conservative label. Instead, I shall call it *reactionary*.

It will be interesting to examine the program of a reactionary critic. The movements he opposed favored a conception of poetry as something that could be polished, complicated, and played with. All of this was most reprehensible to our critic. But if a poem was not a plaything for Jūng Húng, what was it? We shall consider the *SP*'s positive program in two parts; the explicit prescriptions in the preface, and the implicit picture that emerges by collating the filiation-statements.

The negative program of the work, detailed above, implies its positive counterpart; prosody and allusiveness are both presented in the *SP* as violating simplicity of utterance, and impersonal "light" poetry, portable style, and hermitical insincerity are all offenses against straightforwardness. The negations thus boil down to the single positive ideal of directness; an ideal which is articulated, fittingly, at the beginning of the preface — "Spirit moves the external world, and the external world moves mankind, stirring his innate emotions, and taking shape as dance and song." This is to be compared with the beginning of the preface to the Confucian *Classic of Poetry* (*SJ*):

> Poetry is the outcome of an intention. In the mind, it is intent; realized in words, it becomes poetry. Emotion stirs within and takes shape in words. As the words are inadequate, one sighs them; as the sighing is inadequate, one sings them; as the singing is inadequate, one mimes them with his hands, and dances them with his feet.

In both views, poetry is essentially the outer dimension of an inward feeling. The *SJ* preface formula, however, with its successive stages of adequacy in the expression, could be construed as envisioning a mediated, gradual attainment of the final poem. Jūng Húng has firmly suppressed this possibility. He has also ruled out any play element in the emotion by making that an equally unmediated response to an outward stimulus, which in turn is merely an aspect of the inherent dynamism of the cosmos. This effectively closes the door against trifling; it has won him acclaim as progressively "materialistic" in certain hemispheres,[9] and though this judgment is itself trifling of a sort, it is not as far wrong as it might be.

In practice, of course, poetry cannot exist without a certain measure of deviousness, or artistry, or what one will. The only other positively stated section of the preface (except for a brief historical sketch, a survey of subject matter, and a list of approved poems) is one which attempts to satisfy this need. It goes:

> There are thus three cardinal principles of poetry — image, analogy, and narration. When the rhetorical figure ceases but the conception continues [in other terms], we have an *image* (*syìng*). When the intention is expressed [throughout] in terms of some external object, we have an *analogy* (*bǐ*). When a matter is stated directly, or an outward manifestation described by way of metaphor, we have *narration* (*fù*). Judiciously extending these three principles, basing them on spontaneity and adorning them with embellishments, we can make the reader savor the poem without satiety, and the hearer be stirred at heart. This is the perfection of poetry.
>
> If we use images and analogies exclusively, the conception will be too deep, and if the conception is too deep, the verse will stumble. If we use narration only, the conception will be too superficial, and if the conception is too superficial, the poem will collapse. Further, if one is fond of drifting from one mode to another, the poem will suffer from diffuseness.

None of this is new. Even the strange definition of narration (misinterpreted by Lwó, I, 245) is no more than a summary of the way the term is actually used in explicating the *SJ* preface. An image, in the *SJ* preface sense, is an evocative introductory figure drawn from the nonhuman world, the human counterpart being given in the immediately following lines. *SJ*, 6 桃 夭 , is a typical example.

---

9 See for example Lwó 羅根澤 , 中國文學批評史 (上海 : 古典文學出版社 , 1958), vol. 1, p. 243.

peachtree, fair-fair	桃 之 夭 夭
radiant, its bloom —	灼 灼 其 華
yon maid, marrying,	之 子 于 歸
suits the bride's room	宜 其 室 家
peachtree, fair-fair	桃 之 夭 夭
graceful, its fruits —	有 蕡 其 實
yon maid, marrying,	之 子 于 歸
bride's room she suits	宜 其 家 室
peachtree, fair-fair	桃 之 夭 夭
its leaves, rife-rife —	其 葉 蓁 蓁
yon maid, marrying,	之 子 于 歸
suits her new life	宜 其 家 人

Rather than alternating with the thing of which it is a symbol, such a nature-image can also be extended so as to comprise a whole poem; this is "analogy." It is the mode of *SJ*, 5 螽斯 , which is understood as being addressed entirely to the locusts (though ultimately symbolic of the numerous progeny of a royal house).

locust-wings	螽 斯 羽
clust'ring, oh	詵 詵 兮
your descendants	宜 爾 子 孫
blust'ring, oh	振 振 兮
locust-wings	螽 斯 羽
whirring, oh	薨 薨 兮
your descendants	宜 爾 子 孫
flurry'ng, oh	繩 繩 兮
locust-wings	螽 斯 羽
streaming, oh	揖 揖 兮
your descendants	宜 爾 子 孫
teeming, oh	蟄 蟄 兮

Contrariwise, the entire poem may be within the human realm. Even here, however, one part of it may be a metaphor for another. Thus the plantain-gatherers of *SJ*, 8 芣苢 , are taken as symptomatic of peace and normality (plantain makes a preparation used in childbirth), and ultimately symbolic of the "virtuous influence of the Queen," which is considered to be the esoteric meaning of the poem.

strip the plantain	采 采 芣 苢
sing we, strip it	薄 言 采 之
strip the plantain	采 采 芣 苢
sing we, grip it	薄 言 有 之

strip the plantain	采 采 芣 苢
sing we, pluck it	薄 言 掇 之
strip the plantain	采 采 芣 苢
sing we, shuck it	薄 言 捋 之
strip the plantain	采 采 芣 苢
sing we, lap it	薄 言 袺 之
strip the plantain	采 采 芣 苢
sing we, wrap it	薄 言 襭 之

There are, then, these three rhetorical types. Suitably tricked out with embellishments, discreetly applied, they constitute the entire weaponry of the poet in his quest for the perfection of his art. The technical advice (as distinct from technical interdictions) in the *SP* does not go beyond these paragraphs.

The *W̤n-syīn Dyāu-lúng* (*WSDL*), produced under eclectic auspices while Lyóu Syé was a member of Syāu Tǔng's entourage, and warmly commended by Sh̤n Ywē, who had been Subtutor to the Heir Apparent since 506, contains a considerably more sophisticated view of the relation between idea and technique. The beauty of the poem, in this view, is not an afterthought to be tacked onto the poem after its completion; it is rather a necessary and inseparable aspect of the poet's sensitivity to the emerging poetic entity. The epistrophe to *WSDL*, 33 聲 律 (the tonal prosody chapter) sums up this modernist approach in a quaintly archaist meter.

Emotion ranges far and wide	標 情 務 遠
Euphony is at your side	比 音 則 近
sound the keynote in your heart	吹 律 胸 臆
tune the lips with this as guide	調 鍾 脣 吻
when the sounds are blended well	聲 得 鹽 梅
and the echoes smoothly slide	響 滑 楡 槿
the poem's faults will all be gone	割 棄 支 離
and its music hard to hide	宮 商 難 隱

Behind this, of course, lay Sh̤n Ywē's grammar of euphonic patterns, to guide the poet in achieving the kind of perfection he describes.

Jūng Húng, on the other hand, faced with a growth of poetry far beyond the confines of the *SJ*, and a subtle and persuasive theoretical text to codify the development, contents himself with a ritual recitation of a theory designed to help explicate the hidden meaning of a thousand-year-old classic. Such a stance is typical of Confucian criticism, whose instinct is always to assert, not to adapt. Development of these theories would not have been out of the question. Politics aside, the rhetorical modes fit the *SJ* poems not too badly, and could have been extended to deal realistically with a wider corpus. Nor is mere ignorance involved, since the *WSDL* had been very much in the picture for about a decade; its omission from the list of earlier critical works in the *SP* preface is a self-conscious Confucian criticism-by-omission, a well-established historical technique in the *Spring and Autumn*, as then understood. The point is simply that a reactionary critic denies the necessity of adapting what to him is a wholly satisfactory account of things, familiar enough to be considered "direct" in application, unlike the obvious artificiality of the newfangled. Evolutionary compromise is the method, not of the reactionary, but of the eclectic.

So much for the uncontemporaneousness of the *SP*. As to whether its archaic theories were adequate to underlie its archaic idea of poetry, or to rationalize its assignation of praise and blame, we may notice the case of Syè Líng-yẁn. The preface states that vacillation between rhetorical modes produces the evidently serious fault of diffuseness. The only poet to be accused of this fault is Syè Líng-yẁn, whose notice reads:

> He derives from Tsáu Jŕ (A4). He has some miscellaneous influence from Jāng Syé (A10); hence he emphasizes skillful description, but in his facile extravagance he surpasses Syé; he suffers considerably from diffuseness. I would comment that a man like this, whose inspirations are many and whose talent is lofty and comprehensive, provided that his perceptions issue directly into poetry, with no inner distortion or outer omission, is actually justified in his lavishness. To be sure, obtrusive lines do rise here and there out of his famous stanzas, and novel sounds constantly bolt away from his lovely verses, like green pines emerging from a thicket, or white jades glittering in the dust, but these are not enough to vitiate his lofty purity.

The "stumbling" supposed to result from overuse of indirect rhetoric is predicated of Yén Yén-jŕ and Syè Tyàu, both ranked in B, and both thoroughly trounced in the preface. Syè Líng-yẁn, on the other hand, is not only ranked in A, but singled out in the preface as one of the giants of pentameter. This might seem to be clear evidence of the inadequacy of Jūng Húng's theory, even on Jūng Húng's terms. We may notice, however, that the author is thoroughly aware of his dilemma. He intervenes in person ("I would comment . . . "), which occurs in the *SP* only at points of considerable danger, and his unwillingness to let the resulting exception stand (Syè's extenuating genius is instantly qualified for the worse, before finally being reinstated as an exception) is very manifest. The case reflects not a theoretical inadequacy, but a practical necessity. The whole purpose of the *SP* is to influence the direction of contemporary poetry; in order to succeed, it must get the ear of the moderate majority. This in turn requires

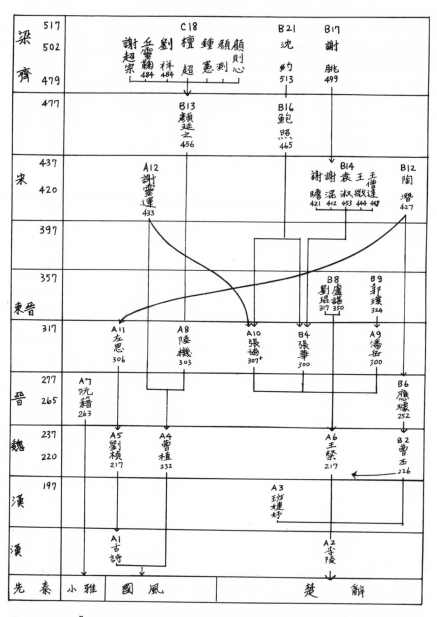

Chart 2. — Shī Pǐn Internal Geometry. Main filiation-statements (those whose wording occurs more than once in the book) are shown as orthogonal lines, supplementary ones (immediately following the main ones) as curved lines. The chart is divided vertically into 40-year periods, counting backwards from the putative *SP* date, A.D. 517. Poets are chronologized by date of death (given, when known, below. the name). Names, as throughout the paper, are standardized according to the most common form of the personal name (also for emperors). Slightly different versions of the filiation-chart appear in Lwó (I,248) and Takamatsu (pp. 161–162).

that he at least seem to praise the poets most venerated by the moderates.
Those he can safely downgrade, he downgrades. The rest he keeps, leaving
it to the preface and the wording of the notice to imply that these people
are not, after all, very safe models to follow. Lù Jī (*WS* no. 1) is another case
in point; ranked in A, characterized in the preface as "the hero of the 280's"
— but described in his notice as "in some ways violating the integrity of
direct expression," while the contemporary poet Jāng Syé (A10) is said,
in *his* notice, to be "definitely the best of a rather desolate era." The theory
remains intact, only seemingly violated by the strategy of the crooked brush.

When this has been said, it still remains true that the *SP* is not centrally
concerned with theory, but rather with value; the title of the work says
as much. If we wish to see it at its most consistent, we must turn from the
rather token theorizings of the preface to the implicit value-system that
emerges from the text itself, upon collation of the filiation-statements.
These are schematized in Chart 2. Explication of the chart has usually been
attempted on a point-to-point basis. It will be somewhat simpler to begin
with the whole picture, and work inward to the specifics.

Perhaps the most immediately obvious feature of the chart is its division
into two nearly unrelated streams, one stemming from the *Chǔ Tsź* (*CT*),
and the other (slightly more fragmented) from various parts of the *SJ*.
This "double origin" theory was a critical commonplace, but the separation
of the two strands had never been so extensively insisted on. Since the poetics
of the *SP* derive largely from the *SJ*, we would expect to find this the
preferred development. This is confirmed by the preface, which says of the
followers of Syè Tyàu and Bàu Jàu (*CT* side) that they "foolishly turn away
from all that is lofty or wise, and never get into the mainstream of literature."

Secondly, it is a rule that no B poet derives from a C poet, no A from a B.
This is equivalent to saying that the movement of poetic history is never from
bad to good, but always the reverse. The *SJ* preface says, "But when the
Kingly Way declined, rites and righteousness were disused, and statecraft
was lost; the states were governed in divers ways, and the families practiced
varying customs — then the changed Airs and the changed Graces arose."
For Jūng Húng, too, citizen of a politically fragmented age, change (*byèn* 變)
is precisely decadence. Decadence affects the two traditions differently,
however. That of the *CT* is light poetry and tonal prosody, imitations and
insincerities, for none of which Húng spared a kind word. The *SJ* stream
issues in Yén Yén-jr̄'s overallusiveness, which is also criticized. The criticism,
however, concludes, "Still, a fresh natural style is seldom met with, and since
their verse has lost all loftiness, they may as well stick in their allusions

instead. Though it is a decadent sort of genius, they at least succeed in displaying their learning, which is after all one way of going about it." Even in its decline, the *SJ* remains the good side.

Each side has a characteristic virtue, and a characteristic mode of erosion of that virtue. The most common attribute of *SJ* poets is loftiness, to be understood in a political and moral sense, which Yén Yén-jr̄ and followers were said, in the passage just quoted, to have finally lost. The hallmark of the *CT* side (its prototype being Chyw̄ Ywáen himself) is "resentment," the suffering of the loyal minister alienated from his ruler's favor. The respective modes of decline are given in *Analects*, 6/16, a passage which occurs ubiquitously in Six Dynasties critical contexts, from Tsáu Pǐ (letter to Wú Jr̀) to Syāu Tǔng (letter to Syāu Yì, quoted above). The original goes, "The Master said, 'When substance exceeds style, you get crudeness; when style exceeds substance, you get pedantry. When style and substance are in harmonious balance, *then* you get the gentleman.'"

"Substance exceeding style" is the *SJ* mode of decline; "style over substance" that of the *CT*. Taken as a whole, these are the most consistent features of the notices themselves; in difficult cases, only a similarity in type (rather than specifics) of shortcoming will be found to connect two poets.

We can run through the main branches of the chart briefly, to see how these two types work out in practice. Beginning with Tsáu Jr̀, at the bottom of the main *SJ* stem, will afford us an idea of how the *SP* describes a poet it really likes.

He derives from the Airs of the *SJ*; his spirit is sublime and his diction gorgeous; his moods include courtly resentment and his work has both style and substance. Solitary and preeminent, he ranges brilliantly over the old and the new. Indeed, Tsáu Jr̀ in literature is like the Prince of Jōu and Confucius in the moral sphere, cithern and syrinx in music, sacrificial robes among the womanly arts. He makes the hacks and poetasters clutch their odes and verses and look up at him in awe, holding up their little candles against the sunset. Applying to poets the metaphor of *Analects*, 11/14, Lyóu Jr̄n (A5) has ascended the hall, but Tsáu Jr̀ has entered the inner chamber — and Jāng Syé, Pān Ywè (A9) and Lù Jí are sitting somewhere in the corridor outside.

With both style and substance, Tsáu Jr̀ is obviously unassailable. In Lù Jǐ, however, substance begins to preponderate; "he emphasizes principles but does not prize verbal delicacy, and thus in some ways violates the integrity of direct expression," the balance of style and substance being equated with the earlier ideal of directness. To Lù's "principles" (moral-political) corresponds Yén Yén-jr̄'s statesmanliness; "he is definitely a statesmanlike and a courtly talent — but a man whose courtly talent is so diminished as this, is bound to stumble in his stride." The imbalance is clearly more severe. The seven poets of C18 are "the heirs of Yén Yén-jī," and "achieve the refinement of Officers and Dignitaries" (a slight reduction in rank); that they also continued to exalt substance at the expense of style can be inferred from the cryptic last line — "Yén Tsì in particular carried on the family tradition."

The parallel *CT* development, if one may use the term, is from Lǐ Líng to Shìn Ywē. Lǐ Líng, corresponding schematically to Tsáu Jí, represents the virtues of his type without the associated vices — "his style has much sorrow in it; his is the tradition of resentment." His resentment is valid because it springs from personal experience — "he had a remarkable talent, but fate was unkind to him; his reputation was sullied and his lifework destroyed. Had Líng not experienced such hardships, how could his poetry ever have achieved so much?" He is, we remember, the one "promotion" in the *WS* list, obviously due to his value as a symbol of sincerity and directness. Bān Jyé-yẃ, supplanted in the Emperor's favor by Jàu Fēi-yèn 趙 飛 燕, also has legitimate cause for grief — "her resentment is deep and her style is delicate; she perfectly expresses the feelings of a wife." With Wáng Tsàn, though "he turns out verses of melancholy," the characteristic *CT* imbalance sets in — "his style is graceful but his substance is feeble." What form this feebleness took we are not told, but in Jāng Syé, following, it is nature-poetry (idle, impersonal) — "his style is smooth, with few flaws; he is also skilled at framing descriptive similes." This, as we have seen, makes him the proximal ancestor of Syè Líng-yẁn, who appears on the *SJ* side (the honorable side) for special reasons. In Jāng Hwá, on the other hand, "feebleness" yields to sensuality — "his style is opulent, but his inspiration nothing wonderful; he is skilled at using words, but his concern is with the merely pretty." Bàu Jàu derives from the two Jāngs together, and thus is also a completely exterior poet; a "stylist" — "he is good at descriptive verses; he has Jāng Syé's arabesque and Jāng Hwá's profusion." The latter's penchant for the merely pretty comes out later, in the claim that Bàu "did not altogether avoid the perilously oblique, greatly violating the pure, courtly mode." Finally comes Shìn Ywē, from whom a great deal of the "devious" (erotic) and "miscellaneous" (quasi) must be pruned before he can be ranked as high as B. There is also the tonal prosody thing, not directly mentioned in the notice. He is something like an inversion of the original banished-minister type — "not at ease in the statesmanly, and best at detached resentment." Detached resentment 清 怨 is, of course, fake resentment, devoid of poetic validity.

The progressive stages of immoderateness of expression that culminate in Syè Tyàu are also easily discernible. The lines that expire before reaching the top of the chart, however, offer some difficulties. Some of these are with special *SP* meanings of words ("vulgarity" for "overrefinement," *passim*); some are simply in the smoothness with which the crooked brush is plied.[10]

Tsáu Pĭ, for example, has a supplementary derivation from Wáng Tsàn (ten years his senior), and thus embodies one form of the style/substance imbalance — "his more than a hundred novel and curious pieces are all as blunt as everyday speech"; that is, are too fancy. "Only the ten-odd titles including 'North and west are full of drifting clouds' are notably piquant and enjoyable, and begin to show his skill." The poem quoted is a "Miscellaneous Poem" 雜詩 written while Tsáu Jŕ was challenging him for their father's favor, and Pĭ had been sent out on a military campaign.

north and west are full of drifting clouds	西北有浮雲
level and high, like carriage-canopies	亭亭如車蓋
alas indeed, the times are out of joint	惜哉時不遇
violent whirlwinds are the only breeze	適與飄風會
they blow me on a journey south and east	吹我東南行
south to Wú and Gwèi Commanderies	南行至吳會
Wu and Gwei are not my native land	吳會非我鄉
how could I stay in places such as these?	安能久留滯
put it by, nor speak of it again —	棄置勿復陳
the wanderer goes in fear of other men	客子常畏人

The ninth line of this occurs almost identically in the "Old Poems" and in Tsáu Jŕ's poetry. It is thus not on the basis of "textual borrowings" that Tsáu Pĭ is separated from them and put in the opposite camp. Nor is it the resentment of the poem itself that links him to the *CT*, since "resentment" occurs in the wording of the Tsáu Jŕ and "Old Poems" notices.[11] It is rather by virtue of the ratio of genuine feeling to mere poetry that he is linked with the style-over-substance people (from figures in the notice, he is 90 per cent style) rather than with his brother (perfect 50/50). His modicum of genuineness, however, is insisted on — "how otherwise could he

---

[10] The fact that Syè Lĭng-yẁn has no followers in the *SP* scheme of things, for instance, though descriptively absurd, is polemically intelligible. Any poet with a Syè Lĭng-yẁn pedigree would be all but impossible to criticize, at least to eclectics. This will perhaps help explain why Húng felt constrained, above, to argue for transferring Shẹn Ywē's filiation to Bàu Jàu.

[11] Where, to be sure, it is differentiated from the *CT* type by various *SJ*-ish qualifying adjectives; so also Dzwǒ Sẓ.

have assigned ranks to the several worthies, or competed successfully with his brother?" This is the familiar Confucian idea that poetic and public talent are interchangeable aspects of a man's inner character, in contrast to the Six Dynasties conception of the independence of the literary realm.

Yìng Chyẃ's case is more obscure because most of his work has been lost, including the poem quoted in the notice, but he too has his artificiality of style ("good at archaisms"), and his element of personal genuineness ("diligent in referring to events," of his satires against the evil minister Tsáu Shwǎng). The lost poem is described as "ornate, but not without a taste of satire." Note that he is variously "archaic" and "ornate," a suggestion of portability which doubtless counts against his sincerity quotient.

Some similarities in wording can be found between Yìng Chyẃ and Táu Chyén, notably the repetition of the seemingly desirable words "antique" and "sincere." In Táu's case, however, they occur in the description of his persona, his public image, which is later exposed as actually insincere. Further, if we take these stylistic descriptions as the crux of the filiations, we shall be at a loss to explain how the two of them derive from Tsáu Pǐ, of whom neither term is used, sarcastically or otherwise. Common to all three, however, is an unfavorable style/substance ratio, not too unfavorable in Tsáu Pǐ's case, not too much worse with Yìng Chyẃ, but pretty despicable in Táu Chyén. Then there is the biographical side; Tsáu Pǐ was an emperor, Yìng Chyẃ was a minor minister, and Táu Chyén entirely renounced public life; this, in a work that lists poets complete with their official rank (the name of the work is, according to the preface, an allusion to the Han system of classifying civil service candidates), may also be in the picture.

I can now answer my question of some pages above. A poem, to Jūng Húng, was ideally a medium for the unmediated venting of deep personal sorrows. In practice, it was also an index of the degree of deviousness of the writer's moral character, and in a wider sense a symptom of the ever-worsening decadence of the times and the customs. His advice to the poets of his generation was, in effect, to return to the early third century — if not, indeed, to the earlier layers of the *SJ* itself.

It is not hard to see what sustains a critic of the avant-garde school; precisely his notion of an evolving literature, his faith in the future. Shn̆ Ywē's manifesto on the euphonic ideal climaxes on an already triumphantly confident note — "Jāng Hn̆g, Tsài Yūng, Tsáu Jŕ, and Wáng Tsàn never had an inkling of it, and Pān Ywè, Lù Jǐ, Yén Yén-jr̄, and Syè Líng-yẁn were far from the mark indeed, but devotees of literature now have the means to attain it. This is the truth; if you think I am wrong, just wait for the geniuses to come!"

But what sustains the critic who believes in a constant decline of culture; why does he bother? A clue to the psychology of such cases may be had in the profoundly Confucian fable of *Analects*, 18/6, where Dž-lù, twitted on his activism by two recluses of the Dàuist type, is told by Confucius, "If the world possessed the Truth, I should not be trying to change it (*yi*)." The fact that its kind of perfection is to be achieved by retrogressive movement to a pristine state does not deny Confucianism a strong evangelistic potential. The sense of having cast his lot with mankind, "such as he is," rather than with the morally insentient (and thus morally pure) birds and beasts, will impel the convinced Confucian to try to point out, to a world in need, the road back.

There is some excuse for thinking that Jūng Húng saw himself in this light. Besides the symptoms, here and there in the *SP*, of an awareness of contravening current taste or opinion, some of which have been noticed above, there are points at which the tone of the writing seems to betray the presence of deeply felt convictions. The most striking of these is the "justification" of B11—"none of the five has written very much, but their spirit is remarkable. If I grant them admission, then no Bàu Jàu or Jyāng Yēn can forbid them (see *Analects* 7/29) — I have promoted them to B, and all will concede the rightness of the decision."

Syè Shř-jī (B11c), the third of these poets, was sentenced to death together with his uncle Syè Hwèi 謝 晦 in 426. Their "Last Poem" is in linked verse, Shř-jī supplying the first quatrain and Hwèi the second. This poem, referred to in the *SP* notice, goes:

great the fins that over oceans crossed	偉 哉 橫 海 鱗
strong the wings that through the heavens wended	壯 矣 垂 天 翼
in a moment, lost to wind and wave	一 旦 失 風 水
as the food of ants they now have ended	翻 爲 螻 蟻 食
work well done is worthy of the Past	功 遂 侔 昔 人
shrinking from it cannot be defended	保 退 無 智 力
we have gone beyond the Tài-háng Height —	旣 涉 太 行 險
This Road is not easily ascended	斯 路 信 難 陟

Tài-háng is a stock metaphor for the all but unclimbable; here, for the superhuman demands of the Confucian vocation, which compelled a man to labor for the world's good at whatever personal cost, and against whatever obstacles. Such a sense of high duty would well agree with Húng's behavior as reported in the *History of the South*, especially the courage shown in his two protests to Emperor Wǔ.

Precisely apropos the *SP*, however, the *History* suggests a different sort of motivation. It relates that "Húng had once sought a recommendation from Shĭn Ywē, but Ywē had rebuffed him. When Ywē died, Húng did an evaluation of ancient and modern poetry, in which he assessed his worth in the following terms." After quoting the less obviously sarcastic portions of B21, the passage concludes, "This was how he evened the old score with Ywē." This does not, to be sure, claim that the whole *SP* grew out of a personal grudge. But Jūng Húng's defenders have felt him to be generally endangered by the charge, and have been at some pains to discredit the *History*. Since the *History of the South*, official or no, is a late and virtually secondary work, and since the corresponding part of the earlier *Lyáng History* makes no such statement, it is easy enough to dismiss the whole thing as a myth.

Even as myth, however, it still stands as evidence that the treatment of Shĭn Ywē is such as to suggest vindictiveness rather than mere critical disapproval; the particular legend invented may be fanciful, but the patent antipersonal tone of the *SP* that inspired the legend remains, and demands to be explained one way or another. Apart from Shĭn Ywē's notice proper, there are the oblique and hostile references under Syè Tyàu and Bàu Jàu, noted above, and others besides. Ywē's prosody manifesto, for instance, was promptly challenged in a letter of rebuttal from Lù Jywé (C27), of whom the *SP* says admiringly, "We are everywhere aware of the presence of an intrepid spirit. If his actual poetry is not too good, it is not the fault of his opinions." Then there is C9, less a critique of its nominal subject than one more chance for a sidelong thrust against Ywē—"I have never bothered to look into Fù Lyáng's works, but Shĭn Ywē's collection incorporates several titles by him, which are nothing if not plain." On the whole, it must be said that the *SP*, by placing so many caustic criticisms in so many out-of-the-way corners, conveys a strong impression of being out to get Shĭn Ywē, in any and all possible ways. The myth is thus not at all unintelligible, or even implausible, and it is accepted as true by so thorough a student of the work as Takamatsu.

Between the manifest antipathy and the unreliable anecdote, I know of no further evidence that would aid in a solution. The point is too central to be left to impressions, however; Jūng Húng is either a Confucian critic or a scorned sycophant, depending on the probity of the rumor. As the case lies beyond human resources, in the present state of our knowledge, recourse has been had to divination. The question of the nature of Jūng Húng's dislike for Shĭn Ywē was submitted to the *Book of Changes* by myself in May of 1963, obtaining as answer hexagram 7, with the second line emphasized. In this hexagram, then, and in the oracle texts associated with it, we are to seek an image of the relationship between Húng and Ywē.[12]

Hexagram 7 is called The Army; it suggests many men grouped around a strong leader, struggling against opposition to achieve their purpose. This must symbolize the avant-garde forces, bent on the cultivation of techniques of conscious literary artistry, and noisily opposed to the conservative majority. The emphasized second line of the hexagram represents the leader of the Army; this, again, can only refer to Shĭn Ywē, around whom the avant-garde movement had gathered since its inception. The line reads, "In the Army; successful; no blame; the king thrice bestows the mandate." It is not possible to doubt Shĭn Ywē's success; virtually all the younger poets of early Lyáng were much influenced by his ideas. The three bestowings of the mandate, similarly, can be taken as representing the three principal stages in his success, under three different kings — first, Syāu Dž-lyáng 蕭子良 , king of Jìng-líng 竟陵王 during the Chí dynasty, patron of Ywē and his group in their early days, 487–493; second, Syāu Yĕn 蕭衍 , Emperor Wŭ of Lyáng, personally indifferent to technical niceties, yet reflecting the popularity of the modern style; and finally Syāu Tŭng, Heir Apparent during Ywē's last days, who presided over the emergence of the *WSDL* and, with it, over Ywe's symbolic acceptance into the mainstream tradition. It was this third bestowing of the mandate, under the third king, that threatened final victory for the avant-garde, and posed a corresponding crisis for the votaries of more ancient ways.

The oracle is thus easy to apply to the over-all Chí and Lyáng literary situation; it is simply a vignette of Shĭn Ywē in his role as leader of the avant-garde. It follows that it was this role, and not the suspected personal grudge, that was the source of Jūng Húng's animus. We may accordingly dismiss the anecdotal explanation in favor of the factional one, more consistent with Jūng Húng's personality, more in keeping with the spirit of the times, and tidier altogether.

---

12 Readers who find this and the following too cabalistic are welcome to regard it as a metaphorical way of stating the paper's final conclusions, rather than as a method for arriving at them. Jūng Húng himself specialzied in the *Book of Changes* during his student days, and probably would not have minded. Modern experts will notice that I do not mention the resultant hexagram, explication of which would go beyond the intended scope of this paper. I hope to return to it on a future occasion.

The *SP*, then, is essentially a Confucian remonstrance with its age. Its position, though strategically hopeless, is both an interesting and a sympathetic one; Jūng Húng is a good case study of the vitality of the Confucian tradition of dedicated intransigeance, in a period intellectually dominated by Buddhism.[13] Whether this intransigeance itself was equally vital as literary theory, let alone stylistic analysis, is very doubtful. It is risky to quote Húng's pronouncements as though he were some kind of authority on the period, rather than one of the combatants—a reactionary trying to infiltrate the moderates. Some objective historian will want to go over the *SP* to see how much of it will stand up to rigorous stylistic analysis, but it will not do to regard Húng himself as such a historian. As a critical treatise, the *SP* is a good critical tract.

This is not to deny it virtues of its own. The Six Dynasties are not to be apprehended solely on the basis of those works, rare in any age, which happen to appeal to posterity's taste for the universal. Chinese poetry was not compounded of any such gossamer quantities; it was rather hammered out on the anvil of passion and counterpassion, and controversy rather than consensus is its native element. For a genuine understanding of the times, the universalist note must not be allowed to drown out the factionalist din, and thus a work like the *SP*, about whose pages there still lingers the smoke of battle, has its uses.

There is another virtue, rather in the nature of a by-product, that might be urged for it. Readers of the *WSDL*, whose undoubted bias is so much

---

13 The ruling houses of Chí and Lyáng were strongly interested in Buddhism; important writers who dallied more or less seriously with it include Yén Yén-jī, Syè Líng-ywn and his brother, Shǐn Ywē and his circle, and Lyóu Syé. The *SP* makes no overtly anti-Buddhist statements, but its treatment of Fàn Jǐn is suggestive. Fàn, who did not believe in spirits of any kind, was the most important anti-Buddhist controversialist of the period. In 487 he argued his doctrine of the extinction of the soul at death before Syāu Dž-lyáng, the king of Jìng-líng. The king brought in learned monks to refute him, but without success. The king then had Wáng Yúng say to him, "The extinction of the soul is contrary to reason, yet you firmly maintain it. One with talent such as yours would have no difficulty becoming a State Secretary, but you insist on going on in this way, ruining your chances." Fàn gave a great laugh, and replied, "When Fàn Jǐn sells his principles for an office, it will be that of Lord Constable Director of the Secretariat; why only State Secretary?" The *SP* does not try to pass Fàn off as a major poet (none of his work now survives), but comments in C22b that he "emulated the antique and simple style, despised the vulgar and delighted in the lucid, and did not lose the cardinal principle of courtliness." This is probably equivalent to endorsing Fàn's anti-Buddhist stand, which above all else would have been associated with his name by contemporaries. It could at the same time be yet another dig at Shǐn Ywē, who (at the king's behest) had been Fàn's principle opponent in 487; his important disquisitions "On the Non-Extinction of the Soul" and "Contra Fàn Jǐn's *On the Extinction of the Soul*" date from this year, and are still extant.

better concealed, may possibly develop a taste for Chinese literary criticism, but they are unlikely to rush out thirsting for a drink of minor-dynasties poetry. The *SP*, on the other hand, abounds with tasty gossip and pungent rejoinder, low intrigue and high dudgeon; its appeal to our faculty of liking and disliking intrigues us in a way that the methodical and balanced nice-chapmanship of the *WSDL* does not. It is hard to put it down without wondering what all that glorious and damnable poetry is really like. It is just possible that it may have the somewhat ironic effect of stirring a flicker of perverse interest in the very poetry it was designed to discredit — or, for that matter, to promote. This, in an age that still tends to regard the *SP* centuries as a bleak sort of wilderness, inhabited solely by Táu Chyén and the "Nineteen Poems," would in itself amount to a quite respectable importance.

The Early History of the Chinese Word *Shih* (Poetry)

CHOW TSE-TSUNG

The Earliest Occurrences of the Word in the Classics

IT is curious that we have not yet identified the Chinese graph 詩 *shih* in its ancient form, i.e., as it was written prior to the Ch'in dynasty (221–206 B.C.), when the Chinese script was radically reformed. The earliest form of the graph known to us is in the so-called "small seal style" (*hsiao chuan*), but the testimony for this form is no earlier than the first century during the Later Han dynasty. Thus the graphic and semantic history of this important word remains obscure. This has troubled many scholars.

Up to now we have discovered about 4,000 different graphs in the earliest known form of the Chinese script, viz. the oracle and other inscriptions on tortoise shells and cattle or deer bones belonging to the late Shang period, from the fourteenth to the twelfth century B.C. About 1,000 of these graphs have been identified with later graphs or otherwise deciphered with more or less certainty. We have also been able to isolate about 3,000 different graphs from the bronze inscriptions of the Shang and Chou dynasties. Of these we have identified about 1,900. By combining these figures, eliminating duplicates, and adding a number of graphs from other early epigraphic sources, we have a total of almost 4,500 different graphs in these archaic forms.[1] This number far exceeds the average number of graphs in pre-Ch'in

---

[1] My estimates are based on a number of different studies. In 1934, Hsü Wen-ching 徐文鏡 included 3,035 entries in his dictionary of ancient epigraphic forms which had been identified with more or less certainty. See his *Ku chou hui-pien* 古籀彙編 , 凡例 , no. 20. Ch'en Meng-chia 陳夢家 estimates the total number of the oracle graphs at 3,000–3,500, among which the identified do not exceed 1,000. See his *Yin-hsü pu-tz'u tsung shu* 殷虛卜

works. For example, the *Book of Poetry* contains about 2,600 different graphs. The *Lun-yü* has only about 1,400, the *Mo-tzu* less than 2,400, the *Mencius* less than 1,800, the *Hsün-tzu* about 2,640, and the *Chuang-tzu* about 2,300. In all of these works, the graph *shih* occurs in the meaning of "a poem," or "poetry," and in many of them it is a key word which occurs frequently. In spite of this, it is believed that this character does not appear in the oracle and bronze inscriptions or in any other surviving epigraphic materials of pre-Ch'in times, such as, for instance, stone monuments, seals, sealing clay, bamboo, or silk. This is even more strange when one considers that other words of similar nature like *ke* 歌 (song), *wu* 舞 (dance), *yüeh* 樂 (music), and *shu* 書 (record) have all been found in those materials.

Some of the passages in the classics in which the word *shih* appears (putting aside for the present those works written after Confucius' time) belong to a quite early period. The word appears twice in the *Book of History*. In the "Yao tien" 堯典, when Emperor Shun ordered his minister K'uei 夔 to take charge of music and to teach his sons, he decreed:

> Poetry expresses intention (inclination, determination, or will) in words, songs prolong the sounds of words for chanting, the notes accompany the chanting, and the pitch-pipes harmonize the notes. Make the eight kinds of musical sounds in accord and let them not interfere with each other, so that spirits and men may be brought into harmony.[2]

辭綜述 (Peking: K'o-hsüeh ch'u-pan-she, 1956), 2:63. Tung Tso-pin 董作賓 thinks the total number of the oracle graphs do not exceed 3,000. He says that Li Hsiao-ting 李孝定 lists 1,377 identified in his MS, *Chia-ku wen-tzu chi shih* 甲骨文字集釋. See Tung, *Chia-ku hsüeh liu-shih nien* 甲骨學六十年 (Taipei: I-wen, 1965), 1:11. But when Li published his book later on (台北 : 中央研究院史語所專刊 之五十, 1965), he listed 1,062 identified and 75 variants; he also listed 567 graphs which he thought did not appear in the *Shuo wen*, and 136 unidentified. Chin Hsiang-heng 金祥恒 in his *Hsü chia-ku wen pien* 續甲骨文編 (Taipei, preface dated 1959) lists more than 2,500 entries, of which 1,022 are identified. The revised and enlarged version of Sun Hai-po's 孫海波 *Chia-ku wen pien* 甲骨文編 (Peking: 中國科學院考古研究所, 1965) lists 4,672 graphs, of which 941 are identified, 782 recognizable only by the root, and 2,947 unidentified. Some of the entries should be considered variants. Jung Keng 容庚 gives 1,894 identified and 1,199 unidentified bronze inscription graphs of pre-Ch'in times in his *Chin-wen pien* 金文編 (Peking: K'o-hsüeh, 1959); 951 identified and 33 unidentified or doubtful ones of the Ch'in-Han period in his *Chin-wen hsü-pien* 金文續編 (Shanghai: Commercial Press, 1935). He also lists 1,241 graphs from stone inscriptions of Han and pre-Han times (some unidentified) in his *Shih k'e chuan-wen pien* 石刻篆文編 (Peking, 1957). Chin Hsiang-heng lists 1,080 pre-Ch'in pottery inscription graphs, of which 408 are identified and found in the *Shuo wen*, 90 are not in, and 582 unidentified. See his *T'ao-wen pien* 陶文編 (Taipei: I-wen, 1964), 編輯凡例, 1b.

2 All translations are my own. Cf. Legge, trans. *The Chinese Classics*, vol. 3: *The Shoo King* (Hong Kong, 1865, 1960), pp. 47–49; Bernhard Karlgren, trans. *The Book of Documents* (Stockholm, 1950), pp. 6–7. The first sentence was cited in *Shih chi*, "Wu-ti pen-chi" as 詩言意.

詩 言 志 ， 歌 永 言 ， 聲 依 永 ， 律 和 聲 。 八 音 克 諧 ， 無 相
奪 倫 ， 神 人 以 和 。

The "Yao tien" was preserved in the Han Modern Text version of the *History*, the authenticity of which has been generally accepted. It has been traditionally attributed to the times of the Yü (*ca.* twenty-third to twenty-second centuries B.C.) and the Hsia (*ca.* twenty-second to eighteenth centuries B.C.) periods. This dating is certainly false. In the opinion of modern scholars the narrative portions of this document belong to a much later date; some even suggest the period after Confucius' death. But in the case of quotations such as the one cited above, a relatively early date would, of course, still be possible. At any rate, the *Tso-chuan*, the *Mencius*, and the poem "The Heavenly Questions" attributed to Ch'ü Yüan all cite this document.[3]

In another section of the *History*, "Chin t'eng" 金縢 ("The Metal-bound Casket"), also in the Modern Text version, it is said that after his quelling of the rebellion in east China (in about 1102 B.C.),[4] "The Duke [of Chou] then wrote a poem and presented it to King [Ch'eng], and it was entitled 'Ch'ih-hsiao' (The Eared Owl)."[5] " 公 乃 爲 詩 以 貽 王 ， 名 之 曰 ' 鴟 鴞 ' " The poem exists in the prevailing version of the *Book of Poetry*.[6] Recent scholarship tends to accept "The Metal-bound Casket" as written in the eleventh or eighth century B.C.[7]

The *Book of Poetry* with *shih* as its title certainly existed before Confucius' time. The word *shih* also appears three times within the book itself. The last lines of "Sung kao" 崧 高 (no. 259), in the "Ta-ya" 大 雅 section, read:

Chi-fu makes this song,	吉 甫 作 誦 ，
Its verse is very great,	其 詩 孔 碩 ，
Its air is extremely fine,	其 風 肆 好 ，
It is presented to the Prince of Shen.[8]	以 贈 申 伯 。

---

[3] Ch'ü Wan-li 屈 萬 里 in his *Shang-shu shih-i* 尙 書 釋 義 (Taipei, 1956), pp. 1–4, dates this document between Confucius' death in 479 B.C. and the time of Mencius (*ca.* 372–*ca.* 289 B.C.). The reasons for this dating seem to be inadequate.

[4] The ancient Chinese calendar prior to Eastern Chou has not yet been convincingly reconstructed. For convenience I have tentatively adopted the view that the Chou dynasty succeeded Shang in 1111 B.C. Others prefer 1122 or 1175.

[5] Cf. Legge, vol. 3, p. 359; Karlgren, *Documents*, p. 36.

[6] No. 155, in "Pin Feng."

[7] Wang Kuo-wei 王 國 維 believes that it was written shortly after the event, i.e., about eleventh century B.C. (see his *Ku shih hsin cheng* 古 史 新 證). Ch'ü Wan-li dates it in about the eighth century B.C., *shih-i*, 67.

[8] Cf. Legge, trans. *The Chinese Classics*, vol. 4: *The She King*, p. 540; Arthur Waley, trans. *The Book of Songs* (London, 1937, 1954), p. 135; Karlgren, trans. *The Book of Odes* (1950), p. 228.

This poem has been dated beyond doubt in the reign of King Hsüan (827–782 B.C.), i.e., before the end of Western Chou. The poet's name has been identified as Hsi Chia 兮 甲 , and his courtesy name (*tzu*) as Po-chi-fu 伯 吉 父 .[9]

In the last stanza of another poem "Hsiang-po" 巷 伯 (no. 200), in the "Hsiao-ya" 小 雅 section, there are these lines:

The *ssu-jen* (attendant) Meng-tzu	寺 人 孟 子
Makes this poem,	作 爲 此 詩 ，
All you hundreds of lords	凡 百 君 子
Carefully listen to it![10]	敬 而 聽 之 ！

The preface to this poem in the Mao edition 毛 詩 小 序 says that it was written to criticize the last ruler of Western Chou, King Yu (r. 781–771 B.C.). Pan Ku (A.D. 32–92) put the poet Meng-tzu in the period of King Li (r. 878–842 B.C.).[11]

In another poem, "Chüan O" 卷 阿 (no. 252) of the "Ta-ya" section, the last two lines read:

I present these verses, which are very few,	矢 詩 不 多 ，
They are merely enough to be sung.[12]	維 以 遂 歌 。

According to the Mao preface to this poem, it was composed by the Duke of Shao 召 公 and presented to King Ch'eng (r. 1104–1068 B.C.). The *Chin-pen chu-shu chi-nien* 今 本 竹 書 紀 年 even records an excursion by the king to Chüan O in the thirty-third year of his reign, i.e. 1072 B.C.[13] This account is of course unreliable. But most scholars, from Chu Hsi to Ma Jui-ch'en, accept the view of the "Preface,"[14] though some have expressed doubts.[15]

---

9 The "Preface" of the *Mao Shih* and other sources say the poem is written by Yin Chi-fu 尹 吉 甫 . Wang Kuo-wei established, and most scholars accept, that this is the Hsi Chia in the inscription on the bronze vessel, *Hsi Chia p'an*. See his " 兮 甲 盤 跋 " in *Kuan-t'ang pieh-chi* 觀 堂 別 集 , vol. 2, pp. 8a–10a; also Kuo Mo-jo 郭 沫 若 , *Liang Chou chin wen-tz'u ta-hsi t'u-lu k'ao-shih* 兩 周 金 文 辭 大 系 圖 錄 考 釋 (Tokyo, 1935; rev. ed. Peking, 1958), "Plates," p. 134, "k'ao-shih," pp. 143b–144b.

10 Cf. Legge, vol. 4, p. 349; Waley, p. 316; Karlgren, *Odes*, p. 152.

11 *Han shu*, "Ku chin jen piao" 古 今 人 表 (*Po-na* ed), 20:16a; Ma Jui-ch'en 馬 瑞 辰 *Mao Shih chuan chien t'ung shih* 毛 詩 傳 箋 通 釋 (*SPPY* ed.), 20:44b–45a.

12 Cf. Legge, vol. 4, p. 495; Waley, p. 184; Karlgren, *Odes*, p. 210.

13 Lei Hsüeh-ch'i 雷 學 淇 , *Chu-shu chi-nien i-cheng* 竹 書 紀 年 義 證 (author's preface dated 1810), 19:144b; Wang Kuo-wei, *Chin-pen chu-shu chi-nien su-cheng* 今 本 竹 書 紀 年 疏 證 (author's preface dated 1917), 2:8a. Wang believes that the passage in the *Chin-pen* is spurious, being copied from the *Mao* "Preface."

14 朱 熹 , *Shih chi chuan* 詩 集 傳 (Peking: Wen-hsüeh ku chi, 1955 reprint of a Sung ed.), 17:18b; Ma Jui-ch'en, *T'ung shih*, 25:27b.

15 E.g., Yao Chi-heng 姚 際 恒 (1647–1715?), *Shih-ching t'ung-lun* 詩 經 通 論 , *chüan* 14.

Many contemporary Chinese scholars, mainly under Fu Ssu-nien's influence, date the poem in the period of King Li or King Hsüan, i.e., the ninth or eighth centuries B.C.[16] I believe, however, that their suggestions are ground-less and that there are reasons for attributing it to the eleventh century B.C.[17]

There are other works such as the *Kuan-tzu* 管 子 , the *I-li* 儀 禮 , and the *Chou li* 周 禮 , parts of which may belong to pre-Confucian times, which contain the word *shih*. These I will discuss later on. It suffices, for the time being, to say that this word was in use in the sense "poem" or "poetry" at the latest before the eighth century B.C. and possibly during or before the eleventh century B.C.

Previous Interpretations and Definitions

From the Chou dynasty on, most authors who discuss the meaning of *shih* base themselves on the formula cited above from the *Book of History*: "*Shih yen chih*" (Poetry expresses intention in words), or at least appeal to a similar idea.[18] This definition became a dominant principle of Chinese poetic criticism and literary theory in general throughout the following centuries.

In the year 554 B.C., according to the *Tso chuan*, Chao Meng 趙 孟 of Chin said, "*Shih i yen chih*" 詩 以 言 志 (Poetry is for expressing intention).[19] The *Kuo yü* has a story to the effect that when King Chuang of Ch'u 楚 莊 王 (r. 613–591 B.C.) appointed a teacher for his crown prince, a certain minister, Shen-Shu Shih 申 叔 時 , advised that the teacher might "teach him (the prince) poetry with a view to broadening his mind and illustrating ancient virtuous examples, so that his intention would be clearly defined." " 敎 之 詩 而 爲 之 導 廣 顯 德 以 耀 明 其 志 . "[20] This further implies that poetry

---

[16] Fu Ssu-nien 傅 斯 年 , *Fu Meng-chen hsien-sheng chi* 傅 孟 眞 先 生 集 , 中 編 乙 , " 詩 經 講 義 稿 " (written in 1928), pp. 35–50; Ch'en Shih-hsiang 陳 世 驤 , " 中 國 詩 字 之 原 始 觀 念 試 論 ," Academia Sinica, *LSYYYCSCK* 中 央 研 究 院 , 歷 史 語 言 研 究 所 集 刊 , no. 4 (Taipei, June 1961), pp. 900–901; see also his "In Search of the Beginnings of Chinese Literary Criticism," in Walter J. Fischel, ed., *Semitic and Oriental Studies* (University of California Press, 1951), pp. 45–63.

[17] On this problem I have an article in Chinese "*Shuo Chüan O*" 說 卷 阿 (in MS).

[18] See Chu Tzu-ch'ing 朱 自 淸 , *Shih yen chih pien* 詩 言 志 辨 (Shanghai: K'ai-ming, 1945; Peking: Ku-chi, 1957); also Achilles Fang, "Some Reflections on the Difficulty of Translation," *in* Arthur F. Wright, ed., *Studies In Chinese Thought* (1953), pp. 263–285, *reprinted in* Reuben A. Brower, ed., *On Translation* (Harvard University Press, 1959); see particularly pp. 119, 133.

[19] *Tso chuan* 左 傳 , Hsiang-kung 襄 公 二 十 七 年 . In the same year Po Chou Li 伯 州 犂 said: " 志 以 發 言 ， 言 以 出 信 ， 信 以 立 志 · 參 以 定 之 ."

[20] *Kuo yü* 國 語 (A.D. 1800 wood-block ed. based on A.D. 1033 ed.), 楚 語 上 , 17:1b.

can also influence the reader's intentions or inclinations. Similar interpretations may also be found in early Confucian writings. Mencius says:

Therefore, one who explains the [*Book of*] *Poetry* must not rely on its embellishment so as
to do violence to the language, nor on the language so as to do violence to the intention
[of the poet]. If he uses his mind to trace the meaning to the intention [of the poet], he will
be successful.

故說詩者，不以文害辭，不以辭害志；以意逆志，是爲得之。[21]

Although Mencius does not actually define *shih* in terms of *chih* (intention)
in this passage, the juxtaposition of the two terms shows his understanding
of the traditional definition of *shih*.

Another leading Confucian philosopher, Hsün-tzu, who paid more
attention to the *Book of Poetry*, and probably exerted more influence upon
its interpretation in later centuries than any other ancient philosopher,
is elaborating the same definition when he says: "The sage is the controls
to the *tao*. . . . What is expressed in the [*Book of*] *Poetry* is his intention."
"聖人也者，道之管也. …. 詩言是其志也."[22]

Hsün-tzu's relating *chih* with the sage and the *tao* is significant enough,
but the significance of his description of the *Book of Poetry* in another passage
seems to have never been fully understood: "The [*Book of*] *Poetry* is the
impression (or repository) of correct sounds." "詩者，中聲之所止也."[23]
Here his use of *chih* 止 may not be irrelevant if the origin of *shih* is clarified,
a task I am going to undertake.

---

21 The *Mencius*, 萬章上, 5A, 4. Almost all English translations of this passage interpret
wen as "term" or "word" and *tz'u* as "sentence" or "phrase" (see Legge, vol. 4, p. 359;
James R. Ware, Mentor paperback, 1960, p. 117). They probably follow Chu Hsi's commentary: "文, 字也；辭, 語也." (四書集註) W. A. C. H. Dobson translates the first
part of the passage as: "those who interpret the *Book of Songs* should not do violence to the
poet's intention, by singling out one line" (*Mencius*, University of Toronto Press, 1964,
p. 97). He seems to have left out one line. I believe rather that *wen* means something like
"rhetoric" as Chao Ch'i's 趙岐 commentary suggests. Mencius himself in a sentence
immediately following the above passage identifies *tz'u* with *yen*: 如以辭而已矣，
"雲漢"之詩曰："周餘黎民，靡有孑遺."信斯言也，是周無遺民也.
This strongly supports the view that *wen* means "embellishment" or "rhetoric." Cf. the
passage in the *Tso chuan*, Hsiang Kung 25th year: "Confucius said, 'The record has this:
"Language is to complement one's intention, and embellishment to complement the
language." Without language, who can know one's intention? If one expresses himself in
language without embellishment, he will not go very far.' " 仲尼曰："志有之：
'言以足志，文以足言.' 不言，誰知其志? 言之無文，行而不遠."
(左傳, 襄公二十五年, 548 B.C.) Here *yen* is similar to Mencius' *tz'u*.
22 *Hsün-tzu*, chap. 8, "Ju hsiao" 儒效.
23 *Ibid.*, chap. 1, "Ch'üan hsüeh" 勸學.

When Hsün-tzu used the word *shih*, he, like many other authors of the late Chou period, more often meant the book. Since no other existing writings of that time were called *shih*, the term then actually could be regarded as generic.

The Taoist work, the *Chuang-tzu*, in summarizing the ancient Chinese learning, gives a statement similar to that in the *Tso chuan* but changes 言 into 道: "The [*Book of*] *Poetry* is to tell intentions; the [*Book of*] *History*, events; the *Rites*, behavior; the *Music*, harmony; the [*Book of*] *Changes*, yin and yang; and the [*Annals of*] *Spring and Autumn*, title and obligations [name and boundaries]." "詩 以 道 志 ，書 以 道 事 ，禮 以 道 行 ，樂 以 道 和 ，易 以 道 陰 陽 ，春 秋 以 道 名 分 ."[24]

Moreover, the "Great Preface" of the Mao edition of the *Book of Poetry* not only defines *shih* in terms of *chih* 志, but also used the word *chih* 之 (go) in the following definitions:

Poetry is where the [poet's] intention goes. Existing in the mind it is intention; expressed in words it is poetry. When one's emotions move within, they are expressed in words; when words are inadequate, one may use exclamations to express them; when exclamations are inadequate, one may express them in song by prolonging the sounds; when singing is inadequate, one may unconsciously express them in dance by gesturing with one's hands and beating with one's feet.

詩 者 ，志 之 所 之 也 。在 心 爲 志 ，發 言 爲 詩 。情 動 於 中 而 形 於 言 ；言 之 不 足 ，故 嗟 嘆 之 ；嗟 嘆 之 不 足 ，故 永 歌 之 ；永 歌 之 不 足 ，不 知 手 之 舞 之 ，足 之 蹈 之 也 。[25]

As the authorship and dating of this preface are in dispute, we may suspend judgment on whether it was written during the fifth century B.C., as believed by the scholars of the Han dynasty, at the end of the third century B.C. as

---

24 莊 子 "T'ien-hsia" 天 下 . In the *Kuo yü* there is a passage which says that in 522 B.C. the Entertainer Chou-chiu 伶 州 鳩 told King Ching of Chou 周 景 王 : " 聲 以 和 樂 ，律 以 平 聲 ，金 石 以 動 之 ，絲 竹 以 行 之 ，詩 以 道 之 ，歌 以 詠 之 ，匏 以 宣 之 ，瓦 以 贊 之 ，革 木 以 節 之 ." The commentator Wei Chao 韋 昭 of the third century, while recognizing 之 in all cases to be a pronoun referring to 聲 (the sound), after the sentence 詩 以 道 之 comments: 道 己 志 也 . 書 曰 ：詩 言 志 , and after 歌 以 詠 之 comments: 詠 詩 也 . 書 曰 ：歌 永 言 ，聲 依 永 . Considering the 詩 以 道 志 in the *Chuang-tzu*, the passage from the "Yüeh chi," and the " 天 之 " in the *Mo-tzu* cited below, we may allow the possibility that the 之 in 詩 以 道 之 was intended in the sense of 志 .

25 *Mao Shih* "Ta hsü" 毛 詩 大 序 . The term 不 足 (inadequate) may be compared with 足 (to complement, or to express adequately) in the *Tso chuan* cited in n. 21 above.

suggested by Chu Tzu-ch'ing,[26] or by Wei Hung 衛宏 in the first century A.D. as believed by other modern scholars.

Similar interpretations can be found in another classic, the *Li chi* 禮記, the authorship and date of which are also very uncertain. For the sake of expediency we may tentatively follow Pan Ku in supposing that most of its chapters were written by Confucian scholars after the time of Confucius' disciples.[27] The chapter "K'ung-tzu hsien-chü" 孔子閒居 may lie in this category. In that chapter there is this passage:

Confucius said: "Where the intention reaches, there poetry reaches; where poetry reaches, there propriety reaches; where propriety reaches, music (joy) reaches; and where music (joy) reaches, grief reaches. Grief and joy give birth to each other. These, therefore, are correct (or normal). Intention (*chih*) and passion-vitality (*ch'i*) pervade the universe. This is what I call the 'five reaches.' "

孔子曰：「志之所至，詩亦至焉；詩之所至，禮亦至焉；禮之所至，樂亦至焉；樂之所至，哀亦至焉。哀樂相生，是故正。… 志氣塞乎天地。此之謂「五至」」。[28]

In another chapter of the same book, the "Yüeh chi" 樂記, there is a statement about poetry which is also close to that in the "Great Preface" of the *Mao Shih*. We are not sure whether this is the version which Pan Ku says was composed during the time of Emperor Wu (r. 140–87 B.C.).[29] The source materials used, however, are believed to be from the records of the late Chou period:

Virtue is the beginning of man's nature. Music is the flower of virtue. Metal, stone, silk, and bamboo are the instruments of music. It is poetry which expresses his intention, songs which carry his voice, and dance which animates his appearance. These three originate in the mind, and therefore the instruments follow them.

德者，性之端也。樂者，德之華也。金石絲竹，樂之器也。詩言其志也，歌咏其聲也，舞動其容也。三者本於心，然後樂器從之。[30]

---

26 See Chang Hsin-ch'eng 張心澂, *Wei shu t'ung k'ao* 僞書通考 (Shanghai: Commercial Press, 1939; rev. and enl. ed. 1957), pp. 271–309; Chu Tzu-ch'ing, *Shih yen chih pien*, 3:19–20; Ch'ü Wan-li, *Shih ching shih i* 詩經釋義, "Introduction," pp. 20–21.

27 Chang Hsin-ch'eng, pp. 389–403.

28 阮刻十三經注疏, 禮記, chap. 29, *chüan* 51. K'ung Ying-ta 孔穎達 (A.D. 574–648) interprets 樂 in all of the cases as "joy." According to the traditional way of reading 是故正 is not punctuated as a complete sentence but is connected with the words following, i.e.: 是故正明目而視之，不可得而見也；傾耳而聽之，不可得而聞也. I think 明目 instead of 正明目 makes better parallelism with 傾耳. "Yüeh cheng" 樂正 is a frequently used term in the classics.

29 *Han shu*, "I wen chih," 30:7a.

30 *Li chi*, chap. 19, *chüan* 38.

All the citations above merely maintain that *shih* is to express *chih* 志 . There is at least, however, one example in which the two terms are virtually identified. According to the *Tso-chuan*, at a diplomatic gathering in 526 B.C., Han Ch'i 韓 起 of Chin asked the officials of Cheng each to recite something so that he "might rely on it to know the *chih* (intention) of Cheng" 亦 以 知 鄭 志 . Then each of the six officials chanted in turn a verse from the "Cheng feng" 鄭 風 section in the *Book of Poetry*. When they had finished, Han remarked that what the gentlemen "chanted does not fall outside of the *chih* of Cheng." " 賦 不 出 鄭 志 ."[31] Thus Han used the word *chih* in the first case in the meaning of "intention" and in the second case of "recorded poem."

From the above examples it is clear that during the pre-Ch'in period, i.e., before the third century B.C., the meaning of *shih* was closely related to 志 which meant, on the one hand "intention" and, on the other, "a recorded poem" or simply "a record." In the latter sense, the two words *shih* and *chih* are almost interchangeable. The above examples, taken together, also suggest a relationship between the meaning of 詩 and the meanings of 之 and 止 .

A number of authors of the early Han period elaborated on these definitions in one way or another. Chia I 賈 誼 (201–169 B.C. or 200–168 B.C.) writes:

The [*Book of*] *Poetry* records the pattern of virtue and makes clear its point, so that man may follow it to perfect himself. That is why I say: The [*Book of*] *Poetry* is the record of this [virtue].
詩 者 ， 志 德 之 理 而 明 其 指 ， 令 人 緣 之 以 自 成 也 。 故 曰 ： 詩 者 ，
此 之 志 者 也 。[32]

Tung Chung-shu 董 仲 舒 (176–104 B.C.), in discussion of the six kinds of teachings, says:

The men of virtue knew that those in power were unable through evil to make men submit, so they chose the Six Arts to help and cultivate them. The [*Book of*] *Poetry* and the [*Book of*] *History* are to set their intentions (purposes) in order; the *Rites* and *Music* are to purify their cultivation; and the [*Book of*] *Changes* and the [*Annals of*] *Spring and Autumn* are to enlighten their intellect. These six learnings are all great, but each excels in its own way. The *Poetry* expresses the intentions, so excels in substance; the *Rites* is to restrain, so excels in embellishment. . . .

---

[31] 左 傳 , 昭 公 十 六 年 . Cf. Legge, *The Ch'un Ts'ew, with the Tso Chuen*, Book X, year XVI, p. 664.

[32] *Hsin shu* 新 書 (明 ： 程 榮 校 本), " 道 德 說 ," *chüan* 8, p. 13a.

君子知在位者之不能以惡服人也，是故簡六藝以贍養之。詩、
書序其志，禮、樂純其養，易、春秋明其知。六學皆大，而各
有所長。詩道志，故長於質。禮節制，故長於文。···³³

As we can see, even such moralistic interpretations of *shih* (poetry) still
preserve its association with the word *chih* ("intention" or "record") passed
down from ancient times.

This meaning of *shih*, however, was made much more explicit by the
lexicographers of the Han dynasty. Hsü Shen 許慎 (*ca.* 30–*ca.* 124) listed
shih as an entry in his *Shuo wen chieh tzu* 說文解字 which was written in
A.D. 96–100: "*Shih* 詩 is *chih* 志 [intention or a recorded poem?]. It is made
with *yen* 言 (words), and the phonetic *ssu* 寺 . 𤔋 is a simplified ancient
form of 詩 ." " 𤔋 , 志也 . 从言 , 寺聲 . 𤔋 , 古文詩省 ."³⁴ Hsü's entries
are written in the "small *chuan*" form, and his explanations were originally
in the "clerical" (*li*) form popular in his time. Furthermore, since Hsü's
book has been transmitted to us through many hands and was not printed
until A.D. 986, the text is quite corrupt.³⁵ But the form of the character
shih in this entry is attested by existing epigraphs dating from A.D. 123, i.e.,
Hsü's time:³⁶ 𤔋 𤔋

The definition, as it stands above, follows the text of all early or later
Shuo wen editions, including those dating from the late tenth century.
But in a citation from this passage in the *Ku chin yün hui* 古今韻會 by Huang
Kung-shao 黃公紹 of the thirteenth century, there appears one more
phrase, "intention expressed in words" 志發於言 , between 志也 and 从言 .
It has been suggested by Yao Wen-t'ien (1758–1827) and Yen K'o-chun
(1762–1843) that these four characters must originally have been a commen-
tary by Hsü Ch'ieh (920-974 or 975) mistakenly introduced into Hsü Shen's

---

³³ *Ch'un-ch'iu fan-lu* 春秋繁露 (凌曙注 , 皇清經解續編 , *chüan* 865), 玉杯第
二 , 2:21.

³⁴ 3A 三上 , 言部 . See Ting Fu-pao 丁福保 , comp. *Shuo wen chieh tzu ku-lin* 說文解
字詁林 , p. 968a–b.

³⁵ In this year Hsü Ch'ieh's brother Hsü Hsüan 徐鉉 (917–992 or 916–991) presented
to the throne the book he and others had edited under the order of the Emperor. It was
published and since then has become the sole source of all later editions, except for some
variants preserved in Hsü Ch'ieh's book mentioned below and a few citations appearing in
other works.

³⁶ The two graphs appear respectively in 少室石闕銘 and 開母廟石闕銘 .
Both the stone tablets were made in the second year of Yen-kuang during the reign of
Emperor An of the Han dynasty 漢安帝延光二年 (A.D. 123), and uncovered in Teng-
feng county of Honan Province 河南登封 . See Jung Keng, *Shih k'e chuan-wen pien*,
chüan 3, p. 7a.

text.[37] But this theory is not borne out by the present text of Hsü Ch'ieh's work, the *Shuo wen chieh tzu hsi-chuan* 說文解字繫傳 which lacks these four characters. Thus their origin remains unknown. It has been argued by Yang Shu-ta and accepted by other contemporary scholars that they must have stood in the original text, principally on the ground that they reflect the well-known definition in the "Great Preface" to the *Mao Shih* quoted above, i.e., "Existing in the mind it is intention; expressed in words it is poetry."[38] But this argument is hardly convincing in view of the fact that the "Preface" was so well known later.

The most important doubt raised by the *Shuo wen* definition concerns the sense in which Hsü Shen meant *chih* to be taken; that is, whether he meant it as unexpressed "intention" or in the sense of "a recorded poem" (or "a record"). Unfortunately, this question cannot be solved by the *Shuo wen* itself because *chih* does not occur there as an independent entry. Although *chih* is also used to define *i* 意 , this does not help us very much to decide the present case because the meaning of *i* is not clear either. As Tuan Yü-ts'ai points out, there both *i* and *chih* may mean 識 , which Hsü Shen defines as 常 . This last word probably means "a banner," hence "a marker," "a record," "to record" or "to remember."[39] The presence of 志發於言 in the definition of *shih* would narrow *chih* itself to the sense of "*unexpressed* intention." Thus these four characters which mean, in effect, "expressed intention," must represent an alternative definition. But in such cases Hsü Shen's normal usage is to prefix a phrase 一曰 (or 或曰 , or 一說) or to add a final 也 , or both, to the second definition. Without either of these markers, the four characters can only be read as an explanation of 志也 , in which case they contradict the definition itself.[40]

---

[37] 姚文田 , 嚴可均 . *Shuo wen chiao-i* 說文校議 (姚氏咫進齋刻本), cited in *Ku-lin*, p. 968a.

[38] 楊樹達 , "Shih shih" 釋詩 , written on Sept. 16, 1935, in his *Chi-wei chü hsiao-hsüeh chin shih lun-ts'ung* 積微居小學金石論叢 (enl. ed.; Peking: K'o-hsüeh ch'u-pan she, 1955), pp. 25–26. Yang's theory is accepted by Chu Tzu-ch'ing (see n. 58, below) and Ch'en Shih-hsiang (see n. 16, above).

[39] 段玉裁 , *Shuo wen chieh tzu chu* 說文解字注 (經韻樓藏版 , 1808; reprinted I-wen, 1958). 心部 :意字 , 10A:506–507; 言部 :識字 , 3A:92; 巾部 :常字 , 7B:362. 識 reads 記 or 志 , see 漢書"匈奴傳上" 顏師古注 ;廣雅 , "釋詁二" ;郭嵩燾 , 史記札記 :關於 "屈原傳" : "博聞彊志" 及 "三王世家" : "博聞彊記." See also Chang Ping-lin 章炳麟 , *Wen shih* 文始 (浙江圖書館景印手稿本 , 1913), 8:5a–b.

[40] For definitions followed by a supplementary explanation in the *Shuo wen*, see for example: "天 :顚也 , 至高無上" (一上 , 一部). "蒲 :水草也 , 可以作席" (一下 , 草部). "音 :聲也 , 生於心有節於外謂之音" (三上 , 音部).

There is, however, one possibility, and that is, he may be using, as Han
Ch'i did in the *Tso chuan*, the first *chih* in 志也，志發於言 as "a record"
(or "a recorded poem") and the second in the sense of "unexpressed intention." Therefore the definition can be translated as "*shih* is a record (or
a recorded poem), i.e., intention expressed in words." But in this case, it
would have been enough to say 志發於言也 without the redundant 志也.
In sum, it is unlikely that Hsü Shen was giving two different definitions
(as Yang Shu-ta suggests) by saying 志也，志發於言 ; nor could he say
this without self-contradiction or redundancy if he intended to give *shih*
a single definition. Consequently, the four words in question may be best
thought of as an interpolation. The single *chih* in the definition probably
either means "a recorded poem" if the current usage of Hsü Shen's time is
taken into consideration, or is used in the double sense, "intention" and "a
recorded poem," if he chooses to follow the earlier practice of the *Tso chuan*.

This simple definition of *shih* as *chih* (a recorded poem, or a record) is
given by another prominent scholar of the Eastern Han, Kao Yu 高誘 ,
in his commentary to the *Lü-shih ch'un-ch'iu* 呂氏春秋 . The *Lü-shih
ch'un-ch'iu*, edited by Lü Pu-wei 呂不韋 (d. 235 B.C.), tells of a very interesting event in antiquity. When King Chieh (r. *ca* 1802–*ca*. 1752 B.C.) of the
Hsia dynasty became tyrannous, T'ang, the ruler of Shang (*ca*. 1751–*ca*. 1739
B.C.), shot his confidant Yi Yin with an arrow as a cover for his design to
send him to Hsia to do intelligence work. Three years later Yi Yin returned
to report to T'ang, saying that Chieh was bewitched by beautiful women:
he "does not regard the multitude and in their hearts the multitude can bear
him no more." " 不恤其衆，衆志不堪 ." He then goes on to say that the
people circulate rhymed sayings that the Heaven will end Hsia's mandate.
Upon hearing this T'ang said, "You are telling me that the great Hsia is
going to be finished as the folk poems say." " 若告我曠夏盡如詩 ." Here
again *chih* and *shih* are related indirectly.[41] But Kao Yu, who wrote a

---

For alternative definitions see " 帝：諦也，王天下之號也 " (一上，上部). In all
editions including *Ku chin yün hui's* quotations, the second 也 appears in this kind of definition.
Only Hsü Ch'ieh's version does not have 也 , which is considered a mistake. See T'ien
Wu-chao 田吳炤 , *Shuo wen erh Hsü chien i* 說文二徐箋異 (1909), in *Ku-lin*, 1:21b.
But most alternative definitions take the following form: " 識：常也，一曰知也 "
(三上，言部). For the last category see Ma Hsü-lun, *Shuo wen chieh tzu yen-chiu fa* 說文
解字研究法 , pp. 110b–112a.

[41] Hsü Wei-yü 許維遹 , *Lü-shih ch'un-ch'iu chi-shih* 呂氏春秋集釋 (1935, reprinted
Taipei: Shih-chieh, 1962), " 慎大覽第三 ", 15:2a–3a. I have not interpreted the *chih*
in 衆志不堪 as 記 (to record), because the sentence is followed by 上下相疾
民心積怨 . 皆曰：" 上天弗恤，夏命其卒 ." Otherwise the writing would be
out of sequence.

commentary for the book after 212, made a note at this point. He says: "*Shih* is *chih*." " 詩 ,志也 ." It is very possible that Kao Yu was simply following Hsü Shen's definition. If so, he must have understood *chih* in the sense of "a recorded poem" or "expressed intention."[42]

Apart from the word 志 , another important and perplexing point concerns the variant form of *shih* which Hsü gives at the end of his definition. This form is composed of 屮 (modern form: 之) as a major root and 𡿨 , which is supposed to be an unusual ancient form of 言 .[43] It is not possible to discuss this problem in detail in this article, but we will have to come back to the question of 屮 .

At about the same time as Kao Yu, Liu Hsi 劉 熙 in his dictionary, the *Shih ming* 釋 名 , says: "*Shih* is *chih* 之 (to go), i.e., where the *chih* 志 (intention) goes." " 詩 ,之也 ,志之所之也 ." Following this he lists a few other terms, *hsing* 興 , *fu* 賦 , *pi* 比 , *ya* 雅 , and *sung* 頌 , and concludes that "these are variant terms [for *shih*] which are named according to the author's intention." " 隨 作 者 之 志 而 別 名 之 也 ."[44] Though Liu is following the "Great Preface" of the *Mao Shih* almost literally, his definition of *shih* in terms of *chih* (to go) should be noticed.

As the *chuan* form of this word *chih* 之 is 屮 or 屮 , we can easily see that both 詩 and 志 (*chuan* form: 㞢) have it as a root. Furthermore, from our knowledge of the oracle inscriptions, it has been well established that 之 and 止 are of the same origin.

---

[42] *Ibid.* Yü Yüeh 俞 樾 (1821–1907) considers Kao Yu's note too far-fetched and argues that the *shih* in the text actually means rhymed folksongs or proverbs. I think Yü Yüeh misunderstands the meaning of *chih* in Kao's definition. That Kao Yu is very familiar with Hsü Shen's works is quite clear from the fact that he follows Hsü Shen to write a commentary to the *Huai-nan-tzu*.

[43] This odd form of *yen* appears quite often in the *yen* category of the *Shuo wen*. Shen T'ao 沈 濤 of the Ch'ing dynasty says that the *Han chien* 汗 簡 by Kuo Chung-shu 郭 忠 恕 of the Sung dynasty cites the word 詩 from the *Shuo wen* as 𧥡 instead of 𡿨 , so he wonders whether the latter is a corrupt form. See Shen's *Shuo wen ku pen k'ao* 說 文 古 本 考 (1884). Ch'ien Tien 錢 坫 (1741–1806) thinks that, since the ancient form of the radical 言 resembles that of 心 , the word 𡿨 is probably a corrupt form of 志 . See his *Shuo wen chieh tzu chiao-ch'üan* 說 文 解 字 斠 詮 , in *Ku-lin*, 3A:968b. See also Ma Hsü-lun, *Shuo wen chieh tzu liu shu su cheng* 說 文 解 字 六 書 疏 證 (Peking: K'o-hsüeh ch'u-pan she, 1957), *chüan* 5, pp. 37–39. Ma accepts Ch'ien's view, but also suggests, without adequate evidence, that Hsü Shen might have defined 詩 as 諸 也 . Karlgren gives the pronunciations of 志 during early Chou, A.D. 600, and modern times: *ţiəg/tśi-/chï (Grammata Serica Recensa, no. 962e, p. 254). In Japanese 之 , 詩 , and 志 are all pronounced *shi*; but other words with similar corresponding sounds are often pronounced the same too.

[44] *Shih ming*, *chüan* 3, chap. 20, " 釋 典 藝 第 二 十 ". For general information about this book see Nicholas Cleaveland Bodman, *A Linguistic Study of the Shih ming* (Harvard University Press, 1954). Cf. *Ch'un-ch'iu shuo t'i-tz'u* 春 秋 說 題 辭 : " 詩 之 爲 言 志 也 ," cited by K'ung Ying-ta.

With the help of Ch'ing scholarship and the advantage of the new epigraphic data that have come to light in this century, modern scholars have traced the origin of *shih* with more precision than was previously possible. Yang Shu-ta, commenting on the definition of *shih* in the *Shuo wen*, said in 1935:

The graph *chih* 志 is made with *hsin* 心 and the phonetic *chih* 止. The graph *ssu* 寺 also has its phonetic 止. The ancient pronunciations of 止, 志, and 寺 are the same. The ancient form [of 詩] is made with 言 and 止; actually 言止 is 言志. (In the *Mo-tzu* the term "the Heaven's intention" 天志 is written as 天之). The *chuan* form of 詩 is made with 言 and 寺; actually 言寺 is also 言志. .... Since *"Shih* 詩 is for expressing (言) *chih* 志 " is a prevailing belief in ancient times, those who created the written language made the graph with 言 and 志. As for the fact that sometimes 止 and sometimes 寺 are used instead of 志, it is because the pronunciations of the former two were similar to that of the latter and so they were borrowed for it.

志字从心，止聲。寺字亦從止聲。止、志、寺古音無二。[詩]古文從言、止，言止即言志也。（墨子 "天之" 即 "天志"）篆文詩從言、寺，言寺亦言志也。… 蓋詩以言志爲古人通義，故造文字者之制字也，即以言志爲文。其以止爲志，或以寺爲志，音同假借耳。[45]

Wen I-to, writing in 1939, asserted that *shih* 詩 and *chih* 志 were originally the same word, which developed three meanings in various times, i.e., to remember 記憶, to record 記錄, and what is cherished in the mind (emotion) 懷抱.[46] To prove that *chih* means "to remember," Wen reasons that the two elements of the graph mean "stay (stop) in mind" 停止在心上. So he cites the *Hsün-tzu*: "*Chih* is to store," "志也者，臧［藏］也，"[47] and regards it as meaning "to store (keep) in mind." By extension the word has the meaning "to remember." For example, in the *Li chi*, Duke Ai of Lu implored Confucius to remember the duke's inability to understand: "You keep it in mind." "子志之心也."[48] And the *Kuo yü* cites the decree of Duke Wu of Wei (r. 812–758 B.C.), made when he was already ninety-five

---

45 "Shih shih," see n. 38, above. Yang's opinion in many aspects is similar to those of Ch'ing scholars such as Sung Pao 宋保, *Hsieh-sheng pu i* 諧聲補逸 and Tai Ko-heng 戴果恒, "Shih shih" 釋詩. In addition to the example *t'ien chih* mentioned by Yang, we may find also in the *Mo-tzu* that 志功 is sometimes written in the form 之功.

46 聞一多 "Ke yu shih" 歌與詩, in *Wen I-to ch'uan chi* 聞一多全集 (Shanghai: K'ai-ming, 1948), vol. 1, p. 185.

47 荀子, chap. 21, "Chieh pi" 解蔽.

48 禮記, *chuan* 15, chap. 27, "Ai-kung wen" 哀公問. Karlgren translates it as "May you make it registered in my heart" ("Loan Characters in Pre-Han Texts," *BMFEA*, 35 [1963], 48). I think "my" is the wrong word.

years old, as follows: "When you hear any comments on me, you must recite and remember [record?] them and present them to me in order to admonish and guide me." "聞一二之言，必誦志而納之，以訓導我."[49] Here Wen I-to interprets *chih* as "to remember," but from the context, it might mean "to record" as well.[50]

The use of 志 as "a record" (記) certainly can be proved by citing a number of passages of the late Chou period and commentaries of the Han dynasty. The relating of *shih* with "to record" or "a record" is clearly shown in Chia I's writing, as has been cited above. To support this, Wen further quotes from the *Kuan-tzu*: "The [*Book of*] Poetry is for recording things." "詩所以記物也."[51]

As for *shih* in the meaning of "emotion," Wen thinks that this is what the ancient writers meant by *i* 意 when they employed it to define *shih*, e.g. "詩以達意."[52] "詩所以言人之意志也."[53] "詩,意也."[54] According to Wen, all the *i*'s in these passages equal Lu Chi's (261–303) *ch'ing*: "Poetry follows emotion and tends to be elegant and exquisite." "詩緣情而綺靡."[55] As all these quotations belong to the Han dynasty or later (see also n. 2, above), I shall support Wen's case with one from the *Kuo yü*: "The [*Book of*] Poetry is for uniting minds, and songs are for singing the poems." "詩所以合意也，歌所以詠詩也."[56] A similar example occurs in the *Hsin yü* by Lu Chia 陸賈 of the early Han dynasty.[57]

---

[49] 國語, *chüan* 17, "Ch'u yü, A" 楚語上, p. 9a.

[50] Wei Chao in his commentary to *Kuo yü* says in this case: "志,記也."

[51] 管子, *chüan* 22, chap. 75, "Shan ch'üan shu" 山權數. See Tai Wang 戴望, *Kuan-tzu chiao-cheng* 管子校正 (reprinted Taipei: Shih-chieh, 1958), p. 366.

[52] A saying by Tung Chung-shu as cited in the "Biography of Ssu-Ma Ch'ien" (32) in the *Han shu*.

[53] Cheng Hsüan's commentary on 詩言志 in the "Yao tien" of the *Book of History*.

[54] Chang I 張揖 (fl. 227–232), *Kuang Ya* 廣雅, "Shih yen" 釋言. The original text reads 詩,志:意也. Wang Nien-sun 王念孫 says, "The pronunciations of 詩 and 志 are close, so that many books define 詩 as 志, but none of them defines it as 意." "案詩, 志聲相近,故諸書皆訓詩爲志. 無訓爲意者." He consequently changes the text into 詩,意:志也. See his *Kuang Ya su cheng* 廣雅疏證 (author's preface dated 1796, *SPPY* ed.), *chüan* 5A, p. 8a. There seems to be no reason to change the text (see n. 2, above).

[55] 陸機, "Wen fu" 文賦. Achilles Fang translates this sentence as: "*Shih* (lyric poetry) traces emotions daintily." See his translation "Rhyme-prose on Literature: The *Wen-fu* of Lu Chi," *HJAS*, 14 (1951), reprinted in John L. Bishop, ed., *Studies in Chinese Literature* (Harvard University Press, 1965), pp. 12, 32.

[56] *Chüan* 5, "Lu yü, B" 魯語下, p. 10a.

[57] Lu says, "When it is latent it is *tao*, when it is expressed it is literature and poetry. In the mind it is *chih*, spoken out it is words." Then he goes on to say that if this is done well,

Another contemporary writer, Chu Tzu-ch'ing, after consulting and accepting the views of Yang Shu-ta and Wen I-to, summarizes his own view as follows:

The graph *shih* (poetry) does not appear in the shell and bone inscriptions, the bronze inscriptions, nor in the *Book of Changes*. . . . This graph has probably existed only since the Chou dynasty. . . . The graph *chih* 志 and the graph *shih* were not distinguished originally, but by that time there was probably a need to distinguish between the two, so by adding the radical *yen* to *chih* a new graph was made; the meaning of this radical *yen* is precisely what the *Shuo wen* implies when it says "[It is] *chih* expressed in *yen*."

"詩" 這 個 字 不 見 於 甲 骨 文 金 文 , 易 經 中 也 沒 有 。 … 這 個 字 大 概 是 周 代 纔 有 的 。 … "志" 字 原 來 就 是 "詩" 字 , 到 這 時 兩 個 字 大 概 有 分 開 的 必 要 了 , 所 以 加 上 "言" 字 偏 旁 , 另 成 一 字 。 這 "言" 字 偏 旁 正 是 說 文 所 謂 "志 發 於 言" 的 意 思 。[58]

To sum up, it may be said that, except for some less common interpretations which will be discussed later, traditional and contemporary views of the history of the word *shih* generally agree in suggesting that 詩 and 志 were originally graphic variants of the same word and that 之 was the ancestor of both. But these views are based mainly on the semantic values, implicit or explicit, of *shih* found in the classics with inadequate epigraphic evidence. Although we have been able to identify the word 之 in the earliest inscriptions, the intermediate form corresponding to 寺 has been traced only to the bronze and stone inscriptions of the Chou period. Without identification of this main element of 詩 in its earliest form we are at a loss to explain the evolution of 之 into 詩 , and the original meaning of the latter remains unclear. These are problems very difficult to solve. All I shall attempt in the following sections is to establish the missing link and discuss some of its implications.

Identification of 寺 (邿 、 詩) in the Oracle Inscriptions

There is a graph in the oracle inscriptions which has not been identified. It is written in the form 㞢 or 㞢 . Almost all students of the oracle inscriptions know that it is the name of a state located north of Shang but think that there is no such word in the *Shuo wen* or other written records. So it is always

---

"then the emotion will be benefited and personality cultivated." " 隱 之 則 爲 道 , 布 之 則 爲 文 詩 . 在 心 爲 志 , 出 口 爲 辭 . . . . 而 情 得 以 利 而 性 得 以 治 ." 新 語 , chap. 6, "Shen wei" 愼 微 第 六 . (Or punctuate after 文.)

58 Chu Tzu-ch'ing, *Shih yen chih pien*, 1:10. The last statement is based on Yang Shu-ta's theory (see n. 38, above).

copied in its original form in their discussions. In 1914, Lo Chen-yü 羅 振 玉 first listed it as a name of a place but without transcription and identification in his study of the oracle vocabulary and history of Shang.[59] In this he has been followed by all other scholars in this field and by historians of Chinese antiquity.[60]

The graph in question appears on two large oracle bones, photographs of which were first published in 1914 by Lo Chen-yü and reprinted in several other collections (see Figs. 1 and 2).[61] In addition, there are two or three small shell fragments with the graph (see Figs. 3 and 4).[62] From the style of writing and other evidence we can be sure that all these inscriptions belong to the time of King Wu-ting 武 丁 (r. *ca.* 1339– *ca.* 1281 B.C.) of the Shang dynasty, i.e., probably the earliest of the periods from which oracle inscriptions have been discovered.

This graph 坣 or 坣 can be identified with certainty with the later graph 寺 . For convenience of discussion I have transcribed the two large inscrip-

[59] Lo Chen-yü, *Yin-hsü shu-ch'i k'ao-shih* 殷 虛 書 契 考 釋 (1914, 1927), pp. 54, 303.

[60] These include Wang Hsiang 王 襄 , *Fu-shih Yin ch'i cheng wen k'ao-shih* 簠 室 殷 契 徵 文 考 釋 (1925). " 征 伐 篇 ", p. 5b; Kuo Mo-jo, *Pu-tz'u t'ung-tsuan* 卜 辭 通 纂 (Tokyo, 1933), "考 釋", pp. 91, 112; Chu Fang-pu 朱 芳 圃 , *Chia-ku hsüeh Shang shih pien* 甲 骨 學 : 商 史 編 (Shanghai: Chung-hua, 1935), 5:10a–b; Tung Tso-pin, *Yin li p'u* 殷 曆 譜 (Academia Sinica, 1945), 下 編 , 卷 九 , 日 譜 一 , 武 丁 日 譜 , pp. 5b, 40a–b, 41b; T'ang Lan 唐 蘭 , *Yin-hsü wen-tzu chi* 殷 虛 文 字 記 (1934). p. 23a; Ch'en Meng-chia, *Yin-hsü pu-tz'u tsung shu*, pp. 270, 272; Kaizuka Shigeki 貝 塚 茂 樹 , *Kyōto daigaku zimbun kagaku kenkyūsho zō kōkotsu mo-ji* 京 都 大 學 人 文 科 學 研 究 所 藏 甲 骨 文 字 (Kyoto University, 1960), "Text," p. 209; Shirakawa Shizuka 白 川 靜 , *In: kōkotsu-bun shū* 殷 . 甲 骨 文 集 (Tokyo, 1963), Text, p. 9. All the above use the form 坣 without identification. Tseng I-kung 曾 毅 公 lists it in the category of unidentified words in his index to place names appearing in oracle inscriptions, *Chia-ku ti ming t'ung-chien* 甲 骨 地 名 通 檢 (1939), " 待 考 ", p. 9. So do the lexicographers Sun Hai-po, *Chia-ku wen pien* (Peiping: Yenching University, 1934), " 附 錄 ", p. 75a (1965 revised version, 3:18); Chin Hsiang-heng, *Hsü Chia-ku wen pien*, 3:21b and " 說 文 所 無 之 字 ", p. 15b; and Li Hsiao-ting, *Chia-ku wen-tzu chi shih*, 3:0947. See also Li Hsüeh-ch'in 李 學 勤 , *Yin-tai ti-li chien lun* 殷 代 地 理 簡 論 (Peking: K'e-hsüeh ch'u-pan she, 1959), 1:22–23, 3:61–64, 95. Kuo Mo-jo discusses the place in a similar manner in his "P'ing *Ku shih pien*" 評 古 史 辨 (1930) in *Ku shih pien*, vol. 7, pp. 366–367. See also Wu Tse 吳 澤 [Chung-kuo] *Ku-tai shih* 古 代 史 (Shanghai: T'ang-li, 1953), pp. 35, 57.

[61] Fig. 1 is from Lo Chen-yü, *Yin-hsü shu-ch'i ching-hua* 殷 虛 書 契 菁 華 (1914), no. 5. This is also reproduced in Kuo Mo-jo, *Pu-tz'u t'ung-tsuan*, no. 513. Fig. 2 is from Lo's same book, no. 6. It also appears in Shirakawa Shizuka, *In: kōkotsu bun shū*, p. 19. This is also reprinted in Kuo's book, no. 431. All the above items are printed from photographs, except Shirakawa's which is a photoprint from a rubbing.

[62] Fig. 3 is from Lo Chen-yü, *Yin-hsü shu-ch'i hsü-pien* 殷 虛 書 契 續 編 (1933), *chüan* 5, p. 8, no. 1. This has been published earlier in Wang Hsiang, *Fu-shih Yin ch'i cheng-wen* (1925), *chüan* 9, no. 41. Fig. 4 is from Kaizuka Shigeki, *Kyōto* (1960), "Plates," 0306 (Plate 8).

tions and the two fragments into modern Chinese script with punctuation added and have translated them into English. It will be noticed that the original inscriptions are read from the left and down.

Inscription A (Figure 1 — only the lower central portion transcribed)

Four days later,[63] on the day *Keng-shen* [i.e., the thirteenth day of the sixth month in the twenty-ninth year of King Wu-ting in the lunar calendar, or May 27, 1311 B.C. in the solar calendar[64]] there was also an alarm of war[65] coming from the north; Tzu-chien[66] reported

---

Tseng I-kung (*T'ung-chien*, p. 9) and Chin Hsiang-heng (*Hsü*, 3:21b) mistakenly list both the graphs from Wang Hsiang's and Lo Chen-yü's works as separate inscriptions. Tseng also lists a 𩥉 from 明義士 (James Mellon Menzies, of Canada), *Yin-hsü pu-tz'u* 殷虛卜辭 (Shanghai, 1917), p. 77. Chin lists a similar graph from Lo Fu-i 羅福頤, *Ch'uan ku p'ieh-lu ti-erh chi* 傳古別錄第二集 (1928), 2:9. I have not been able to check whether these two are duplicates. Menzies' book is printed from hand-copied versions. All the others mentioned in this note are printed from rubbings.

63 According to the usage in shell and bone inscriptions, when a phrase mentioning a "certain number of days" precedes a date, it indicates the number of days that have passed since an immediately previously mentioned date. In calculating this interval of time both dates are counted. This way of counting the number of days is still popular among many Chinese people.

64 The solar date equivalent to the lunar date recorded in the Shang dynasty is tentatively based on Tung Tso-pin's *Yin li p'u*, 下編卷九，日譜一，武丁日譜, pp. 2a–43b, esp. pp. 4a–9a. The reconstruction of the calendar of the Shang period is certainly disputable. It is fortunate that from the oracle inscriptions we have found three dated lunar eclipses during King Wu-ting's period, and one of them very likely falls in the same year in which T'u-fang's attack on Ssu took place. Tung's dating seems to be supported by a study by Homer Dubs, in "A Canon of Lunar Eclipses for Anyang and China, –1400 to –1000," *HJAS*, 10:2 (1947), 162–178; but Ch'en Meng-chia suggests that this should be in 1229 B.C. see his *Tsung-shu*, 6:215. For Tung's reasoning see his *Yin li p'u*, 下編卷三，交食譜, pp. 1a–35b; and his article "殷代月食考," in *Tung Tso-pin hsüeh-shu lun-chu* 董作賓 學術論著, vol. 2 (Taipei: Shih-chieh, 1962), pp. 847–867.

65 I choose to translate 尌 as "alarm of war" for the following reasons: The *Shuo wen* defines 侸 as 立; the *Yü p'ien* 玉篇 gives 侸 for 侸 and says that it is now written as 樹; the *Kuang yün* 廣韻 identifies 侸 with 尌; the *Shuo wen* also defines 尌 as 立 with the explanation: 寸，持之也，讀若駐. So the graph 侸 may mean a man or woman holding a drum on guard; the drum is for warning. The fact that drums were used by guards for raising alarms is recorded in *Mo-tzu* ("雜守篇") and the wooden slip documents of the Han dynasty (see Lao Kan 勞榦, *Chu-yen Han chien k'ao-shih* 居延漢簡考釋, 1960, "K'ao-cheng," p. 36). The word 侸 is comparable to 戒 (to guard against, to warn), which the *Shuo wen* defines as: 警也，从𠬞戈．持戈以戒不虞. Kuo Mo-jo identifies 尌 as 鼓, which the *Shuo-wen* defines as a night guard with a drum 夜戒守鼓也. This is also very close to the meaning of 侸. See Kuo, *T'ung-tsuan*, 考釋, p. 88.

66 Kuo Mo-jo transcribes the graph as 豩 which is quite different in form (*T'ung-tsuan*, 考釋, p. 112). Tung Tso-pin transcribes it as 嬎 without identification. I think this must be the earlier form of 僭 which is listed in the *Shuo wen* 人部.

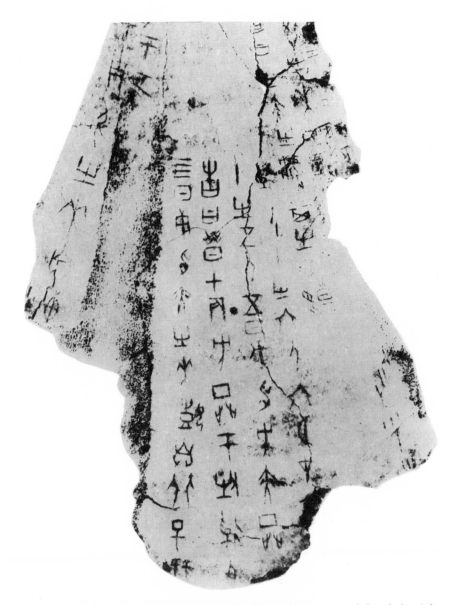

Fig. 1. — Oracle inscription on bone, from the **Shang** dynasty, termed Inscription A in the text (see also n. 61).

saying, "On the last *Chia-ch'en* [i.e., the twenty-sixth day of the fifth month, or May 10] Fang attacked Ssu[67] and captured fifteen men. Five days later, on the day *Wu-shen* [i.e., the first day of the sixth month, or May 15], Fang attacked again and captured sixteen men." In the sixth month [the King] was in [Ch'un].

四日庚申，亦之（有）來戫（值）自北 ； 子姚（僭）
告曰 ：「昔甲辰，方征于寺，俘人
十之（又、有）五人。五日戊申，方亦征，
俘人十之（又、有）六人。」六月，在[亶]。

Inscription B (Figure 2 — only the lower left portion transcribed)

The King divined, asking, "There is killing.[68] Is there an alarm of war coming? Pray descend [to show me]!"[69] Nine days later, on the day *Hsin-mao* [i.e., the fourteenth day of the seventh

---

[67] I have romanized all the graphs according to their modern pronunciations, since the exact manner in which they were pronounced during the Shang period is virtually unknown. Phonologists' efforts to reconstruct the sound system of even the Chou dynasty have not produced conclusive results.

[68] The graph 求 has been mistakenly identified by Lo Chen-yü and Wang Kuo-wei as 求. Kuo Mo-jo accepts Sun I-jang's identification as 希, and thinks that it is loaned as 祟 (evil spirits, calamities). Sun's identification may be acceptable, but the meaning is probably different. The *Shuo wen* defines 希 as a kind of porcupine and gives its ancient form as 希. Under the entry 殺 (to kill) it gives an ancient form 希. This last is probably derived from the name of the animal 希 or it may denote a similar one. At any rate, 求 seems to be closer to 希 (希) than 希 both in form and in meaning. It could sometimes have the meaning 祟. See Yang Shu-ta, *Pu-tz'u ch'iu i* 卜辭求義 (Shanghai, 1954), p. 17a–b.

[69] The graph 三 here has been before identified as 三 (three), 彡 (the name of a sacrifice), 彤 (the sailing of a boat), or 川 (a stream). Later Yü Hsing-wu 于省吾 identifies it as 气 (earlier form of 乞 and 氣). Independently I reached a conclusion similar to Yü's. But he reads the graph in this case as 迄 (reach to, until) and thus punctuates the sentence as 气至九日辛卯 (until nine days later on *Hsin-mao*) (see his *Shuang chien i Yin ch'i p'ien-chih* 雙劍誃殷契駢枝 (1940), "Shih ch'i" 釋气, pp. 55–58). This has been followed by others such as Yang Shu-ta, *Pu-tz'u ch'iu i*, pp. 45b–46a; Shirakawa, *In: kōkotsu-bun shū*, Text, p. 9, and Ch'en Meng-chia, *Tsung-shu*, 2:71. (Tung Tso-pin reads 乞 in the sense 繼, i.e. "continue." See his " 漢城大學所藏大胛骨刻辭考釋 ," 史語所集刊, no. 28, May 1957.) Because 迄 itself means 至 and would be better not to be followed by 至 (爾雅 " 釋詁 "： " 迄：至也." 詩 " 大雅," 245, " 生民 "： " 以迄于今." 毛傳： " 迄, 至也." 尚書 " 召誥 " uses " 越 " as in " 越三日戊申."), because other cases in the oracle inscriptions also show that 迄至 is not needed to express the idea "until" (see 四日庚申 and 五日戊申 in Inscription A and n. 63, above), and because this term is often preceded by a question in divination, 气 should be read in its usual meaning of "implore" or "beg," which Yü recognizes in such cases as 气雨 and 气正 (征). This meaning of the word might have developed from its original sense of sacrificial "vapor" or "air" ascending to the divinities. Hence the word acquired the meaning of "implore.' I suggest, therefore, that 气至 is a standard phrase at the end of a prayer similar to such phrases as 來各 (格) (pray descend!) or 來假來饗 (they [the ancestors] come and enjoy the offerings) (詩 " 商頌 ," 302, " 烈祖 "). Waley translates the latter as: "They come, they accept." Karlgren's translation is "We come forward, we come and present our offerings." In another poem (no. 245) the *Mao Commentary* defines 歆 as 饗. K'ung Ying-ta

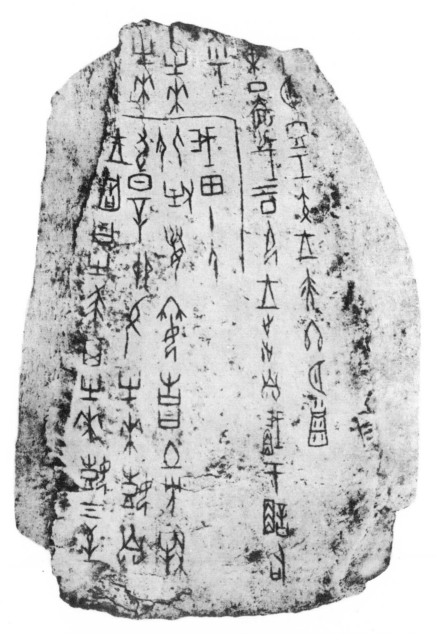

Fig. 2. — Oracle inscription on bone, from the Shang dynasty, termed Inscription B in the text (see also n. 61).

month in the twenty-ninth year of Wu-ting, or June 27, 1311 B.C.], truly there was an alarm of war coming from the north; Ch'i-no[70] of Ssu reported, saying: "T'u-fang invaded our territory and captured ten men."

王固曰：「之（有）希，其之（有）來戜（偉）？乞至！」
九日辛卯，允之（有）來戜（偉）自
北；寺妻娚（娜）告曰：「土方侵
我田十人。」

Inscription C (Figure 3 — only the left portion transcribed)

... Ssu .... also attacked. Captured.... In the sixth month ...

… 寺 …
　… 亦 征　俘 …
　　六 月 …

Inscription D (Figure 4)

.. asked the oracle, "We .... go not .... from Ssu in the fourth month.

… 貞 我 …
　… 行 勿
　　… 从 寺 四 月

The dates mentioned in these inscriptions are so close and the hand so similar that we can be certain that they refer to the same event. Because in A it is recorded that "Fang attacked Ssu," and in B that "Ch'i-no of Ssu reported, saying, 'T'u-fang invaded our territory,'" it is safe to identify the "Fang" in A with the "T'u-fang" in B. Moreover, it is said in A that "Four days later, on the day *Keng-shen*, there was also an alarm of war from the north"; therefore, there must have been a previous alarm on the day *Ting-ssu*, i.e., the tenth day of the sixth month, or May 24, 1311 B.C. It may

---

notes: "歆 means that the spirits and gods eat the vapor (air)." 鬼 神 食 氣 謂 之 歆. The *Shuo wen* also says: 歆，神 食 氣 也. Cf. the graph 餀 (the smell of a sacrificial animal). The *Tso chuan* mentions the term 乞 靈 under the year 471 B.C. (哀 公 二 十 四 年). The *Li chi* mentions the practice of 乞 言 in sacrificial ceremonies (" 文 王 世 子 ").

70 Kuo Mo-jo transcribes this name as 敏 笭 ; Tung Tso-pin and others, 妻 娚 without further identification. I think 妻 is the earlier form of 郪 . The *Spring and Autumn Annals* says that on May 20, 611 B.C., there was a conference in 郪 丘 . (春 秋 經：文 公 十 六 年 六 月 戊 辰，" 盟 于 郪 丘 .") The *Tso chuan* mentions the same. The place was in the state of Ch'i 齊 , and located in the present Tung-o 東 阿 county of Shantung (see Wang Hsien-ch'ien 王 先 謙 , *Han shu pu chu* 漢 書 補 注 , " 地 理 志 " 第 八 上 , 東 郡 , 28A:78a). The tribe later might have moved southward to present Honan. In the Warring States period the state of Wei 魏 had a 新 郪 . The military tally 新 郪 (釁) 兵 符 belongs to about 230–221 B.C. The Han emperors honored the Yin (Shang) remnants in the place and changed its name into 宋 (see Wang, *Pu chu*, 汝 南 郡 , 28A: 6b–7a; also *Shuo wen*, 6B). For the other graph 娚 , see *Ku-lin*, 12B:5575b–5577a.

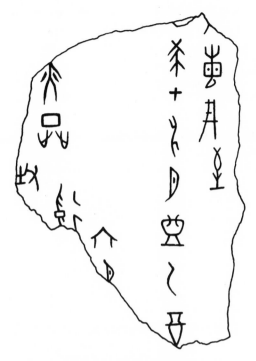

Fig. 3. — Inscription on shell fragment,
from the Shang dynasty, termed Inscription C
in the text' (see also n. 62).

Fig. 4. — Inscription on shell fragment,
from the Shang dynasty, termed Inscription D
in the text (see also n. 62).

even be possible that the *Ting-ssu* alarm resulted from the invasion of the day *Chia-ch'en* and the *Keng-shen* alarm from the invasion of the day *Wu-shen*.[71] From the context we may also infer that Ssu was a dependent state or tribe of the Shang.

The invasion of Ssu by the state T'u started in the third month probably of the twenty-ninth year of King Wu-ting of Shang. Next spring, the king sent Chih Chia 沚戛 , a commander, and others to attack T'u-fang. The war ended in the winter of the thirty-second year with the surrender of T'u. During these four years Shang also waged wars with two other hostile states on its northwestern border. Although the exact chronology of Wu-ting's reign by the Western calendar is, as has been mentioned in note 64 above, still uncertain, the sequence of the events concerning T'u-fang's attack on Ssu during the first year of the war may reasonably be reconstructed as follows (I have omitted the references to the wars with the other two states and some minor events):[72]

Third month (day unknown):

[A diviner] asked the oracle, "The King to make an inspection in Ch'un?" "Small fortune."
[A diviner] asked the oracle, "Should the King not inspect the cattle?" In the third month.

Third month, 18th day (Ting-yu). *March 5*:

Truly there was an alarm of war coming from the west; Chih Chia reported, saying, "T'u-fang attacked our eastern frontier and ruined two regions."
[Two diviners made separate divinations asking the same question:] "This year draft five thousand men to attack T'u-fang. Will we receive grace and protection?"

Fourth month, 5th day (Kuei-ch'ou). *March 21*:

[The diviner] Cheng asked the oracle, "No misfortunes in the next ten days?" The King divined, "There is killing, there is a dream."

Fifth month, 26th day (Chia-ch'en). *May 10*:

A great windstorm .... In the fifth month the King was in Ch'un.
[T'u] Fang attacked Ssu, captured fifteen men. [A][73]

Sixth month, 1st day (Wu-shen). *May 15*:

[T'u] Fang again attacked [Ssu], captured sixteen men. [A][74]

---

71 Kuo Mo-jo, *T'ung-tsuan*, "K'ao-shih," p. 112.

72 The outline is adapted from a table by Tung Tso-pin, *Yin li p'u*, 下編卷九 , 日譜一 , 武丁日譜 , pp. 4a–9a, and *Chung-kuo nien li tsung-p'u* 中國年曆總譜 (Hong Kong, 1960), p. 91. I have made some minor revisions which are indicated in the notes. I have also omitted all the notes on sources which can be found in Tung's *Yin li p'u* except for those inscriptions reprinted above.

73 Tung leaves out this reference under this date.

74 This item is also left out under this date.

Sixth month, 8th day (Yeh-mao). *May 22*:

There is a warning; the people of Shan-ting performed a military ceremony [?] in Lu.

Sixth month, 10th day (Ting-ssu). *May 24*:

[There was an alarm of war coming from the north.] [implied by A][75]

Sixth month, 13th day (Keng-shen). *May 27*:

There was also an alarm of war coming from the north; Tzu-chien reported, saying, "On the *chia-ch'en* Fang attacked Ssu and captured fifteen men. Five days later, on the day *wu-shen*, Fang attacked again and captured sixteen men." [A]

In the sixth month the King was in Ch'un. [A]

Sixth month, 17th day (Chia-tzu). *May 31*:

Truly there was [an alarm of war?] coming from the east.

... Ssu ... also invaded, captured ... in the sixth month ... [?] [C]

Seventh month, 2nd day (Chi-mao). *June 15*:

Divined and asked the oracle: "Order Chih-chia to march?" The seventh month.

Seventh month, 6th day (Kuei-wei). *June 19*:

[A diviner] asked the oracle, "The next ten days no misfortunes?"[76]

The King divined, asking, "There is killing. Is there an alarm of war coming? Pray descend [to show me]." [B]

Seventh month, 14th day (Hsin-mao). *June 27*:

Truly there was an alarm of war coming from the north; Ch'i-no of Ssu reported, saying, "T'u-fang invaded our territory and captured ten men." [B]

Ninth month, 25th day (Hsin-ch'ou). *September 5*:

An evening sacrifice.[77]

Ninth month, 26th day (Jen-yin). *September 6*:

The King was also in silence for the whole evening.

Twelfth month, 4th day (Chi-yu). *November 12*:

[A diviner] asked the oracle, "This year the King to attack T'u-fang?"

Twelfth month, 15th day (Keng-shen). *November 23*:

A lunar eclipse.

Thirteenth month, 17th day (Hsin-mao). *December 24*:

[Diviner] Yung asked the oracle, "In this thirteenth month Chih Chia will arrive?"

---

75 Tung does not list this item.

76 Tung's note number 六 二 (referring to the inscription on p. 21b) must be wrong; it should be 三 九 (on p. 21b), i.e., from Shang Ch'eng-tso 商 承 祚 , *Yin ch'i i ts'un* 殷 契 佚 存 (1933), no. 386.

77 For this and the following item I have adopted Tung's own revised version as listed in his " 漢 城 大 學 所 藏 大 胛 骨 刻 辭 考 釋 " (p. 832). He has assigned them previously under the Seventh Month in *Yin li p'u*.

There are both linguistic and historical grounds for identifying 屮 in the above inscriptions as 寺 . Linguistically, it is a well-known fact that, when the ancient form of writing was transcribed into the clerical form during the third century B.C., the position of a secondary element in a graph was sometimes changed optionally. In fact, the position of such an element in the ancient form itself was often variable. Thus, for instance, the oracle form of the graph 專 *chuan* (to roll, a roll) can be 專 , 專 , 專 , or 專 . The oracle inscription has an unidentified graph 專 . Although it unfortunately exists alone in a fragment with its context entirely lost, I think the graph must be a variant of 屮 and an immediate ancestor of 寺 .[78] The above example, *chuan*, also shows us that the element 又 (modern form: 又 or 手 , a hand) may be transcribed into 寸 (small *chuan* form: 寸 or 寸 , an elbow). Other similar examples abound. Consider, for instance, the graph 得 *te* (obtain) which appears in the following early forms: 得 , 得 , 得 , 得 , or 得 .[79] Actually, in the bronze inscriptions of the Chou dynasty, 寺 was written more often with 又 than with 寸 . The following are some examples.[80]

(a) 寺   (b) 寺   (c) 寺   (d) 寺   (e) 寺   (f) 寺

Ancient pottery inscriptions give the graph as 寺 , 寺 , 寺 , or 寺 .[81] In the *Stone Monuments Inscriptions* this appears in the form 寺 .[82]

In addition, on a piece of silk, written in the area of the state of Ch'u, during the Warring States period (403–221 B.C.) the graph appears as 寺 .[83]

---

[78] For *chuan* see Tung Tso-pin, *Yin-hsü wen-tzu i-pien* 殷虛文字乙編 , 109, 811; Tung, *Chia-pien* 甲編 (1948), 2863; and Sun Hai-po, *Ch'eng-chai Yin-hsü wen-tzu* 誠齋殷虛文字 (1940), 483, respectively. For 寺 see Sun Hai-po, *Chia-ku wen lu* 甲骨文錄 (河南通志 , 文物志之一 , 1937; I-wen reprint, 1958), no. 814.

[79] The first is an oracle inscription from Tung, *I-pien*, 3776. The second and the third are bronze inscriptions from 虢弔鐘 , Lo Chen-yü, *San-tai chi-chin wen ts'un* 三代吉金 文存 (1937), 1:57, and 臼鼎 , *San-tai*, 4:45. The fourth is from a stone inscription made in 221 B.C. 秦始皇帝二十六年泰山刻石 , in Jung Keng, *Shih k'e chuan wen p'ien*, 2:30. The last is from an ancient seal inscription 牛得鈢 , Ting Fo-yen 丁佛言 , *Shuo wen ku-chou pu pu* 說文古籀補補 . Ancient seal inscriptions should not be confused with the so-called "seal" (*chuan* 篆) style, which is not necessarily used on seals and is not necessarily epigraphic.

[80] These are respectively from (a) 洗伯寺𣪘 , *San-tai*, 8:13; (b) 寰㽔𣪘 , same, 10:14; (c) 吳王光鑑 , 安徽省博物館 , 壽縣蔡㽔墓出土遺物 , 39; (d) 邾公牼鐘 , *San-tai*, 1:49; (e) 邿季𣪘 , same, 8:21; (f) 䮂羌鐘 , same, 1:32. All these are listed in Jung Keng, *Chin-wen pien*, 3:32a (163).

[81] The first two 古匋 , in Hsü Wen-ching, *Ku chou hui pien*, 3B:34a; for the remaining two see Chin Hsiang-heng, *T'ao-wen pien*, 3:22a.

[82] *Shih ku wen* 石鼓文 , " 遄車 " and " 田車 ."

[83] Jao Tsung-i 饒宗頤 , 長沙出土戰國繒書新釋 ("A Study of the Ch'u Silk Manuscript: with a new reconstruction of the text") (Hong Kong, 1958); also Shang

In view of these considerations it seems certain that 㞢 should be identified with 寺 .

From the historical evidence of epigraphic and transmitted records we know that during the Chou period there existed a small state named Ssu 寺 . Up to the present at least eleven bronze vessels with such a name in their inscriptions have been discovered.[84]

1. *Ssu Chi ku-kung kuei*　寺季故公設
2. *Ssu Chi li*　寺季鬲
3. *Ssu Po li*　寺伯鬲　(4 similar cauldrons)
4. *Shih Po ting*　郣伯鼎
5. *Shih Po Ssu ting*　郣伯祀鼎
6. *Shih Tsao Ch'ien ting*　郣造遣鼎
7. *Shih Ch'ien kuei*　郣遣設
8. *Shih Ch'ien p'an*　郣遣盤

In the above list, as we can see, the last five vessels give the name of the place as *Shih* 郣 (㝡). This is a late form of 寺 , because the right-hand element *i* 阝 (<邑 , a region, a state) was certainly added as a classifier in order to show that the graph stood for a place name. This was almost standard practice in late Chou. For example, early bronze inscription forms of the place names 邾 , 鄒 , 酇 , 邢 , 鄧 , 廓 , 郊 , 聊 , 鄲 , all occur without the right-hand element.[85] I regard this kind of added element as a pure semantic classifier, which as such ought to be distinguished from principles of graph construction like *hsieh sheng* 諧聲 or *hsing sheng* 形聲 .[86]

Although 寺 and 郣 are pronounced differently in Mandarin as *ssux* and *shih*,[87] their pronunciations probably were similar or very close to each

---

Ch'eng-tso, " 戰國楚帛書述略 ," *Wen-wu* 文物 (Peking, September 1964), pp. 8–20 and illustrations.

[84] Nos. 1, 4, 5. 6, and 7 can be found in Kuo Mo-jo, *Liang Chou chin wen tz'u ta hsi t'u-lu k'ao-shih* 兩周金文辭大系圖錄考釋 (Tokyo, 1935, rev. ed., Peking, 1958), Plates, pp. 222–224; most of them are reprinted from Lo Chen-yü, *San-tai chi chin wen ts'un*, Liu T'i-chih 劉體智 , *Hsiao chiao chin ko chin-wen t'o-pen* 小校經閣金文拓本 (1935), and Tsou An 鄒安 , *Chou chin wen ts'un* 周金文存 (1916). For the rest see Tseng I-kung, *Shan-tung chin-wen chi ts'un* 山東金文集存 (n.d.). For a list of proper names related to 郣 and their bronze sources see Wu Ch'i-ch'ang 吳其昌 , *Chin-wen shih-tsu p'u* 金文氏族譜 (1936), 第二篇 , " 姬姓 ": " 郣氏 ," 1:29b–30a.

[85] See Jung Keng, *Chin-wen pien*, 6:23b–25b (354–358).

[86] See my pamphlet *Shuo "wu-i" yü "lai"*: *chien lun "pi-yeh" yü "kuei-ch'ü-lai hsi"* 說 " 無以 " 與 " 來 ": 兼論 " 必也 " 與 " 歸去來兮 ," mimeographed, 1965), p. 18.

[87] I have added a letter to the romanization in order to indicate its tone for the Wade-Giles system: 1st tone: no mark; 2nd: *q* (i.e., ′); 3rd: *v* (˘); and 4th: *x* (ˋ).

other in pre-Han times. Both the *Ch'ieh yün* 切 韻 and the *Kuang yün* 廣韻 list 寺 in the rhyme category 志 , and 郣 in the 之 category. The *Kuang yün* gives the pronunciation of 寺 as 祥吏切 , the *Ch'ieh yün* as 辝吏反 ; the initials of both these values are voiced dental fricatives in the third division 邪母三等 .[88] The two dictionaries, however, give the pronunciation of 郣 as 書之切 , which implies a voiceless palatal fricative in the third division, i.e., 書母三等 .[89] Bernhard Karlgren reconstructs the "archaic" and "ancient" pronunciations of 寺 and 郣 and lists them with their modern values as follows:[90]

$$寺 \quad *dz\underaccent{\cup}{i}əg \ / \ zi- \ / \ sï$$
$$郣 \quad *ś\underaccent{\cup}{i}əg \ / \ śi \ / \ shï$$

The archaic and ancient values of 寺 are considered dentals, and those of 郣 palatals. As we know now, in the *hsieh-sheng* system dental fricatives in the third division and palatal fricatives in the same division may be related with dental stops. An example is that 似 *dzi̯əg / zi : / sï and 始 *śi̯əg / śi : / shï are related with 治 *d'i̯əg / d̂'i / ch'ï.[91] We have here a very similar phonetic situation, i.e., 寺 and 郣 are related to 持 *d'i̯əg /d̂'i /ch'ï, though we do not consider, as has been said above, 郣 a word constructed according to the so-called *hsieh-sheng* principle.[92] Therefore, it is at least clear that 寺

---

[88] See Liu Pan-nung 劉半農 , etc., eds. *Shih yün hui pien* 十韻彙編 (Peiping, 1936), pp. 17, 192; *T'ang hsieh-pen Wang Jen-hsü K'an-miu pu-ch'üeh Ch'ieh yün* 唐寫本王仁昫刊謬補缺切韻 (1948).

[89] There is, however, one copied fragment of the *Ch'ieh yün* discovered in Tunhuang, i.e, 切 三., which lists the word 郣 as 所之反 (*Shih yün hui pien*, p. 17). Karlgren reconstructs 所 as *si̯o / si̯wo: / so, i.e., a supradental in its archaic and ancient values. Since the *Ch'ieh yün* version is incomplete, we do not know the exact value of the 所 used in the 切 三 . In the *Kuang yün*, 所 belongs to 生母 in the second or third divisions. But the rhyme category 之 in the medieval belongs to the third division; so the value represented by 所之 probably does not belong to the second division. If it does, then, as the 照 category in the second division and the 精 category were related in *hsieh-sheng* and *chia-chieh* in pre-Han times, 寺 and 郣 might be related in a similar manner. For this see Tung T'ung-ho 董同龢 , *Chung-kuo yü-yin shih* 中國語音史 (Taipei, 1954, 4th ed. 1961), 10:172. In many present southern dialects, the graph 郣 is read as *ssu*, like 所 and 寺 , with a dental initial.

[90] Karlgren, *Grammata Serica Recensa* (1957), pp. 253–254, nos. 961m, e′. Karlgren's theory that the ancient initial *z* was developed from the archaic *dz* has been rejected by Tung T'ung-ho; see Tung's *Yü yin shih*, 10:174.

[91] Karlgren, *Grammata*, p. 257, nos. 976h, e′, and z respectively.

[92] *Ibid.*, p. 253, no. 961p; see also Tung T'ung-ho, *Shang-ku yin-yün piao kao* 上古音韻表稿 (史語所集刊第十八本) (Shanghai, 1948), pp. 15, 30, and 125. Yang Shu-ta has suggested that the vowels of the words belonging to the 之 and 咍 rhyme categories were not distinguished in pre-Han times; thus 之 was "read" 臺 , 以 (㠯) read 台 , 寺 read 待 , 持 read 臺 , 時 read 待 , 恃 read 待 , 侍 read 待 , 止 read 戴 , and 詒 , 怡 , 飴 ,

and 郘 are phonologically so close that there is no problem in assuming that 郘 could be used in place of 寺 as a name of a state, even if we refrain from speculating that the pronunciation, or one of the pronunciations, of 寺 was exactly the same as that of 郘 during the late Shang or early Chou times when 郘 was first used.

Furthermore, the graph 寺 (郘) on the vessels listed above has long been recognized as the state 郘 and is mentioned in the *Annals of Spring and Autumn* under the reign of Duke Hsiang of the State of Lu 魯襄公 : "The thirteenth Year [560 B.C.]: In spring, the Duke arrived from Chin. In summer, we took Shih."[93] " 十 有 三 年 : 春 ， 公 至 自 晉 · 夏 ， 取 郘 ."

The *Tso chuan* says in this connection:

In summer, Shih was in disorder and divided into three. A force [was sent from Lu] to rescue Shih, then took the opportunity to take it. When "to take" was used, it means that it was done with ease; it would be called "to subdue" if a large force was used, and "to enter" if the territory was not retained.

夏 ， 郘 亂 ， 分 爲 三 。 師 救 郘 ， 遂 取 之 。 凡 書 取 ， 言 易 也 ； 用 大師 焉 曰 滅 ； 弗 地 曰 入 。

The *Ku-Liang chuan* in this case merely repeats the *Annals*, saying, "In summer, we took Shih." " 夏 ， 取 郘 ."

It is, however, very interesting to notice that the *Kung-Yang chuan*, in referring to the same event, has 詩 for 郘 :

The thirteenth Year [of Duke Hsiang]: In spring, the Duke arrived from Chin. In summer, [Lu] took Shih. What was Shih? It was a district of Chu-lou. Why then was it not recorded in connection with Chu-lou? It was to avoid the mention of an extreme action.

十 有 三 年 : 春 ， 公 至 自 晉 。 夏 ， 取 詩 。 詩 者 何 ？ 邾 婁 之 邑 也 。曷 爲 不 繫 乎 邾 婁 ？ 諱 亟 也 。

This variation in writing is hardly a mistake. The *Han shu* in its "Treatise on Geography" lists K'ang-fu as one of the seven districts of the Tung-p'ing State and Pan Ku himself makes a note following the entry:

Tung-p'ing State: . . . K'ang-fu ([In this district there is a] Shih-t'ing [Shih post station], the ancient site of the State of Shih).

東 平 國 … 亢 父 (詩 亭 ， 故 詩 國) 。[94]

貽 ， 治 were all read 台 . He thinks that the *a* in the diphthong *ai* of the words in the 之 category was later dropped. See his " 之 部 古 韻 證 " in *Ku sheng-yün t'ao-lun chi* 古 聲 韻討 論 集 (1933), also in 積 微 居 小 學 金 石 論 叢 .

[93] Cf. Legge, *The Chinese Classics*, vol. 5: *The Ch'un Ts'ew, with the Tso Chuen*, p. 457.

[94] 漢 書 (*Po-na* ed.), " 地 理 志 下 ," *chüan* 28B, p. 14b.

The *Shuo wen chieh tzu*, under the graph 䢵 *Shih*, reads:

Shih is a dependent state. It is located at the present Shih-t'ing, in K'ang-fu of Tung-p'ing. It is made with 邑 as a root and with 寺 as a phonetic. The commentary to the [*Annals of*] *Spring and Autumn* says, "We took Shih."

䢵 ，附 庸 國 。 在 東 平 亢 父 䢵 亭 。 从 邑 ， 寺 聲 。 春 秋 傳 曰 ： " 取 䢵 " 。 95

Thus Pan Ku and Hsü Shen refer to the same place with different graphs. Later scholars also write it with these variants. For instance, Tu Yü 杜 預 (A.D. 222–284) annotated this passage in the *Annals* by adopting the spelling similar to that used by the *Annals*, the *Tso chuan*, the *Ku-Liang*, and the *Shuo wen*:

Shih is a small state. Now the K'ang-fu district of Jen-ch'eng [in A.D. 84 a part of Tung-p'ing was separated from it and became 任 城 國] has a Shih-t'ing.

䢵 ， 小 國 也 。 任 城 亢 父 縣 有 䢵 亭 。 96

Whereas on the other hand, Li Tao-yüan 酈 道 元 (A.D. 483?–527), in his famous *Shui ching chu* 水 經 注 , follows the version similar to the *Kung-Yang* and the *Han shu*:

In the K'ang-fu ... district there is a Shih-t'ing and it is the location of Shih State of the Spring and Autumn period.

亢 父 … 縣 有 詩 亭 ， 春 秋 之 詩 國 也 。 97

At any rate, we may assert with confidence that 䢵 and 詩 , which are pronounced the same in the *Ch'ieh yün* and the *Kuang yün*, are both later variants of 寺 .

There also seems to be no reason to doubt the Han view that K'ang-fu was the site of the ancient state of Shih (see map), even though the exact

---

95 說 文 解 字 (*Ku-lin* ed.), 6B, " 邑 部 ," p. 2859a–b. I think Tuan Yü-ts'ai has no grounds for suggesting " 按 前 志 當 作 ' 詩 亭 ， 故 䢵 國 .' 許 書 當 作 ' 東 平 亢 父 詩 亭 .' 杜 預 左 注 亦 當 本 作 ' 詩 亭 .' 皆 寫 者 亂 之 耳 . 䢵 ， 詩 ， 古 今 字 也 ." (說 文 注 , *ibid.*) Yang Shu-ta says that the *Kung-Yang* is in the Modern Text version, so it uses 詩 , a graph of the Han times. 蓋 公 羊 爲 今 文 ， 故 用 漢 時 字 也 . But then how can we explain the fact that the *Ku-Liang*, also in the Modern Text, uses 䢵 ? Yang says, "This is probably changed after the *Annals* of the *Tso chuan*." 蓋 從 左 氏 經 改 (積 微 居 金 文 說 , p. 40) He has no evidence to support this assumption. (I wonder whether the graph 傳 in Hsü Shen's passage cited here means *Ku-Liang chuan*.) Ma Tsung-huo 馬 宗 霍 takes a similar view to Yang's in *Shuo wen chieh tzu yin ch'un-ch'iu chuan k'ao* 說 文 解 字 引 春 秋 傳 考 (Peking, 1958), 1:29a–b.

96 杜 預 , 春 秋 左 氏 經 傳 集 解 , 襄 公 十 三 年 經 . (Shanghai: Shih-chieh, 十 三 經 註 疏 ed.), p. 1954.

97 *Shui ching chu, chüan* 8, " 濟 水 篇 ," 荷 水 下 注 .

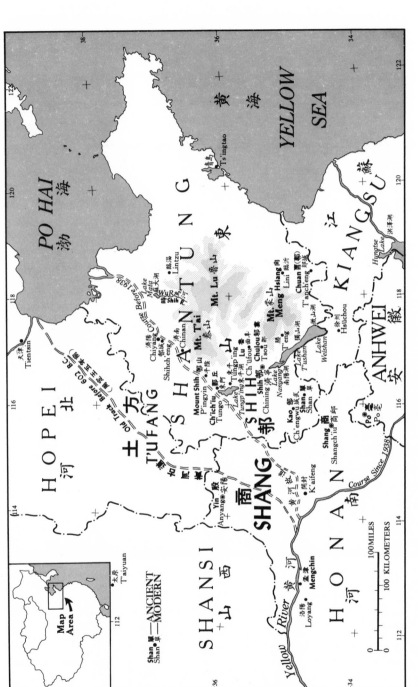

Shang, Shih, and T'u-fang. Map by the University of Wisconsin Cartographic Laboratory.

boundaries of that state can no longer be determined with certainty. K'ang-fu is referred to in the *Chan-kuo ts'e*, which records a conversation between Su Ch'in 蘇秦 (d. 317 B.C.) and King Hsüan of Ch'i (r. 342–324 B.C.) in which the former says that K'ang-fu was a very important strategic pass where neither chariots nor horses could pass abreast, and which a hundred soldiers could defend against a thousand.[98] The *Shih chi*, which also has this story, mentions K'ang-fu again in connection with the collapse of the Ch'in dynasty. It says that in 208 B.C. Hsiang-Liang 項梁 led troops to attack K'ang-fu from the south and defeated the Ch'in forces in the adjacent district of Tung-o 東阿 .[99] Chang Shou-chieh of the T'ang dynasty, in commenting on this passage, cites the *Kua ti chih* 括地志 , a geographical work by Hsiao Te-yen 蕭德言 (A.D. 558–654) and others: "The old city of K'ang-fu lies fifty-one *li* to the south of Jen-ch'eng of Yen-chou." " 亢父故城 , 在兗州任城縣南五十一里 ."[100] A later work, the *I-t'ung chih* 一統志 gives this identification of K'ang-fu in modern terms, placing it "fifty *li* southeast of present Chi-ning Prefecture 濟寧州 ."[101] This has been accepted as the site of the ancient state of Shih by most modern scholars.

But, besides this Shih 郋 , there was also a Shih 郋 in the state of Ch'i, mentioned in the *Tso chuan* under the year 555 B.C. Tu Yü's commentary at that point states: "In the west of the present P'ing-yin there is a Mount Shih." " 平陰西有郋山 ."[102] This, as many commentators maintain, was probably a different place from the state of Shih.[103] Yet, since P'ing-yin is so close to Tung-o, we may wonder whether the K'ang-fu attacked by Hsiang Liang lay there instead of at Chi-ning. This is very possible, since we have known that Tung-o was the location of Ch'i 鄆 , the antecedent of which is mentioned in Inscription B (see n. 70, above). To further complicate the situation, there is, at the present time, a place called Shih-ch'eng 郋城 in Chi-yang county in Shantung, twenty-five *li* to the west of the county seat. The people there traditionally regard it as the location of the ancient state of Shih.

In this connection, we may bring into consideration the sites where the Ssu (Shih) bronze vessels were uncovered. The *Ssu Po li* (no. 3 of the above

---

98 *Chan-kuo* ts'e, " 齊策 ."
99 史記 , *chüan* 7, " 項羽本記 " (會注考證 ed.), p. 12.
100 張守節 , 史記正義 (Chang's preface dated A.D. 736), *ibid.*
101 Cited in Wang Hsien-ch'ien. *Han shu pu chu*, 28B, 2:35a.
102 杜預 , 集解 , 襄公十八年 , p. 1965.
103 Wang Hsien-ch'ien, *Han shu pu chu*, same.

list) was found in the present T'eng 滕 county, the *Shih Ch'ien kuei* (no. 7), in Ch'ü-fou 曲阜 county, both very close to Chi-ning. In 1817, Feng Yün-p'eng secured a bronze tripod *Chou Ch'ien-shu ting* 周遣叔鼎 in Chi-ning. "Ch'ien-shu" is very probably the same person "Ch'ien" who appears on the Shih vessels (nos. 6–8).[104] The *Shih Tsao Ch'ien ting* (no. 6) itself was uncovered in present Tung-p'ing county, which lies between Chi-ning and P'ing-yin.[105] This evidence indicates that the area with the present Chi-ning as its center was the location of the Shih state in the Ch'un-ch'iu period.

This area might also have belonged to the state of Ssu in the time of King Wu-ting of the Shang dynasty, but, as the tribes of that period were often in danger of outside attack and needed to shift periodically to new land for agricultural and other reasons, it is quite possible that the Ssu of Shang times moved on a number of occasions and occupied over a period of time an area much larger than that of the Ssu (Shih) state during the Ch'un-ch'iu period. This movement would have been roughly from north to south because of pressure from T'u-fang, which apparently occupied a large area in the present Hopei, Shansi, and northern Shantung provinces.[106] Therefore, the claim of modern Chi-yang to be an early site of Ssu (Shih) cannot be disregarded.[107]

If the above assumption is true, a serious question arises. Since the oracle bones and shells consulted here were all uncovered in An-yang, which lies to the west of the Shih area, why then do they imply that Ssu lay to the north? It is, or course, possible to say that T'u-fang was to the north of both Shang and Ssu. But when Ssu was attacked by T'u-fang, it could hardly be said, from the point of view of An-yang, that that alarm came from the north.

As is well known, the Shang moved their capital on a number of occasions.

---

104 馮雲鵬, *Chin shih so* 金石索, 金索, pp. 33–34.

105 Tseng I-kung, *Shan-tung chin-wen chi-ts'un.*

106 Cf. Tung Tso-pin, *Yin li p'u*, 下編卷九, 日譜一, 武丁日譜, p. 40b. Ch'en Meng-chia thinks that the Fang in Inscription A is not T'u-fang and that T'u-fang and Ssu lay in present southern Shansi (*Tsung shu*, 8:270–273).

107 In early times the area of Ssu (Shih) might also have included the present Wu River 烏河, which was called Shih River 時水 during the Chou dynasty. The river name 時 appears in the *Chou li, chuan* 33, "夏官：職方氏." I also wonder whether this is the river mentioned in *Ch'u tz'u* "天問," which says, "黑水玄趾, 三危安在?" Some editions have 沚 or 阯 for 趾. The oracle inscriptions have a place name which Yu Hsing-wu interprets as 下危 and regards as one of the 三危. See his *Shuang chien i Yin-ch'i pien chih*, "釋下危," p. 22a–b. 下危 is mentioned very often in Wu-ting's oracles about the time when T'u-fang attacked Ssu.

Different sources record eight changes of location between the earliest times and the conquest of the kingdom by King T'ang, while between his reign and that of King P'an-keng 盤庚, there were five more changes. The exact positions of the sites and their present whereabouts are still a matter for conjecture. We only want to mention here three important places which at one time or another were, without question, used as capitals by the Shang. Two of them, Po 亳 and Shang 商, are south of the Yellow River and to the southwest or south of the Shih state we just discussed. The other one, Yin (present An-yang), is north of the river. There is no question that the former two were used as capitals before T'ang's conquest; whether Yin was so used in that period is uncertain.

What concerns us here is the problem of where the Shang Kingdom, and in particular its capital, lay during the reign of P'an-keng's nephew, King Wu-ting. To answer this question, we have first to settle the question of the location of P'an-keng's capitals, i.e., his old and new capitals. The location of the former is still in dispute. The *Ku-pen chu-shu chi-nien* places it at Yen 奄, which according to some modern scholars, lies in the present Ch'ü-fou 曲阜 or at least in the Chou period state of Lu, i.e., in the southwestern Shantung.[108] Two other sources, the "Preface" to the *Book of History* and the "Chronicle of Yin" of the *Shih chi*, give it another location which Wang Kuo-wei believes to be modern Wen 溫 county in Honan, on the north bank of the Yellow River.[109] As for the place P'an-keng moved to, the *Ku-pen chu-shu chi-nien* and an early citation from the "Preface" to the *Book of History* give Yin or Yin-hsü 殷虛.[110] The "Preface" in its received version, however, indicates that the new capital was Po-yin 亳殷. This could be a corruption of *chai* Yin 宅殷 (made a dwelling at Yin), so it cannot be taken as evidence that P'an-keng moved to Po.[111] But the "Chronicle of Yin" of the *Shih chi* says definitely this is the case:

In King P'an-keng's time, the Yin dynasty has already made its capital in the north of the Yellow River. P'an-keng crossed the River to the south and lived at the old residence of King T'ang. . . . So he crossed the River to the south and ruled from Po. . . . [Later when] King Wu-i ascended the throne [about fifty years after Wu-ting's reign], the Yin dynasty again left Po and moved to the north of the River.

---

108 Chao T'ieh-han 趙鐵寒, "說殷商亳及成湯以後之五遷," *Ta-lu tsa-chih* 大陸雜誌, 10:8 (Taipei, April 30, 1955), 259.

109 Wang Kuo-wei, *Kuan-t'ang chi-lin* 觀堂集林 "說耿," 12:5a–b.

110 Fan Hsiang-yung 范祥雍, *Ku-pen chu-shu chi-nien chi-chiao ting-pu* 古本竹書紀年輯校訂補 (Shanghai, 1956), p. 20; Ch'en Meng-chia, *Shang shu t'ung-lun* 尚書通論 (Shanghai, 1957), pp. 193–197.

111 Wang Kuo-wei, *Kuan-t'ang*, "說殷," 12:5b–7a.

帝盤庚之時，殷已都河北。盤庚渡河南，復居成湯之故居。…
乃遂涉河南治亳。…帝武乙立，殷復去亳，徙河北。[112]

Contemporary scholars from Wang Kuo-wei on, arguing mainly from the
fact that the oracle bones and shells and the ruins of palaces were uncovered
at An-yang, which is believed at least to be a part of the ancient place Yin,
dismiss the account of the *Shih chi* as a mistake.[113]

But there are many other independent sources, such as *San-tai shih-piao*
三代世表, *Ti-wang shih-chi* 帝王世紀, *Shui ching chu*, and *Kua ti chih*,
which all mention that either King Wu-ting or King Wu-i, or Wu-i's father
King K'ang-ting 康丁 did move from south of the river to the north. Yet
modern scholars reject them all, without adducing sufficient reasons.[114]

They accept, on the other hand, two later pieces of historical testimony.
One is Chang Shou-chieh's statement allegedly based on the *Ku-pen chu-shu
chi-nien* to the effect that "From P'an-keng's move to Yin to the extermination
of Chou, the last king, in seven [two] hundred and seventy-three years,
the capital was not moved any more." "自盤庚徙殷，至紂之滅，七
[二]百七十三年，更不徙都."[115] The second is a quotation by P'ei
Yin 裴駰 (fifth century A.D.) from Cheng Hsüan 鄭玄 (A.D. 127–200)
which says that, after P'an-keng moved to Yin, the dynasty changed its
name Shang into Yin.[116]

The above conclusion that Yin was the capital of the dynasty during its
later days is certainly well supported. I only want to point out here, however,
that we still have no confirmation of Chang Shou-chieh's testimony that after
P'an-keng the capital was never changed. The mere fact that oracle documents dating from the reigns of all twelve kings after P'an-keng have been
found at An-yang does not exclude the possibility of the documents having
been brought from elsewhere. Beneath the names of almost all the kings after

---

[112] "殷本紀"（會注本），3:19–24.

[113] Wang Kuo-wei, "說殷"; Tung Tso-pin, "卜辭中的亳與商," *Ta-lu tsa-chih*,
6:1 (Jan. 15, 1953), 11; reprinted in *P'ing-lu wen ts'un* 平廬文存 (Taipei: I-wen, 1963),
chüan 3, p. 288; Ch'en Meng-chia, *Tsung-shu*, 8:252.

[114] See quotations in Ch'en Meng-chia's *Tsung-shu*, 8:252. Ch'en rejects them all as
textual errors.

[115] *Shih chi cheng-i* 史記正義, "殷本紀" (*Po-na* ed.); other editions give 二百七
十五年 or 二百七十三年. See Fan, *Ku-pen chu-shu*, p. 21. In fact, the sentence is not
in the *Chu-shu* style. Wang Kuo-wei merely suggests that this might be a summary by Chang
based on the *Chu-shu*. 雖不似竹書原文，必纍括本書爲之.（"說殷"）He
thought it might be Chang's comment. 國維案：此亦注文，或張守節隱括本書
之語.（古本竹書紀年輯校, 9a).

[116] *Shih chi chi chieh* 史記集解, "殷本紀"（會注本），3:20–21.

P'an-keng, the *Ku-pen chu-shu chi-nien* records the comment "Resided in Yin," 居 殷 , but curiously enough Wu-ting's name is not mentioned at all, or to be more precise, he is not referred to in any of the surviving quotations from that book. This is particularly strange in view of the fact that Wu-ting's reign was one of the longest among the Shang kings and that, as all other evidence attests, he was the most famous and active king after T'ang.

Moreover, some pre-Han records show that Wu-ting stayed in Po in the south. The *Kuo yü* quotes a conversation of Pai-kung Tzu-chang 白公子張 with King Ling (r. 540–529 B.C.) of Ch'u 楚靈王 : "Formerly, King Wu-ting was able to achieve such lofty virtue that he could communicate with the gods. Then he entered the Yellow River area, and from the River he went to Po. There he remained silent for three years to meditate on the *tao*." "昔 武丁能聳其德,至於神明．以入於河,自河徂亳．於是乎三年 默以思道．"[117] The commentator Wei Chao 韋昭 (A.D. 204?–273?) has a note under Po in the text saying, "From the area north to the River went to the capital Po." "從河內往亳都．"[118] We do not know if Wei had any basis for calling Po "the capital," but the *Kuo yü* at least makes it clear that Wu-ting moved from the north of the Yellow River to Po in the south and remained there for at least three years.

Wu-ting's three-year silence is mentioned in several other classics, often referred to as *liang-an* 亮陰 . It is very likely that he had some difficulty of speech and this is sometimes related with his stay outside of the capital.[119]

---

117 國語 , "楚語上 ," (A.D. 1800 reprinting from A.D. 1033 ed.), *chüan* 17, p. 10a.
118 *Ibid.*
119 The term appears in the "Wu-i" 無逸 of the *Book of History* in the Modern Text, in which the Duke of Chou says, "其在高宗 [武丁], 時舊勞於外, 爰暨小人． 作其即位．乃或亮陰,三年不言．其惟不言,言乃雍." The "Yüeh ming" 說命 of the allegedly forged Ancient Text version has similar records. The term also occurs in a number of variants in other classics: 諒陰 (論語 , "憲問 ," 14:40), 諒闇 (禮記 , "喪服四制 "; 呂氏春秋 , "審應 "), 梁闇 (尚書大傳), 亮闇, 涼陰 . The interpretation of the event itself and of this expression has been in dispute for centuries. Early sources imply that Wu-ting's silence was due to his caution in speech. But the Confucians, including the Master himself and Mencius, believe it to be an ancient imperial mourning custom and a political institution. Contemporary Chinese scholars like Hu Shih, Fu Ssu-nien, and Ch'ien Mu have various interpretations. An interesting one is suggested by Kuo Mo-jo, viz., that Wu-ting's remaining dumb for so long might have been caused by a disease, aphasia. His interpretation of 陰 (or 闇) as 瘖 seems to me convincing. Wu-ting did at times, a study of the oracles reveals, have trouble with his speech. But Kuo finds it difficult to understand the graph 亮 or 諒 in the compounds, and makes a conjecture that it meant "definitely" 明確 or "truly" 眞正 . Karlgren defines 亮 in the sense "brightness" and interprets the term as "*liang* the light *yin* was obscured (the ruler withdrawing into seclu-

There is further evidence from the very oracle documents which we have examined that Wu-ting was frequently in the south. The notation, "The king was in Ch'un," appears several times in the inscriptions. Although this place has not been identified precisely, Tung Tso-pin believes that it must have been located between present T'eng 滕 county and Hsü-chou 徐州. The king often made hunting trips to this area.[120] During the first half of the Twenty-ninth Year of Wu-ting, when T'u-fang started to attack Shih, as the oracles show, the king stayed in Ch'un. Since Ch'un was much closer to Po and Shang than Yin, the king's frequent trips to that area might have started from either of the former two places. In any event, when he received the news of the invasion, both Shih and T'u-fang were almost precisely to his north.

Besides this, the time-honored belief that, after P'an-keng moved to Yin, the Shang dynasty changed its name permanently to Yin cannot be confirmed through any reliable evidence. Lo Chen-yü already doubted this long ago and believed that well after Wu-ting's time the dynasty was still called Shang.[121] It is well known that the word *Yin* 殷 does not appear in the oracle inscriptions. Its ancient form 衣 in the oracle inscription stands only for the name of a sacrifice or for a place name. So far, we have not found it used as the name of the dynasty. In transmitted records attributed to the late Shang period in the *Book of History*, we find that after P'an-keng's time the people of the dynasty themselves referred to the dynasty sometimes as Shang and sometimes as Yin.[122] But more important, an oracle inscription

---

sion)." I believe rather that, in this case, the graph should be 𡲢 (small *chuan* form: 𢓊), which the *Shuo wen* defines as "to have hardships in speech when one performs a duty." "事有不善言𡲢也." Hsü Hsüan and others have already pointed out that this character is the ancient form of 亮. See Kuo Mo-jo, *ch'ing-t'ung shih-tai* 青銅時代, "駁 '說儒'" (written May 19–24, 1937), revised in *Mo-jo wen chi* 沫若文集 (Peking, 1962), vol. 16, pp. 129–134; Hu Shih 胡適, "說儒," written in July 1930, *Wen ts'un*, 4th Collection, pp. 18–21, 27–35, 95–103; Ch'ien Mu 錢穆, "駁胡適之說儒" *Tung-fang wen-hua* 東方文化, 1:1 (Hong Kong, 1954); Ts'en Chung-mien 岑仲勉, "三年之喪'的問題," in his *Liang Chou wen shih lun ts'ung* 两周文史論叢 (Shanghai: Commercial Press, 1958) pp. 300–312; Hu Hou-hsüan 胡厚宣, "殷人疾病考," *Chia-ku hsüeh Shang shih lun-ts'ung* 甲骨學商史論叢 (1944); Karlgren, *Glosses on the Book of Documents* (1949), p. 107, also *Loan Characters in Pre-Han Texts*, 2 (1964), 86; *Shuo wen*, 8B, "兄部" (*Ku-lin*), 3905a–3907a.

120 *Yin li p'u*, 下編卷九, 武丁日譜, p. 37a–b.

121 Lo Chen-yü, "殷虛書契考釋序" (dated 1915).

122 Chao T'ieh-han 趙鐵寒 in his "說殷商亳及成湯以後之五遷," *Ta-lu tsa-chih*, 10:8 (Taipei, April 30, 1955), 250–260, suggested that, in these cases, Shang was used when the affairs of the ancestors of the dynasty were being referred to and was imbued with connotations of nostalgia and ancestral piety, whereas Yin was used when

made in Wu-ting's time says, "On the day *Kuei-mao* a divination is made; the diviner Cheng asks, 'This year will Shang have a good harvest?' " "癸 卯 卜 ， 爭 貞 ： ' 今 歲 商 受 年 ? ' "[123] It is very likely that Shang here refers to the kingdom instead of the old capital. The fact that the late Shang people still actually called their kingdom Shang is also evident in the oracle inscription 尸 其 臣 商 .[124]

I might also mention another fact noticed by many. In the oracle inscriptions, when a king went to hunt, it usually says "went" 往 or "went out" 出 , but when he went to Shang, it commonly says "the king entered Shang," 王 入 于 商 , "returned to Shang," 歸 于 商 , "did not return to Shang," 勿 歸 于 商 , "came to Shang," 至 于 商 , or "did not come to Shang" 不 至 于 商 . All these examples belong to Wu-ting's time.

From all these records, it seems reasonable for us to say that Wu-ting moved his residence to the south, i.e., to the old capital Shang or Po, at least temporarily, and that the oracle documents which refer to Shih and which were found at the Yin site, were actually inscribed in the south and later moved to the royal archive at Yin.

This conclusion not only explains well the direction from which the news of the T'u-fang attack on Shih came but also makes the length of time that this news took to reach the court somewhat more credible. As can be seen from the schedule of events given above, in one case it took fourteen days (May 10–24) for the news to arrive, and twelve days (May 15–27) in another. With these records Kuo Mo-jo has estimated that the southern limits of T'u-fang were 1,000 *li* north of An-yang; and Chu Fang-pu estimated 1,200–1,300 *li*.[125] These figures are based on an estimate of 80

---

current events were under discussion and was devoid of such connotations (also in his *Ku shih k'ao shu* 古 史 考 述 , Taipei, 1965). This theory can hardly hold if one considers the following examples: "Shang now will have a calamity" 商 今 其 有 災 , "Shang will probably decline and be exterminated" 商 其 淪 喪 , "Yin therefore became so much declining and decay" 殷 遂 喪 越 (all from " 微 子 "); "The Heaven has terminated its mandate to Yin" 天 既 訖 我 殷 命 , and "The immediate extermination of Yin" 殷 之 即 喪 (both from " 西 伯 戡 黎 "). See also Ch'en, *Tsung-shu*, 8:259,262–264.

123 Jung Keng, *Yin ch'i pu-tz'u* 殷 契 卜 辭 (Peiping, 1933), no. 493; also Kuo Mo-jo, *Yin ch'i ts'ui-pien* 殷 契 萃 編 (Tokyo, 1937), no. 907. There is also the sentence 受 年 商 , in Hu Hou-hsüan, *Chan hou nan pei so chien chia-ku lu* 戰 後 南 北 所 見 甲 骨 錄 (Peiping, 1951), " 師 友 ," 2:47. Ch'en Meng-chia interprets it as 受 年 于 商 (*Tsung-shu*, 3:129). But since we can also find 受 年 王 (乙 編 , 98), which seems to mean 王 受 年 , the above example may be regarded as a structural variant of 商 受 年 .

124 Hu Hou-hsüan, *Chan hou Ching Chin hsin huo chia-ku chi* 戰 後 京 津 新 獲 甲 骨 集 (1954), no. 1220. See also Ch'en, *Tsung-shu*, 8:257–258.

125 Kuo Mo-jo, *T'ung-tsuan*, "K'ao-shih," p. 112; Chu Fang-pu, *Chia-ku hsüeh Shang shih pien*, 5:10a–b.

or 100 *li* per day traveling speed. But in view of the probable difficulties that faced the traveler in Shang times it seems safer to estimate lower speeds. Tung Tso-pin believes that in ancient times troops could move only 30 *li* per day. It is possible of course that a messenger would travel faster. Now it is known that King Chou took at least two days to travel from Shang to Po, which are only 100 *li* apart.[126] At this speed, 50 *li* per day, twelve days would represent a distance of about 600 *li*. This fits well with the assumption that the news was received in Shang or Po, assuming that the T'u-fang attack took place in the north of the Shih region, i.e., around modern P'ing-yin and Chi-yang. On the other hand, however, even from Chi-yang hardly more than eight days would have been needed to bring the news to An-yang.

For all the above reasons, therefore, I feel that the 𠃬 of the Shang oracle inscriptions ought to be identified positively with the 𨙭 of the Chou sources, while recognizing, of course, that the exact boundaries of the state may have changed between Shang and Chou times.

The Origin of the Word 詩 and a Suggested Interpretation

We can now say that 𠃬 is the ancestral form of 寺 , 𨙭 , and 詩 . Since it was the name of a state or tribe in Wu-ting's time, it is very likely that it represented a common word in the language long before the fourteenth century B.C. Extant records, however, are inadequate to tell us what semantic value it might have had at such an early time.

According to epigraphic records of the Chou dynasty, the word 寺 did have various meanings besides its use as a proper name:

1. In the *Stone Monuments Inscription*, which possibly belongs to the eighth or seventh century B.C.,[127] two passages should be noticed:

Now my bow is already waiting [*or* held in position]　　弓兹目 [已] 寺 [待、持] ，
I strike at that bull.　　　　　　　　　　　　　　　　避毆其特 。 [128]

---

[126] Tung Tso-pin, " 卜 辭 中 的 亳 與 商 ," *Ta-lu tsa-chih*, 6:1 (Jan. 15, 1953), 9; also *Yin li p'u*, 下 編 卷 九 , pp. 37, 62. Even during the Han dynasty, as the epigraphic records on wooden strips show, an official messenger's speed was usually set at 4.5 or 6 *li* per hour. (The Han dynasty *li* is roughly a quarter of a mile and the modern *li* ,one third of a mile.) *Chu-yen Han chien chia pien* 居 延 漢 簡 甲 編 , nos. 767, 916. Cf. Mo-tzu, 50.

[127] Chen Chun 震 鈞 and Ma Hsü-lun attribute it to 秦 文 公 三 至 四 年 (763–762 B.C.); Ma Heng 馬 衡 to 秦 穆 公 (r. 659–620 B.C.) 時 ; Kuo Mo-jo to 秦 穆 公 八 年 當 周 平 王 元 年 (770 B.C.). See Kuo. *Shih ku wen yen-chiu* 石 鼓 文 研 究 (Peking, 1955), " 弁 言 ," pp. 4a–5b; " 石 鼓 之 年 代 ," pp. 14b–18b; " 再 論 石 鼓 之 年 代 ," pp. 48a–62b. T'ang Lan attributes it to 422 B.C.; see No Chih-liang 那 志 良 , *Shih ku t'ung-k'ao* 石 鼓 通 考 (Taipei, 1958), pp. 38b–41b, 45a–67b.

[128] *Shih ku wen*, " 避 車 ," Kuo, pp. 70a–b, 28b–29a, 36b. Also No Chih-liang, pp. 84b,

I stretch the bow and wait for shooting.   秀弓寺[待]射。[129]

In both cases 寺 (𠂢) seems to mean "be ready" or "to wait for" 待 .

2. The *Chu Kung K'eng chung* 朱公怪鐘 , which was cast by the middle of the sixth century B.C., has: "The vessel which fits to his lot [social position] is thus held in position [*or* preserved]." " 分器是寺 ."[130] Here 寺 definitely means 持 (to hold, to hold in position, or to support).

3. In the manuscript written on silk in the State of Ch'u during the Warring States period, which we have mentioned before, 寺 is used for the later word 時 (a season, or seasonal) as in 四寺 and 寺雨 .[131] This word 時 , however, already appears in the shell and bone inscriptions in the form 𡿨 , or 𡿨 , and in the pottery inscriptions of pre-Ch'in times, 嗶 .[132]

4. On the 麤氏鐘 the word 寺 appears to be used in the sense 恃 (depend on).[133]

5. On the 竇侯作叔姬寺男段 , the same word seems to have the meaning of 侍 (attend on).[134]

Among the above five values of 寺, the second (to hold) and the last (to attend on) are probably earlier. The unaugmented graph occurs in the latter sense in many classics of the Chou dynasty. The term *Ssu-jen* 寺人 , for instance, appears in the present texts of the "Ch'e lin" 車鄰 in the *Book of Poetry*,[135] of the *Tso chuan*,[136] and of the *Ku-Liang chuan* .[137]

89b–90a. The graph 特 in the sense of a "bull" might have derived from the fact that 生 was related to archery and hunting; see discussion and n. 187, below.

[129] *Ibid.*, " 田車 ." Kuo. pp. 82a, 30a, 36b. Also No Chih-liang, pp. 116a, 123b–125a. In the pre-Ch'in pottery inscriptions there is the graph 𠂢 which is identified as 侍 (see Chin Hsiang-heng, *T'ao-wen pien*, 8:59b). The *Shuo wen* defines the latter as 待 (待也，从人寺). See n. 194, below.

[130] Kuo Mo-jo, *Liang chou*, "Tu-lu," pp. 213–215; "K'ao-shih," pp. 190–191. Chu Kung K'eng died on Feb. 2, 556 B.C. See *Tso chuan*, 襄公十七年春王二月庚午.

[131] See n. 83, above.

[132] From Hu Hou-hsüan, *Chan hou Ching Chin*, nos. 1548, 2483; for the last see Chin Hsiang-heng, *T'ao-wen pien*, 7:49a.

[133] The inscription reads 入䟴 [長] 城先會于平陰武侯寺力. Kuo Mo-jo interprets 寺 as 鄀山 which is close to 平陰 (*Liang Chou*, "Tu-lu," pp. 277a–278a "K'ao-shih," pp. 234a–239a). Liu Chieh·劉節 reads it 恃 (" 麤氏編鐘考," 北平圖書館館刊 , vol. 5, no. 6, reprinted in *Ku shih k'ao ts'un* 古史考存 , Hong Kong, 1963, pp. 90–92). Wu Ch'i-ch'ang reads it 之 (" 麤羌鐘補考," 北平圖書館館刊 , vol. 5, no. 6). Yang Shu-ta agrees with Wu (積微居金文說 , pp. 161–162).

[134] Hsü Wen-ching, *Ku ch'ou hui-pien*, 3B:34a.

[135] " 秦風 ," no. 126.

[136] Hsi-kung 僖公二十四年 (636 B.C.); the *Tso chuan* mentions five 寺人 : 寺人披 (勃鞮，伯楚) (僖五，二十四，二十五); 寺人孟張 (成十七); 寺人柳 (昭六，十); 寺人貂 (僖二，十七); and 寺人羅 (哀十五).

[137] Hsiang-kung 襄公二十九年 (544 B.C.).

In all three cases, however, Lu Te-ming (556–627) in his *Ching-tien shih wen* 經 典 釋 文 (A.D. 583) gives the variant 侍 人 from other editions. It is interesting to note that the term 侍 人 appearing elsewhere in the *Tso chuan* is supported by all the textual evidence.[138] In the *Mencius* there is allusion to a rumor that Confucius once stayed in the home of a 侍 人 in the State of Ch'i. Liu Hsiang (77–6 B.C. or 79–8 B.C.) however, in citing this story in the *Shuo yüan* 說 苑 , edited by him in about 16 B.C., gives the term as 寺 人 .[139]

The author of the poem "Hsiang-po" in the *Book of Poetry* which was quoted earlier referred to himself as 寺 人 孟 子 . Because the *Mao Shih Commentary* explains 寺 (侍) 人 in the "Ch'e lin" as *nei-hsiao-ch'en* 內 小 臣 , and the *Chou li* lists the latter as *yen* 奄 (castrated, or eunuch), and because Cheng Hsüan's commentary on the term in the "Hsiang-po" is garbled, many later scholars have interpreted 寺 人 as "a eunuch." Other scholars, however, maintain that the term merely means "an attendant" or an official, whose duty as listed in the *Chou li*, was to supervise and assist within the palace but who was not a eunuch.

Bernhard Karlgren, in discussing the 寺 (侍) 人 in the "Ch'e lin," notices the two different interpretations. But, in commenting on the view of the *Mao Shih*, he says:

Chouli: T'ien kuan records four functionaries (all eunuchs) of the interior: 內 小 臣 , 閽 人 , 寺 人 , 內 豎 — here the nei hsiao ch'en is distinguished from (and of higher rank than) the si jen. *Chouli* is probably of the 3rd c. B.C., *Mao* is of the 2nd. Neither can be relied on for the details of the early Chou functionaries. Suffice it to say that the si jen 寺 人 was some kind of eunuch functionary of the interior, an attendant.[140]

With all this cautiousness Karlgren still chooses to translate the term as "the eunuch."[141] As a matter of fact, the "T'ien kuan" of the *Chou li* itself does not specify that the four functionaries are "all eunuchs." The *Chou li* indicates all the eunuch functionaries in the book with *yen*, but 閽 人 , 寺 人 , and 內 豎 are not indicated.[142] Moreover, the Mao and Ch'eng commentaries are apparently corrupted and cannot be taken as evidence

---

138 Ai-kung 哀 公 二 十 五 年 (470 B.C.).

139 Chiao Hsün 焦 循 , *Meng-tzu cheng-i* 孟 子 正 義 , *chüan* 9, "萬 章 上 ," pp. 388–392; *Shuo yüan*, " 至 公 篇 ."

140 *Glosses on the Book of Odes* (*BMFEA*, no. 14, 1942, reprinted 1964), p. 210.

141 *The Book of Odes* (1944, 1950), p. 81.

142 The total list of those indicated with *yen* consists of fourteen: 酒 人 , 醬 人 , 籩 人 , 醢 人 , 醯 人 , 鹽 人 , 冪 人 , 內 小 臣 , 司 內 服 , 縫 人 (以 上 " 天 官 "); 舂 人 , 饎 人 , 槀 人 , (以 上 " 地 官 "); 守 祧 (以 上 " 春 官 ").

that *ssu-jen* was a eunuch functionary.[143] But on another occasion, the *Chou li* does mention that "the castrated are designated to guard the interior" 宮 者 使 守 內 ,[144] although we are not sure whether this refers to *nei-hsiao-ch'en* or *ssu-jen*. In addition, according to other records of the Chou period *ssu-jen* was a punished and mutilated man. In the year 636 B.C. the *ssu-jen* P'i 寺 人 披 called himself "a punished subject" 刑 臣 in the *Tso Chuan*[145] and "a criminal" 罪 戾 之 人 in the *Kuo yü*.[146] The *Ku-Liang chuan* also identifies a doorkeeper 閽 as a 寺 人 who was "a punished man" 刑 人 .[147]

On the basis of all this evidence, what we can conclude is that 寺 人 is identical with 侍 人 in the sense of "an attendant," who was usually a punished and disfigured man. It is also possible, however, that he was castrated if his duty was to attend on women. The graph 寺 is the earlier form of 侍 and one of its early meanings must be "attend."[148] In the opinion of some Ch'ing scholars this meaning was derived from the fact that an attendant had to "hold" or serve by using his hands.[149] Through further extension it probably came to mean "depend on" 恃 .

Early classics do not seem to have retained the form 寺 in the sense 持 (to hold) in the manner of the epigraphic documents. But writers in the late

---

143 For this see Ma Jui-ch'en, *Mao Shih chuan chien t'ung-shih*, *chüan* 20, pp. 44b–45a. Although the *Mao Commentary* says that the *ssu-jen* in the "Ch'e lin" is *nei-hsiao-ch'en*, the poem itself is written on the court life of a local feudal state instead of the central government of the kingdom, hence *nei-hsiao-ch'en*, as Ma notices, may be regarded as the *hsiao-ch'en* 小 臣 of the local states mentioned in the *I-li* (*chüan* 6 " 燕 禮 第 六 "). The latter title corresponded in the local governments to the *ta-p'u* 大 僕 in the central government. See Ma, *T'ung-shih*, *chüan* 12, p. 2a–b.

144 *Chüan* 9, " 秋 官 : 掌 戮 ."

145 The 24th Year of Hsi-kung 僖 公 二 十 四 年 .

146 *Chüan* 10, "Chin yü" 晉 語 四 , pp. 267–269.

147 Hsiang-kung 襄 公 二 十 九 年 (544 B.C.). The *Ku-Liang* says: 閽 , 門 者 也 , 寺 人 也 .... 禮 : 君 不 恥 無 恥 , 不 近 刑 人 , 不 狎 敵 , 不 邇 怨 .... 吳 子 近 刑 人 也 . The *Kung-Yang* says: 閽 者 何 ? 門 人 也 , 刑 人 也 .... 君 子 不 近 刑 人 , 近 刑 人 則 親 死 之 道 也 . So if this is the case it is curious that a eunuch is usually close to the sovereign. 閽 and 寺 are also related in other classics; one of the commentaries to the *Book of Changes* says: 艮 爲 閽 寺 (" 說 卦 "). The *Ching-tien shih-wen* notes here that some version gives 閽 for 寺 . Scholars such as Tu Yü and Chu Hsi often consider *ssu-jen* 寺 人 a 奄 官 . In some writings of the Chou and Han times 刑 could mean "castration." See *Tso chuan*, 襄 公 十 九 年 : " 婦 人 無 刑 ."

148 寺 is mentioned with women in a poem of the *Book of Poetry* (no. 264, " 瞻 卬 "): " 時 維 婦 寺 ," on which the *Mao chuan* comments: " 寺 , 近 也 ." Cheng Hsüan's note in the *Chou li*, "T'ien kuan," says: " 寺 之 言 侍 也 . 詩 云 : 寺 人 孟 子 ." This shows that Cheng regards *ssu-jen* in the "Hsiang-po" as an "attendant."

149 See for example Hsü Hao 徐 灝 , *Shuo wen chieh tzu chu chien* 說 文 解 字 注 箋 , in *Ku-lin*, p. 1309b. The graphic element "hand" in 寺 , however, may not be regarded as the origin of the meaning of 侍 ; see my explanation below.

Han period at least give definitions to the word which are quite relevant to "hold" or "support."[150] Moreover, and more interesting, in a few classics of the late Chou or early Han times the word 詩 is used in a similar sense. The *I-li*, in describing the procedure of a gentleman's sacrifice to his ancestor, says that, when the assistant who impersonates the dead in the ceremony holds out a platter of glutinous millet and says a prayer to him, "he with his left hand holding the wine cup, saluting twice and knocking his head, receives the platter; then he returns to position, *shih* and cherishes it in his bosom, wrapping it with his left sleeve . . . " "主人左手執角,再拜稽首, 受;復位,詩懷之,實於左袂 . . . ."[151] Here Cheng Hsüan's commentary on the word *shih* reads: "*Shih* is similar to 'hold'; [the sentence] means to hold and put [the platter] in the bosom." " 詩猶承也;謂奉納之懷 中 ."[152]

In another of the ritual classics, the *Li chi*, the celebration of the birth of a feudal king's crown prince is described with the word *shih* in a similar way. It says that three days after the birth, a diviner "*shih* and carries [the infant] on his back" 詩負之 .[153] Cheng Hsüan also makes a comment here: 詩之言承也 .[154]

I believe that the above two uses of *shih* are not merely equivalent to "hold" or "carry" in the ordinary sense, but also indicate such an action in a specific religious context. Later on 詩 is sometimes defined as "to hold" in general and at the same time has the meaning of "poetry." The *Shih wei han shen wu* 詩緯含神霧 , a prognostic work of the Han dynasty which gives the *Book of Poetry* religious and mystic interpretations, says:

> *Shih* (poetry) is to hold. This means the teaching of honesty and generosity [by the *Book of Poetry*] enables one to hold [firm or in position] one's own heart, and the principle of satire and remonstration [of the same book] may support and hold [firm or stable] the state and the royal house.

> 詩者 ,持也 。在於敦厚之教自持其心 ,諷刺之道 ,可以扶持邦 家者也 。[155]

---

150 *Shih ming*, " 釋宮室 ": " 寺,嗣也.治事者相嗣續於其內也 ." *Feng-su t'ung i* 風俗通義 : " 寺,司也 ;諸官府所止皆曰寺 ." Also the *Kuang Ya*: " 寺, 治也 " (cited in 一切經音義).
151 *I-li chu su* 儀禮注疏 , *chüan* 45, " 特牲饋食禮第十五 ," 十三經注疏 , p. 1185.
152 *Ibid.*
153 *Li chi cheng i* 禮記正義 , *chüan* 28, " 內則 ," p. 1469.
154 *Ibid.*
155 Cited in *Ku wei shu* 古微書 and *Yü han shan-fang chi i-shu* 玉函山房輯佚書 .

This definition of *shih* is also used by the literary critic Liu Hsieh (A.D. 465?–520?) when he says:

Shih (poetry) is to hold: it holds [firm or in position] man's emotion and nature. The central theme of the three hundred odd poems [in the *Book of Poetry*] is [as Confucius says] "without deviation." Hence the meaning of "hold" is to keep [the mind] in agreement [with the rightness] like fitting the two halves of a tally as credentials.

詩者，持也；持人情性。三百之蔽，義歸無邪。持之爲訓，有符焉爾。[156]

Liu's use of the word *fu* 符 (tally) may not be of special significance; but since it also means "a charm," "a spell," or "an auspicious omen," it coincides curiously with the religious meaning of the word *shih* which we have seen above, that is to say, in the sense of holding a sacred object in certain rites or ceremonies.

On the basis of these considerations, I am inclined to hypothesize that the graph 寺 was coined in the sense of "to hold something which indicates the direction or intention of an oracle or omen in certain religious ceremonies." The fact that the graph 寺 is related with religious ceremonies or sacrifices is shown in quite a few cases. A later word *chih* 峙 , which means "a mound on which sacrifices to the heaven and earth are carried out," is made with this graph. [157] There is also the possibility that the 峙 in the *Stone Monuments Inscription* was used in this sense. [158] In another case, 侍 is often employed in the classics to describe the act of serving in religious ceremonies.

---

[156] *Wen-hsin tiao-lung* 文心雕龍 , *chuan* 2, " 明詩第六," 范文瀾注 edition, p. 65; 劉永濟，校釋 (1962) edition, pp. 12–13. Cf. Vincent Shih, trans. *The Literary Mind and the Carving of Dragons* (New York, 1959), p. 32. K'ung Ying-ta in his commentary to Cheng Hsüan's *Shih p'u hsü* 詩譜序 gives three meanings of 詩 : (1) to bear (receive), (2) intention, and (3) to hold; he explains that the poets "bear" the effects of their sovereign's government, write the poems to express their own "intentions," and to "maintain" (i.e. hold) man's proper behavior. 詩有三訓：承也，志也，持也. 作者承君政之善惡，述己志而作詩，爲詩所以持人之行，使不失隊，故一名而三訓也. (*Mao Shih cheng i, Shih-san ching* ed., p. 262).

[157] Chu Chün-sheng points out that in the classics 峙 is sometimes loaned for 庤 , 偫 (both mean "to store") or 沚 (var. 渚 , "an islet"). In the *Tso chuan* the name of a place 平峙 appears several times. Since some editions give 疇 or 壽 for 峙 , Chu thinks 峙 is a mistake (*Ting-sheng*, 5:121; *Ku-lin*, pp. 6198b–99b). But Yen Chang-fu 嚴章福 of the Ch'ing dynasty believes that 峙 here is a variant of 邿 and the place referred to is the 邿亭 , which has been mentioned above (see his *Ching-tien t'ung-yung k'ao* 經典通用考 , cited in *Ku-lin*, 補遺 , p. 940b). If Yen's view is accepted, it will provide one more link between 邿 (詩) and 峙 , a word associated with sacrifice. In Kuo Mo-jo's opinion, in primitive times a storehouse also served as a place for sacrifice or worship.

[158] T'ang Lan, *Chung-kuo wen-tzu hsüeh* 中國文字學 (reprinted Hong Kong, 1963), 26:154. Kuo Mo-jo interprets 峙 here in the sense of a "sty" 庤 (see his *Shih ku wen*, p. 29).

The *Hsün-tzu* says that in a certain sacrifice a hundred offering-carriers served in the west side-room. 五祀，執薦者百人侍西房 .[159] The *Li chi* mentions that in a funeral for a dead official-candidate a clerk must help serve: 士之喪 ，胥爲侍 .[160] And the *Law of the Han Dynasty* specifies, "Those who have [just] seen menses shall not serve in offering sacrifices." "見姅變不得侍祠 ."[161]

Further support for this hypothesis can be gained by analyzing the structure of the graph 寺 itself.

We have already seen that in the oracle inscriptions there is the graph 㞢 . The left-hand element as a root or independent word is possibly written 㞢 , 㞢 , 㞢 , or 㞢 in the bronze and stone inscriptions of the Chou dynasty. The last form was also used in the "small *chuan*" form during the late Chou and Ch'in times. This small *chuan* form is sometimes given as 㞢 . By the end of the third century B.C. when the *li* (clerical) form was established, the word had been transformed into 之 . This is the direct antecedent of the modern 之 .

㞢 is a very common independent graph in the oracle inscriptions, where it seems to occur with a number of variants, of which the following have been suggested by Wu Ch'i-ch'ang (d. 1944):[162] 㞢 , 㞢 , 㞢 , 㞢 (or 㞢). Of these, the first two may be simple graphic variants, but the last, consisting of a "foot" or "footprint" 㞢 and a base line which probably signifies the ground or a position, is recognized by some scholars today as a more primitive form of 㞢 . Although 㞢 and 㞢 are used as distinct and separate characters in many cases in oracle inscriptions, there is also notable evidence in such inscriptions that they were sometimes interchangeable.[163]

---

159 " 正論第十八 ."

160 " 喪服大記 ," 十三經注疏 ed., p. 1580.

161 Cited in *Shuo wen*, 12B, 女部 姅 ; see Ma Tsung-huo, *Shuo wen chieh tzu yin ch'ün-shu k'ao* 說文解字引羣書考 , 2:31b–32a.

162 吳其昌 , *Yin-hsü shu-ch'i chieh-ku* 殷虛書契解詁 (Peiping, 1934–1937, reprinted Taipei, 1960), pp. 4–6.

163 Hu Kuang-wei 胡光煒 points out that in the oracle inscription no. 2918 of Menzies' *Yin-hsü pu tz'u* appears the sentence: 㞢 于 㞢 . See Hu's *Chia-ku wen-li* 甲骨文例 (Canton, 1928), and Chu Fang-pu, *Wen-tzu pien*, 2:7. Kuo Mo-jo thinks 㞢 is 之 and differs from 㞢 . I believe this is true in most cases. But Wu Ch'i-ch'ang believes the phrase " 徣 㞢 于 " should be regarded as similar to " 徣 于 㞢 ." See his *Chieh-ku*, p. 5. In pottery inscription 之 is often written 止 or 㞢 ; but in P'u Ju's 溥儒 *Ku t'ao t'a-pen* 古陶搨本 (no. 192), it appears as 㞢 . The relationship between 㞢 and 㞢 , it seems to me, is still not well established, almost like the relationship between 㞢 and 㞢 as discussed in the text below. It is not impossible that 㞢 is closer to 㞢 than to 㞢 . Plants, life, and fertility could have been objects of worship in early times. It is also possible that 㞢 is simply a different graph having no etymological relation with the other two. I must acknowledge that my interpretation in the following passages is tentative.

Perhaps due to the difficulties of carving on shells and bones, the graph ᵂ ,
like many others in such inscriptions, is a linear simplification of the earlier
pictograph which is still preserved in bronze inscriptions. The following
examples provide a partial view of the evolution of the graph:[164]

Bronze: ♥ , ♂ , ᵂ , ∨ , ᵠ , ᵠ
Stone: ⨖
Small *chuan* form: ⨖
Clerical form: ⻊ , ⻌
Modern: 止 (止)

From the fact that, in some compound graphs in the oracle inscriptions,
as is shown in 先 and 往 below, the base line is optional, we may assume
that ᵂ might be the original form of ᵠ (and ⨖). Distinguishing the two
characters by adding the line probably involved a long process. This line,
as both the bronze inscriptions and the transcribed records of the Chou
dynasty show, had been established in an overwhelming number of cases
as a necessary element for the character which was later transcribed as 之 .[165]
It is also possible that the modern 止 was a descendant of ᵠ and antecedent
of 之 , and that, as the descendant of ᵂ without the base line, its historically
correct modern form should be 止 .[166] The two words 之 and 止 in both

---

164 The bronze graphs are from *Chih chih* 彶 觶 (Shang dynasty), *Cheng kuei* 征 毁 (in
上 海 博 物 館 藏 青 銅 器 , 1964, 附 冊 , p. 3), 卣 文 (in Jung Keng, *Chin-wen pien*,
p. 887), *Fu I ting* 父 乙 鼎 (*ibid.*), *Ya hsing tsun* 亞 形 尊 (in Hsü Wen-ching, *Ku chou*,
2A:34b), and 尨 毁 (*ibid.*). The stone graph is from 石 鼓 文 , " 田 車 ." For the small
chuan see *Shuo wen*. The first clerical form is from Ma Heng, *Han shih ching chi ts'un*, 漢 石 經
集 存 , 圖 版 , p. 85; see also Ch'ü Wan-li, *Chou I ts'an-tzu chi-cheng* 周 易 殘 字 集 證 ,
2:19a; the second is from Lao Kan, *Chu-yen Han chien*, Plate, no. 562–3A, on p. 47.

165 Karlgren says that the graph ᵂ "is mostly used both in the bone and the bronze
inscriptions as loan for the homophonous 之 in its various meanings." (no. 961). He also
considers ⨖ a variant of ᵂ (no. 962). These points do not seem quite true. ᵂ (ᵠ) and
⨖ are distinguished in both types of inscriptions. (The *Tzu-chang chung* 子 璋 鐘 has 之 as
⨖ , but it is still distinguishable from ᵠ .) The fact that 先 has both variants as its upper
part in the oracles proves that this is possible in compounds. Also, his identification of
the ⨖ in the 中 (南 宮) 鼎 (no. 961d) and the 止 in the 小 克 鼎 (no. 961e) as ᵠ is
doubtful. It might be 之 , because in both texts the graph appears in the phrase 之 年 .
His reference to the oracle graph ᵠ (no. 961c) which he says appears in *Yin-hsü shu-ch'i
ch'ien-pien* 殷 虚 書 契 前 編 , 7:19, 1, appears to be inaccurate, because there we can only
find a ᵂ , which should be transcribed as 涉 . (This may be a mistake copied from Sun
Hai-po, *Chia-ku wen pien*, 6:5b.) See Karlgren, *Grammata Serica Recensa*, pp. 253–254.

166 Yü Hsing-wu points out that the 止 in the Sung dynasty and later editions of the
Book of Poetry appeared as 止 in all earlier editions. Some of these, he suggests, should be
止 in the sense of "a foot" or "to stop"; others should be 止 , i.e. 之 . See his article " 詩 經
中 「 止 」 字 的 辨 釋 ," *Chung-hua wen shih lun-tsung* 中 華 文 史 論 叢 , vol. 3
(Shanghai, 1963), pp. 121–132.

medieval and modern times possess similar phonetic values, differing only in tone, the former in the "even" and the latter in the "rising" tone. Whether this tonal difference existed in these two words during the early Chou and late Shang times is still unknown.[167]

Another alleged graphic variant of 屮 in the oracle inscriptions, 丫 , has been denied as such by Ch'en Meng-chia and others in later studies, and is identified as a different word, i.e. modern 生 (to beget, to grow, birth, life, etc.)[168] This is probably correct.[169] But the confusion of 屮 and 丫 seems to have taken place at a very early date, perhaps since the Shang dynasty. Evidence for this is provided by characters in which they occur as elements. Notice for example the variants in oracle inscriptions of the following two graphs:[170]

先 (*hsien*): ꁯ , ꁰ , ꁱ
往 (*wangv*): ꂐ , ꂑ , ꂒ , ꂓ

Further evidence may be found by comparing the different forms of three graphs which represent words related to divination or sacrifice. The first example is a graph which has among others the following forms:[171] ꂔ , ꂕ , ꂖ . At least from the small *chuan* on, this graph has been transcribed into a form essentially resembling 叡 in the sense of divination. This means that the upper left part has been regarded as 出 (go out), of which the bronze form is ꂗ and the oracle form, ꂘ . Two other examples are the following graphs which in their early stages sometimes had the same meaning:[172]

---

167 Karlgren reconstructs the pronunciations of 止 as *t̯i̯əg / t́si: / chǐ and those of 之 as *t̯i̯əg / t́si / chǐ. See *Grammata*, pp. 253–254. See also Tōdō Akiyasu 藤 堂 明 保 , *Kanji gogen jiten* 漢 字 語 源 辞 典 (Tokyo: Gakutōsha 学 燈 社 , 1965), pp. 69–74.

168 *Tsung-shu*, 3:117–118.

169 Wu's reason for identifying the two graphs is that the sentence pattern of " 求 丫 于 高 妣 丙 " (前 編 , 3:33, 3) and " 丫 于 高 妣 □ " (續 編 , 2:15, 2) is similar to that of " 屮 于 高 妣 庚 " (燕 京 , no. 287). But actually this similarity does not guarantee that 丫 and 屮 had the same meaning.

170 For *hsien* see *Yin-hsü wen-tzu chia pien*, nos. 3338, 2874, and 7767, respectively. For *wangv* see *ibid.*, 799; *Fu-shih Yin ch'i cheng wen* 簠 室 殷 契 徵 文 , 10:46; Chin Tsu-t'ung 金 祖 同 , *Yin ch'i i-chu* 殷 契 遺 珠 (Shanghai, 1939) 493; and *Yin ch'i ts'ui-pien*, 1169, respectively. For additional examples see 峀 in Hsü Wen-ching, *Ku chou*, 7B, 1b–2a; 紫 and 襚 in *Shuo wen* and inscriptions.

171 *Ch'ien-pien*, 1:8, 5; 1:18, 3; *Chia-pien*, no. 2416, respectively.

172 For *feng*, the oracle form is from *Chia-pien*, no. 2902; the bronze: *Shao-po Hu kuei* 召 伯 虎 敦 ; the ancient seals: Ting Fo-yen. *Shuo wen ku chou pu pu*; the rest in *Shuo wen*, 13B. For *pang*, the oracle is from *Ch'ien-pien*, 4:17, 3; the bronze: *Shu Pang ting* 叔 邦 鼎 , *Feng ting* 封 鼎 , *Yü ting* 盂 鼎 , *Mao-kung ting* 毛 公 鼎 ; the ancient seal: Ting Fo-yen, *Pu pu*; the rest in *Shuo wen*, 6B.

封 (*feng*, to sacrifice on a mound, a fief):
   Oracle: 𡉚
   Bronze: 𡉙
   Ancient seal stamp: 𡉉 , 𡉙
   Ku-wen (ancient graph): 𡉉
   Chou-wen: 𡉙
   Small *chuan*: 𡉙
邦 (*pang*, a state):
   Oracle: 𡉚
   Bronze: 𡉙 , 𡉙 , 𡉙 , 𡉙
   Ancient seal stamp: 𡉙
   Ku-wen: 𡉚
   Small *chuan*: 𡉙

From these examples the confusion of 屮 and 止 is quite obvious. It is also interesting to notice this in several explanations in the *Shuo wen*. Hsü Shen regards the left-hand part of 封 as a combination of 之 and 土 , which is the same as 𡉙 (往). In spite of this, he defines 𡉙 as "grass and trees grow wildly." He also mentions that both 邦 and the *chou-wen* form of 封 contain the element "grass." Moreover, in his definitions of 止 , 之 , 出 , and 生 , he considers them all as having their origin in a picture of a grass stalk or a plant. It is easy for us to understand that 生 (small *chuan*: 𡉙) is made of a blade of grass above the earth. Hsü defines 之 as 出 也 . He also defines both 出 and 生 as 進 也 . Thus all these words mean "go forward." Grass and plants, as he explains, grow in such a manner. In this way he seems to have regarded the element 屮 in the graph 生 as close to 止 , which he defines in the sense of a "foundation" or a "foot," i.e., the picture of a grass stalk or a plant with its lower part shown.[173] Although in the definition of 正 he says, "A human foot is also a 止 " (足 者 亦 止 也), he still seems to believe that the original meaning of 止 is the bottom of a grass stalk or a plant.

With this long history of confusion, it is very difficult to say with certainty that 屮 had no connection with the formation of 出 in the early days. But from the evidence of the oracle inscriptions and later records, it seems more likely that 𡉙 is the original element of 出 . At any rate both 屮 and 𡉙

---

173 *Shuo wen*, 6B: " 往 : 艸 木 妄 生 也 , 从 之 在 土 上 "; 2B: " 止 : 下 基 也 , 象 艸 木 出 有 址 , 故 以 止 為 足 "; 6B: " 之 : 出 也 , 象 艸 過 屮 , 枝 莖 益 大 , 有 所 之 , 一 者 地 也 "; " 出 : 進 也 , 象 艸 木 益 滋 , 上 出 達 也 "; " 生 : 進 也 , 象 艸 木 生 出 土 上 ."

have been used as elements of words denoting some kind of sacrificial function.

These points will be clearer, if we consider the meanings represented by 出 and its variants in the shell and bone inscriptions. The first six of the meanings given below are generally known and are mainly based on studies by Sun I-jang 孫 詒 讓 (1848–1908) and Wu Ch'i-ch'ang.[174] The seventh is an addition of my own:

1. The name of a sacrifice, usually to an ancestor but sometimes to the gods, or to make such a sacrifice (similar to 祭). 出 出

2. "To offer," usually an animal or animals, in (such?) a sacrifice (similar to 侑 or 用). 出

3. "To go" or "to arrive at" (similar to 往 or 至). 出

4. "To have," or "there is" (similar to 有). 出

5. "And" as used in "ten and five" (i.e., fifteen) (similar to 又). 出

6. "This" or "such" (similar to 此 or 是). 出

7. "Blessing," "blessed," or "fortune" (similar to 祉). 出

The seventh meaning is based on my interpretation of the frequently used term in the oracles: *Shou chih yu* 受 出 又 . Following the interpretation of Wang Kuo-wei and Lo Chen-yü, recent scholars are almost unanimous in reading the term as 受 此 祐 (receive this help, protection, or happiness). Only Hu Kuang-wei and Kuo Mo-jo interpret 出 as 有 (to have).[175] There is also in the inscriptions the shorter term 受 又 . We also can find in the oracle inscriptions such terms as 受 年 , 受 又 年 , 受 禾 年 , and more interesting, 受 出 年 . This last phrase is obviously a parallel expression to the 受 又 年 . As the latter means "to receive a helped (or prosperous) year," it seems better to interpret the former as "to receive a blessed (or happy) year." There may exist an oracle phrase 受 出 , in which 出 must mean "blessing" or the like; but the phrase seems to be fragmentary. Yet there is the case " 王 受 又 隹 出 ," in which 隹 (維) may mean "and" 與 as is used in some classics.[176] The character 止 in the classics, in my opinion, sometimes stands for 祉 (blessedness, happiness). In the "Ta ming" of the *Book of Poetry*, 止 in the lines " 文 王 嘉 止 , 大 邦 有 子 " seems better

---

174 Sun I-jang, *Ch'i-wen chu-li* 契 文 舉 例 (1917); Wu Ch'i-ch'ang, *Chieh-ku*, pp. 6–11.

175 See Lo Chen-yü, *K'ao-shih*, pp. 300–301; Wu Ch'i-ch'ang, *Chieh-ku*, pp. 10, 252–255; Ch'en Meng-chia, *Tsung-shu*, 9:313–316; 17:568; Hu Kuang-wei, *Wen-li*; Kuo Mo-jo, *Ts'ui-pien*, "K'ao-shih," 138b; Chin Hsiang-heng, *Hsü Chia-ku wen pien, chüan* 4, appendix 1, 35b.

176 Lo, *K'ao shih*; Chin, *Hsü*, 46b. The 受 出 年 appears in *Yin-hsü wen-tzu i-pien* 殷 虛 文 字 乙 編 , 3290 and others; Chin mixes it up with 受 又 年 . See also Ch'en, *Tsung-shu*, 16:525–529, 532–535, 540. There is a case " 我 逐 豕 , 出 又 ." (Kuo, *Ts'ui-pien*, no. 948).

interpreted in this sense.[177] In the same book the line "*Chi tuo shou chih*" 既 多 受 祉 (Has received abundant blessing) appears twice. The *Mao Commentary* interprets 祉 here as 福 . It might also mean "reward."[178] There is also the line "*Chi shou ti chih*" 既 受 帝 祉 (Has received God's blessing). Cheng Hsüan interprets the word as Mao does. In the *Book of Changes* both 祉 and 祐 are used as oracle terms.[179] In a mirror inscription of the Ch'in or Han period, there is also the term "*shou ta chih*" 受 大 祉 (receive great blessing).[180] Moreover, the words 祉 and 又 (右) are sometimes still used in close relationship in the classics. The "Yung" of the *Book of Poetry* has " 綏 我 眉 壽 ， 介 以 繁 祉 ， 既 右 烈 考 ， 亦 右 文 母 ，" though the 右 here may only mean "to wait on."[181] All these suggest that 受 止 又 should be interpreted as 受 祉 祐 (receive blessing and help). That the graph 止 acquired the meaning "blessing" from its earlier meaning "a sacrifice," is actually easy to understand. A parallel development may be found in 福 (good fortune, happiness), the oracle form of which depicts a jar for wine 畐 , either by itself or with two hands holding it 𥄕 , in a sacrificial ceremony, and the meaning of which during the Shang dynasty was such a sacrifice.[182] The *Shuo wen* actually defines 福 as 祐 (又) which, as has been shown above, was closely related with 止 in the oracles. The term 祉 福 also appears in the *Book of Poetry* (no. 269).

Of the seven meanings of 止 , the third (to go) seems to be the one most directly related to the idea of "a foot" or "a footprint" carried by the com-

---

Here 止 could be interpreted as "to have" (see Ch'en, *Tsung-shu*, 3:130), but 祉 祐 might also be considered two verbs or a compound verb. For 受 止 see Wang Hsiang, *Fu-shih Yin-ch'i cheng wen*, 游 1:3; Lo Chen-yü, *Hsü-pien*, 3:10, 1. For 受 又 佳 止 see Li Ya-nung 李 亞 農 , *Yin ch'i chih i hsü-pien* 殷 契 摭 佚 續 編 (Shanghai, 1950), 141; Hu Hou-hsüan, *Chan-hou nan pei so chien chia-ku lu*, "wen," 100. The existence of a 𦰩 (*Chia-pien*, no. 2947) may not exclude the possibility that 止 has a similar meaning, just as the case of 福 shown below.

177 No. 236, 大 雅 : " 大 明 ." Several Chinese commentators interpret 止 here as " rite" (禮), and particularly "a wedding." Waley translates the lines as "Wen wang was blessed. A great country had a child." Karlgren thinks Waley's interpretation of *chia* 嘉 as "blessed" can scarcely be supported; so he follows the *Mao Commentary* and renders the lines as "Wen Wang was fine; and in a great state there was the young lady." Both consider 止 a particle almost without meaning. I prefer to interpret the lines as "It was King Wen's fine blessing that a great country had the young lady [as his consort]."

178 No. 177, "Liu-yüeh" 小 雅 : " 六 月 "; no. 300, "Pi-kung" 魯 頌 : " 閟 宮 ."
179 No. 241, "Huang-i" 大 雅 : " 皇 矣 ." *Chou I* 周 易 , nos. 11, 12, and 14.
180 " 子 孫 順 息 家 富 戠 ， 予 天 無 極 受 大 祉 ," from *Chiao-wang Chü-hsü ching* 角 王 巨 虛 鏡 (Ch'in-Han period), in *Ch'ang-an huo ku pien* 長 安 獲 古 編 , cited in Huang Fin-hung 黃 賓 虹 , *Pin-hung ts'ao t'ang hsi yin shih wen* 賓 虹 草 堂 鉥 印 釋 文 .
181 No. 282, 周 頌 : " 雝 ."
182 Lo Chen-yü, *Yin-hsü shu-ch'i k'ao-shih*, 2:17a-b; Yang Shu-ta, *Pu-tz'u ch'iu i*, 38b.

ponent 止. With the combination of a footprint and a line below, the notion of "going in a certain *direction*" seems to be conspicuous. Meanings 1, 2, and 7, which all have religious connotations, may be related to this in the sense of "the *direction* in which supernatural powers *tend*," hence (*a*) a ceremony which reveals, (*b*) an offering which elicits, or (*c*) a blessing which results from such a *tendency* or *intention* of those powers. In this connection it is interesting to notice the later use of 坒 in the highly religious classic *Mo-tzu*, where 天 之（志）"the Will (intention, or law) of Heaven" might well be understood in the sense of "the Tendency of Heaven."

In interpreting the origin and evolution of related graphs such as we have here, we must of course acknowledge the difficulties of judging whether they are merely phonetic loans or semantic extensions. Chinese philologists in the past usually tended to emphasize semantic extension, particularly with regard to the more basic graphs created in early times. To a certain degree this seems to be justifiable, as the meaning and the sound of a word are closely related and most of the early Chinese characters are pictographic and ideographic. In our case, i.e., with a group of early graphs consisting of the basic element 屮, it seems likely that they all developed from a meaning which the ancients chose to represent with a picture of "a foot" or "a footprint." This fundamental meaning may very well have been "a sign." A Chinese legend relates the invention of the script itself to "footprints." Hsü Shen in his postscript to the *Shuo wen* says: "The Yellow Emperor's scribe Ts'ang Chieh, observing the footprints of birds and animals, and recognizing that their patterns could be distinguished from one another, invented the written language." "黃帝之史倉頡，見鳥獸蹄迒之迹，知分理之可相別異也，初造書契．"[183]

Though this is hardly satisfactory as a total explanation of the origin of the Chinese script, it reflects an ancient feeling for animal tracks as a kind of communication. To primitive people footprints presented information, in particular the direction from which blessings in the form of food might come or in which danger in the form of wild animals or an enemy might lie. The oracles of the Shang dynasty often ask 𠂤（屰、迉）(sign of harm) or 亡屰 (no sign of harm).[184] The *Shuo wen* in defining the graph 它 (a

183 *Shuo wen*, 15A. A similar view appears in Wang Ch'ung's *Lun heng* 論衡 "感應篇," Kao Yu's commentary to *Lü-shih ch'un-ch'iu*, "君守篇" and to *Huai-nan-tzu*, and many later works, see Kuei Fu 桂馥 (1733–1802), *Shuo wen chieh tzu i-cheng* 說文解字義證, in *Ku-lin*, p. 6744b. See also Huang K'an 黃侃 (1886–1935), *Huang K'an lun hsüeh tsa chu* 黃侃論學雜著 (Peking: Chung-hua, 1964), pp. 1–4.
184 See Kuo Mo-jo, *Yin ch'i ts'ui-pien*, nos. 11, 61, and 75, "K'ao-shih," p. 4b; Yang Shu-ta. *Pu-tz'u ch'iu i*, pp. 13b–14a. The upper element of the graph may of course represent

reptile, a snake) says, "In antiquity, people lived in swamps and suffered
from snakes, so they often greeted each other with the question: 'No snakes
(harm)?'" "上 古 艸 居 多 蛇，故 相 問：無 它 乎？"[185] Modern scholars
believe that this greeting is similar to the question appearing in the oracle
inscriptions. The combination of a footprint or trail with a snake here is
self-explanatory. Moreover, footprints could tell the ancient people the
location, direction, and movement of nomadic hunters. Such symbols
might also be useful for marking and helping to remember the way.

Therefore, it seems very possible that the ancients regarded these signs
as a natural written language and imbued them with all the supernatural
powers as ascribed to spells and later to other writings. As a legend circulated
by the royal house of the Chou dynasty says, the lady Chiang Yüan 姜 嫄 gave
birth to Ch'i 棄 , the ancestor of the Chou tribe or virtually of humanity,
after she trod on the big toe of God's (or "a giant's," according to another
version) footprint in the field and was inspired. In Wen I-to's opinion, this
legend of Chiang Yüan's impregnation may refer to a sacrificial ceremony
concerned with the cultivation of the land in which she was supposed to
have performed a symbolic dance of following the "footsteps" of a priest
impersonating God, with whom she then had sexual relations. Wen also
relates the sacrifice to 時 and suggests that the surname of the Chou royal
house, Chi 姬 , is also written as 址 , which implies "born from a footprint."
In quite a few writings of the Han dynasty, there is a similar story which
says that the legendary Emperor Fu Hsi 伏 羲 who is credited with the
invention of the eight trigrams, which were considered to be the predecessor
of the written language, was born after his mother Hua Hsü 華 胥 trod
on a huge footprint in a marsh in a place which was identified as lying in or
around the 郤 area. Wen I-to believes Fu Hsi and Ch'i probably belonged
to the same tribe. In a recent study, Yü Hsing-wu dismisses the idea of
sacrifice. Citing the example of a rock pit in the shape of a huge footprint
on Adam's Peak in southern Ceylon, which has been worshiped by many
religious people, Yü thinks that the Chiang Yüan legend reflects the common
practice of footprint worship by the primitives as described by modern
folklorists and that it might have developed from ancient totemism. In
this connection I also would like to draw attention to the fact that traditional-

---

a foot instead of a trail or direction, and so the graph may mean "the harming of a foot."
But considering the fact that the word 迆 means go awry or out of a straight line (see
Shuo wen and *Kuang Ya*), I am inclined to interpret its original meaning as "the arrival or
trail of a snake" and hence a potential harm.
[185] *Shuo wen*, 13B, 它 部 .

ly the people of 郤 were considered descendants of the tribe which had 姬 as its surname.[186] And more important, in these legends the power of a footprint to cause birth seems revealing in view of the relationship between the graphs 𝕍 and 𝚈 in writing as we have discussed above.

If the graph 𝚿 had been ascribed to some supernatural power, then it would also be possible to use it as a concrete ceremonial symbol. The *Book of History* cites a decree by King P'an-keng of the Shang dynasty, in which he solicits the people to behave according to a certain goal or standard as one is guided by a target or marker in archery. 若 射 之 有 志 .[187] The graph 志 in the sense of an object in archery also appears in the *I-li*, where the term 志 矢 is mentioned in connection with a standard funeral for a knight.[188] The *Erh-ya* defines 志 as "an arrow with bone head and untrimmed feather." 骨 鏃 不 翦 羽 謂 之 志 .[189] In ancient China archery was closely related to sacrifice and divination. The classics on rites say that archery was practiced before sacrifice or divination was made, and actually the outcome of an archery contest decided who were eligible to attend a sacrifice.[190] We are not sure whether the meaning of 志 (i.e. 𝚿) as a target or marker in archery and sacrifice was derived from the graph 𝚿 in the sense of a sacrifice, or vice versa. But it is quite possible that 𝚿 had denoted a concrete object in ceremonies. We have mentioned above the graph 叙 . The *Shuo wen* defines it by saying, "The people of Ch'u used 叙 in the sense of 'asking for an omen by divination.' It is formed with a hand holding a 祟 ." " 楚 人 謂 卜 問 吉 凶 曰 叙 . 从 手 持 祟 ."[191] The same book defines 祟 as "a misfortune caused by gods."[192] Lo Chen-yü already noticed that a misfortune could not be held in the hand and hinted that it might be some concrete object used in a divination or a sacrifice.[193] In a sense, the case of 寺 may be similar

---

186 *The Book of Poetry*, no. 245, "Sheng min" 大 雅 " 生 民 "; *Shih chi*, 4, Chou pen-chi 周 本 紀 ; Wen I-to, " 姜 嫄 履 大 人 跡 考 ," in *Ch'üan-chi*, vol. 1, " 神 話 與 詩 ," pp. 73–80; Yü Hsing-wu, " 詩 ' 履 帝 武 敏 歆 ' 解 ," *Chung-hua wen shih lun-tsung*, 6 (Aug. 1965), also Wu Ch'i-ch'ang's work as cited in n. 84, above; Lü Ssu-mien 呂 思 勉 , *Hsien-ch'in shih* 先 秦 史 (1941), 6:53–54; and Ts'en Chung-mien, " 周 初 生 民 之 神 話 解 釋 " in his *Liang Chou wen shih lun ts'ung*, pp. 1–17.

187 " 盤 庚 上 ." See n. 128 above.

188 *Chüan* 13, " 既 夕 禮 ": " 志 矢 一 乘 , 軒 輖 中 亦 短 衛 ."

189 Chap. 6, " 釋 器 ."

190 See *Li chi*, chap. 46, " 射 義 "; chap. 11, " 郊 特 性 "; *Chou li*, 夏 官 , " 司 弓 矢 "; also Ch'en Meng-chia, " 射 與 郊 ," *Ch'ing hua hsüeh-pao* 清 華 學 報 , 13:1 (April 9, 1941), 115–126.

191 3B, " 手 部 ." Cf. Yü Hsing-wu, *Shuang-chien-i Yin ch'i p'ien chih*, p. 43a, " 釋 叙 ."

192 1A " 示 部 ": " 祟 , 神 禍 也 ."

193 *Yin-hsü shu-ch'i k'ao-shih*, *chüan* 2, p. 18a–b; also Chu Fang-pu, *Wen-tzu pien* 3:9a–b; Yang Shu-ta, *Pu-tz'u ch'iu i*, p. 47b.

to that of 尌 . That is to say, adding a hand 又 (寸) to the symbol 止 may be interpreted as the holding of such a sign or object in a ceremony.

Nevertheless, before this addition, 止 or even 止 must have been used in the sense of 寺 for some time. Yang Shu-ta has suggested that the frequently employed graph 祉 in the bronze inscriptions should be identified as 侍 .[194] This reminds us of the statement in the *Shuo wen* which says, " 𡉞 is a simplified ancient form of 詩 ." Although we still have not found direct epigraphic proof for this statement, we may acknowledge that it is quite reasonable to have such an ancient form without the hand element. The tribe which during Shang times was named by the graph 㞢 might have used the left-hand element as its totem sign or to indicate its desire for blessings from the supernatural power. Whether the hand element was added much earlier than the graph was adopted as a propor name still remains a question. In the oracle inscriptions there are also the terms 止 邑 , 止 族 , and 屮 白 . Whether this area, tribe, and prince were related with 㞢 is not clear to us.[195] We know from the classics, however, that the graph 又 (有) had the meaning of "state" or "area."[196] It was very often used at the beginning of a name of a tribe or state (probably to indicate the owner of something) in ancient China, such as 有易 (有鳫) , 有任 , 有娀 , 有苗 , 有夏 , 有商 , 有周 . If we follow this practice, the title 㞢 might be regarded as 有 之 as well as 寺 .

We may also notice here that both 止 and 又 have the meanings "to have" and "and." It is also curious that the phrase 受 止 又 consists of the two elements of 㞢 . The graph 止 as the name of a sacrifice was widely used during King Wu-ting's time. But, when his younger son Tsu-chia 祖 甲 came to the throne, the word in this sense was substituted with 又 , which before had usually been used in the meaning of "prosperity" or "help."[197]

---

[194] *Chi-wei chu chin-wen shuo, chüan* 1, p. 22; *chüan* 5, pp. 131–132. The oracle inscription has " 多 子 其 祉 學 ?" Ch'en Pang-huai 陳 邦 懷 interprets 祉 as " 徙 ." See his *Yin-tai she-hui shih-liao cheng ts'un* 殷 代 社 會 史 料 徵 存 (Tientsin, 1959), *chüan* 2, pp. 9b–10a. I wonder whether this may also mean 侍 . The *Ts'ang Chieh p'ien* 蒼 頡 篇 defines 侍 as 從 也 (cited in 華 嚴 經 音 義 下). See also n. 129, above.

[195] See *Yin-ch'i i ts'un* 殷 契 佚 存, 627; *Chan hou Ching Chin hsni huo chia ku chi* 戰 後 京 津 新 獲 甲 骨 集, 3078; Chin Hsiang-heng, *Hsü chia ku wen pien*, 13:10a, appendix 1, 41b. I wonder whether 止 邑 is an early form of 郣. 之 , 時 , and 詩 were all surnames during Han and later times. See also Ch'en Meng-chia, *Tsung-shu*, 9:322–323, 329. Ch'en does not identify 止 , but he thinks that another place name 㞢 , which denotes a hunting area, is the same as 㞢 (*ibid.*, 8:270, 272, 330). This last point is still uncertain.

[196] The term 九 有 in the sense of 九 域 appears in a number of classics such as *The Book of Poetry*, no. 303, 商 頌 , "玄 鳥 "; *Kuo yü*, "楚 語 "; *Hsün-tzu*, chap. 21, "解 蔽 ." See Liang Ch'i-hsiung 梁 啓 雄 , *Hsün-tzu chien shih* 荀 子 簡 釋 , p. 289.

[197] Tung Tso-pin, *Yin li p'u*, 上 編 卷 一 , pp. 3a–4a; 卷 三 . pp. 13a, 14a; also *Chia ku hsüeh liu-shih nien*, 4:115.

From this fact we might infer that prior to Tsu-chia's time the graph or element 又 probably already had had some connections with sacrifices.

On the other hand, it is also quite interesting to notice that 寺 is made with the symbols for a foot *and* a hand. As we have cited earlier, the "Great Preface" of the *Mao Shih* in its explanation of the meaning of poetry with reference to singing and dancing, says, "when singing is inadequate, one may unconsciously express them [emotions] in dance by gesturing with one's hands and beating with one's feet." The author of this passage probably was not conscious of the etymology of 詩 as he wrote it, but the word does coincidentally contain the elements "foot" and "hand" in its ordinary form. We should not ignore that fact that ancient odes were often sung and chanted accompanied with dance and gesture. When the ancient Chinese used 寺 as a graph or element to indicate poetry, it is not impossible for them to have had this fact in mind. Charms, prayers, and oracles, such as those included in the *Book of Changes*, are often made in rhyme or rhythm, and probably were at one time chanted or sung with dance and gesturing. A few oracles in the shell and bone inscriptions are also in simple verse form and could be chanted in such a manner. This is certainly one of the reasons for the classification of the religious odes in the *Book of Poetry* under the title *sung* 頌 , which meant songs accompanied with acting or performance.

But besides dance and gesture, the ancients might also have grown conscious of the accompanying musical elements and the wishes expressed in their ceremonial performance. As has been shown above, we are quite sure that both 詩 and 志 are derived from the single element 㞢 . If Ch'ien Tien's assumption cited in note 43 above is true, 詩 and 志 would really have been the same word during a certain stage of its development. The ancients sometimes used the elements 言 and 心 with similar implications; thus 訧 and 忨 are only different forms of a single word, as are 訴 and 忻 , and 說 and 悅 . More instructive is the last pair, because it occurs in an earlier form simply as 兌 . The reasons for adding such elements are sometimes very obscure. For instance, the two ancestors of the Shang royal house, 王亥 and 王亙 in the oracle inscriptions, appear as 該 and 恆 in later records.[198]

In the case of 詩 , however, the addition of the element 言 (big flute, hence "word," "speech") to the graph 寺 seems easy to understand. The difficult question is when it was added. Although the graph 詩 is not found in the Chou bronze inscriptions, it probably exists in a slightly different form. The *Ch'u Wang Hsiung-chang chung* 楚王能章鐘 which was evidently

---

198 See Wang Kuo-wei, " 殷卜辭中所見先公先王考 ," *Kuan-t'ang chi lin*, *chüan* 9, pp. 4a–8b.

made in 433 B.C., has a sentence, " 其 永 㲋 用 旨 ." A similar bell made on the same occasion has the same sentence but the third graph appears as ᛃ .[199] Juan Yüan 阮 元 (1764–1849) and his disciple Chu Wei-pi 朱 爲 弼 transcribe it as 峕 .[200] Kuo Mo-jo transcribes it as 峕 and says: " 峕 is a variant of 詩 , and here is loaned as *ssu* 寺 . *Ssu* means 'to preserve.' The *Chu Kung K'eng chung* says, 'The vessel which fits to his lot is thus preserved.' " " 峕 乃 詩 之 異 , 此 假 爲 寺 . 寺 , 守 也 . 朱 公 牼 鐘 : ' 分 器 是 寺 .' "[201] Since this identification is uncertain and still in dispute, the graph does not seem to have been noticed by many. Jung Keng does not include it in his *Chin-wen pien*. I think 峕 is not merely a variant of 詩 , it may even be an earlier form. Nor is it here loaned as 寺 . Instead, it is probably used in its original meaning, such as the 詩 used in the books on the Rites. These bells were cast on the occasion when King Hui of Ch'u 楚 惠 王 (r. 488–432 B.C.) made a sacrifice to one of his ancestors, before he moved his capital. On many bronze sacrificial vessels " 其 永 保 用 旨 " (forever preserve it and use it for making offerings) is used as a standard ending. But for bells such endings sometimes make reference to the bell's special function, such as " 永 保 鼓 之 " (forever preserve and toll it) or " 其 聿 其 言 " (be rhythmic and harmonic). It may be noticed that besides the inscription on the *Chu* bell which ends with 寺 and the two *Ch'u* bells which have 峕 , the latter graph also appears on *Tseng Hou chung* 曾 侯 鐘 as 㞢 and ᛃ and on *Ch'i Hou i* 齊 侯 彝 as 㞢 .[202] Except for the last, all of these are bells, i.e., musical instruments. It seems possible then that because such an instrument was used in certain sacrificial ceremonies to accompany songs, the graph 峕 became suitable to such vessels. In the *Book of Poetry* there is a poem describing a presacrificial archery ceremony which we have referred to above. Bells are mentioned as being used in that ceremony. In the poem there is the line " 以 奏 爾 時 ." Waley suggests: " 時 for 詩 ?" and translates the line as "that you may perform your songs." I think he is correct and suggest further that the graph might have been 峕 and mistakenly transcribed 時 as Juan Yüan has done in the bronze inscriptions.[203] A development similar to that from

---

199 Kuo Mo-jo, *Liang Chou*, pp. 179b–180b.

200 *Chi-ku chai chung ting i ch'i k'uan shih* 積 古 齋 鐘 鼎 彝 器 款 識 (嘉 慶 九 年 刊 本 , 1804) *chüan* 3, pp. 16b–18b.

201 Kuo, *Liang Chou*, "K'ao-shih," p. 166a.

202 Wang Li-ming 汪 立 名 of the Ch'ing dynasty, *Chung ting tzu yüan* 鐘 鼎 字 原 , cited in Hsü Wen-ching, *Ku chou*, 7A:2.

203 詩 , no. 220, 小 雅 , " 賓 之 初 筵 ." Waley, *The Book of Songs*, p. 295, "Notes," p. 29. Ma Jui-ch'eng supports the *Mao Commentary* definition 時 , 中 者 也 by citing the *Ta Tai li* 敎 士 履 物 以 射 .... 時 以 斅 伎 . 時 有 慶 以 地 , 不 時 有 讓 以 地

寺 to 峙 can be seen in the graphs 又 (𠂇) and 右 (𠮢) . The *Shuo wen* says that 𠮢 means "the hand and the mouth help each other." " 手口相助也 ."[204] The graph is later written 佑 or 祐 (to help, to protect). A magic word, a prayer, or a laborer's song all coming from the mouth were believed to have the power to do things as a hand does. This symbol 口 as an element is sometimes interchangeable with 言 in epigraphs and usually stands earlier than the latter. For example, the *chuan* and later forms have the graph 詠 , but the bronze and oracle inscriptions only give 咏 . Indeed, 言 is scarcely employed as a root and never as a "classification element" in the shell and bone inscriptions. So far as the records show, we may doubt whether the form 詩 exists in them at all.

As a tentative conclusion, perhaps we may suggest that the Chinese word *poetry* develops from the basic symbol ㄓ to 㞢 and 𡳾 (寺), with the meaning of a particular action in a sacrifice accompanied with a certain sign, music, songs, and dance. Later, when the aspect of music, song, and words was emphasized, 峙 was coined, and the latter ultimately became 詩 .

Poetry probably begins with man's spontaneous expression of emotions. The primitive men's strong emotions and desires are expressed through magic and ceremony-making. When they stamp in a strange rhythmical dance around a camp fire and mark the beat with cries and grunts, they are making a spell, in the hope that their prayer, their imitation of animals, or nature's sounds and gestures will provide them power over animals or nature and fulfill their wish. This kind of magic-making or mimic hunt is believed by many modern writers to be the beginning of art, of, for instance, music, poetry, painting, and the drama.[205] It is therefore very natural that the ancient Chinese adopted for "poetry" a word associated with sacrifice or an action in religious ritual.

As we know, the earliest men lived mainly by instinct, and one of the strongest instincts of mankind is the instinct to create things, to make things. Magic and religious ceremonies were believed to be able to satisfy this instinct. In the earliest days the magicians were probably also the fighters

---

(" 虞戴德第六十九 ") and the *Li chi* 射中者得與於祭，不中者不得與於祭．不得與於祭者有讓，削以地；得與於祭者有慶，益以地 (" 射義第四十六 "). I tend to believe that this 時 is also 峙 which means to ring a bell, make some music, or sing a song when one hits the target in archery.

204 3B, " 又部 "; the same entry also appears in 2A, " 口部 ," where Hsü Shen defines it as " 助也 ."

205 See for example C. M. Bowra, *Primitive Song* (London, 1962), chaps. 2, 5 9, and 10; C. Day Lewis, *Poetry for You* (New York, 1954), pp. 12–20.

and doers of the tribe, and most of its members probably participated in magic-making.[206] But those who were physically handicapped, and prevented from making and doing practical things, were compelled to find some other outlet for their creative instincts. So, with their abnormally developed sensibility and imaginative faculty, they made images of things by sounds or signs. We believe this is how the first poets were born. To a certain extent, as Homer in ancient Greece, the blind in ancient China, according to many classics, also performed the function of poetic chanting, music-making, or record-keeping.[207] It then may not be an accident that a "disfigured attendant" (寺 人) was also a poet (詩 人) and that perhaps the two were called by the same name 寺 人 . The disfigured attendant in the *Book of Poetry* might have been just carrying on this long tradition of poetry-making.[208]

---

[206] James George Frazer, ed. with notes by Theodor H. Gaster, *The New Golden Bough* (New York, 1959), pp. 5 ff.

[207] For the blind person's function in poetry and music in ancient China see *Book of Poetry*, no. 280, 周 頌 , " 有 瞽 "; *Tso chuan* , 襄 公 十 四 年 (559 B.C.) : 師 曠 對 晉 侯 曰 : " 史 爲 書 , 瞽 爲 詩 "; *Kuo yü,* " 周 語 上 ," 邵 公 [邵 康 公 之 孫 穆 公 虎] 告 周 厲 王 (r. 878–842 B.C.): " 天 子 聽 政 , 使 公 卿 至 於 列 士 獻 詩 , 瞽 獻 曲 , 史 獻 書 , 師 箴 , 瞍 賦 , 矇 誦 , 百 工 諫 , 庶 人 傳 語 , 近 臣 盡 規 , 親 戚 補 察 , 瞽 史 教 誨 , 耆 艾 修 之 , 而 後 王 斟 酌 焉 ." " 周 語 下 ," 魯 成 公 十 七 年 (574 B.C.) 單 襄 公 謂 成 公 曰 : " 吾 非 瞽 史 , 焉 知 天 道 "; same: 伶 州 鳩 對 周 景 王 (r. 544–520 B.C.) 曰 : " 古 之 神 瞽 , 考 中 聲 而 量 之 以 制 , 度 律 均 鍾 , 百 官 軌 儀 "; *Chou li* " 春 官 ": " 瞽 矇 : 掌 播 鼗 , 柷 , 敔 , 塤 , 簫 , 管 , 弦 , 歌 , 諷 誦 詩 , 世 奠 繫 , 鼓 琴 瑟 , 掌 九 德 六 詩 之 歌 , 以 役 大 師 ." same: " 大 師 ": " 大 祭 祀 , 帥 瞽 登 歌 , 令 奏 擊 拊 ." Also Ch'en Pang-huai, *Yin-tai she-hui shih-liao cheng ts'un*, " 敎 瞽 矇 ," *chüan* 2, pp. 8b–9a.

[208] In this connection I would like also to point out a possible coincidence in the early histories of the words for "poetry" in ancient Chinese and Greek. It is a well-known fact that the Greek word ποιεῖν (*poiein*: "to make," "to do") is the origin of the words ποίημα (*poēma*: "anything made or done," "poem") and ποιητής (*poiētēs*: "a maker," "a poet"). That is to say, a poet composes a poem as a carpenter makes a table. I do not know when the word *poēma* started to have this literary meaning, but at least Plato already uses it in the sense of "a poetical work" or "a poem." The root *poi* can be traced to the Indo-European *quei* (variant: *quoi*). And the Greek word ποίη (Ionic), which means "grass," seems very close in sound to the root of the word "poetry," just as the Chinese graphs discussed above are very close in form.

The Chinese word 詩 does not seem to derive from sources with the meaning "to make." Yet we still can find some comparable explanations. In the *Book of Poetry* the composition of a poem or song is mentioned at least eight times, and each time the word *tso* 作 (to make) is used, e.g. 作 誦 , 作 歌 , 作 爲 此 詩 . (Chu Tzu-ch'ing cites twelve passages, but I find that four of them do not directly refer to "composing" a poem or a song. See his *Shih yen chih pien*, pp. 3–5.) Similar examples can be found in other classics. In both oracle and bronze inscriptions there is the title of a functionary 乍 冊 (a recorder), whose duty is to make records. (*Ch'ien-pien*, 4:23, 3, etc.; see Ch'en Meng-chia, *Tsung-shu*, 15:518.) No other functionaries have 乍 in their titles in pre-Ch'in times. A close one is the 柞 氏 in the *Chou li*, whose duty is to take care of forests (攻 木). The word 作 in the classics is often defined as 爲 (do, make), 始 (start, create), or 生 (beget). To make handicraft or to till the land may be called 作 , and in divination to prepare the tortoise shells is called 作 龜 . (*I-li*, " 士 喪 禮 "; *Chou li*, " 大 卜 "; *Li chi*, " 郊 特 牲 .")

   As we know, the word 作 in epigraphs is written 乍 , and the *Shuo wen* defines the latter as 止 也 . If that were the case, the word 作 would be immediately related to the basic root of 詩 . We do not know on what authority Hsü Shen bases himself in this definition. The oracle inscriptions have 乍 in the form 乚 , ㇏ , or probably 𢦏 . The bronze inscriptions sometimes give 乚 but more often 乚 . This last form certainly resembles 止 . More interesting is the fact that 乍 in the bronze inscriptions also has the form 㞢 , 㞢 , or 㞢 . (The first graph is in 楚 王 能 肯 鼎 , the rest in 能 肯 簠 ; Kuo, *Liang Chou*, Plates, p. 185, also 補 遺 ; "K'ao-shih," p. 170.) This last form resembles 㞢 very closely. Ma Hsü-lun wonders whether the foot symbol 止 on the bronze vessel *Mu yu* 母 卣 might mean 乍 (see his " 中 國 文 字 之 原 流 與 研 究 方 法 之 新 傾 向 ," in *Ma Hsü-lun hsüeh-shu lun-wen chi* 馬 叙 倫 學 術 論 文 集　 Hong Kong, reprinted 1963, pp. 13–18).

   On the other hand, some bronze inscriptions give 作 in the form of 㞢 or 㞢 . (姑 氏 𣪘 and 仲 鑠 盨 , in Jung Keng, *Chin-wen pien*, 8:4b; cf. Kuo Mo-jo's explanation cited in Li Hsiao-ting, *Chi-shih*, 2637–41.) These seem to indicate a hand holding a knife and other tools. The foot symbol in *Mu yu* also actually follows a picture of carving tools, which Ma regards as the graph 契 (a notch knife, to cut and carve [tortoise shells for divination], hence a written record). It is also interesting to notice that the *Mo-tzu* often regards the 天 志 (the Heaven's will or law) as a wheel-maker's compass and a carpenter's square (see " 天 志 " 上 , 中 , 下).

The *Yüan-hun Chih* (Accounts of
Ghosts with Grievances):
A Sixth-Century Collection of Stories

ALBERT E. DIEN

THE origin of Chinese fiction and the novel has been traced to the early short stories dealing with the supernatural, popular during the Six Dynasties Period (A.D. 220–581), and fully developed by the T'ang.[1] The *Yüan-hun chih* 冤 魂 志 by Yen Chih-t'ui 顏 之 推 merits our attention, for, compiled in the Sui, it is one of those works which provided a transition between the early origins and the full flowering of this genre. It also serves as a unique source for material on the society of the time. Finally, an examination of this collection against the background of the intellectual milieu of the period will require us to revise the judgment of modern critics who classify it simply as Buddhist propaganda.[2]

The compiler of this collection of stories, Yen Chih-t'ui (531–*ca.* 591), was a member of a Shantung family which had gone south in 317, when

---

[1] James R. Hightower, *Topics in Chinese Literature* (Harvard University Press, 1950), pp. 76 ff.

[2] Recent studies of the *Yüan-hun chih*, now known as the *Huan-yüan chi* (hereafter *HYC*) include the following:

a) Chou Fa-kao 周 法 高 ,"Yen Chih-t'ui *Huan-yüan chi* k'ao-cheng 顏 之 推 還 冤 記 考 證 ," *Ta-lu tsa-chih* 大 陸 雜 誌 , 22:9 (1961), 1–4, 22:10 (1961), 13–18, and 22:11 (1961), 14–22. These are referred to as Chou, 1; Chou, 2; and Chou, 3 in the notes below.

b) A Tun-huang fragment, Bibliothèque nationale, no. 3126, has been reproduced in *Tun-huang pi-chi liu-chen hsin-pien* 敦 煌 秘 籍 留 眞 新 編 , pp. 101–109. It was entitled *Ming-pao chi* 冥 寶 記 , but its fifteen stories are all in *HYC*. The scroll has an inscription dated 882, and is important both for textual reasons, and because it may well follow the original sequence of the stories. The following items are concerned with this fragment.

c) Wang Chung-min 王 重 民 , *Tun-huang ku-chi hsü-lu* 敦 煌 古 籍 叙 錄 (Peking: Commercial Press, 1958; revision of the 1936 edition).

north China fell into the hands of the nomads. The Yen family maintained its status as one of the lesser émigré clans by the learning of its members, and through it, their service in the southern courts. As a young man, Yen Chih-t'ui was made prisoner during the wars between the south and the north, and was taken to Ch'ang-an. He managed shortly to escape to the northeast, to the Northern Ch'i, where he spent his mature years. At the fall of this state in 577, he was once again taken to Ch'ang-an. Here he witnessed the successful establishment of the Sui dynasty, during which dynasty he spent the last years of his life. Yen Chih-t'ui is best known for his book of instructions, Yen-shih chia-hsün 顏氏家訓, which was directed towards the junior members of his family.[3] He was apparently involved in a historical compilation; in addition he took part in the establishing of the principles for the famous dictionary, the Ch'ieh-yün 切韻, as well as writing his own lexicographical and etymological studies. The tradition of learning which he embodied, and which he urged on his family, was perhaps best personified by his grandson, Yen Shih-ku, the famed commentator of the Han shu.

Textual History

The history of the text of the Yüan-hun chih resolves itself into three stages: (a) the earliest notices; (b) a change in name during the Sung; (c) the loss of the text and a new recension at the end of the Ming and beginning of the Ch'ing.

The earliest notices of the collection of stories by Yen Chih-t'ui appear under the title Yüan-hun chih. We find this listed in the bibliographic essay

---

d) Shigematsu Shunshō 重松俊章,"Tonkōhon Kan'enki zankan ni tsuite 敦煌本還冤記殘卷に就いて," Shien 史淵 ,17 (1937), 120–139.

e) Kuan Te-lien 關德棟, Su wen-hsüeh 俗文學, no. 77, Chung-yang jih-pao 中央日報 (Shanghai, 1948). I have not seen this, but according to Chou, 1:1, it is a collation of the Tun-huang fragment with the editions of HYC in Han Wei ts'ung-shu 漢魏叢書 and Wu-ch'ao hsiao-shuo 五朝小說 .

[3] There have been a few articles on this work, and it has been cited frequently for the valuable information which it contains on the period. Recently Chou Fa-kao has published a new collation of the text, Yen-shih chia-hsün hui-chu 顏氏家訓彙注, Special Publication no. 41, Institute of History and Philology, Academia Sinica, Taipei, 1960. See also Miao Yüeh 繆鉞 , "Yen Chih-t'ui nien-p'u 顏之推年譜," Chen-li 眞理, 1 (1944), 411–422; Satō Ichirō 佐藤一郎 , "Ganshi kakun shōron 顏氏家訓小論 ," Tōkyō shinagakuhō 東京支那學報 , 1 (1955), 192–205; Albert E. Dien. "Yen Chih-t'ui: His Life and Thought" (unpublished Ph.D. dissertation, University of California, Berkeley, 1962).

in *Sui shu*, compiled in 656.[4] It is also found listed among the works of Yen
in a family temple inscription of 780.[5] The bibliographic essays of the Old
and New T'ang histories, of 945 and 1041–1048 respectively, also list it.[6]
All of these notices describe the work as being in three *chüan*. The *Fa-yüan
chu-lin* 法 苑 珠 林 , an encyclopedia of Buddhism completed by Tao-shih
道 世 in 668, however, lists the *Yüan-hun chih* as being in one or two *chüan*,
depending upon the edition of the *Fa-yüan chu-lin*. Another work of Yen,
the *Chieh-sha hsün* 戒 殺 訓 , "Instructions Warning against Killing," in one
chüan, and the *Ch'eng-t'ien ta-hsing lun* 承 天 達 性 論 are also noted in the
Fa-yüan chu-lin.[7] It was suggested by Yao Chen-tsung 姚 振 宗 that these
three titles were combined into one work with three *chüan*.[8] However, judging
from its title, the *Ch'eng-t'ien ta-hsing lun* would not appear to be involved
in this problem. Assuming that the original edition of *Yüan-hun chih* was
in two *chüan*, then the increase to three *chüan* may have been the result of
the *Chieh-sha hsün* being joined to it. The *Kuang Hung-ming chi* 廣 弘 明 集 by
Tao-hsüan 道 宣 (596–667), completed in 664, includes the *Chieh-sha hsün*,
which appears as a short chapter of 485 graphs, consisting of some prefatory
remarks and a few illustrative stories.[9] One of these stories is listed in the
T'ai-p'ing kuang-chi 太 平 廣 記 as being from the *Yüan-hun chih*.[10] While
there is the possibility, of course, that some stories may have appeared both
in the *Yüan-hun chih* and in the *Chieh-sha hsün*, the story in question does
not concern "a ghost with a grievance," thus adding weight to the conjecture

---

4 *Sui shu*, 33:20b (I-wen yin-shu kuan reprint from Wu-yin Palace ed.). In some editions
魏 appears for 魂 .

5 *Chin-shih ts'ui-pien* 金 石 萃 編 , 101:25a (wood-block print, Ching-hsün t'ang 經 訓 堂,
1805).

6 *Chiu T'ang shu*, 46:38a; and *Hsin T'ang shu*, 59:19a. These were all cited by Chou, 1:1.

7 *Fa-yüan chu-lin*, *chüan* 100, *Taishō Daizōkyō*, 53:1021a–b, 120:14a (*SPTK* ed.). For the
Fa-yüan chu-lin, see *Bussho kaisetsu daijiten*, 10:5, and *Taishō Daizōkyō*, 98:619c. For the *Yüan-hun
chih* listing in *Fa-yüan chu-lin*, the Korean edition of 1151, which is the basic text of *Taishō*,
has two *chüan*, while the other editions collated, of 1239, 1290, a Ming edition of 1601, and
a Japanese palace edition of 1104–1148, have one *chüan*. The 1591 Ming edition, reproduced
in *SPTK*, also has one *chüan*.

8 Yao Chen-tsung, *Sui-shu ching-chi chih k'ao-cheng* 隋 書 經 籍 志 考 證 , *Erh-shih-wu
shih pu-pien* 二 十 五 史 補 編 , 5384c (4:346). This was cited by Chou, 1:1.

9 This same text, without its title, appears in the *Kuei-hsin p'ien* 歸 心 篇 , an apologia
for Buddhism included as the sixteenth section of the *Yen-shih chia-hsün*. Yao mentioned this,
but did not refer to its occurrence in *Kuang Hung-ming-chi*.

10 *T'ai-p'ing kuang-chi*, 120:5a (Wen-yu t'ang photolithographic edition of 1934). It
tells of an official who cut the hands off thieves, and then had a son born without hands. It
should be noted that the story is found in *T'ai-p'ing kuang-chi*, and not *Fa-yüan chu-lin*,
which drew on stories from the original edition.

that the two works were early combined under the title *Yüan-hun chih.*
Besides mentioning the *Yüan-hun chih* in its short bibliography, the *Fa-yüan
chu-lin* included many of the stories in its text, a point to which we will return.

In the second stage of the textual history, during the Sung, the name of the
collection changed from *Yüan-hun chih* (*Accounts of Ghosts with Grievances*)
to *Huan-yüan chih* 還冤志 (*Accounts of Requiting Grievances*). For the new
name, we may cite the *Ch'ung-wen tsung-mu* 崇文總目 of 1034–1038, three
chüan; *T'ung chih* 通志, twelfth century, three *chüan*; *Chih-chai shu-lu chieh-t'i*
直齋書錄解題 of 1234–1236, two *chüan*; and derived from this, the
Wen-hsien t'ung-k'ao 文献通考 of the end of the Sung, two *chüan*; and
finally, the *Sung shih*, three *chüan*.[11] Of much importance, too, many of the
stories were included in the *T'ai-p'ing kuang-chi*, compiled in 977–978;
these stories are attributed to the later title.[12]

Thus, during the Sung, the collection received a new title, and was
recorded at times as having two *chüan*, rather than three. More recent notices
of a version in three *chüan* appear, but need to be accepted with caution.
The *Ssu-k'u ch'üan-shu* editors claimed to have based their account of the
HYC on a three *chüan* edition, which derived from Ho T'ang's 何鎧 *Han
Wei ts'ung-shu* 漢魏叢書, but the *HYC* in the *Ssu-k'u ch'üan-shu* of the Palace
Museum in Taichung is actually the one *chüan* edition described below.[13]
There is also a reference to an edition of three *chüan* in the late Ming
collectanea, *T'ang Sung ts'ung-shu* 唐宋叢書, but the edition available to
this writer did not contain the *HYC*.[14]

The modern text of the *HYC*, as we have it, appears first in the works of

---

[11] *Ch'ung-wen tsung-mu* (*Yüeh-ya t'ang ts'ung-shu* 粤雅堂叢書 ed.), 3:34a; *T'ung-chih*
(*Wan-yu wen-k'u* ed.), 65:780b; *Chih-chai shu-lu chieh-t'i* (*Kiangsu shu-chü* ed.), 11:2; *Wen-
hsien t'ung-k'ao*, 215:1756b (this cites the *Chih-chai*); *Sung shih*, 206:1a. Ch'ien T'ung 錢侗,
in a note in *Ch'ung-wen tsung-mu*, pointed out that *Chih-chai* and *Wen-hsien t'ung-k'ao* both
precede the title with Pei Ch'i 北齊. *Ssu-k'u ch'üan-shu* (*Ta-tung* ed.), 142:18a, noted that
this was misleading, for the collection was not limited to events of that period.

[12] While I cannot find any reason for the change, there is no doubt that the two titles,
Yüan-hun chih and *Huan-yüan chih*, represent the same work. Many of the stories found in
Fa-yüan chu-lin under the former title also occur in *T'ai-p'ing kuang-chi* under the latter.

For the Ming, the *Kuo-shih ching-chi chih* 國史經籍志 (*Yüeh-ya t'ang ts'ung-shu* ed.),
3:66b, lists the *Yüan-hun chih* in three *chüan*. This catalog, however, listed lost works together
with titles still available; the name *Yüan-hun chih* indicates that this was one of the former
category.

[13] *Ssu-k'u ch'üan-shu*, 142:18a The title is not entered in the *Ssu-k'u ts'ai-chin shu-mu*
四庫採進書目 (Peiping, 1960). See also *Ssu-k'u chien-ming mu-lu piao-chu* 四庫簡明
目錄標注 (Shanghai, 1959 ed.), p. 604.

[14] The *T'ang Sung ts'ung-shu*, by Chung Jen-chieh 鍾人傑, and edited by Chang
Sui-ch'en 張邃辰, both of the Ming, has a version in three *chüan*, according to the *Hui-k'o
shu-mu* 彙刻書目 (Shanghai, Fu-ying shu-chü blockprint edition of 1886–1889), 4:10a,

two contemporaries, Ch'en Chi-ju 陳繼儒 and T'ao T'ing 陶珽 .[15] Ch'en Chi-ju (1558–1639), known for his interest in popular literature, printed the *HYC* in his *Pa-kung yu-hsi ts'ung-t'an* 八公遊戲叢談 , and in the *Pao-yen-t'ang pi-chi* 寶顏堂秘笈 , *keng* section, which has a preface dated 1615.[16] T'ao T'ing also included the *HYC* in his edition of *Shuo-fu* 說郛 , printed in 1621.[17] Thus credit for the recension of this text should probably be given to Ch'en, as well as responsibility for slightly altering the title once more, *chih* 志 being changed to *chi* 記 .

---

and *Ts'ung-shu chii-yao* 叢書舉要 , 36:18a. However, according to the *Ts'ung-shu shu-mu hui-pien* 叢書書目彙編, pp. 321–322, this edition of the *T'ang Sung ts'ung-shu* has only a one *chüan* version of *HYC*. In *Ts'ung-shu chii-yao* there is a note that one edition of the *ts'ung-shu* was made up using the blocks of the *Shuo-fu* 說郛 , changing only the sequence of the items included. Pelliot, in another connection, distinguished between the genuine and spurious *T'ang Sung ts'ung-shu*: "Quelques remarques sur le *Chuou Fou*," *T'oung Pao*, 23 (1924), 217–219. This later edition of the *ts'ung-shu* also contains the *HYC*, but in one *chüan*, according to the *Chung-kuo ts'ung-shu tsung-lu* 中國叢書綜錄 , pp. 56–57.

15 Ching P'ei-yüan 景培元 , "*Shuo-fu* pan pen k'ao 說郛版本考 ," *Chung Fa Han-hsüeh yen-chiu so t'u-shu-kuan kuan-k'an* 中法漢學研究所圖書館館刊, 1 (1945), 7–8.

16 I have not seen the former work; see Arthur Hummel, ed., *Eminent Chinese of the Ch'ing Period* (Washington, D.C., 1943, 1944), pp. 83–84.

17 This discussion is based upon the history of the *Shuo-fu* as set forth by Pelliot and Ching. The *HYC* does not appear in the table of contents of *Shuo-fu* in the *P'ei-lin t'ang shu-mu* 培林堂書目 , which Pelliot believes to be a list of the contents of T'ao Tsung-i's edition; see Pelliot, pp. 184–187. This confirms the point that *HYC* was included in *Shuo-fu* by T'ao T'ing. While the *HYC* was probably complete, as far as the modern text is concerned, when T'ao printed the work in 1621, the 1646 edition is marred by the loss of half of page 6b and all of pages 7 and 8. Wu Yung 吳永 , who printed his *Hsü Pai-ch'uan hsüeh-hai* 續百川學海 between 1628 and 1643 from the very blocks of *Shuo-fu*, does not lack these pages (cf. *Chung-kuo ts'ung-shu tsung-lu*, 1:4–6). Ch'ang Pi-te 昌彼得 , *Shuo-fu k'ao* 說郛考 (Taipei, 1962), p. 20, points out that the *Hsü Pai-ch'uan hsüeh-hai* and other *ts'ung-shu* printed from the *Shuo-fu* blocks between the two printings of *Shuo-fu* have the names of collators below the title of individual works, and the texts are punctuated—features which were cut from the blocks before the subsequent printings of *Shuo-fu*. The *Wu-ch'ao hsiao-shuo* 五朝小說 , printed during the Ch'ing, made use of the *Shuo-fu* blocks after the loss of those pages, and thus does not include this portion of the text, nor is the collator mentioned or the text punctuated (cf. *Chung-kuo ts'ung-shu tsung-lu*, 1:761, and Pelliot, p. 219). Chu Hsüeh-chin 朱學勤 , in *Lü-t'ing chih-chien ch'uan-pen shu-mu* 邱亭知見傳本書目 , 10:15a, as cited in Pelliot, pp. 217–218, said that many *ts'ung-shu* were created by selecting works out of the *Shuo-fu*. It is clear now that what he meant was that the very blocks of the *Shuo-fu* were used for this purpose (cf. Ch'ang, *Shuo-fu k'ao*, p. 21).

The *Han Wei ts'ung-shu* of Wang Mo 王謨 , printed in 1791, is said by Wang himself to have derived the text of *HYC* from the *T'ang Sung ts'ung-shu*. The *Han Wei ts'ung-shu* text is the same version as that of the later *Shuo-fu*, as proven by the missing portion. As Wang pointed out, he changed the sequence of the stories and added a line to one story which was incomplete. The edition of *HYC* in the *Hsü Pai-ch'uan hsüeh-hai* has Yao Ying-jen 姚應仁 listed as collator of the text, but no information relating to him has been found.

The text of the *HYC* is very obviously a recension, rather than a fragment which has been preserved from an earlier date. The sequence of the thirty-six stories contained in this edition is the same as that found in the first ninety-one *chüan* of the *Fa-yüan chu-lin*, the T'ang encyclopedia of Buddhism mentioned above.[18] The *Fa-yüan chu-lin* is contained in the Tripitaka, as well as having independent editions,[19] and thus was readily available to the editor of the text.[20] It has been noted that T'ao T'ing made use of encyclopedias to recover texts; for example, the *Pao-ying chi* 報應記 of *Shuo-fu* 73 obviously comes from *T'ai-p'ing kuang-chi* 102–103.[21] But *HYC* is the only

---

[18] All but six stories in the *Fa-yüan chu-lin* which were attributed to *HYC* were copied into the new edition.

[19] See n. 7, above. Both Ming editions differ from the preceding versions in that they are divided into 120, rather than 100, *chüan*.

[20] Shigematsu mentioned the occurrence of *HYC* in *Fa-yüan chu-lin*, and made use of this text in his collation of the Tun-huang fragment. Chou also cited the *Fa-yüan chu-lin*, and listed the occurrences of some of the stories. This is the first time, as far as I know, that the origin of the modern text of *HYC* has been noted. The statement in various histories of Chinese literature that this work is the only one of its genre and period to have survived as an integral text must therefore be emended.

A comparison of the available texts fails to reveal which edition of the *Fa-yüan chu-lin* provided the basis for the recension, but such an examination does seem to support the conjecture that the *Pao-yen t'ang* edition was the earlier one, since it resembles more closely the *Fa-yüan chu-lin* texts. In the following table, P = *Pao-yen t'ang*; S = *Shuo-fu*; F = the *Taisho* basic text; a, b, c, and d are the *Taisho* collation texts of 1239, 1290, 1601, and 1104–1148, respectively; and M = the *SPTK* edition of 1591 (see n. 7, above). Within some 224 collational notes for the *HYC*, we find the following contact points:

| PM: 100 | Pd: 83 | Pc: 100 | Pb: 89 | Pa: 90 | PF: 84 |
| SM: 82 | Sd: 68 | Sc: 78 | Sb: 71 | Sa: 70 | SF: 70 |

While the *HYC* agrees most closely with the Ming editions of *Fa-yüan chu-lin*, either the compiler ranged over many editions or he used an edition which itself was a collation of previous ones. One may also note that the *Shuo-fu* and *Pao-yen t'ang* texts differ 73 times, of which *Shuo-fu* agrees with *T'ai-p'ing kuang-chi* 46 times and *Pao-yen t'ang* agrees with *T'ai-p'ing kuang-chi* only 8 times. (In 14 cases all three texts differ, and for 5, there is no *T'ai-p'ing kuang-chi* version.) This would further bear out the earlier date for the *Pao-yen t'ang* recension, since it would indicate that the *Shuo-fu* text had undergone more extensive collation with *T'ai-p'ing kuang-chi* after the text had been copied out from the *Fa-yüan chu-lin*. Such a conclusion would also agree with the statement in Ch'ang, *Shuo-fu k'ao*, p. 28, which lists *Pao-yen-t'ang pi-chi* as a source for the contents of the recension of the *Shuo-fu*.

[21] The *Pao-ying chi* was by T'ang Lin 唐 臨, who was also the compiler of *Ming-pao chi* 冥 報 記. Sun Yü-hsiu 孫 毓 修, in his edition of *Ming-pao chi* in *Han-fen lou pi-chi*, said that the text of *Ming-pao chi* in *Shuo-fu* was copied out of the encyclopedias. I have been unable to find *Ming-pao chi* listed in *Shuo-fu*; Sun may have had *Pao-ying chi* in mind.

Hu Ying-lin 胡 應 麟 (1551–1602) in his *Chia-i sheng-yen* 甲 乙 剩 言 (*Hsü Shuo-fu* 續 說 郛, section 16), p. 15b, admitted to Yao Shih-lin 姚 士 粦, T. Shu-hsiang 叔 祥 (fl. 1550–1612), that the *Sou-shen chi* 搜 神 記 in his collection was a recension compiled by putting together the quotations contained in the *Fa-yüan chu-lin*, *T'ai-p'ing yü-lan*, *I-wen*

title of more than twenty collections of short stories represented both in *Fa-yüan chu-lin* and *Shuo-fu* which can be shown to have been derived from the former. This would perhaps confirm the suggestion that Ch'en, rather than T'ao, made the original recension.

Table I is a chart of the stories and their place of occurrence in various texts. Chou Fa-kao has pointed out that there are a number of stories in *Fa-yüan chu-lin* which are attributed to *Ming-hsiang chi* 冥祥記 , but which in *T'ai-p'ing kuang-chi* are credited to *HYC*. These, marked on Table I with brackets, are stories 42–46, 48–50, 52–56, and 62. Chou points out that a number of these refer to events after the time of Wang Yen 王琰 , the compiler of *Ming-hsiang chi*, and with adequate reason decides that the *Fa-yüan chu-lin* is in error. Stories 59–61 are not in *T'ai-p'ing kuang-chi*, Chou continues, but are in close association with some of the above in *Fa-yüan chu-lin*; however, without confirmation from *T'ai-p'ing kuang-chi*, Chou believes that these should be considered doubtful. *T'ai-p'ing kuang-chi* does indeed have one of these stories, but lacks an identification for it, and for another, cites the T'ang work, *Kuang ku-chin wu-hsing chi* 廣古今五行記 .[22] We can thus be certain of forty-five stories, reasonably certain of another fourteen, and include the last three only as possibilities.

Theme and Content

The *HYC* is one of the many works in the same tradition as the *Sou-shen chi*; that is, a collection of tales dealing with the supernatural.[23] But unlike

---

lei-chü, and *Ch'u-hsüeh chi*; and he continues by saying that this was true of almost all of the books on curiosities which had later appeared. We now see that the *HYC* is to be also included in this category. Hu's remarks were quoted in the item on the *Sou-shen chi* in the *Ssu-k'u ch'üan-shu tsung-mu* (Ta-tung ed.), 142:14b–15a, and subsequently translated by Lionel Giles, "A T'ang Manuscript of the *Sou Shen Chi*," *New China Review*, 3 (1921), 385. I differ from Giles in crediting the statement to Hu, rather than to Yao. This ascription is confirmed by Yao's rather uncomplimentary recasting of the incident in his *Chien-chih pien* 見只編 (*Ts'ung-shu chi-ch'eng* photolithographic ed.), p. 96.

[22] By Tou Wei-wu 竇維鋈 , this work is also listed in the bibliographies of *Hsin T'ang shu*, 59:28b, and *Sung shih*, 206:14a. Another version of story 12 is contained in *T'ai-p'ing kuang-chi* 127:3a–b, and the *Kuang ku-chin wu-hsing chi* is cited as the source. This need not indicate any specific relationship between *HYC* and the latter compilation, for the story is to be found originally in the *Lo-yang ch'ieh-lan chi* (see below). Another story, *T'ai-p'ing kuang-chi* 383:4b–5a, is credited to *Huan-i chi* 還異記 ; but its theme, recovery from death, makes it probable that the title should be *Shu-i chi* 述異記 . See Harvard-Yenching Index No. 15, Part II, p. 8, n. 1, which credits the story to *HYC*.

[23] See Derke Bodde, "Some Chinese Tales of the Supernatural, Kan Pao and his *Sou-shen chi*," *HJAS*, 6:3/4 (1942), 338–357, and Bodde, "Again Some Chinese Tales of the Supernatural," *JAOS*, 62 (1942), 305–308.

TABLE I
Textual Occurrences of Stories in *HYC**

No.	*Pao*	*Tun-huang* (sequence)	*Han-Wei* (sequence)	*Fa-yüan*	*T'ai-p'ing*
1	1a	–	6	27:483c	119:4a
2	1a	10	7	32:536b–c	127:2a–b
3	1a	–	8	62:756b	119:4a
4	1b	–	5	63:764b	–
5	1b	–	1	64:772a	–
6	1b	–	2	67:798b	119:2a
7	1b–2a	–	9	798b–c	–
8	2a	–	10	798c	119:4b–5a
9	2a	12	11	798c	5a–b
10	2b	13	12	798c	5b
11	2b	14	13	799a	–
12	2b	15	14	(799a)	–
13	2b–3a	–	–	70:821a–b	–
14	3a	–	–	821b–c	–
15	3a	–	–	821b–c	119:4b
16	3a	–	–	821c	4b
17	3a–b	–	15	821c	–
18	3b–4a	1	16	821c–822a	–
19	4a	2	17	822a	–
20	4a	7	18	822a	119:6b–7a
21	4a	8	19	822a–b	120:1b
22	4a–b	9	20	822b	127:2b–3a
23	4b	3	21	73:841b	126:2a
24	4b–5a	–	3	74:845c–846c	127:1a–b
25	5a	–	4	846a–b	127:2a
26	5a–b	11	22	75:852a–b	120:3a–b
27	5b	–	23	77:866a–b	119:3b
28	5b	6	24	866b	6b
29	5b	5	25	78:875a	6a–b
30	6a	–	26	(91:961c)	129:1a
31	6a	–	27	(961c)	119:2b
32	6a–b	–	28	(962a)	[129:1b–2a] †
33	6b	–	29	(962a)	–
34	6b	–	30	(962a–b)	126:1a–b
35	6b	4	31	(962b)	119:6a
36	7a	–	32	(962b–c)	– ‡
37	–	–	–	(961c)	119:1a–b
38	–	–	–	(44:628b)	2a
39	–	–	–	–	2b
40	–	–	–	(76:858c–859a)	2b–3a
41	–	–	–	31:520a	119:3a–b
42	–	– ·	–	[77:866b]	7b–8a
43	–	–	–	([91:962c])	8a

TABLE I–*Continued*

No.	Pao	Tun-huang (sequence)	Han-Wei (sequence)	Fa-yüan	T'ai-p'ing
44	–	–	–	([78:870a–b])	120:2a
45	–	–	–	([78:870b])	2a–b
46	–	–	–	([91:962c–3a])	2b
47	–	–	–	–	3b–4a
48	–	–	–	([78:870a])	4a–b
49	–	–	–	([78:870c])	4b
50	–	–	–	([78:870c–871a])	4b–5a
51	–	–	–	–	5a
52	–	–	–	([78:869c])	5a–b
53	–	–	–	([78:869c–870a])	5b–6a
54	–	–	–	([91:962c])	6b
55	–	–	–	([78:870c])	6b–7a
56	–	–	–	([91:963a])	7a–b
57	–	–	–	(44:628b)	–
58	–	–	–	(94:978c)	–
59	–.	–	–	([78:870b–c])	[126:2b–3a]§
60	–	–	–	([78:871a])	–
61	–	–	–	[78:870a]	[129:2b–3a] ‖
62	–	–	–	[46:640a–b]	129:3a–b

* The numbering of the stories follows Chou, 1:1–2, with numbers 61–62 added. *Pao* = *Pao-yen-t'ang pi-chi; Han-Wei = Han Wei ts'ung-shu; Fa-yüan = Fa-yüan chu-lin; T'ai-p'ing = T'ai-p'ing kuang-chi*. Brackets mark stories which the sources either attribute to collections other than *HYC*, or which have no attribution. Parentheses mark the stories in *Fa-yüan chu-lin* noted by Chou, 1–3.

† This is attributed to *Ming-pao chi*.

‡ Chou, 1:2, indicates that this story is in *T'ai-p'ing kuang-chi*, but I have been unable to locate it.

§ No source cited.

‖ This is attributed to *Kuang ku-chin wu-hsing chi*.

---

other works, the collection by Yen Chih-t'ui included only one category of the supernatural; that is, stories which tell of those murdered or wrongfully executed, and of their spirits returning to seek justice. This theme, of course, occurs also in the West; one may think immediately of Hamlet's father's ghost, or the Nun's Priest's tale in *Canterbury Tales*. In China there is evidence that the spirits of the dead were regarded as malevolent, and a dissatisfied spirit with a grievance was especially dangerous. Thus the topic of spirits seeking justice was a dramatic and compelling one.

The general pattern and nature of these stories appear in the earliest ones, those culled from a variety of classical texts. Two are from *Mo-tzu* (37–38),[24] one from the *Tso chuan* (5),[25] and one from *Wu-yüeh ch'un-chiu* (6).[26] In *Tso chuan*, Duke Hsiang 襄 of Ch'i, some time after having Duke Huan 桓 of Lu assassinated, shot a boar which then stood up on its hind legs like a man and howled. This presaged the death of Duke Hsiang. From the *Wu-yüeh ch'un-ch'iu* comes the story of Fu-ch'ai 夫差, king of Wu, who unjustly killed his vassal Kung-sun sheng 公孫聖, and later would not pass the spot where the spirit of the murdered man hovered. The two stories from *Mo-tzu* are even more explicit in their moral. King Hsüan 宣 of Chou, in one case, and Duke Chien 簡 of Yen, in the other, unjustly killed vassals. In the latter case, before his death, the vassal stated that if there were cognition in death, he would seek to return. Spirits of both vassals returned, the former shooting the king with a vermilion arrow from a crimson bow, the latter beating his duke with a crimson stick, and both princes died. *Mo-tzu* concludes that no one, knowing of these examples, could carry out unjust executions.

In these anecdotes from the Chou, one can see the typical format of the majority of the stories in the collection. Whatever the historical circumstances, the spirit returns to wreak vengeance. He may hit the victim with a stick, stab him with a knife, shoot him with an arrow, force him to drink poison, or jump into his mouth inducing convulsions. In a large number of cases, merely his appearance is enough to bring on death. Retribution may be sought indirectly, as when the spirit of the murdered person complains to a relative or to a passing official. A less typical means of revenge (story 12) is translated below:

Yüan Hui 元徽,[27] Prince of Ch'eng-yang 城陽 of the Wei, had earlier helped Emperor Hsiao-chuang 孝莊 plot the murder of Erh-chu Yung 爾朱榮. When Erh-chu Chao 兆 arrived at Lo[-yang] and put Hsiao-chuang to death, Hui became frightened and fled, throwing himself on [the mercy of] K'ou Tsu-jen 寇祖仁, Commandant of Lo-yang. Tsu-jen's father and two uncles had all been prefects through Hui's doing, and yet, when Erh-chu Chao posted a reward for Hui of a marquisate of 10,000 households, Tsu-jen beheaded Hui and sent in [his head]. At the same time he concealed 100 *chin* of gold and 50

---

24 *Mo-tzu* (*SPTK* ed.), 8:2b–3a and 4a. These two are cited frequently by Wang Ch'ung in his *Lun-heng*; see for example *SPTK* ed., 21:1a.

25 *Tso chuan* (I-wen yin-shu kuan reprint), 7:25b–26a.

26 *Wu Yüeh ch'un-ch'iu* (*SPTK* ed.), 5:27a–b.

27 Yüan Hui has biographies in *Wei shu*, 19C:19b–21b, and *Pei shih*, 18:21a–22b. There it says that he fled to a former official, K'ou Mi 寇彌, who murdered him. Chou, 3:16, points out that the story in *HYC* is from *Lo-yang ch'ieh-lan chi* 洛陽伽藍記 (*SPTK* ed.), 4:2b–4a. The numerous textual variants for this and the following stories have not been noted; these will be included in a translation of the stories which I plan to publish.

head of horses [which had been Hui's]. When Chao obtained Hui's head, he still did not give the reward of the marquisate. Chao later dreamed of Hui saying to him, "My 200 *chin* of gold and 100 head of horses are in Tsu-jen's household. Your Lordship might seize them." Chao awakened and said, "The house of [the prince of] Ch'eng-yang was originally large and prosperous, but yesterday when I ordered the confiscation and seizure [of his property] it was entirely without gold and silver. This dream may be true." At daylight he ordered the confiscation of Tsu-jen's [property]. Tsu-jen also saw Hui who said, "This will be adequate to obtain requital." Tsu-jen in good faith handed over the 100 *chin* of gold and 50 horses but Chao did not believe him. Tsu-jen took his own and collected what his relatives and dependents had, but only obtained 30 *chin* of gold and 30 horses, which he gave over to Chao. As this still did not complete the [required] number, Chao became angry and had him suspended by his head from a tree, with stones weighing down his feet, and had him bastinadoed to death.

From this story it can be seen that retribution need not be meted out directly by the aggrieved. One story (no. 43) even tells of a person who cut out and swallowed the eyeballs of a fugitive slave and gagged and finally died from them. These forms of less direct retribution usually occur in the stories of the later periods, and allow for more variety and interest.

The time of occurrence and the themes of the stories are outlined in Tables II and III. The large number from Chin may reflect the interest in the supernatural of that period, while the number from the Liang may stem from Yen Chih-t'ui's own background. In the *Yen-shih chia-hsün*, too, most of the anecdotes seem to have been drawn from the south, where he had spent his youth.

The formulaic curse (see Table III) appears, as was said, in one of the stories from *Mo-tzu*, and is repeated at later periods. The aggrieved victim, at the time of the execution, says, "If there is no cognition after death, then this is all, but if there is cognition, then you will suffer for this," or words to this effect. The appeals to Heaven, the use of written documents, for which

TABLE II

Times of occurrence of stories in *HYC*

Period	No. of stories	Period	No. of stories
Chou	4	Liang	10
Han	9	Ch'en	3
San-kuo	4	Northern States	2
Chin	13	N. Wei	2
Sung	8	N. Ch'i	4
S. Ch'i	1	N. Chou	2

TABLE III
Themes of stories in *HYC*

Theme	No. of stories
Types of retribution	(67)
1. Appearance	(40)
a) to give warning of death	19
b) at time of death	21
2. Physical retribution	(16)
a) shot by bow and arrow	2
b) clubbed with stick	5
c) stabbed with knife or rod	3
d) made to drink posion	1
e) spirit jumps into mouth	2
f) bitten by dog	2
g) chokes on eyeballs	1
3. Indirect retribution	(8)
a) guile	1
b) appeal to officials	2
c) revelation to relatives	3
d) prevents escape	2
4. No obvious cause	3
References to Buddhism	6
Appeals to Heaven	11
Written charges	4
Formulaic curse	6

purpose paper and ink are placed in the coffin, and the occasional dispatch of ghostly lictors to seize the culprit, are all on the pattern of what one found on earth. The vision of Heaven being a typical bureaucratic office, with red tape and official errors, may seem an amusing conceit in the West, but it is the accepted pattern for these stories.

The stories, especially the later ones which were probably written by Yen himself, are often fascinating. The events of one of these may well have been witnessed by Yen. In 554 the capital of the Liang state was captured by the Western Wei armies, and thousands of prisoners were taken north to Ch'ang-an; among these was Yen Chih-t'ui, who was suffering from beri-beri and riding an old nag.[28] The story (no. 46) deals with this trek northward.

---

[28] Yen's prose-poem, *Kuan wo sheng fu* 觀 我 生 賦 , line 99, notes, *Pei Ch'i shu*, 45:23a.

When Chiang-ling fell there was a man from Within the Passes [named] Liang Yüan-hui 梁 元 暉 29 who took as prisoner a grandee with the surname Liu. This man had previously encountered Hou Ching's rebellion, and had lost his family. Only a small boy several years old remained, whom he now personally carried. When they reached snow and mud, he could not go on. Liang Yüan-hui was supervising [the trek] to enter the Passes. He pressingly ordered him to cast away the child. Liu so loved [the child] that he asked to die himself. They then forcibly took the boy and threw him into the snow, and beat Liu with a succession of blows to force him to go on. Liu at every step looked back, wailing so as to break [one's heart]. The hardships had strained and overtaxed him, and adding to it his grief, he died after several days. Later, Yüan-hui saw Liu daily stretching out his hands to take his child. He became ill from this, and although he repeatedly expressed his regrets, it was too late. Bearing this illness, Yüan-hui returned home and died.

The stories are also valuable as a source of information for the society of the time. While the stories may not have been factual, they were presented as such, and so must have been at the least believable in terms of their mundane settings. The position of slaves, the relationship of landowners and those who worked the land, and the uncertainty of the merchant's position often come to light, for these were groups which could be mistreated with impunity, and whose only recourse for justice might often be their appearance as ghosts. There appear cases even of officials who fell victim to unjust accusations, revealing the helplessness of the official in the face of the bureaucratic structure of the state. The stories also contain anecdotes about important persons of the time which do not appear in the histories.[30] The collection, then, is a valuable social and historical document of this period.

The HYC and Buddhism

There now remain to be said some words about Yen's motivation in compiling this group of stories, and related to this question, the evaluation of the *HYC* by later critics. The belief in the existence of ghosts, and a supernatural apparatus for exacting retribution for misdeeds, were identified during the Six Dynasties Period as being Buddhist. Yen's selection of this theme for a collection of stories has meant that the *HYC* has been categorized as being Buddhist. Thus as early as 668, Tao-shih included the *HYC* in a

---

29 Liang Yüan-hui has no biography in the standard histories, but he may have been related to Liang Hsin 昕 , cognomen Yüan-ming 元 明 , who has a biography in *Chou shu*, 39:2b–3b.

30 This was mentioned by Wang Mo in his postface to *HYC* in *Han Wei ts'ung-shu*. See, for example, the stories about Yü-wen T'ai, Ch'en Pa-hsien, Yang Hsin, and others. The value of the short stories as source material for another period has been noted by F. Schurmann, "On Social Themes in Sung Tales," *HJAS*, 20 (1957), 241.

special bibliography in the *Fa-yüan chu-lin* made up of books which were in accord with the principles of the Buddhist faith.

The editors of the *Ssu-k'u ch'üan-shu,* in their discussion of the book, mentioned how widespread Buddhism was from the time of Emperor Wu of the Liang, and how Yen revealed his Buddhist sympathies in section sixteen of his *Yen-shih chia-hsün;* this section is an apologia for Buddhism. Thus, they continued, "What this book records are all stories of the Buddhist retribution *pao-ying* 報 應 ." The ghost stories in the classics, they say, were merely the attempt of the spirits to correct the wrongs, and had no trace of Heavens or Hells, nor was there an attempt to probe the unknowable. Nevertheless the editors conclude, the style of writing is good, not like other, verbose, collections of stories, and, read only as an exemplary work, it could do no harm.[31]

Cheng Chen-to 鄭 振 鐸 , in his *Chung-kuo wen-hsüeh shih* 中 國 文 學 史 , page 226, mentions how the Buddhist ideas of karma and retribution entered the minds of the people, replacing the native Chinese fatalistic viewpoint. He includes the *HYC* among those collections which recorded the efficacy of praying to the Buddha, reciting the scriptures, or making sacred images. Thus, he concludes, under this religious impetus, a new type of story grew up in the Six Dynasties Period.

Lu Hsün was somewhat more cognizant of its nature when he said that it quoted from the classics and history to validate the idea of retribution, and unites the Confucian and Buddhist points of view.[32] Lu Hsün's book had much influence on subsequent writers about Chinese literature, but these critics frequently went beyond Lu Hsün's prudent analysis. T'an Cheng-pi 譚 正 璧 said that Yen made use of these stories to teach Buddhism;[33] Kuo Chen-i 郭 箴 一 said that this book was merely Buddhist propaganda.[34] Liu Ta-chieh 劉 大 杰 said that in content and appearance, Yen's book was similar to Wang Yen's *Ming-hsiang chi,* and was written to aid the propagation of the faith.[35]

In several of these histories of Chinese literature, there are representative stories from the *HYC* and other works classified with it in this genre of Buddhist literature; these stories might well cause one to doubt the validity

---

[31] *Ssu-k'u ch'üan-shu,* 142:18b–19a.

[32] *Chung-kuo hsiao-shuo shih-lüeh* 中 國 小 說 史 畧 (1933), p. 64.

[33] *Chung-kuo hsiao-shuo fa-ta shih* 中 國 小 說 發 達 史 (1935), pp. 116–118.

[34] *Chung-kuo hsiao-shuo shih* 中 國 小 說 史 (1939), p. 106. Ko Hsien-ning 葛 賢 寧 , *Chung-kuo hsiao-shuo shih* 中 國 小 說 史 (1956), p. 32, has a similar statement.

[35] *Chung-kuo wen-hsüeh fa-chan shih* 中 國 文 學 發 展 史 (1941–1949) pp. 241–244.

of placing the *HYC* in this category of proselytistic works. The *Ming-hsiang chi*, *Hsüan-yen chi* 宣 驗 記 , and the *Ching-yi chi* 旌 異 記 are openly Buddhist in nature, and their surviving stories tell of the efficacy of faith in Buddha and in the sutras.[36] The following is a story from the *Ming-hsiang chi*, by Wang Yen of the later fifth century, which may be compared with the stories from *HYC* translated above.[37]

Chou Tsung 周 宗 was a man of Kuang-ling 廣 陵 Commandery. In the seventh year of Yüan-chia 元 嘉 of Sung (430) he followed Tao Yen-chih 到 彥 之 [38] to campaign in the north. When the imperial troops lost, he and five others of the same city fled to hide. On their way, they came on an empty temple north of P'eng 彭 City. There were no monks or followers [about], but inside was an image with a piece of rock crystal for the figure. They thereupon stole it, and going to a village, bartered it for something to eat. One man who was weak and ill was despised by the others, and only he did not get a share. Within three or four years after their return home, Tsung and the four others, one after the other, became ill and died. Only the one who had not shared in the food escaped.

In the *HYC*, on the contrary, the lack of overt references to Buddhism stands in sharp contrast to such stories.

There are in all only five references to Buddhism in the *HYC*. These are:

Story No. 2: The name of a murderer is Fa-seng 法 僧 , a Buddhist name.

Story No. 23: The head of a temple was executed. Later, the man responsible flees to the temple and hangs himself.

Story No. 29: A śramana is unjustly killed; his ghost kills the murderer with a sword.

Story No. 32: A man attempts to hide from a vengeful ghost by becoming a monk.

---

36 For these works, see Kuo, pp. 99 and 104–107. The *Chi-ling chi* 集 靈 記 , by Yen Chih-t'ui, is also usually placed in this category. It is listed in *Sui shu*, 33:20b, in twenty *chüan*; in *Chiu T'ang shu*, 46:38a, and *Hsin T'ang shu*, 59:19a, as being in ten *chüan*. *T'ung chih* notes it in twenty *chüan* (65:780b). One story survives in *T'ai-p'ing yü-lan* 太 平 御 覽 , 718:7b; it tells of the ghost of a man appearing to his wife to ask for food. On leaving he promised to send on any valuables he might obtain. A month later, the daughter of the family found a gold ring. This story is quoted in Lu Hsün, *Ku hsiao-shuo kou-ch'en* 古 小 說 鉤 沈 , *Lu Hsün ch'üan-chi*, 8:447. This same story and five others are included in *Shuo-fu*, p. 118. These others tell of the same sort of supernatural oddities that one might find in *Sou-shen chi*. Only one has a reference to Buddhism, relating of an encounter between a monk and a sylph. The sylph tells the monk of a well of immortality. Another story, dated 821, was certainly not originally in Yen's work; perhaps others are also not authentic. To include the *Chi-ling chi* in this genre on the basis of the one story in *T'ai-p'ing yü-lan* seems unjustified.

37 Kuo, pp. 104–105; Chou, 1:2.

38 Tao Yen-chih (d. 433) has a biography in *Nan shih*, 25:4a–5b. The defeat occurred in the same year as the start of the campaign, *Sung shu*, 5:8a, not 433 as given in his biography, 25:5b.

Story No. 52: A merchant is executed on trumped up charges and his goods are confiscated to provide materials for building a temple.

Not even in the cases of the murdered monks do we find the intervention of the Buddha or bodhisattvas. Instead, appeal is made to Heaven, *t'ien* 天 , or to *shang-ti* 上帝 . In general, one may say that these references to Buddhism occur only as might be expected in a society in which Buddhism was as important as it was in the Six Dynasties Period. To say then that the *HYC* is to be classed with such works as the *Ming-hsiang chi* is perhaps an over-simplification.

As Liebenthal has pointed out,[39] the debates on the survival of the souls during the Six Dynasties Period were a Chinese phenomenon, rather than a conflict between Indian and Chinese thought. Striving to find immortality, the disputants saw in the ancient Chinese belief in the survival of spirits an argument to defend the theory of transmigration. This view was defended by Confucians with Buddhist commitments, and these men were able to buttress their arguments by citing instances from the classics, including the story from *Tso chuan* that we mentioned above. While the intellectuals among the Buddhist clergy heeded Kumarajīva's dictum that survival of souls was incompatible with Buddhist theory, the disputation continued with the conservative Confucians who would ignore these stories in their tradition, or would go no further than Confucius had in remaining noncommittal on supramundane matters. What is not to be overlooked is that both parties to the disputes were Confucians. The problem of the survival of souls and retribution had been argued for centuries by Yen's time, and, while still discussed, was no longer a burning issue. There is some evidence in contemporary texts that the idea was generally accepted, certainly by the majority of the populace who had Buddhist leanings.[40]

---

39 Walter Liebenthal, "Chinese Buddhism during the 4th and 5th Centuries, "*Monumenta Nipponica*, 11 (1955), 44–83; and "The Immortality of the Soul in Chinese Thought," *Monumenta Nipponica*, 8 (1952), 327–397.

40 We find some indication of this general acceptance of a belief in retribution by ghosts in the sources for the period. In a state document of the Northern Chou of 564, the ruler of the Northern Ch'i was threatened that if the mother of the chancellor Yü-wen Hu were not allowed to return, Yü-wen Hu, when he died, would become a "ghost with a grievance," *yüan-hun* (*Chou shu*, 11:9b). This was evidently meant to be a dire threat. Another example is that of Chiang Yen 江淹 (444–505), who was implicated in a crime and sentenced to death. He wrote a petition stating his innocence, and ended with a request that the prince show understanding so that "the ghosts of Wu-ch'iu will not be ashamed of their buried heads, and the spirit of Ku-t'ing will be without hatred about her ashes and bones." The first refers to a story in *Yen-tzu* 晏子 about five men who were unjustly put to death (*Yen-tzu, SPTK* ed., 6:28a–b; *SPPY* ed., 6:1b). The passage also occurs in *Shuo-yüan* (*SPTK* ed.),

Related to this point is the problem of whether the *HYC* was compiled to prove the principle of karma; or whether, taking this for granted, it was meant to emphasize a traditional precept of social morality. It may be impossible to decide that either one of these was Yen's motive, to the exclusion of the other. But from what we learn of Yen Chih-t'ui from his *Yen-shih chia-hsün*, one may be inclined to think that the emphasis on social morality was at least an important factor in the compilation. Yen lived as a Confucian in a Confucian society, but he also had religious and even intellectual commitments to Buddhism. As Buddhism did not supply a code of behavior for the lay person, Yen evolved in the *Yen-shih chia-hsün* a pattern of life which did not conflict with his Buddhist commitments. It was a system which was primarily Confucian but, in the areas of individual responsibility and ultimate goals, avoided conflict with Buddhism.[41] In

---

18:25b–26a, with some minor changes.

The second allusion made by Chiang Yen is to a Han story of an official who stopped overnight at a lodging place. The ghost of a woman reported that she had been murdered by the village headman of the place. This story appeared in a lost *Hou Han shu* of the San-kuo period, and in *Sou-shen chi*. Yen Chih-t'ui copied the *Sou-shen chi* version into his own collection.

The petition by Chiang Yen occurs in his biography in *Liang shu*, 14:2b, and in *Wen-hsüan* (*SPTK* ed.), 39:24b–30a. While mentioned in Chiang's preface, it apparently does not appear in his collected works, *Liang Chiang wen-t'ung wen-chi* 梁 江 文 通 文 集 (*SPTK* ed.). In the *Wen-hsüan* commentary of Li Shan 李 善 , a version of the story is cited from the *Hou Han shu* of Hsieh Ch'eng 謝 承 . Hsieh Ch'eng was a brother-in-law of Sun Ch'üan 孫 權 ; cf. *San-kuo chih*: Wu, 5:2b, where his *Hou Han shu* in over 100 *chüan* is mentioned. Li Shan ended his note by saying that for Ch'üeh-ch'ao t'ing 鵲 巢 亭 , where the official, Chou Ch'ang 周 敞 , encountered the ghost, the *Lieh-i chuan* 列 異 傳 had Ku-pen 鵠 奔 t'ing. Chang Hsien 張 銑 , in his notes to *Wen-hsüan*, gives more details of the story about Chou Ch'ang, and uses the name Ku-pen t'ing, but gives no source. The story is quoted from Li Shan's commentary in *T'ai-p'ing yü-lan*, 194:6b–7a, as being from Hsieh Ch'ang's *Hou Han shu*, and includes Li Shan's comment about the *Lieh-i chuan*. Lu Hsün, in his *Ku hsiao-shuo kuo-ch'en*, quoted the story as being from *Lieh-i chuan*, only changing the name to Ku-pen t'ing, to accord with Li Shan's note, and mentioned its occurrence in the *T'ai-p'ing yü-lan* and the commentary of *Wen-hsuan*. The version of Chang Hsien, which has details not included in Li Shan's version, is not mentioned or used. Lu also noted the version in *Fa-yüan chu-lin* as cited from *HYC*, with the name of the official given as Ho Ch'ang 何 敞 , and another change of a place-name, Kao-yao 高 要 for Kao-an 高 安 .

Chou Fa-kao, 2:314 (16), is thus apparently not entirely correct in saying that a comparison of the version originally from Li Shan's commentary, which he takes to be from *Lieh-i chuan*, with that in *Sou-shen chi*, demonstrates the way in which the story was expanded and elaborated. We do not have the *Lieh-i chuan* form, and the version in Li Shan's commentary may well be a summary of what he found in the *Hou Han shu* of Hsieh Ch'eng.

[41] For a treatment of the effect of Yen's religious commitments on his thought, see Albert E. Dien, "Yen Chih-t'ui, A Buddho-Confucian," *in* Arthur F. Wright and Denis Twitchett, eds., *Confucian Personalities* (Stanford University Press, 1962).

the *HYC* we may see a further extension of this activity. As in the *Yen-shih chia-hsün*, Yen, the Confucian, brought together material from the ancient works and similar examples from later history bearing on a specific problem. He could feel that he was within the ancient tradition, for belief in the "ghosts with grievances" was an old one in China, and had only been taken up and given a rationale by the Buddhists, not invented by them. In accepting this phenomenon, the Buddhist rationale would seem to Yen rather to support the tradition than to supplant it. It is important here too that the belief in "ghosts with grievances," appearing as early as the Chou in China, was not necessarily to be related directly to the area of efficacy of the Buddhist faith. For this reason, Yen did not find it necessary to relate parochial tales of miracles. Indeed, these would have blunted the lesson which he had to teach, which was the applicability of this principle in society without regard to religion.

The collection, then, is to be classified as Buddhist insofar as the tradition of "ghosts with grievances" had been taken up by the Buddhists and its workings explained by them. One may or may not accept the position that the *HYC*, like the *Yen-shih chia-hsün*, is a didactic work, selecting and systematizing elements from the Confucian tradition as it had come down, to be forged into a pattern of social behavior. But to consider the *HYC* merely as Buddhist propaganda is to impose on the thought of Yen's time clear categories which did not exist in Yen's mind or in his time. It is to make a distinction between Buddhism and Confucianism which would in effect obscure the position of Yen Chih-t'ui and the other literati of the period who believed that faith in Buddhism was no obstacle to their acceptance of the Confucian tradition.

New Perspectives on Two Ming Novels:
Hsi Yu Chi and *Hsi Yu Pu*

C. T. HSIA *and* T. A. HSIA

Editor's note: The two parts of this article are revised versions of papers by the Hsia brothers, presented at the Panel on Chinese Myths and Fictional Imagination, the Sixteenth Annual Conference of the Association for Asian Studies, held in Washington, D.C., March 21, 1964. The discussion of *Hsi yu chi* is by C. T. Hsia. That of *Hsi yu pu* is by T. A. Hsia, whose untimely death in 1965 prevented him from enlarging his paper as he had planned. T. A. Hsia was on the faculty of the University of California, Berkeley, at the time of his death.

MONSTROUS APPETITE: COMEDY AND MYTH IN THE *HSI YU CHI*

IN his pioneer study published over forty years ago,[1] Hu Shih crystallized the modern attitude toward *Hsi yu chi*, compounded of an enthusiastic endorsement of its comedy, a less than adequate appreciation of its mythological content, and a summary dismissal of its religious allegory. What the recent Communist critics have done is to elaborate on the political aspects of the comedy, with especial attention given to the revolutionary implications of its satire on traditional bureaucracy, but they have not gone beyond Hu Shih in attempting a total comprehension of the work in mythical and religious as well as in comic terms.[2] On the surface, it is true, the Communist critics have praised highly the author's fertile imagination as seen in his use of myth, but they regard myths primarily as political fables and

---

[1] Hu Shih completed his second, enlarged version of "*Hsi yu chi* k'ao-cheng" (西 遊 記 考 證) on February 4, 1923. It is included in *Hu Shih wen-ts'un* (胡 適 文 存), vol. 2 (Taipei, 1953).

[2] *Hsi yu chi yen-chiu lun-wen chi* (西 遊 記 研 究 論 文 集), compiled by 作 家 出 版 社 編 輯 部 (Peking, 1957), is a representative volume of Communist criticism on the novel. See also Li Hsi-fan (李 希 凡), *Lun Chung-kuo ku-tien hsiao-shuo te i-shu hsing-hsiang* (論 中 國 古 典 小 說 的 藝 術 形 象 , Shanghai, 1961), which devotes three essays to *Hsi yu chi*. [*Editor's note*: The criticism of this novel from a simple political viewpoint does not seem to have satisfied all scholars in mainland China. For a somewhat more complex view and a moderate protest against this trend, see Hu Nien-i 胡 念 貽 , "T'an *Hsi yu chi* chung ti shen mo wen-t'i" 談 " 西 游 記 " 中 的 神 魔 問 題 , in his *Chung-kuo ku-tien wen-hsüeh lun-ts'ung* 中 國 古 典 文 學 論 叢 (Shanghai: ku-tien wen-hsüeh ch'u-pan she 古 典 文 學 出 版 社 , 1957), pp. 71–88.]

are completely unaware of the kind of criticism being practiced in the West today which interprets a work of literature at the level of myth in order to arrive at its deeper human significance.[3] With all the admirable work done in recent years to illustrate its wealth of comedy, *Hsi yu chi* is nevertheless becoming as much misunderstood through our preoccupation with its overt satiric meaning as it was misunderstood by traditional commentators through their preoccupation with its recondite meaning. These commentators may have blundered in their quest for allegory, but they were, I believe, prompted by the right instinct that a novel of this sort could not have been written without some religious purpose in view. In this paper, therefore, I propose to examine the mythical and religious aspects of the work, with the intention not so much to slight its comic element as to accord the comedy a fuller view of its total significance. Indeed, I believe it is Wu Ch'eng-en's unique distinction that, writing in the unsophisticated tradition of the Chinese novel, he could have so expertly interwoven the diverse strands of comedy, myth, and allegory into the rich fabric of his fiction.

To avoid possible misunderstanding, I would say first of all that, as used in this paper, the term "myth" means "a narrative resurrection of a primeval reality" — a definition which has found much currency among literary critics since Bronislaw Malinowski first coined it.[4] I am therefore concerned not so much with the author's synthetic adaptation of existing Indic, Buddhist, and Taoist mythologies as with the "mythic" content of his many

---

[3] I have in mind the work of such critics as Richard Chase, Leslie A. Fiedler, Northrop Frye, and Stanley Edgar Hyman. *Myth and Mythmaking*, edited by Henry A. Murray (New York, 1960), offers a good general introduction to "myth" criticism. For a more guarded appraisal of its usefulness, see William K. Wimsatt, Jr., and Cleanth Brooks, *Literary Criticism: A Short History* (New York, 1957), chap. 31, "Myth and Archetype."

[4] "Myth" criticism draws upon the findings of modern psychology and anthropology. A prominent anthropologist deeply influenced by Sir James Frazer, Bronislaw Malinowski wrote in 1926 an important paper on "Myth in Primitive Psychology," directing our attention to the role of myth in a primitive culture located in northeast Melanesia: "Studied alive, myth, as we shall see, is not symbolic, but a direct expression of its subject matter; it is not an explanation in satisfaction of a scientific interest, but a narrative resurreciton of a primeval reality, told in satisfaction of deep religious wants, moral cravings, social submissions, assertions, even practical requirements. ... Myth is thus a vital ingredient of human civilization; it is not an idle tale, but a hard-worked active force; it is not an intellectual explanation or an artistic imagery, but a pragmatic charter of primitive faith and moral wisdom." — Malinowski, *Magic, Science and Religion* (New York, Doubleday Anchor Books, 1954), p. 101. Richard Chase has adopted Malinowski's definition of myth as "a narrative resurrection of a primeval reality" in *Quest for Myth* (Louisiana State University Press, 1949), which was one of the first books to urge the adoption of "the mythical method" in the study of literature.

large and small episodes insofar as they are suggestive of the archetypical
situations of primordial humanity. It goes without saying that, while nearly
all mythological narratives of early antiquity possess a mythical meaning,
folk tales and mythological fabrications of a later date are not necessarily
mythically significant. Thus with all its endless round of fantastic combats
between opposing ranks of celestial and human warriors, *Feng shen yen yi*,
a work roughly contemporaneous with *Hsi yu chi*, seems to me to be devoid
of mythical significance, with the notable exception of a few episodes such
as the story of No-cha 哪 吒 and his father, a myth of Oedipal import
derived from Indian sources. With *Hsi yu chi*, however, even a reader of
Arthur Waley's abridged translation, *Monkey*, will be immediately struck
by the resemblance of all its major episodes to classic embodiments of
mythic reality in Western and Indic literature. In his defiance of Heaven,
Monkey suggests Lucifer, Ravana, and possibly Prometheus. Tripitaka —
though the story of his birth is quite conventionalized in the form of a
romance and is almost certainly not from the pen of Wu Ch'eng-en[5] —
shares nevertheless the miraculous fate of a discarded infant with Oedipus
and Moses. The story of the Crow-Cock Kingdom (烏 雞 國 ; Chapters
37–40) has the makings of a Hamlet myth — a foully murdered king,
a crafty confidant who usurps his throne and his conjugal bed, and an
estranged prince enjoined with the task of revenge. In the story of the
Cart-Slow Kingdom (車 遲 國 ; Chapters 44–47), the Buddhist inhabitants
suffer the same fate as the Israelites in their Egyptian captivity, and Monkey
and Pigsy eventually triumph over the three Taoists in a contest of magic
skill just as Moses and Aaron triumphed over Pharaoh's priests. And as
for the monster that rules over the T'ung-t'ien River (通 天 河 ; Chapters
47–49), his demand for an annual sacrifice of live children makes him kin
to many familiar figures in Western as well as Chinese mythology.

But in the last three episodes instanced, and numerous other episodes of
this type excluded from *Monkey*, their possibly coincidental resemblance to
earlier myths is a less impressive proof of their mythical status than their
striking suggestion of the fertility cults of primitive man. Thus the monster
at the T'ung-t'ien River has to be propitiated because failure to observe

---

[5] The story of Tripitaka's birth and early life, which now forms chap. 9 of *Hsi yu chi*,
was not incorporated into the Wu Ch'eng-en text until the K'ang-hsi period. For a study
of this textual problem see Cheng Chen-to (鄭 振 鐸), "*Hsi yu chi* te yen-hua" (西 遊 記
的 演 化), included in his *Chung-kuo wen-hsiieh yen-chiu* (中 國 文 學 研 究) vol. 1,
Peking, 1957.

the annual sacrifice will bring agricultural ruin to the area under his control. Similarly, the three Taoists have won the confidence of the ruler of the Cart-Slow Kingdom because, as rain-makers of proved competence, they guarantee the fertility of his country. And the magician in the story of the Crow-Cock Kingdom breaks a long siege of drought upon entering that country and immediately earns the gratitude and trust of the king. In this respect, he is even more suggestive of Oedipus than of Claudius in that his clearly manifested mana entitles him to the slaying of the powerless king and the possession of his wife.

But, as every reader of *Monkey* is aware, the story of the Crow-Cock Kingdom only goes through the motions of primitive ritual and tragic murder. Though the king is pushed into the well, he reposes down there quite unharmed and is eventually revived. The usurper is a castrated lion so that, with all the lewdness implicit in his violation of the queen and the harem, the ladies are actually left in the cold and complain of his neglect. And with the aid of the pilgrims, the prince, who, unlike Hamlet, is filial to his mother rather than obsessed with her supposed perfidy, restores the old order without bloodshed. Thus we may say of this episode as of most other episodes in the novel that a primeval reality is resurrected so that its unreality may be the more effectively exposed.

If we examine the novel in the aspect of myth, therefore, we can at least distinguish two types of comedy: one denying the reality of mythical experience and one reinforcing the impression of its reality. Included in the first type are, first, the kind of political satire with which modern readers are in ready sympathy, a good-natured representation of the stupidities of the government on earth in the guise of a celestial court, and secondly, the kind of comedy suggested by the story of the Crow-Cock Kingdom, an oblique religious commentary exposing the falsity of appearance and the absurdity of man's inordinate appetite. The Buddhist character of this comic mode will be later discussed; for the present we shall be concerned with the second type of comedy which, in its positive celebration of man's elementary appetites, exaggerates and seemingly affirms the life-sustaining energies of myth.

No critic has to my knowledge made any serious attempt to compare Wu Ch'eng-en (*ca.* 1500–1582) with Rabelais (*ca.* 1494–1553) though the two authors were almost exact contemporaries and have bequeathed to their respective national cultures two comic masterpieces unsurpassed for their sheer animal exuberance. In the episode of the Cart-Slow Kingdom, for example, we have the Rabelaisian comedy of the three prankish pilgrims gorging themselves on the offerings at the Taoist temple, posing as gods before the stupefied Taoist priests, and eventually favoring them with an enormous quantity of their urine. Pigsy, especially, shares with Gargantua and Pantagruel a limitless appetite for food: in the episode of the T'ung-t'ien River, despite the apprehension of his host over the fate of his daughter and nephew, Pigsy eats unconcernedly one of his heartiest meals in the novel, prepared from "a ton of flour, five bushels of rice, and a load or two of vegetables."[6] And some of the monsters do even better. Hurling defiance at Heaven, the Lion of the Lion-Camel Cave 青毛獅子怪 once opened his mouth and swallowed a celestial army of a hundred thousand troops — a conceit worthy of. Rabelais at his best. And his comrade, the Roc 雲程萬里鵬, once swallowed a king and his entire court and then proceeded to devour every inhabitant in his capital.[7]

But despite the comparable gusto in their description of food, Wu Ch'eng-en and Rabelais are nevertheless quite different in their moral attitude toward appetite. Turning away from the ascetic monkish existence to which he himself had been subjected, Rabelais intends his characters of almost limitless capacity for food and wine and limitless sexual prowess to be unqualified positive metaphors for man's emancipation from the life-denying disciplines of the Church. Gargantua, Pantagruel, and their friends are giants rather than monsters, and their giant appetite unambiguously corresponds to their giant intellectual powers. Compared with the Chinese novelist, Rabelais is also far more ribald and scatological because, placing his faith in a nonreligious humanism, he finds the anatomical functions of man not only infinitely amusing but worthy of the most serious contemplation. Wu Ch'eng-en, on the other hand, is not a humanist in the manner of the European Renaissance. In point of moral sensibility he is far more Chaucerian than Rabelaisian in that he finds man's insatiable appetite ultimately laughable as a negative confirmation of his comic absurdity. However lovable, his major symbol of appetite, Pigsy, has no spiritual or intellectual pretensions; his gluttony is quite inseparable from his lust, sloth, and selfish cunning. Though the author good-humoredly indulges his appetite for food, he never once gives free rein to his equally strong desire for sex, so that in the two fine episodes of his temptation by, respectively, the three transformed Bodhisattvas (Chapters 23–24) and the Spider-spirits (Chapters 72–73) he undergoes the exquisite comic torture of

---

[6] Arthur Waley, trans. *Monkey* (New York, 1958), p. 253.

[7] The said exploits of the Lion and the Roc are mentioned in chap. 74.

unfulfilled concupiscence. Far from being intellectual giants in the Rabelaisian sense, the gluttons and lechers in the Chinese novel are monsters in
their physical appearance as well as in the sheer monstrosity of their uncon-
trollable appetite.

But precisely because he contemplates lust from the viewpoint of traditional wisdom, Wu Ch'eng-en is able at the same time to invest many of
his monsters with a kind of fierce mythical life denied the Rabelaisian
giants of humanist enlightenment. The numerous man-eating monsters,
as well as Monkey, Pigsy, and Sandy in their unregenerate state, embody
a boundless will to live, in defiance of all restraint and authority, and of
death itself. Many of them are voluntary exiles from Heaven because they
hate their servile state there and want to enjoy their sensual delights and
practice their magical arts without let or hindrance. They live on human
flesh because in accordance with the magical view that food is mana they
believe that human flesh confers greater power and intelligence than the
flesh of any other animal. Moreover, since human flesh is forbidden as food
in the heavenly court, they regard their cannibalism; if one may use that
word, as a proud badge of their defiant freedom. Many a monster, when
finally captured, finds the prospect of resuming his servitude in Heaven
extremely repellent. Thus the Roc to his captor Tathagata Buddha (Chapter
77), "Over at your place, keeping fasts and sticking to a vegetarian diet,
one leads an extremely poor and miserable existence. Over here, I live
on human flesh and enjoy myself infinitely. If you starve me, you will be
held responsible for your crime." To him, energy is eternal delight and is
equated with the condition of cannibalism.

To the monsters, inevitably, Tripitaka represents the supreme temptation.
Known as the Elder Golden Cicada (金蟬長老 , or 金蟬子) in his
original heavenly state, he has for ten incarnations on earth lived a life of
strict purity so that, in the monsters' eyes, to eat his flesh or absorb his
semen is to acquire the gift of automatic immortality. Throughout his
journey, therefore, Tripitaka is a mana object under perpetual cannibalistic
and sexual assault by the male and female monsters. But their desire is
always stultified, and they forfeit their life or their earthly freedom as a
consequence. In this respect, the novel must be seen as a comic critique
of the life-force itself: the monsters' ferocious aggressiveness only magnifies
the hideousness of that craving seen in every one of us, that craving which,
according to Buddhist teaching, is the cause of all suffering.

The novel pokes fun not only at the monsters but also at Tripitaka as the
embodiment of a no less deluded, and ever fearful, self-consciousness. Early

on his journey (Chapter 19), after he has taken Monkey and Pigsy as disciples but before his encounter with Sandy, Tripitaka is instructed to seek out the Ch'an Master Crow Nest 烏 巢 禪 師 and to receive from him the Heart Sutra, which is duly recorded in the novel in the historical Hsüan-tsang's own standard translation. The monk appears so transported by its truth that he immediately composes a poem to indicate his new state of spiritual illumination. What so far has escaped the notice of modern critics is that, like his monster-disciples, the sutra is a spiritual companion appointed for Tripitaka's protection on his perilous journey. And in the Buddhist allegory, it is a far more important guide than even Monkey himself insofar as a true understanding of its teaching will have rendered unnecessary the service of his disciples and automatically exposed the illusory character of his calamities.

The Heart Sutra, despite its brevity, is perhaps the most central of the prajna paramita texts. Historically, it was a text dear to Hsüan-tsang; "for when he was crossing the desert in 629," writes Arthur Waley in his biographical study of *The Real Tripitaka*, "the recitation of it had routed the desert-goblins that attacked him far more effectively than appeals to the Bodhisattva Avalokitesvara."[8] With its historical association with Tripitaka, we are not surprised that in the primitive Sung version of his legend, *Ta-T'ang San-tsang ch'ü-ching shih-hua* 大唐三藏取經詩話 , the receiving of the Heart Sutra constitutes the crowning success of his quest.[9] By the time the storytellers' version was recorded in the Yuan dynasty,[10] we may presume that, in view of its climactic importance in the primitive

[8] *The Real Tripitaka and Other Pieces* (London, 1952), p. 98.

[9] This episode takes place in section 16 of the *Shih-hua*. Tripitaka has already been to the kingdom of T'ien-chu (天 竺 國) and received 5,048 scrolls of Buddhist scriptures; though none of these are identified by name, it is pointedly mentioned in section 15 that the Heart Sutra is still missing. Now on his return journey, he stops by the Fragrant Grove Market (香 林 市 ; the sectional heading identifies the place as the Fragrant Grove Temple 香 林 寺) of the P'an-lü Kingdom (盤 律 國), and a god informs him in a dream that he is going to receive the Heart Sutra the next day. And the next day a Buddha titled Ting-kuang (定 光 佛), who looks like a fifteen-year-old monk, descends upon a cloud and hands Tripitaka the Sutra, saying, "I transmit to you this Heart Sutra. When you return to court, you must protect it and cherish it. Its power reaches to Heaven and Hell. It is compact with the mysterious forces of *yin* and *yang*, and therefore do not lightly transmit it to anybody. It will be extremely difficult for the less fortunate multitudes to receive it."

[10] This version is extant only in two fragments, preserved in the *Yung-lo ta-tien* (永 樂 大 典) and a Korean reader of Chinese texts. See *Chung-kuo wen-hsüeh shih* (中 國 文 學 史 , 中 國 科 學 院 文 學 研 究 所 中 國 文 學 史 編 寫 所 編 寫 , Peking, 1962), vol. 3, pp. 903–905.

version, the episode of the transmission of the sutra must have been transposed to a much earlier section of the narrative so that the meaning of that sutra could be further expounded by the pilgrims on their journey. And we may further maintain that, in adapting this source, Wu Ch'eng-en has done nothing less than make his whole novel a philosophical commentary on the sutra. George Steiner has brilliantly observed that the major characters in Tolstoy and Dostoevsky, when confronted with personal problems of crucial moral importance, often recite and discuss passages from the New Testament, which in turn keynote and illuminate the meaning of the novels in which these characters appear.[11] In *Hsi yu chi*, the Heart Sutra is a subject of repeated discussion between Tripitaka and Monkey and serves the same novelistic function.

Tripitaka is indeed Everyman, as Mrs. Yi-tse Mei Feuerwerker has aptly observed,[12] but the clear religious implications of this designation can only be understood by reference to the Buddhist wisdom of the Heart Sutra. Though Tripitaka constantly recites the sutra, its transcendent teaching that "form is emptiness and the very emptiness is form"[13] is so far beyond his mortal understanding that every calamity demonstrates anew his actual incomprehension. During pauses between adventures, therefore, it is Monkey with his far superior spiritual understanding that repeatedly asks his master to heed the sutra. Thus, in Chapter 43, he makes another attempt:

Old teacher, you have forgotten the verse, "no eye, ear, nose, tongue, body, mind." Of all of us who have forsaken the world, our eyes should not see color, our ears should not hear sound, our nose should not smell, our tongue should not taste, our body should not feel cold and heat, and our mind should not harbor vain illusions: this is known as "routing the six thieves." Now your mind is constantly occupied with the task of seeking the scriptures, you are afraid of the monsters and unwilling to give up your body, you beg for food and move your tongue, you are fond of sweet smells and provoke your nose, you listen to sounds and excite your ear, you see things around you and strain your pupils. Since you have welcomed these six thieves on your own invitation, how could you hope to see the Buddha in the Western Paradise?[14]

---

11 See George Steiner, *Tolstoy or Dostoevsky* (New York, 1959), particularly pp. 58–59, 300–305.

12 Yi-tse Mei Feuerwerker, "The Chinese Novel," *in* Wm. Theodore de Bary, ed., *Approaches to the Oriental Classics* (New York, 1959), p. 178.

13 I follow the translation given in Edward Conze, *Buddhist Wisdom Books, Containing The Diamond Sutra and The Heart Sutra* (London, 1958) p. 81. "FORM (*rūpa*)," Mr. Conze explains on p. 82, "covers the 'material' or 'physical' aspect of the world, and it comprises chiefly the four material elements, the five sense organs and the five sense objects."

14 *Ibid.*, p. 89.

Measured against this standard of nonattachment, Tripitaka's every manifestation of fear and credulity, of fanatical obsession with correct conduct and peevish concern over his stomach and physical comforts is as much part of a deliberate comedy as the obviously gross behavior of Pigsy. Indeed, to the end, Tripitaka remains self-obsessed. Even while he is being ferried to the Further Shore of Salvation, he is resentful of the fact that Monkey has pushed him into the bottomless boat and got him wet, and so "sitting there miserably, he wrung out his clothes, shook out his shoes, and grumbled at Monkey for having got him into this scrape."[15]

But his is not the aggressive selfishness of the monsters who aspire to complete autonomy. In his very human fashion, he has a good heart. Upon joining Tripitaka, Monkey's first act is to slay the same six thieves of Eye, Ear, Nose, Tongue, Mind, Body — an allegorical event indicative of his superior spiritual detachment in comparison with the other pilgrims. But Tripitaka is horrified because, among his other frailties, he is still obsessed with love and therefore compassion for phenomenal beings. This episode causes the first temporary rift between master and disciple, and on two further occasions Tripitaka dismisses Monkey for his seemingly merciless killing of brigands and a demon in human disguise. Even at his best, therefore, Tripitaka shows himself under the delusion of compassion. Whereas in nearly every Christian allegory of comparable scope the hero attains definite spiritual progress at the end of his journey, *Hsi yu chi* demonstrates the paradoxical character of the Buddhist imagination in that its nominal hero is granted Buddhahood precisely because he has done nothing to earn his Buddhahood. To consciously strive for Buddhahood would have placed him under another kind of bondage.

In the novel, therefore, Wu Ch'eng-en exercises his right to mock, albeit good-naturedly, every monster, pilgrim, and celestial because everything that exists is but maya with which we are infatuated. Even the most serious character in the book and the one nearest approaching an understanding of the doctrine of emptiness, Monkey, is not spared his affectionate ridicule. To readers conditioned to accept the reality of literary fiction, this attempt at constant negation can be at times very unsettling. Writing from the Christian viewpoint which accords reality to every soul, be it suffering eternal damnation in Hell or rejoicing in eternal bliss in Paradise, Dante, for example, creates a massive comedy of substantive reality designed to elicit our strongest emotional responses. Wu Ch'eng-en, on the other hand,

---

[15] *Monkey*, pp. 281–282.

provides in episode after comic episode the illusion of mythical reality, but
then he inevitably exposes the falsehood of that reality in furtherance of his
Buddhist comedy. Every time he kills off a particularly fascinating monster
or arbitrarily returns him to his heavenly master, we are justified to feel
that he is mocking our emotional attachment to that monster. Like Tripitaka
himself, we are too much creatures of the senses and of humanitarian
sympathy to be able to adjust adequately to the Buddhist reality of
emptiness. The reason why, of all the monsters blocking the path of Buddhist
enlightenment, nearly every modern critic has betrayed a special affection
for the Bull Monster King 牛 魔 王 is that, for once, we are trapped in an
emotional situation that seems to defy the Buddhist assumption of unreality.
The Bull Monster remembers Monkey as an old friend and he further
remembers the humiliating subjugation of his son by the same Monkey
with divine aid; moreover, living with two women, he has his domestic
problems to attend to. He inhabits the epic world of human continuity and
therefore holds for us extraordinary human interest. For the duration of three
chapters (59–61), the mythical drama of primeval reality almost prevails
over the comedy of Buddhist illusion, and we applaud the author for his
uncharacteristic lapse.

But to complain so is to be less than just to the Buddhist design of the
book and to the author's genial comic vision stemming from a proper awareness of the delusions of the self. Even in the story of the Bull Monster, as
in the far more sympathetic account of Monkey's defiance of Heaven, a
careful reader will find a sufficient amount of material in the style of
burlesque, mockery, and comic exaggeration to warn him against total
emotional involvement. Possibly, we are too much in love with the irrational
and mythic, too much inured to the disintegration and chaos of modern life
to fully appreciate the sanity of the Buddhist vision. But place Wu Ch'eng-en
with a self-obsessed precursor of modern fiction like Poe, and we can immediately see the tremendous difference. Allen Tate has admirably called Poe
a writer in possession of the angelic imagination in that he aspires to the
condition of an angel, if not of God.[16] He peoples his serious stories with
characters that are actually vampires.[17] Like the female ogres in *Hsi yu chi*

---

16 See the essays, "The Angelic Imagination" and "Our Cousin, Mr. Poe," *in* Allen
Tate, *The Man of Letters in the Modern World* (New York, Meridian Books, 1955).

17 Tate says (p. 115) that "Poe's heroines — Berenice, Ligeia, Madeline, Morella, with
the curious exception of the abstemious Eleanora — are all ill-disguised vampires; his
heroes become necromancers (in the root meaning of the word) whose wills, like the heroines'
wills, defy the term of life to keep them equivocally 'alive.' "

determined to assault Tripitaka in order to enrich their own vitality, these vampires cling desperately to life so as to vindicate Poe's favorite epigram, "Man does not yield himself to the angels nor unto death utterly, save only through the weakness of his feeble will."[18] Wu Ch'eng-en would have found this arrogance quite laughable, and his monsters are actually far less monstrous than the morbid human beings in Poe's stories, with all their philosophic intensity. Whereas Poe has neither humor nor kindness nor generosity of spirit, it is possibly Wu Ch'eng-en's supreme claim to comic distinction that he destroys or reclaims his monsters before they turn introspective philosophers, before they take themselves too seriously in the fashion of the heroes of modern fiction. They remain plain monsters, amenable to a religious interpretation in the dual modes of myth and comedy.

THE *HSI YU PU* AS A STUDY OF DREAMS IN FICTION*

Hsi yu pu 西遊補 by Tung Yüeh 董說 (1620–1686) is a book in sixteen chapters concerning one episode on Tripitaka's pilgrimage to the West. The episode is supposed to take place after the episode of the Flaming Mountain (Chapter 61 of *Hsi yu chi*). But except for this link in plot, the familiar characterization of Tripitaka, Monkey, and Pigsy, and a certain allegorical representation of a Buddhistic view of life, *Hsi yu pu* borrows very little from *Hsi yu chi*. It is a work that follows its own logic and is sustained by its own structure. A new world of wonders is here opened up which bears very little resemblance to the charmed world of *Hsi yu chi*. It has a different kind of humor, suspense, bizarreness and even absurdity. The story of the bedevilment of Monkey by the Ch'ing Fish Spirit 鯖魚精,

---

[18] This quotation from Joseph Glanvill (1636–1680) forms part of an epigraph to "Ligeia." It appears twice in the story itself, but with a slight change in wording. D. H. Lawrence, who was probably the first modern critic to call attention to the vampiric character of Poe's heroes and heroines, discusses "Ligeia" and its epigraph at some length in his chapter on Poe in *Studies in Classic American Literature* (New York, Doubleday Anchor Books, 1953).

* [*Editor's note*: The *Hsi yu pu* text which T. A. Hsia used seems to be the original version published in 1641 which was reprinted in lithography by Wen-hsüeh ku chi k'an hsing she 文學古籍刊行社, Peking, 1955. The reprint appends a biography of Tung Yüeh by Liu Fu. This version and the biography are also reprinted in separate volumes by Taipei: Shih-chieh shu-chu 世界書局 in 1958. For a later study of Tung Yüeh's life the reader may consult Hsü Fu-ming's 徐扶明 article "Kuan-yü *Hsi yu pu* tso-che Tung Yüeh ti sheng-p'ing" 關于西遊補作者董說的生平 in *Wen-hsüeh i-ch'an tseng-k'an* 文學遺產增刊, vol. 3 (Peking: Tso-chia ch'u-pan she 作家出版社, 1957), pp. 109–118.]

which is the theme of *Hsi yu pu*, does not fit in with *Hsi yu chi*, any more than
the boudoir scenes of *Chin p'ing mei* belong properly with *Shui hu chuan*.
It cannot be said that Tung Yüeh did not approve of the way *Hsi yu chi*
was written. Like many of its readers, he was probably an admirer of *Hsi
yu chi*'s many good qualities. It must have been a labor of love for him to
compose these supplementary chapters. Judging from the references he
makes to earlier episodes in *Hsi yu chi*, he must have known the original
work very well. But he distinguished himself by not being an imitator.
He did not simply invent another episode to extend a pilgrimage which,
in the original, was anything but short. In his book the pilgrimage is used
for a new purpose. It is used as a framework to present certain truths about
dreams. Since such truths are rarely touched upon in Chinese literature,
Tung Yüeh's conscious reworking of the myth of the Pilgrimage may be
said to be a unique contribution.

To create another adventure for the pilgrims is by no means an easy task,
especially if the writer of the supplementary chapters wishes to stay independent of the method of *Hsi yu chi* which had already been so elaborated
and perfected by Wu Ch'eng-en himself. The perils encountered by the
pilgrims in *Hsi yu chi* follow a pattern recognizable to even the casual
reader. Merely to repeat that pattern would not have justified the creation
of an additional episode. The pattern centers upon the predicament of
Tripitaka, the pious and serious-minded holy man, who is nevertheless
utterly defenseless (except for his borrowed magic power over Monkey)
and innocent both of the demonic world and of the human world, and is at
times exasperatingly stupid. But to the evil spirits, a more tempting morsel
of flesh never traveled the road from China to mythical India. He remains,
of course, unharmed, and that creates the charming fairy-tale quality of
Hsi yu chi. The suspense hangs principally on the contest between Monkey
as the protagonist and a variety of spirits and monsters as the antagonists.
Monkey is brave, loyal, resourceful, irritable, but amenable to discipline,
and powerful without necessarily being brutal. He may get worsted in
battles, but dauntless, he always fights back, with or without celestial
reinforcements. One great virtue he possesses is the alertness and perceptive-
ness which enable him to detect evil whenever he sees it. No illusion can
deceive him, not even the false Lei-yin Temple 雷音寺 which means to
the naïve Tripitaka the end of the journey. Indeed, he was deluded once
when he mistook the fingers of Lord Buddha's hand for the peaks of a
mountain, but then Lord Buddha's magic power is supposed to be irresistible.
Now in *Hsi yu pu*, Tung Yüeh revises this pattern. Monkey, instead of

Tripitaka, becomes the victim, and he is ensnared in delusions much more weird than anything found in *Hsi yu chi*.

So far as the outward action is concerned, the plot of *Hsi yu pu* can be summarized in a few lines. There is a Ch'ing Fish Spirit who, like many other monsters, harbors a cannibalistic lust after Tripitaka. He appears as a handsome young monk, and pretends to have the Bodhisattva Kuan Yin's recommendation to become Tripitaka's disciple. Monkey, who has been away for a while, then returns. With one stroke he kills the impostor. The corpse of the fish that is left behind convinces Tripitaka that once again he has been saved by Monkey.

If it were placed in *Hsi yu chi* this episode would be brief and unexciting. The poor Ch'ing Fish is simply no match for Monkey. Such an incident might have found a place in *Hsi yu chi* to make up the predestined number of eighty-one perils or to have served as an entr'acte before the reader is led to another high adventure where Tripitaka's safety is placed in greater jeopardy and Monkey has to exert his whole being to meet the challenge. But as Tung Yüeh conceives it, the Ch'ing Fish 鯖魚, which reads Ch'ing 情, or *love*, in his allegorical scheme, is the most formidable adversary that Monkey has ever encountered since his conversion to Buddhism. The Spirit's power is so great and its evil influence so subtle that Monkey does not know where he is or what has happened even when it is almost completely subjugated. To do full justice to Monkey's temptation by, and struggle with, the Ch'ing Fish Spirit requires a narrative method which Tung Yüeh has to devise for himself. There is little he can borrow from Wu Ch'eng-en. His method is the creation of dreams, dreams with features familiar to dreamers all over the world: distortions, discrepancies, inconsequence, irrelevance, and preposterous happenings imbued with emotional tensions. Wu Ch'eng-en's method, brilliant as it is, turns out to put too much emphasis on outward action. Monsters in *Hsi yu chi* have their personal histories, they live at certain addresses, and they move, eat, and fight like human beings, albeit the more crude and villainous kind of human beings. Apparitions and shadows that emerge and vanish without reason have no place in the *Hsi yu chi*. Wu Ch'eng-en's method is built squarely on the logic of wakeful life. It does not provide for all the horrors and strange beauties that occur only to a dreamer.

The Ch'ing Fish is indeed a devious monster. It is obvious that once Monkey is put out of the way, Tripitaka will become a much easier victim. One wonders why no monster in *Hsi yu chi* ever comes up with the idea of disposing of Monkey first and getting at Tripitaka later. But it takes the

Ch'ing Fish or Tung Yüeh in his demonic imagination to think up this
strategy and set it in operation.

The predicament of Monkey in *Hsi yu pu* is most ingeniously conceived.
Each episode in *Hsi yu chi* poses a problem which is clearly defined, and the
solution, after some initial frustration, comes at a fast pace. There is always
a case: Tripitaka has disappeared and he must be found and saved. But
in *Hsi yu pu* Monkey begins by going out to beg for alms while Tripitaka,
Pigsy, and Sandy are taking a nap. Monkey is aware of no danger except
for the bafflement caused by the name of the T'ang Empire where he now
finds himself. Does it mean that after so much toil over so many strange
lands the pilgrims have not really left Ch'ang-an, the capital of T'ang?
Moreover, the reigning emperor is no longer T'ai-tsung, but somebody who
calls himself "the thirty-eighth emperor of T'ang, the restorer of the
Dynasty." It seems that more years have elapsed than the twenty which
Monkey somehow still remembers as the number of years which he has
spent on the journey. Something is wrong somewhere, but Monkey can
find neither what the trouble is nor precisely where it is. Bafflement presently
gives way to anxiety, and his anxiety certainly increases when there is
no one who can give him direction. He tries to summon the local deity
(*t'u-ti* 土 地), but the usually obedient petty god fails to appear.
No other deity is available either. In anger he leaps to Heaven, to the Jade
Emperor's Palace; there he finds the gates of Heaven closed. A voice comes
from behind him, saying that the Palace has been stolen and the thief
is none other than the notorious Monkey himself!

Anxiety, indeed, sets the tone of the whole book. Monkey has a number of
reasons to feel insecure: the journey yet to be accomplished with all its
dreaded difficulties, his duty to protect his defenseless but gullible master
Tripitaka, the tension in the master-disciple relationship caused by past
misunderstandings, especially by the unjust punishments he has received
at the hands of Tripitaka, and his suspicion of the purity of Tripitaka's
motives, though after their experience in the Women's Kingdom 西 梁 女 國 ,
it should not seem likely that the holy man will give up his monastic vows
and marry or take a mistress. His close association with Tripitaka may also
have awakened his Buddhist conscience, so that he perhaps feels his hands
stained with the blood of many lives and his effort to humanize himself
a failure. All these anxieties, repressed in Monkey's conscious life, appear
in riotous symbols in his dream. And the spatial and temporal dislocation
of finding himself in the T'ang Empire is only the beginning of a very long
and strange dream.

The Ch'ing Fish is, or course, the spirit that creates the dream world to entrap, weaken, and destroy Monkey. But at this juncture of the pilgrimage, Monkey is particularly susceptible to temptation. The episode is supposed to follow the episode of the Flaming Mountain 火燄山 . The reader of *Hsi yu chi* will remember how during that adventure Monkey had assumed the shape of a little insect and climbed into the body of Lo-sha-nü 羅剎女 , or Mme. Rakshas, the Princess of the Iron Fan 鐵扇公主 , and how a little while later in the shape of her husband Niu-mo-wang 牛魔王 , the Bull Monster King, Monkey had even made love to her. Such experiences perhaps did not have any special significance in Monkey's restless and mischievous life, and they would probably soon have been forgotten by him. But the devilish Ch'ing Fish knows that this is the moment to cast a spell over the invincible and ever alert Monkey. Here is a weakness, an almost fatal one, in Monkey's psyche which the subtle Fish knows how to exploit. So in his dream, Monkey hears reference to his five sons. He is in consternation, because he has no son. And then, horror of horrors, he has to face in battle an enemy general who proudly declares himself to be the son whom Monkey allegedly sired after his dalliance with Mme. Rakshas.

This allusion to Monkey's loss of innocence in sexual matters and his sense of guilt, together with a variety of dream symbols which have either explicit or implicit libidinous associations, naturally impresses a modern reader who expects things of this kind in a dream. But it should be borne in mind that *Hsi yu pu* is not an attempt to reproduce an actual dream. Tung Yüeh's half-facetious and half-serious reconstruction of Monkey's dream, supposedly induced by the Fish's evil influence, has no necessary relation to any theory of dreams. His novel is rather to be appreciated as a tour de force, a marvelous creation of art using materials drawn from the author's uncommonly rich imagination and based also upon the logic of Monkey's character and the precedents in Monkey's life from *Hsi yu chi*.

Tung Yüeh's accomplishment is no less than the cleaning away of an obstacle which stood in the way of a proper treatment of dreams in Chinese fiction. Dreams in Chinese fiction are rarely wild or absurd, and they tend to become flat. The convention is nearly always observed that whatever occurs in a dream is conformable to the logic of wakeful life. Too much conscious manipulation in this manner has deprived readers of Chinese fiction of a kind of beauty that can be found only in dreams. Dreams in Chinese fictional imagination are generally of two kinds: they are either short or long. A short dream usually gives one incident which serves the practical function of communication between this world and the supernatural world.

A typical example from *Hsi yu chi* is T'ang T'ai-tsung's dream encounter
with a suppliant dragon king in Chapter 10. A long dream is one that
summarizes a man's life in its natural time sequence, from youth to age,
from prosperity to decline and ruin, with all hopes, desires, ambitions
ending in the final defeat which is the common lot of humanity. Two of the
most famous long dreams in Chinese fiction are the T'ang tales "The
World in the Pillow" (枕 中 記) and "The Kingdom of Ants" (南 柯 太 守
傳), but the dreamers of these dreams simply live out their wished-for
earthly existence during their sleep. Life passes and leaves not a trace
behind, and it is likened to a dream. But only a dream which pictures forth
a man's whole career can be fittingly used as a metaphor to illustrate this
kind of pessimism. The result is that in order to strengthen the force of the
comparison, dreams are made to look like life. A feeling of melancholy
about the vanity of human wishes is inevitable if such a richness of life as
is found in *Dream of the Red Chamber* is to be accepted merely as a dream,
as the title of the book clearly indicates it should, but the reader is not in
any way helped to appreciate dreams as dreams.

Tung Yüeh may have suffered from some kind of neurosis as Liu Fu
劉 復 maintained in his admirable biographical study. But it takes a writer
of original mind to see the literary possibilities of dreams and to break away
from an established literary convention. Whether he succeeds in doing this
because of his neurosis or in spite of his neurosis does not concern us here.
Tung Yüeh wrote two other works about dreams: *Chao-yang meng shih*
(昭 陽 夢 史) and *Meng hsiang chih* (夢 鄉 志). But even judging by *Hsi
yu pu* alone, it is fair to say that never before in China was the essence of
dreams so well studied in fictional terms. Monkey's dream in *Hsi yu pu* may
be an unusual one, possible only to the superhuman Monkey, but its psychological validity has unmistakable human significance.

The structure and content of Monkey's dream require detailed study.
After Monkey has wandered into the Ch'ing Fish's magic world, he enters the
Tower of a Myriad Mirrors 萬 鏡 樓 . In each looking glass are reflected
scenes of people and landscapes, glimpses of a strange world. Each contains
a microcosm, but in none can Monkey see his own image. He transforms
himself into a hard-biting insect, gnaws into a mirror, and arrives in the
"World of the Past" 古 人 世 界 . From there he falls into the "World of
the Future" 未 來 世 界 . Only the *Meng tung shih-chieh* 矇 瞳 世 界 or the
"World of Oblivion," remains beyond his reach. Returning to the Fish's
Ch'ing ch'ing shih-chieh 青 青 世 界 (the "Green Green World") he discovers
to his disgust that Tripitaka has indeed taken a mistress. He does not wake

up until he has experienced a most chaotic battle where the landscape is bare and no individual warrior is singled out for attention, but flags in black, purple, yellow, and blue fly, clash, and fall upon each other, and are bespattered with blood. This riotous melee of colors, dominated by the red of blood, represents a kind of visual imagination which one usually does not associate with Chinese painting or poetry.

Within such a structure, Tung Yüeh's fancy roams free. I have mentioned that Monkey is accused of stealing the Jade Emperor's Palace, but actually the palace has fallen down from Heaven. What has happened is this: a tribe of sky-walkers is conscripted to make a hole in the solidified sky. The hole is made, but af the wrong place, so that the edifice loses its support and rolls down like a ball. And the sky-walkers at work are quite a spectacle too. With their feet in the air, their necks strained, their faces upward, they hack away, in that grotesque posture, with axes against a metal sky, endeavoring to make another hole.

Such scenes and figures are not found in *Hsi yu chi*. Wu Ch'eng-en is unlike Tung Yüeh in that his imagination is essentially commonsensical though it may be also archetypal. Monkey, for instance, is capable of seventy-two transformations, and much of the suspense of *Hsi yu chi* depends on the transformation contests held between Monkey and some deity or monster. But nothing in *Hsi yu chi* stands comparison, for sheer weirdness, with that scene in *Hsi yu pu* where Monkey is trying to get away from the Tower of a Myriad Mirrors. Anxiety returns when he finds that there is no staircase to allow him to descend. He opens a pair of windows, and tries to go through the delicately designed balustrade. The moment he puts his head through, however, the railings begin to entangle him and tie him down like so many red ropes. Monkey transforms himself into a pearl, and the ropes shrink to form a net. Monkey transforms himself into a sword, and the net hardens and elongates into a scabbard. There is simply no way out. In *Hsi yu chi* Monkey always knows his enemy or guesses what impossible shape his enemy has assumed. But in *Hsi yu pu* it is the universe that has gone topsy-turvy; the enemy is hidden; he is everywhere and he is nowhere. In spite of its happy ending, which permits too facile a deliverance from the world of delusions, *Hsi yu pu* at least throws the light of conscious art upon the problem of nameless oppression and anxiety, a malaise which is perhaps more existential than psychological, but which has not won much recognition until modern times. In this respect Tung Yüeh, writing in the seventeenth century, was an exception in China, but it should not be forgotten that interest in existential malaise is also very recent in the West.

A Note on the Dialects of Lo-yang and Nanking During the Six Dynasties[1]

RICHARD B. MATHER

"FROM the Wei (third century) onward variant pronunciations and rhymes came bristling forth, each locality contradicting or ridiculing the others, pointing at a horse (and calling it a deer), until no one knew who was right. They all mixed the speech of the Imperial Court with their local dialects, but if we should investigate past and present usage, selecting and weighing them, there are only the two: Chin-ling (Nanking) and Lo-hsia (Lo-yang)" (*Yen-shih chia hsün*, 18:119b).

In these words Yen Chih-t'ui 顏之推 (A.D. 531–595?) simplified for himself a problem which must have been far from simple even in his day, and which today, after over a millennium of linguistic evolution, is complicated beyond telling. In presuming to deal with it in this brief note, I should warn the reader not to expect a scientific analysis, but rather a rough summary of the problem and a few examples of specific cases, taken mostly from the fifth-century collection of anecdotes, *Shih-shuo hsin-yü* 世 說 新 語 , which it is hoped will throw light on the solution.

The general question of historical dialect geography in China has engaged the attention of many Oriental and Western scholars in the last three or four

[1] This article is partially based on study done in Kyoto during 1963–1964 supported by grants from the U.S. Educational Commission in Japan and the American Council of Learned Societies, and is a revision and expansion of a brief communication originally presented at the one hundred seventy-fifth annual meeting of the American Oriental Society in Chicago, April, 1965. The author is indebted to Fr. Paul Serruys, to Prof. Tse-tsung Chow, and to Prof. E. G. Pulleyblank, for valuable corrections, though they are in no way responsible for the errors still remaining.

decades, and a very illuminating review of their results may be found in Father Paul Serruys' recent article, "Chinese Dialectology Based on Written Documents,"[2] to which the following remarks owe a considerable debt.

The earliest self-conscious attempt to identify dialect areas in China was Yang Hsiung's 揚雄 (53 B.C.–A.D. 18) work, "Local Words" (*Fang-yen* 方言), in which Serruys has isolated six more or less identifiable dialect zones, corresponding roughly to the six suggested for Han times by Lo Ch'ang-p'ei 羅常培 and Chou Tsu-mŏ 周祖謨 in the first volume of their study of the evolution of rhyme categories during the Han and Six Dynasties periods.[3] In this scheme Lo-yang would fit into the western half of the Kuan-tung area (Honan) and Chien-k'ang (Nanking) into Wu-Yüeh (Kiangsu-Chekiang). Especially helpful in relating the Han dialect words of the *Fang-yen* to the pronunciations current in the fourth century are Kuo P'u's 郭璞 (276–342) glosses, included in most editions of the *Fang-yen*. But to assume that what is referred to by Kuo P'u, Yen Chih-t'ui, and other writers of the period as "Northern speech" or "Wu speech" represents the actual local dialects of Lo-yang and Chien-k'ang is to be grossly misled. It is true that Northern court speech at Lo-yang was sufficiently like the local dialect to be scarcely distinguishable from it,[4] but the speech of the Southern court at Chien-k'ang was actually an artificial "Kanzlei-sprache," a conscious imitation of pre-exilic Lo-yang speech affected by the courtiers of Eastern Chin and the succeeding Southern Dynasties as a nostalgic link with the past. It was influenced, to greater or lesser degrees, depending on the origins, social status, and period of the speakers, by the surrounding Wu dialect, which was itself already an earlier import brought by successive waves of immigrants from the North in late Han and Three Kingdoms times. This compound, in its turn, was further influenced by the *original* Wu language which is described in the *Fang-yen*. In addition, there may also have

---

[2] *Monumenta Serica*, 21 (1962, publ. 1964), 320–344.

[3] See P. L.–M. Serruys, *The Chinese Dialects of Han Times According to Fang-yen* (University of California Press, 1957), summarized by the same author as "A Note on Chinese Dialectology," in *Orbis*, 9 (1960); and Lo Ch'ang-p'ei and Chou Tsu-mo, *Han-Wei nan-pei-ch'ao yün-pu yen-pien yen-chiu* 漢魏南北朝韻部演變研究 (Peking, 1958), reviewed by Serruys in *MS*, 20 (1961), 394 ff.

[4] *Yen-shih chia-hsun, chüan* 18 (citations are from *YSCH hui-chu* 顏氏家訓彙注 , edited by Chou Fa-kao 周法高 , Taipei, 1960). See also Ch'en Yin-k'o 陳寅恪 , *Tung-Chin Nan-ch'ao chih Wu-yü* 東晉南朝之吳語 ("The Language of Wu during the Eastern Chin and Southern Dynasties"), *Bulletin of the Institute of History and Philology, Academia Sinica*, 7:1 (1936), 2.

been remnants of vocabulary inherited from the non-Chinese aboriginal inhabitants of pre-Han times.

To find a parallel in our own day we might turn to the present situation on Formosa, where the ruling group is composed of refugees speaking the standard language of their homeland and making this the prestige dialect. The local speech of earlier settlers from different parts of the same homeland is markedly inferior in prestige. In addition there are still pockets of aborigines in the hills speaking a non-Chinese language.

In the Dynastic Histories, cases are recorded of certain Southerners addressing members of the court in the local Wu idiom, but always as evidence of their ignorance or bad breeding. If poems were to be composed, efforts to do so in the local vernacular were met with good-natured derision. Wang Ching-tse 王 敬 則 (439–502), who, though illiterate, had attained very high rank, is said always to have used his native Wu speech "in addressing courtiers or commoners alike." When called upon by the Southern Ch'i Emperor Wu (r. 483–493) to compose a poem, Wang picked up a piece of paper and remarked wryly, "Your servant nearly fell victim to this slavery."

"What do you mean by that?" asked the Emperor.

"If I knew how to read and write," replied Wang, "I should never have become anything more than a clerk in the Court Secretariat. How could I have gotten where I am today?"[5]

On another occasion, reported in the *Shih-shuo hsin-yü*, one of the aides of the Eastern Chin general Huan Wen 桓 溫 (312–373), a certain Hao Lung 郝 隆 , was at a drinking party at which every person unable to compose a line of poetry extempore had to pay a forfeit by drinking three measures of wine. After failure to compose and paying the forfeit, Hao seized a brush and wrote the words,

"The *chü-yü* (M. *tsįu-ngįu*)[6] leaps up from the limpid pool." 娵 隅 躍 清 池 .

---

5 *Nan-ch'i shu* (K'ai-ming ed., *Erh-shih-wu shih*), 26:1713a.

6 The binom *chü-yü* may represent an original monosyllable with an initial cluster, M. *tsngįu* (M., here and throughout this article, indicates Middle Chinese transcriptions), and is apparently cognate with the standard word for "fish," *yü* 魚 (M. *ngįwo*). [*Editor's note*: Tung Yu 董 逌 of the twelfth century says in his *Kuang-ch'uan hua pa* 廣 川 畫 跋 that he saw in the office of the Ch'engtu Prefecture a painting of fishes captioned "Chü-yü t'u" 娵 魚 圖 . Tung, quoting Hao Lung's line, believed the Southwestern Man tribes did call fish 娵 隅 . It is interesting to notice that the painting had 娵 魚 for 娵 隅 , although we should reject, as the *Ssu-k'u ch'üan-shu tsung-mu t'i-yao* 四 庫 全 書 總 目 提 要 does, Tung's suggestion that the painting had belonged to those tribes. One may wonder whether Hao Lung uses a pun in his line, i.e., uses 隅 (*Ch'ieh-yün* and *Kuang-yün*: 語 俱 切) for 魚 (語 居 切)

"What on earth is a *chü-yü?*" asked Huan Wen in amusement.

"That's the [local] Man word for 'fish,'" replied Hao Lung.

Huan Wen sniffed, "Whoever heard of using the Man language to compose poetry?"[7]

The Man 蠻 language was probably not the Wu dialect, since this incident reportedly took place in Hsiang-yang (Northern Hupei), which falls within the Northern Ch'u dialect belt of the *Fang-yen*, where Huan Wen, as Commandant of the Southern Man, was stationed at the time. The principle, however, of using only the standard literary language for composition, except for conscious imitations of folksongs, is clear.

If further evidence for the literary prestige of the "Lo-yang dialect" in vogue at the Southern court were needed, numerous examples could be found of Southern courtiers, especially in the mid-fourth century, reciting poetry in the "style of the scholars of Lo-yang" (*Lo-sheng yung* 洛生詠 , or *Lo-hsia shu-sheng yung* 洛下書生詠). To recite poetry in any other way would have grated even more harshly on cultivated Chinese ears at Chien-k'ang than would be the case today if an actor were to declaim a passage from Shakespeare in an uncultivated Midwestern American drawl.

One of the most celebrated practitioners of the "Lo-yang style" was the statesman and general, Hsieh An 謝安 (320–385). Hsieh is said to have had a congenital malformation of the nose which made his voice naturally "heavy and turgid" (*chung-cho* 重濁).[8] This is the standard characterization of Northern speech in this period, as contrasted with the "buoyant and clear" (*fu-ch'ing* 浮清) quality ascribed to the Southern court speech.[9]

---

for their similarity in pronunciation. The character 娪 might stand for 隅 ; the *Kuang-yün* gives the two the same phonetic value 子 于 切 (also 子 侯 切). The *Ching-tien shih-wen* 經 典 釋 文 version of Cheng Hsüan's commentary to the "Yüeh ling" 鄭 玄 " 月 令 " 注 : 日 月 會 于 隅 訾 ," has 娪 for 隅 . 隅 could imply the Southern Man tribes; Tso Ssu 左 思 , of the third century, in his "Wei-tu fu" 魏 都 賦 says, " 蠻 隅 夷 落 "; Shen Yüeh 沈 約 (441–513) in his "Ch'i ku An-lu Chao-wang pei-wen" 齊 故 安 陸 昭 王 碑 文 also has " 蠻 隅 夷 徼 ." 隅 and 隅 are synonyms, both meaning "a corner" or "a mountain ridge." 隅 隅 is also a compound with the same meanings. The *Shuo wen* says, " 隅 , 阪 隅 也 "; " 隅 , 隅 也 "; and " 卫 , 隅 隅 高 山 之 節 " (the book does not have the word 娪). Both the *Yü-p'ien* 玉 篇 and the *Kuang-yün* define 隅 with the compound 隅 隅 , of which 峨 嵋 might be regarded as a variant. Thus we are not sure whether Hao Lung really employed an ordinary Chinese term to denote the sound of "fish" in the Man language, or simply twisted that term 隅 隅 to mean 蠻 魚 as a joke, which seems to be clear from his answer to Huan Wen: " 千 里 投 公 ， 始 得 蠻 府 參 軍 ， 那 得 不 作 蠻 語 也 ？"]

7 *Shih-shuo hsin-yü* (3B, 9b, *SPTK* ed.), 25:35.

8 *Shih-shuo*, 6:29 (2A, 31b), Commentary of Liu Chün 劉 峻 (sixth century).

9 *Shih-shuo*, 26:26 (3B, 22b), Commentary; *Yen-shih chia-hsün*, 18:120a (quoted below); Lu Te-ming 陸 德 明 (seventh century), *Ching-tien shih-wen hsü-lu* 經 典 釋 文 叙 錄

Most of Hsieh's contemporaries, who hung on his every foible as the last word, eagerly imitated his nasal twang by covering their noses with their hands while they intoned poems. There were some, however, especially members of the older Wu families, who looked on the Northern refugees as uncouth barbarians, and openly laughed at the "Lo-yang style." The famous painter, Ku K'ai-chih 顧愷之 (*ca.* 345–*ca.* 406) was once asked why he did not use that pronunciation when he chanted poems.

"Why should I make a noise like an old serving-maid?" he retorted.[10]

There were still others who seem to have felt uneasy about the "buoyant," even "seductive" (*yao erh fu* 妖而浮), quality of Southern speech, and the fact that everybody was "valuing it" above its Northern model.[11]

A sixth-century view of the two dialects — the actual speech of Lo-yang, and the artificial preservation of the "Lo-yang style" by Southerners in Chien-k'ang — is neatly stated by Yen Chih-t'ui, who had been born in the South and moved to the North in middle life, in the passage cited earlier. He goes on to say:

In the South the streams and soil are moderate and mild, and their pronunciation clear and elevated (*ch'ing-chü* 清舉), incisive and penetrating (*ch'ieh-i* 切詣), though they lose something through buoyancy and shallowness (*fu-ch'ien* 浮淺), and their vocabulary is full of vulgar colloquialisms (*pi-su* 鄙俗). In the North the hills and rivers are deep and dense, and their pronunciation submerged and turgid (*ch'en-cho* 沈濁), deviant and confused (*o-chun* 訛訰), though they gain something in honesty and directness, and their vocabulary is full of archaic expressions. However, in the case of the gentlemen of the court the South is superior, while in the case of commoners in the villages the North is better. Exchange their clothes and converse with them, and gentlemen and commoners in the South may be distinguished after only a few words; but listen to their speech with a wall intervening, and courtiers and provincials in the North would be hard to tell apart even after a whole day. On the other hand, Southern speech is contaminated by the local dialects of Wu and Yüeh, and the Northern is mixed with those of the barbarian caitiffs (*I-lu* 夷虜). They both have serious shortcomings, and I cannot discuss their faults in detail. But as far as losing something through lightness and insubstantiality (*ch'ing-wei* 輕微) is concerned, Southerners pronounce *ch'ien* 錢 , "cash" (M. *dz'iän*), like *hsien* 涎 , "saliva" (M. *ziän*); *shih* 石 , "stone" (M. *dz'iäk*), like *she* 射 , "shoot" (M. *źiäk*); *chien* 賤 , "cheap" (M. *dz'iän-*), they pronounce like *hsien* 羨 , "admire" (M. *ziän-*); and *shih* 是 , "this" (M. *dź'ie:*), as though it were *shih* 舐 , "lick" (M. *źie:*). Northerners on the other hand, pronounce *shu* 庶 , "common" (M. *śiwo-*), like *shu* 戍 . "garrison" (M. *śiu*); *ju* 如 , "like" (M. *ńźiwo*), like *ju* 儒 , "literatus" (M. *ńźiu*) . . . etc.[12]

(*SPTK* ed.), 1:1a; Lu Fa-yen 陸法言 (sixth century), *Ch'ieh-yün hsü* 切韻序 (quoted by Chou Fa-kao, p. 120a).

[10] *Shih-shuo*, 26:26 (3B, 22b).

[11] *Shih-shuo*, 2:104 (1A, 49b).

[12] *Yen-shih chia-hsün*, 18:120a. The reconstructed "Ancient Chinese" [Middle Chinese]

If we should try from this small sample to construct any laws of phonetic alternation between North and South, we could not go far, but even from this a few things are immediately suggested. For example, the affricate initials, M. *dz'*- and M. *dź'*-, distinguished in the North from the simple fricatives, M. *z*- and *ź*-, appear indiscriminately without affrication in the South. Likewise, distinctions between final M. *-i̯wo* and M. *-i̯u*, maintained in the South, coalesce into M. *-i̯u* in the North. This may be part of what is meant by the terms "clear" (*ch'ing* 清) and "turgid" (*cho* 濁), as applied respectively to Southern and Northern speech. Quite evidently they have no reference in this period to the technical meaning of "voiceless" and "voiced" initials which they have in later philological writing, for the archaic voicing was retained in the South long after it disappeared in the North. A rapid glance at Yen's examples, matched with their corresponding Sino-Japanese Kan-on and Go-on readings, and their readings in modern Mandarin and the Wu dialect of Shanghai, seems to bear this out, though hardly in any conclusive sense.[13]

	Ancient Lo-yang	Ancient Chien-k'ang	Kan-on	Go-on	Modern Mandarin	Modern Wu
錢	dz'i̯än	zi̯än	sen	zen	ch'ien	dzie
石	dź'i̯äk	źi̯äk	se-ki	zi-ya-ku	shih	za
賤	dz'i̯än-	zi̯än-	sen	zen	chien	dzie
是	dź'i̯e̯	źi̯e̯	si	zi	shih	dzi
庶	śi̯u	śi̯wo	si-yo	si-yo	shu	zy
如	ńźi̯u	ńźi̯wo	zi-yo	ni-yo	ju	zy

transcriptions (prefixed with M. in this article) are based on Bernhard Karlgren's *Grammata Serica Recensa* (Stockholm, 1957), but with the *reversal* of Karlgren's affricate and fricative initials, after the principles stated by Pulleyblank in "The Consonantal System of Old Chinese," *Asia Major*, 9, Part I (New Series, 1962), 67–69. I realize that this does not necessarily give the values intended by Yen Chih-t'ui, but the transcriptions may serve in a relative sense for purposes of comparison (ṣee n. 13, below).

13 It is widely held among Japanese linguists that Kan-on readings probably represented standard Ch'ang-an speech of the sixth and seventh centuries, but that Go-on is a very broad designation for all nonstandard provincial variations, and should by no means be equated with the single area of Wu. It is also generally held that the *fan-ch'ieh* spellings of the *Ch'ieh-yün* 切 韻 (A.D. 601), on which Karlgren ostensibly built his reconstructions of "Ancient Chinese," in many cases coincided with the Southern version of the so-called "Lo-yang style" of the Six Dynasties, rather than with the seventh-century dialect of Ch'ang-an. See Tōdō Akiyasu 藤 堂 明 保 , *Chūgoku on'in ron* 中 國 音 韻 論 (Tokyo, 1957), pp. 142–144; and Gunther Wenck, *Japanische Phonetik* (Wiesbaden, 1954), vol. 2, pp. 295 ff., cited by Serruys, in *Monumenta Serica*, 21:333 (mimeographed insert).

Perhaps Yen's terms, "clear" and "turgid," applied to some kind of vowel nazalization in the North. From the story about Hsieh An and the trouble with his nose we might conclude that Northerners spoke like persons suffering from a bad head cold, with a stoppage, or denasalization, of nasal initials. Striking confirmation of this seems to show up in certain Kan-on readings:

	Kan-on	Go-on
女	di-yo	ni-yo
年	den	nen
門	bon	mon
文	bun	mon

However, it is generally agreed that such denasalization (Ancient M. *nd-*, M. *ŋg-*, M. *mb-*) was a peculiarity of the Kuan-hsi area (especially Ch'ang-an), persisting even into modern times, but was never typical for Lo-yang.[14]

Perhaps the most plausible explanation of the "turgidity" of Northern speech may be found in E. G. Pulleyblank's reconstruction of a back velar stop, similar to the *q-* of Turkish and Altaic languages, and distinct from the front velar *k-* ,which appears in distinctively Northern transcriptions of Sanskrit, representing the aspirated initial *kh-*.[15] Identifiably Southern transcriptions disregard the distinction. It may well be that such sounds, produced far back in the throat, with resulting coloration of the vowels, represented one aspect of the influence of proto-Altaic languages spoken by the Hsien-pi and other non-Chinese groups in North China during the Six Dynasties, and produced an effect described as "turgid" and "heavy".

On the whole it seems safe to conclude that Southern usage was, in most of the points of contrast, more conservative than the Northern. Since it was relatively free of foreign influence, it preserved features which were changing or dying out in the North. Yen Chih-t'ui, fine pedant that he was, found the general relaxation in the North of distinctions still current in Southern court speech deplorable. For example, the different intonation (still preserved in Mandarin) of *haŏ* 好 "good" (M. *χâu:*), and *è* 惡 , "evil" (M. · *âk*), when used as nouns or adjectives; and *haò*, "to love" (*χâu-*) and *wù*, "to hate" (M. · *uo-*), when used as verbs, was, according to Yen,

---

14 See B. Karlgren, *Grammata Serica* (original edition, Stockholm, 1940), p. 67; and Serruys, in *Monumenta Serica*, 21:335.

15 E. G. Pulleyblank, "The Transcription of Sanskrit *k* and *kh* in Chinese," *Asia Major* (new series), XI, 2 (1965), 199–210.

disregarded north of the Yellow River. In the South people carefully observed a difference between an initial voiceless glottal stop, or a voiced laryngal fricative, in reading *yen* 焉 , "how, why?" (M. *i̯än*), as an initial interrogative adverb, or *yen*, "thereon, thereof" (M. *ji̯än*), as a final particle. Northerners, claimed Yen, read them exactly alike. *Pai* 敗 as a transitive verb, "to defeat" (M. *pwai-*), was distinguished in the South by an unvoiced high-pitched initial; as an intransitive verb, "to be defeated" (M. *b'wai-*), it was voiced, aspirated, and low-pitched. Northerners made no distinction then, and certainly do not now. In the North, said Yen, no one could be sure when he heard the word *kung* 攻 , "attack," whether it might not also be *kung* 工 , "artisan," *kung* 公 , "duke," or *kung* 功 , "merit" (all M. *kung*). But in the South, at least, *kung* 攻 , "attack," was distinguished as M. *kuong*.[16]

There were, as we should expect, differences as well in vocabulary and syntax, just as there are between modern Chinese dialects. Since what remains of the period is mainly literary texts employing a homogenized literary style, it is not possible to document the differences beyond a few scattered examples, recorded in sources like the *Shih-shuo hsin-yü*, where an approximation to contemporary speech is sometimes preserved. Certain expressions typical for the *Shih-shuo*, like *chiang-wu* 將無 , "isn't it?"; *ho-wu* 何物 , "what?" *a-tu* 阿堵 , "that"; and words still occurring in almost the same usage in Mandarin, like *na* 那 (3rd tone), "how on earth?"; *tou* 都 , "altogether, completely"; and *shih* 是 used as the copula, have already been noted by both Chinese and Japanese scholars.[17] Though it cannot be proved, many of these expressions may have fallen into the category of "vulgar colloquialisms" peculiar to Southern usage, about which Yen Chih-t'ui complained so bitterly.

The first Chancellor of the Eastern Chin court, Wang Tao 王導 (276–339), was himself a Northerner, but pursued a conscious policy of rapprochement with the local gentry of Wu, and even attempted (unsuccessfully) to marry his daughter to one of them. He tried hard to learn a few local expressions, and once as the host at a party where most of the guests were apparently Northerners (i.e. refugees of the *yung-chia* era, 307–312), he took special

---

16 *Yen-shih chia-hsün*, 18:125b.

17 E.g , Yoshikawa Kōjirō 吉川幸次郎 , *Sesetsu shingo no bunshō* 世說新語の文章 ("The Style of the *Shih-shuo hsin-yü*"), *Tōhō gakuhō*, 10:2 (1939), 86–89, trans. G. W. Baxter, *HJAS*, 18 (1955), 124 ff.; Li Hsing-chien 李行健 , "Shih-shuo hsin-yü *chung fu-tz'u 'tou' ho 'liao' yung-fa ti pi-chiao* 世說新語中副詞「都」和「了」用法的比較 ("Comparison of the Uses of *tou* and *liao* in the *Shih-shuo hsin-yü*"), in *Yü-yen-hsüeh lun-ts'ung*, 2 (1958), 84–99.

pains to greet one guest, a Southerner from Lin-hai 臨海 (in Chekiang), in his local dialect.

"When you came out to the Capital (Chien-k'ang)," Wang said to him affably, "Lin-hai then had nobody left anymore." (*Lin-hai pien wu fu jen* 臨海便無復人．)[18]

The particle *fu* 復 interrupts the normal syntactic relation between *wu* 無 and *jen* 人 , and seems to have been typical of numerous particles of scarcely translatable meaning in Wu speech which have been analyzed by Yoshikawa Kōjirō and others (see n. 17). That it was Wu speech, and not court speech, seems to be indicated by the fact that at the same party Wang addressed a group of very lonely-looking Central Asian monks, by using what appears to be an Indian or Central Asian greeting, sounding something like, "Rañja! Rañja!" (蘭闍蘭闍), which brought immediate smiles to their gloomy faces (see n. 18).

On another occasion Wang was sitting in his study, trying to keep cool on a sultry summer day. Leaning across a chessboard with his abdomen pressed against it, he exclaimed with delight, "How cool!" (*ho nai ch'eng* 何乃渹).

His visitor, Liu T'an 劉惔 (*ca.* 310–*ca.* 346), a younger, but very proper man, was shocked by both the act and the accompanying remark. After he had withdrawn, someone asked him, "Now that you have seen Wang Tao, what do you think of him?"

Liu snorted, "I didn't observe anything special, except just to hear him talk in the Wu dialect!"[19]

By "Wu dialect" he surely meant the local speech of Wu, not the court speech which Yen Chih-t'ui had in mind, except as it was "vulgarized" by such expressions as this.

In conclusion, it should be remembered that most of the writers and philologists of the Six Dynasties period whose works have come down to us were Southerners, and as such favored the Southern version of what they took to be the standard idiom of Lo-yang before its fall in 311. It was artificial, conservative, even consciously archaistic, and above all, it was a *literary*

---

18 *Shih-shuo*, 3:12 (1B, 5a).

19 *Shih-shuo*, 25:13 (3B, 5a). The story is also quoted in the early Sung repository, *T'ai-p'ing yü-lan*, pp. 21, 34, 371, and 375, where the character for *ch'eng*, "cool," is variously written 瀞 and 韵 . According to Wang Li-ch'i 王利器 , whose annotated collations accompany the Peking reprint of the Sung wood-block edition from the Kanazawa Bunkō (*Shih-shuo hsin-yü chiao-k'an chi* 校勘記 , Peking, 1956, p. 59), *ch'eng* (spelled *ch'u* 楚 – *ching* 敬) is still current (dialect undesignated) for "refrigerate by placing ice on something."

language, used primarily in reading and reciting ancient texts or composing new ones. When persons of rank spoke to each other at court they tried to use this pure creation of academicians, but could not help bastardizing it with "vulgar colloquialisms," many of which must have originated from the local Wu dialect, a blend of several strata of earlier linguistic alluvia from the North. As this transplanted Southern court language grew farther and farther removed from its Northern source, and Lo-yang speech itself was being more and more affected by the speech of barbarian invaders, the difference between Lo-yang and Chien-k'ang speech became so marked as to cause a sixth-century purist like Yen Chih-t'ui to be disturbed by the "heavy and turgid" timbre of Northern voices, and by their "deviant and confused" pronunciations, which glossed over distinctions between voiced and unvoiced initials, as well as differences of intonation and vowel color. At the same time, as a naturalized Northerner, he could not help feeling a certain pride in the fact that even commoners in the North spoke a standard dialect, while Southern gentlemen, to their ineffable discredit, used a very clear and pleasant-sounding language at court or when they composed literary pieces, but when they were in the bosom of their families or at informal gatherings, stooped to a debased local patois that would have made even a scavenger on the streets of Lo-yang blush for shame.

The Great Clod:
A Taoist Conception of the Universe

H. G. CREEL

IN the Western intellectual tradition it has commonly been taken for granted that man's mind, or his essential nature, enjoys a special and rather intimate relationship with the essential nature of the universe. For Judaism and Christianity the basis for this is laid in the first chapter of Genesis, which says both that God created man in his own image and that God created the heaven and the earth. In Greek thought, at least as it is represented by Plato, while the basis may be different the conviction that man stands in a special position with regard to the universe is no less strong.

In philosophic Taoism,[1] on the other hand, as we see it especially in the *Chuang-tzu*, there is no special relationship between man, or man's mind, and the nature of the universe. This difference of view has important consequences for such matters as the theory of knowledge.

---

[1] The term "Taoism" is used to denote a wide variety of doctrines. The most obvious difference is between philosophical Taoism and what is sometimes called "religious Taoism." The latter gives relatively little attention to such problems as that of the nature of the universe, and is largely concerned with the problem of gaining immortality. I have proposed calling it "Hsien Taoism"; see H. G. Creel, "What Is Taoism?" *JAOS*, 76 (1956), 139–152. Within philosophical Taoism, I further distinguish two aspects, "contemplative" and "purposive"; see H. G. Creel, "On Two Aspects in Early Taoism," in *Silver Jubilee Volume of the Zinbun-Kagaku-Kenkyusyo, Kyoto University* (Kyoto, 1954), pp. 43–53. Purposive Taoism seems to me to be a slightly posterior development, found predominantly (but not exclusively) in the *Lao-tzu*; it is chiefly concerned with the control of phenomena, and relatively little with the nature of the universe. The latter is, however, a major concern of contemplative Taoism, which in my opinion represents the earliest and most authentic form of Taoist philosophy; it is found predominantly (but again not exclusively) in the *Chuang-tzu*.

Plato draws a sharp distinction between knowledge and opinion. He speaks of "the very being with which true knowledge is concerned; the colourless, formless, intangible essence, visible only to mind, the pilot of the soul."[2] And, he says, "the soul is like the eye: when resting upon that on which truth and being shine, the soul perceives and understands and is radiant with intelligence; but when turned towards the twilight of becoming and perishing, then she has opinion only."[3]

If "becoming and perishing" do not characterize reality, then it must be that the truly real is unchanging. Thus Plato writes in the *Cratylus*:

Socrates. I myself do not deny that the givers of names did really give them under the idea that all things were in motion and flux; which was their sincere but, I think, mistaken opinion. . . . And can we rightly speak of a beauty which is always passing away, and is first this and then that; must not the same thing be born and retire and vanish while the word is in our mouths?

Cratylus. Undoubtedly.

Soc. Then how can that be a real thing which is never in the same state? for obviously things which are the same cannot change while they remain the same; and if they are always the same and in the same state, and never depart from their original form, they can never change or be moved.

Crat. Certainly they cannot.

Soc. Nor can they yet be known by anyone. . . . But if the very nature of knowledge changes, at the time when the change occurs there will be no knowledge; and if the transition is always going on, there will always be no knowledge, and, according to this view, there will be no one to know and nothing to be known: but if that which knows and that which is known exist ever, and the beautiful and the good and every other thing also exist, then I do not think that they can resemble a process or flux, as we were just now supposing.[4]

The position of Plato is clear and consistent. Thought operates in terms of concepts, but concepts (names) cannot be forever changing to correspond to the phenomena of a universe in constant flux. Thus if the universe were constantly changing, accurate or "absolute" knowledge would be impossible; for this reason, Plato concludes, reality is not in flux. The *Chuang-tzu*, written at the other end of Eurasia perhaps half a century after the death of Plato,[5] made a remarkably similar analysis of the same problem, but

---

2 Plato, *Phaedrus* [Stephanus 247], in *The Dialogues of Plato*, trans. Benjamin Jowett (New York. 1937), 1:252.

3 Plato, *Republic* [Stephanus 508]; Jowett, 1:770.

4 Plato, *Cratylus* [Stephanus 439–440]; Jowett, 1:228–229.

5 I speak of "the *Chuang-tzu*" rather than of the putative author, Chuang-tzu, because it is quite clear that this work was composite. While the man called Chuang-tzu doubtless existed, and wrote some part of this book, our knowledge of him is slight, and perhaps no scholar today would suppose that all of this work was from a single hand. Contemporary

arrived at an opposite result; the *Chuang-tzu* concluded that knowledge, in any absolute sense, is impossible.

Concerning the universal flux, the *Chuang-tzu* says:

The *Tao* has no beginning or end. Things die and are born, never resting in their culmination· . . . Decay is followed by growth, and fullness by emptiness; when there is an end, there is also a beginning. . . . The existence of all creatures is like the galloping of a horse. With every movement there is alteration; at every moment they are undergoing change.[6]

道 無 終 始 物 有 死 生 不 恃 其 成 …… 消 息 盈 虛 終 則 有 始 …… 物 之 生 也 若 驟 若 馳 無 動 而 不 變 無 時 而 不 移 ("秋 水" 第 十 七)

And again:

All the various species of things transform into one another by the process of variation in form. Their beginning and ending is like an unbroken ring, of which it is impossible to discover the principle.[7]

萬 物 皆 種 也 以 不 同 形 相 禪 始 卒 若 環 莫 得 其 倫 ("寓 言" 第 二 十 七)

The meaning of this latter passage is, I think, fairly clear. There is, for instance, a progression that begins with an acorn and ends with dust or soil, when the process begins all over again. But no one can say at what moment the acorn becomes a tree, the tree wood, the wood dust, and so on. These transformations compose a circle in which there is no break into which we can insert our intelligence, so as to form an immutable concept. The sense is quite similar to that of Plato's statement in the *Cratylus*, quoted earlier.

To Plato's propositions the author of our passage in the *Chuang-tzu* would reply, "Precisely!" There is no knowledge, in any absolute sense. And there are no discrete things, which exist in and of themselves without regard to their changing environment; within this total environment, what we call "things" are merely inseparable and constantly changing aspects. Therefore, in any absolute sense it is perfectly true that there is "no one to know and nothing to be known." Thus the *Chuang-tzu* tells us:

There is one respect in which the understanding of the men of antiquity reached the highest point. Wherein did they excel? They believed that things did not exist.[8] This is the

---

scholarship tends to date this work, or at least its earliest portions, as having been written somewhere in the neighborhood of 300 B.C.

[6] *Chuang-tzu* (*SPPY* ed.), 6:11a; cf. also Richard Wilhelm, trans. *Dschuang Dsi* (Düsseldorf/Köln, 1951), p. 129; James Legge, trans. *The Writings of Kwang-zze*, 1 (*Sacred Books of the East*, vol. 39; Oxford, 1927), pp. 382–383.

[7] *Chuang-tzu*, 9:7b; cf. also Wilhelm, *Dschuang Dsi*, p. 207; Legge, *The Writings of Kwang-zze*, 2 (*Sacred Books of the East*, vol. 40; Oxford, 1927), p. 144.

[8] In my opinion most of the translators of this passage — including Fung Yu-lan, Wilhelm, and Legge, whose translations are cited in the following note — have been misled by their

highest point, the culmination; nothing can be added to it. Next below this is the state of believing that things exist, but that there are no distinctions between them.[9]

古之人其知有所至矣惡乎至有以爲未始有物者至矣盡矣不可以加矣其次以爲有物矣而未始有封也("齊物論"第二)

The Taoists call the totality of existence the *Tao*, but in fact it cannot be known and this is not even really its name. The *Chuang-tzu* says:

The *Tao* cannot be heard; what is heard is not it. The *Tao* cannot be seen; what is seen is not it. The *Tao* cannot be talked about; what is talked about is not it. ... There is no name that truly corresponds to the *Tao*.[10]

道不可聞聞而非也道不可見見而非也道不可言言而非也 …… 道不當名("知北遊"第二十二)

Certainly one cannot generalize to the extent of calling the Platonic "the Western," and the Taoist "the Chinese," view of reality. Exceptions can be found both in China and in the West. It is undoubtedly true, as Joseph Needham and others have pointed out,[11] that the recent developments of modern science conduce to a view that has some remarkable similarities to that of early Taoism. Yet, however much we may intellectually reject the concept of absolutes, many of us still feel a strong emotional pull toward such abstract ideas as "truth." The main stream of Western thinking has followed a course that has not paralleled that of the Taoist conception of reality.

This fact has made it difficult for many Western students effectively to understand the Taoist conception. This becomes apparent when we examine the manner in which most of them translate the term *Tao*, as it appears in the *Chuang-tzu* and the *Lao-tzu*. Insofar as one can judge from these translations, most of them appear to have understood the Taoist conception of

---

interpretation of the expression *wei shih* 未始 , which they take in some such sense as "not yet begun." Certainly this is the usual sense of the characters. But *wei shih* is a very common expression in the *Chuang-tzu*, and at some points it quite unmistakably functions as a simple negative, which I think it very clearly is here. James R. Ware, trans. *The Sayings of Chuang Chou* (New York, 1963), p. 23, here renders *wei shih* as a simple negative, but I do not find his translation of the whole passage satisfactory. For other passages in which *wei shih* must be taken as a simple negative, see *Chuang-tzu*, 2:7b and 8:15b. Fung's partial translation of the *Chuang-tzu* includes only the first of these two passages, but in each occurrence of these passages Fung, Legge, and Wilhelm render *wei shih* as a simple negative. See Fung Yu-lan, trans. *Chuang Tzŭ, a New Selected Translation* (Shanghai, 1933), p. 80; Legge, *The Writings of Kwang-zze*, 1:209, 2:100; Wilhelm, *Dschuang Dsi*, pp. 29, 185.

9 *Chuang-tzu*, 1:16b; cf. also Fung, *Chuang Tzŭ*, p. 53; Wilhelm, *Dschuang Dsi*, p. 15; Legge, *The Writings of Kwang-zze*, 1:185.

10 *Chuang-tzu*, 7:28a; cf. also Legge, *The Writings of Kwang-zze*, 1:185.

11 Joseph Needham, *Science and Civilisation in China*, vol. 2 (Cambridge, 1956), pp. 496–505.

the universe as being quite similar to that which is dominant in Western thought: a conception that establishes a special relationship between the essential nature of man and the essential nature of reality. Arthur Waley writes that

In a particular school of philosophy whose followers ultimately came to be called Taoists, *tao* meant "the way the universe works"; and ultimately, something very like God, in the more abstract and philosophical sense of that term. Now it so happens that all the meaning-extensions of this word *tao* (even including the last: "I am the Way") also exist in European languages, so that Western scholars have had no difficulty in understanding it.[12]

And a number of scholars have rendered the term *Tao* as "God."[13]

It was almost inevitable that the term *logos* should be used to render *Tao*. The Gospel of John opens with the words, "In the beginning there was the *logos*." This, and the kindred sense of "reason," have been favored as translations of *Tao* by many.[14] Abel-Rémusat, who was the first Professor of Chinese in the Collège de France, wrote in 1824: "It seems impossible to translate this word *Tao* otherwise than by the word *logos* and its derivatives, in the triple sense of *supreme being, reason,* and *word.*"[15]

Stanislas Julien, who was a student of Abel-Rémusat and his successor at the Collège de France, objected strongly to the rendering of *Tao* as *logos*.

---

12 Arthur Waley, *The Way and Its Power* (London, 1934; reprint of 1949), pp. 30–31.

13 C. G. Alexander, *Lâo-tsze the Great Thinker* (London, 1895), p. 55; Victor von Strauss, *Laò-tsè's Taò Tĕ King* (Leipzig, 1924), xxxiv–xxxv. Ware, *The Sayings of Chuang Chou, passim.* Ware writes (pp. 7–8): "From Chuang Chou (300 B.C.), one of China's great minds, we get the world's most intelligible and diverting discussion of God. In the book translated here, Chuang Chou describes for his contemporaries the almighty, all-embracing, everlasting God comparable to the One defined in the Judaeo-Christian tradition by the equation God–Life. . . . The term usually employed by Chuang Chou is the sobriquet Tao (see 11.70). In addition, he uses about twenty epithets. All of these I am translating 'God' . . . "

14 Abel-Rémusat, "Mémoire sur la Vie et les Opinions de Lao Tseu," in *Mémoires de l'Institut Royal de France, Académie des Inscriptions et Belles-Lettres,* vol. 7 (Paris, 1824), p. 23; G. Pauthier, *Premier Livre du TAO-TE-KING de Lao-TSEU* (1838), p. 7; John Chalmers, *The Speculations . . . of "The Old Philosopher," Lau-tsze* (London, 1868), vol. 1; Paul Carus, *The Canon of Reason and Virtue* (Chicago and London, 1913; reprint of 1945), p. 73; Wilhelm, *Dschuang Dsi,* p. 3. James Legge, in the Introduction to his work *The Texts of Taoism* (*Sacred Books of the East,* 39:12–33) discusses the meaning of *Tao,* and says, "The first translation of the Tâo Teh King into a Western language was executed in Latin by some of the Roman Catholic missionaries, and a copy of it was brought to England by a Mr. Matthew Raper, F.R.S., and presented by him to the Society on the 10th of January, 1788. . . . In this version, Tâo is taken in the sense of Ratio, or the Supreme Reason of the Divine Being, the Creator and Governor." Herbert A. Giles, trans. *Chuang Tzŭ: Mystic, Moralist, and Social Reformer* (London, 1926), pp. xxiv–xxv, indicates that, while he does not translate *Tao,* he finds it to be used very much as Heraclitus uses *logos.*

15 Abel-Rémusat, "Mémoire sur la Vie et les Opinions de Lao Tseu," p. 24.

The best way to see what the term means, Julien said, was to see what the *Lao-tzu* and other early Taoist works had to say about it. After quoting a number of passages he concluded:

It follows from the preceding passages, and from a great many others that I could cite, that in *Lao-tzu* and the oldest philosophers of his school before the Christian Era, the use and the definition of the word *Tao* excludes any idea of *intelligent cause* .... *Lao-tzu* represents the Tao as a being devoid of action, thoughts, or desires and he wishes man, in order to arrive at the highest degree of perfection, to remain like the Tao in a state of absolute quiet, divesting himself of thoughts, desires, and even of the light of intelligence, which according to him is a cause of disorder.[16]

Although it is a century and a quarter since Julien wrote, at a time when those in the Western world who could even read Chinese with real comprehension were few indeed, his understanding of this aspect of Taoism was in my opinion superior to that of most of the scholars who have studied it since his day.[17] It is interesting to note, however, that a somewhat similar view is stated by one of the most recent translators of the *Lao-tzu*, J. J. L. Duyvendak. He writes: "The Way, *Tao*, here remains a formal notion. It is not a First Cause, it is not a Logos. It is nothing but the process of change, of growth. The world is no longer viewed in static, but in dynamic terms."[18]

Tao is not only, however, "the process of change." It is also that which changes. It is, as the *Lao-tzu* (Chapters 21 and 25) tells us, a "thing," *wu* 物. Indeed, since individual things do not really exist as such, it would perhaps be correct to say that the *Tao* is the only thing there is. It may be called, the *Chuang-tzu* tells us, " 'complete,' 'all-embracing,' 'the whole'; these are different names for the same reality, denoting the One."[19] " 周, 徧, 咸, 三者異名同實, 其指一也 ." It is simply — if this is simple — the totality of all that is. It is indeed *mind*, since men have minds. It is also a great many other things.

Tung-kuo Tzu asked Chuang-tzu, "Where is that which you call *Tao*?" Chuang-tzu said, "Everywhere." Tung-kuo Tzu said, "You must be more specific." Chuang-tzu said, "It

---

16 Stanislas Julien, trans. *Le Livre de la Voie et de la Vertu* (Paris, 1842), XIII–XIV.

17 This does not mean that Julien did not share certain mistaken ideas, on such matters as the dating of certain Taoist texts, that were general in his day. He did; it could scarcely have been otherwise.

18 J. J. L. Duyvendak, trans. *Tao Te Ching* (London, 1954), p. 9. While there is much that is good in this work, on a number of points I do not find Duyvendak's translation and interpretation satisfactory. In particular, it seems to me that his rearrangement and editing of the text is based upon a mistaken conception of its character.

19 *Chuang-tzu*, 7:26b; Legge, *The Writings of Kwang-zze*, 2:66–67; Wilhelm, *Dschuang Dsi*, p. 165.

is in this ant." "In what lower?" "In this grass." "In anything still lower?" "It is in tiles." "Is it in anything lower still?" Chuang-tzu said, "It is in ordure and urine." Tung-kuo Tzu had nothing more to say.[20]

東 郭 子 問 於 莊 子 曰 所 謂 道 惡 乎 在 莊 子 曰 無 所 不 在 東 郭 子 曰 期 而 後 可 莊 子 曰 在 螻 蟻 曰 何 其 下 邪 曰 在 稊 稗 曰 何 其 愈 下 邪 曰 在 瓦 甓 曰 何 其 愈 甚 邪 曰 在 屎 溺 東 郭 子 不 應 ("知 北 遊" 第 二 十 二)

This is indeed, in William James's phrase, a "tough-minded" conception of the universe. It makes not the least concession to human vanity or sentiment. The ultimate nature of the universe has just as much, and just as little, relation to my mind as it has to the smallest pebble lying in the road. Certainly other men, besides Chinese Taoists, have been able to accept a view so unflattering to the human race. If most of them have flinched from it, surely one reason is the dark specter of death, which makes men long to believe that elsewhere in the universe, beyond the tiny span of human life, there is something that vibrates in special sympathy to human aspirations. Yet there have been countless mortals who have faced death bravely without this consolation, from philosophers of antiquity to the New England poet, William Cullen Bryant, who wrote in "Thanatopsis":

> Earth, that nourished thee, shall claim
> Thy growth, to be resolved to earth again,
> And, lost each human trace, surrendering up
> Thine individual being, thou shalt go
> To mix forever with the elements,
> To be a brother to the insensible rock
> And to the sluggish clod, which the rude swain
> Turns with his share, and treads upon. The oak
> Shall send his roots abroad, and pierce thy mould.

And the conclusion:

> So live, that when thy summons comes to join
> The innumerable caravan, which moves
> To that mysterious realm, where each shall take
> His chamber in the silent halls of death,
> Thou go not, like the quarry-slave at night,
> Scourged to his dungeon, but, sustained and soothed
> By an unfaltering trust, approach thy grave,
> Like one who wraps the drapery of his couch
> About him, and lies down to pleasant dreams.[21]

---

[20] *Chuang-tzu*, 7:26a; Legge, *The Writings of Kwang-zze*, 2:66; Wilhelm, *Dschuang Dsi*, p. 164.

[21] Quoted from Tremaine McDowell, *William Cullen Bryant* (New York, 1935), pp. 3–5.

Noble words, and brave. But they are brave because death remains, in spite of everything, a prospect in the face of which bravery is needed. The best that we are offered is eternal sleep, with the dubious prospect of "pleasant dreams." To the author of "Thanatopsis" it is clearly a melancholy fate that, after having attained to humanity, one must become "a brother to the insensible rock, and to the sluggish clod."

Not so the Taoist. "When there is an end," the *Chuang-tzu* tells us, "there is also a beginning" (see n. 6, above). Regarding death there seems to be a human tendency to go to one of two extremes: either what happens to the body is said to be of no importance whatever, or attention may be centered upon the rather unpleasant process of its immediate dissolution. But if man's life is short, the time required for the decay of his flesh is shorter. What then? If "the oak shall send his roots abroad," and pierce the mould of what was once a man, that same mould becomes a part of the oak. And why merely an oak? One of the most memorable passages in the *Chuang-tzu*, as translated by Fung Yu-lan, says:

> The universe carries us in our bodies, toils us through our life, gives us repose with our old age, and rests us in our death. That which makes our life a good makes our death a good also. . . . No matter how well you hide things, smaller ones in larger ones, there is always [a] chance for them to be lost. But if you hide the universe in the universe, there will be no room for it to be lost. This is a great truth. To have attained to the human form is a source of joy. But, in the infinite evolution, there are thousands of other forms that are equally good. What an incomparable bliss it is to undergo these countless transitions![22]

夫大塊載我以形勞我以生佚我以老息我以死故善吾生者乃所以善吾死也 … 藏小大有宜猶有所遯若夫藏天下於天下而不得所遯是恆物之大情也特犯人之形而猶喜之若人之形者萬化而未始有極也其爲樂可勝計邪 ("大宗師" 第六)

The expression with which this passage begins, which Fung renders as "the universe," is *ta k'uai* 大塊. James Legge translates it as "the great Mass (of nature)," Léon Wieger as "la grande masse (du cosmos, de la nature, du tout)," and Richard Wilhelm as "das grosse All."[23] Herbert A. Giles renders it as "nature," James R. Ware as "God (The Mass of Greatness),"

22 *Chuang-tzu*, 3:4b–5b; Fung, *Chuang Tzŭ*, pp. 116–117.

23 Legge, *The Writings of Kwang-zze*, 1:242; Léon Wieger, trans. *Les Pères du Système Taoïste: Lao-tzeu, Lie-tzeu, Tchoang-tzeu* (Paris, 1950), p. 253; Wilhelm, *Dschuang Dsi*, p. 48.

and Evan Morgan as "Heaven."[24] Literally it means "the Great Clod."[25]

The expression *ta k'uai* occurs several times in the *Chuang-tzu*, and from the way in which it is used it seems clearly to be a synonym for *Tao*.[26] While the renderings of translators, and the explanations of some commentators, tend to suggest this, none that I know of says explicitly that *ta k'uai* is used as a designation for the *Tao*.[27] This is perhaps scarcely remarkable.

Of all the many terms that have been used to designate the sum total of reality, "the Great Clod" is perhaps the most surprising. At first sight it seems so incongruous that one supposes that of course the characters

---

24 Giles, *Chuang Tzǔ*, p. 75; Ware, *The Sayings of Chuang Chou*, p. 48; Evan Morgan, *Tao, The Great Luminant*: *Essays from Huai Nan Tzǔ* (Shanghai, 1933), p. 33. In the latter work, the expression *ta k'uai* occurs in the quotation of this same passage, with minor textual variations; see *Huai-nan-tzu* (*SPPY* ed.), 2:2a.

25 That *k'uai* early had the sense of "a clod of earth" is clear from a passage in the *Tso-chuan*; see James Legge, trans. *The Chinese Classics*, vol. 5: *The Ch'un Ts'ew* [*Ch'un-ch'iu*], *with the Tso Chuen* (London, 1872). p. 184 (text), p. 186 (translation). This is part of the story of the wanderings of Chung-er, the future Duke Wen of Chin. Legge translates: "Travelling through Wei, Duke Wǎn treated him discourteously; and as he was leaving it by Woo-luh, he was reduced to beg food of a countryman, who gave him a clod of earth [*k'uai*]. The prince was angry, and wished to scourge him with his whip, but Tsze-fan [Hoo Yen] said, 'It is Heaven's gift [a gift of the soil; a happy omen].' On this he bowed his head to the earth, received the clod, and took it with him in his carriage."

26 *Chuang-tzu*, 1:10b, 3:4b–5a, 3:9b; Legge, *The Writings of Kwang-zze*, 1:177, 242, 249; Wilhelm, *Dschuang Dsi*, pp. 11, 48; Fung, *Chuang Tzǔ*, pp. 43, 116, 122. I believe that there are three more instances of this expression in the *Chuang-tzu* but with *k'uai* changed to another character; see the following note.

27 For the opinions of various commentators on the meaning of this expression see Liu Wen-tien, *Chuang-tzu Pu-cheng* (Shanghai, 1947), 1B:2b. The explanation that *ta k'uai* means "Earth" is clearly not adequate to the contexts; most of the others could be taken as equating it with *Tao*, though none says so definitely.

I strongly suspect that *ta k'uai* in an altered form also occurs three times in *Chuang-tzu*, 8:13b. Here the expression is *ta wei* 大隗 . The alteration of the character would involve changing the *t'u* 土, which means "earth," of *k'uai*, to the *fou* 阜, meaning "earthen mound," of *wei*. The T'ang dynasty commentator Ch'eng Hsüan-ying explained *ta wei* as an epithet of "the great *Tao*," and Lu Te-ming of the same dynasty gave "great *Tao*" as one of the meanings assigned to it (Liu, *Chuang-tzu Pu-cheng*, 8B:6b). Some translators have considered *ta wei* to be the name of an individual, but several interpret it as standing for *Tao*. Legge (*The Writings of Kwang-zze*, 2:96, n. 1) transliterates the characters as "Tâ-kwei" and writes: "The whole paragraph is parabolic or allegorical; and Tâ-kwei is probably a personification of the Great Tâo itself, though no meaning of the character kwei can be adduced to justify this interpretation." Giles, *Chuang Tzǔ*, p. 316, simply translates *ta wei* as "Tao." Wilhelm, *Dschuang Dsi*, p. 242, n. 5, says that it is an "allegorische Bezeichnung für den SINN"; SINN is Wilhelm's standard translation for *Tao*. This whole problem can best be resolved, I believe, by the hypothesis that *ta wei* is an altered form of *ta k'uai*.

cannot mean what they seem to, so that some go so far as to interpret them as "God" or Heaven." I believe, nevertheless, that these characters mean exactly what they say, and that if we do not understand them in their literal sense we miss something that is very important indeed.

We find the term k'uai, "clod," elsewhere in the Chuang-tzu. One passage appears to quote Shen Tao as saying, "A clod of earth (k'uai) does not err with regard to the Tao."[28] " 夫 塊 不 失 道 ." Another relates the manner in which Lieh-tzu attained to Taoist enlightenment. "He had nothing to do with what went on in the world. He discarded everything artificial and reverted to primitivity. Like a clod (k'uai) he stood alone, self-contained amid the confusion of the world, holding fast to the One to the end."[29]

If an early Taoist could have read "Thanatopsis," one can well imagine that he would have demurred at the reference to "the sluggish clod." Is not the earth composed of clods, and are they not the ultimate source from which comes life, both vegetable and animal? Sluggish, indeed! It is the very quicksilver stuff of which all things are made. What is the Tao itself but a clod of unimaginable proportions?

By choosing this striking name for the universe, the Taoists threw into strong relief their view of the nature of reality — a conception that stands in sharp contrast to the Platonic view. For Plato, true reality does not lie in the world of things — of clods. This is very clear in The Republic, when he describes the proper way to study astronomy:

And will not a true astronomer . . . think that heaven and the things in heaven are framed by the Creator of them in the most perfect manner? But he will never imagine that the proportions of night and day, or of both to the month, or of the month to the year, or of the stars to these and to one another, and any other things that are material and visible can also be eternal and subject to no deviation — that would be absurd; and it is equally absurd to take so much pains in investigating their exact truth.

I quite agree, though I never thought of this before.

Then, I said, in astronomy, as in geometry, we should employ problems, and let the heavens alone if we would approach the subject in the right way and so make the natural gift of reason to be of any real use.[30]

This is one view of reality, a view that has held sway over a large part of mankind. It holds that the apparent, gross, visible, tangible things of

[28] Chuang-tzu, 10:18a; Legge, The Writings of Kwang-zze, 2:225. I do not agree with Legge's translation of this passage.

[29] Chuang-tzu, 3:19a; Fung, Chuang Tzŭ, pp. 140–141; Legge, The Writings of Kwang-zze, 1:265–266.

[30] Plato, The Republic [Stephanus 530]; Jowett, 1:789–790.

the world are inferior if not contemptible. However beautiful the cup of a flower may seem, it is only an inadequate attempt to imitate a perfect circle. This attitude harmonizes with the view that "beyond this vale of tears, there is a life above," in which the flaws and limitations of this imperfect world will be transcended. It forbids acceptance of nature, and enjoins the struggle against nature. It brands contentment as sin, and lays upon men the never-ending obligation to *know*, to scorn mere opinion, to seek at the center of the universe that final solution to all mysteries that must be there if we could only find it.

The Taoist view is very different. If one could win through to the very center of the universe, and enter the holy of holies, he would find there only a simple clod: utterly simple, because it is essentially like the clod that lies here at my feet; and utterly mysterious because, like everything else, it can never be understood in an absolute sense at all. Nothing can be understood absolutely. Man's mind is not a machine constructed for the purpose of understanding everything; neither is it a bit of the special essence of the universe implanted by special grace in human beings. What we call man's mind is rather a complex of functions, akin to the complex we call "man's digestion." All digestion is good, because insofar as there is digestion at all it solves a human problem. Some digestion is better than other digestion, but there is no perfect digestion and no absolute standard by which to measure it. Similarly, all thought is good insofar as it solves a human problem. Some thought may be better than other thought, but there is no perfect thought and no standard of absolute truth. Thus the opinion of every man is worthy of consideration, and no one is entitled to suppose that his own view must be accepted without question.

This curious Taoist term for the universe has naturally caught the fancy of poets, and been much used by them.[31] A similar attitude is perhaps found in the West most often among poets, who more than the rest of us find excitement in the seemingly trivial, and scorn the pompous. But in China something of this attitude has been found in all who have been touched by Taoism.

Let others be awed by the lofty remoteness of absolute knowledge, and spend their lives in pursuit of it like quixotic knights seeking the Grail;

---

[31] See quotations from T'ao Ch'ien, Li Po, Po Chu-i, and others in *P'ei-wen Yün-fu* (1711), 70:169a. In the works of Li Po, my colleague Professor T. H. Tsien has kindly furnished me with the following references: *Fen-lei Pu-chu Li T'ai-po Shih* 分類補注李太白詩 (*SPTK* ed.), 3:32a, 11:26a, 15:11a, 28:9a.

the Taoist does not believe in it. Let others honor the universe by endowing it with human qualities, calling it "infinite mind" or "absolute reason." The Taoist, with an apparent simplicity that is wholly deceptive, with the approach to the ridiculous that always characterizes the sublime, calls it The Great Clod.

Some Legal Instruments of Ancient China: The *Ming* and the *Meng*

W. A. C. H. DOBSON

MENCIUS protested that the sovereignty exercised by the Paramount Princes was not legitimate; it was merely "borrowed."[1] Throughout the Chou Dynasty, not only in the minds of Confucian moralists but in society at large, legitimacy meant enjoying religious sanction. "Legitimate" political power derived from Heaven. It was Heaven which, through the bestowal of its *ming* 命 (Heaven's charge) invested its regent on earth, the Son of Heaven, with authority to govern "all under Heaven." This authority he exercised directly in the Royal Domain and by delegation to vassals and liegemen in the "states of the four quarters." Delegation was made in the form of *wang ming* 王命 (the king's charges). The Feudatories, in turn, by the issuing of their own charges, *kung ming* 公命 , exercised or delegated authority within their own domains. Throughout the Chou feudal pyramid, from top to bottom, the legal instrument of such authority was the *ming*. The *ming* was the symbol of authority legitimately exercised.

But during the age of the Paramountcy (eighth to sixth centuries B.C.), real authority as opposed to legitimate political power lay not with the Son of Heaven but with the Paramount Princes. This was the "borrowed" sovereignty of which Mencius spoke. Despite this the religious proprieties of legitimacy were still sufficiently strong to prevent the Princes from exercising their sovereignty by the issuing of *ming*. To have done so would have been

---

[1] See the section "The Paramount Princes" in W. A. C. H. Dobson, *Mencius: A New Translation Arranged and Annotated for the General Reader* (University of Toronto Press, 1964), p. 166. The relevant passage in the *Mencius* cited here is in 6:57.

impious, a challenge not merely to the secular power, which in fact if not in form they did challenge, but to the spiritual powers, which neither in fact nor in form were they prepared to challenge. Instead, they used the *meng* 盟 (the blood-oath) as their instrument of authority. The exploitation of this device by the Paramount Princes, and later by other usurpers of power, throws interesting light on constitutional theory and practice in the Chou dynasty.*

The *meng* like the *ming* enjoyed religious sanction. It was an instrument in which the gods could, with propriety, be invoked and involved. It provided a "legal" form, ritually proper, with which real sovereignty might in fact be exercised without recourse to the *ming* by which alone legitimate authority could properly be exercised. By the *ming*, "legal" authority was exercised between superior and inferior. By the *meng*, two parties "legally" bound themselves to an agreed course of action. The *meng* did not contravene the *ming*. The *meng* therefore as the effective instrument of the Paramountcy enabled the Paramount Princes, as "Lords of the *Meng*" (盟主) to exercise *de facto* sovereignty without violating the rites and forms of religiously sanctioned and therefore *de jure* sovereignty.

The feudal "charge" was the basis of tenure both of property and of social and hierarchical standing. But it was not only a title to property or a patent of rank. It was also an expression of the ruler's wishes — moral admonitions and the like. A charge therefore had, in several senses, what we should call the force of law. Such charges were issued in writing, inscribed on sacral vessels, and preserved in the ancestral temples. In this they were, as it were, "registered" in Heaven, and maintained on earth as records for posterity.

---

* [*Editor's note*: The reader who is interested in previous studies of the *meng* may consult such works as Chang Hsin-ch'eng 張 心 澂 *Ch'un-ch'iu kuo-chi kung-fa* 春 秋 國 際 公 法 (Peking, 1924), 360 pp.; Hsü Ch'uan-pao 徐 傳 保, *Hsien-Ch'in kuo-chi-fa chih i-chi* 先 秦 國 際 法 之 遺 跡 (Shanghai: Chung-kuo k'e-hsüeh kung-ssu 中 國 科 學 公 司, 1931), 658 pp. (source material); Ch'en Ku-yüan 陳 顧 遠, *Chung-kuo kuo-chi-fa su-yüan* 中 國 國 際 法 溯 源 (Shanghai: The Commerical Press, 1934), 333 pp. (see particularly pp. 218–261, 331–333); and Hung Chün-p'ei 洪 鈞 培, *Ch'un-ch'iu kuo-chi kung-fa* 春 秋 國 際 公 法 (Shanghai: Chung-hua shu-chu 中 華 書 局, 1937, 1939), 280 pp. See also Shih Chao-ying 時 昭 瀛, "Ch'un-ch'iu shih-tai ti t'iao-yüeh" 春 秋 時 代 的 條 約, *She-hui k'e-hsüeh chi-k'an* 社 會 科 學 季 刊 11:1 (March 1931), 20–37. For a short study in English, we may mention Roswell Britton, "Chinese Interstate Intercourse before 700 B.C.," *American Journal of International Law*, 29 (1935), 626–628. Richard L. Walker, *The Multi-State System of Ancient China* (Hamden, Conn.: The Shoe String Press, 1953), pp. 82–95, has a brief discussion of the *meng*. For more information on relevant materials see his note 2 in chap. vi, pp. 129–132.]

When the Feudal Lords banded themselves in the Paramountcy and submitted litigious matters concerned with their tenure, succession, and status to the arbitration of the Paramount Prince, his decisions (which, if appeal had been made to their feudal overlord the Son of Heaven, would have been delivered in the form of charges) were incorporated into the text of a document issued under the authority of a *meng*. Such documents were preserved in the *Meng-fu* 盟府 , an archive maintained for that purpose.

The student of Chou institutions has at his disposal a number of *ming* documents, thanks to their preservation on bronze sacral vessels, many of which have been recovered. They constitute a very rich, if as yet but poorly exploited, corpus of source documents (elsewhere[2] I have transcribed and translated a selection of them). For the *meng* however, the student is dependent on fragments cited in historical documents. For this the *Tso Chuan* is the principal source. The *Tso Chuan* records some two hundred occasions on which a *meng* was enacted; and, scattered throughout the narrative, there is a great deal of incidental information about the *meng*, its rites, and its uses. In this article I propose to describe the *meng* rite, its components, and the uses to which it was put, from the evidence afforded by *Tso Chuan*.[3]

The *Meng* Rites

The rites of the *meng* in their developed form as practiced by the Paramount Princes consisted in drawing up the terms of agreement in a document, *tsai-shu* 載書 ; slaying a sacrificial animal, *shenq* 牲 ; smearing the lips of the contracting parties with the animal's blood, *sha* 歃 ; attaching the document to the animal and then burying it, *k'eng* 坑 . The document consisted of a preamble naming the participants, *shou* 首 ; the text outlining the terms, *yen* 言 ; and an oath, *shih* 誓, called down on any of the parties if they should abrogate the *meng*, *yü meng* 渝盟 . To this, the gods and spirits, *ming-shen* 明神, were called upon as witnesses. Gifts were offered to the gods. Copies of the *tsai-shu* were then ratified and exchanged, *li meng* 涖盟 , and deposited

---

2 See W. A. C. .H. Dobson, *Early Archaic Chinese* (University of Toronto Press, 1962), particularly chap. 8, "Texts."

3 References in this article to the *Tso chuan* are to the text and paragraph numbering used in the Harvard-Yenching Institute Sinological Index Series, Suppl. no. 11, *Combined Concordances to Ch'un-Ch'iu, Kung-yang, Ku-liang and Tso-chuan* (Peking, 1937). Excerpts cited are from a new translation of the *Tso chuan*, in preparation, which I hope to publish shortly. *Tso chuan* references that are sufficiently brief are interpolated in the text.

in an archive (*meng-fu*). Careful note was taken of the exact day and place of swearing. In some cases the terms were publicly proclaimed in the streets.

But a simpler and presumably earlier form of the rite was performed by two individuals swearing a declaration of intent and smearing their lips with blood drawn from one of them. This covenant, sealed with blood shared, derives, one may suppose, from a blood-brother pact, binding otherwise unrelated parties in the solemn obligations of kinship. Hints of such an origin are seen in the ritual obligations incurred when the *meng* was used to seal pacts of friendship between states. In the first place, if one of the signatories died, his personal name rather than his posthumous name was used in the notification of his death to the other, as of one bound by kinship.[4] In the second place, a *meng* lapsed on the death of one of the principals and had to be resworn, *hsin* 尋 , by his successor, thus stressing the essentially personal nature of the obligation entered into.[5]

What appears to have happened is that the ceremonial blood-pact between two individuals was extended to a pact between two Feudal Lords as a ritual for sealing bilateral agreements between them and then adapted in the "joint blood-pact," *t'ung-meng* 同 盟 , as a device by which the Feudal Lords in confederacy bound themselves to recognize the authority of the Paramount Prince — the rites of the *meng* in the process becoming increasingly complex as this developed.

The blood-smearing was an indispensable feature of the rite. Two occasions are recorded when the blood-smearing was omitted. The first was the famous *meng* sworn at K'uei-ch'iu in 650 B.C. (Hsi IX, 4). For the omission, our authority is the *Mencius*, 6:70 (see n. 1). Apropos of this, Mencius goes on to observe that "the Feudal Lords contravene every article of this agreement." The second was at the reswearing of a *meng* in 540 B.C. (Chao I, 2). On this occasion the Ch'u delegate requested that "a sacrificial animal might be used, the old agreement read, and simply attached to the animal," that is, without shedding its blood and smearing the lips. This is only one of a number of charges of bad faith leveled at the Ch'u delegation in this passage.

The animal used was a red bull (Hsiang x, *fu* iii). Among the niceties observed at the slaying was the duty of "holding the bull's ear." This was a matter of precedence.[6] Two occasions, however, are described in which human blood was used. In the one case, a daughter of the Chang Family

---

[4] See Yin xi, *fu* iv; Chao iii, 1; Chao xxxi, 3, etc.

[5] See Huan xiv, 3; xvii, 2; Hsiang vii, 7, etc.

[6] Ting viii, 10, and Ai xvii, *fu* vii.

"cut her arm and (with her blood) swore the Duke to a blood-oath" (Chuang xxxii, 5); and in the other, "the King made an incision over Tzu-ch'i's heart and with it (i.e. Tzu-ch'i's blood) took the blood-oath with the men of Wei" (Ting iv, 16).

The use of human blood provides further reason for supposing the *meng* to have been in origin a blood-brother pact. The significance of the blood-smearing evidently had to do with the commingling of the blood of the contracting parties in a ritual kinship pact, rather than with the shedding of blood as an act of propitiation to the gods. When a party to an oath died, and the agreement was renewed, the rite used was called *hsin* 尋 (rewarming). The blood, at death, one must suppose, had "grown cold" and needed to be "rewarmed." An improper demand by a Duke of Wu to renew a treaty with Lu during the lifetime of the Duke of Lu who swore to the original treaty is met with the objection, "If an oath needs to be renewed (lit. 'rewarmed') it can equally *han* 寒 'grow cold' (i.e. be repudiated)" and Lu refused to reswear (Ai xii, 3).

As previously mentioned, the document, *tsai-shu*, consisted of a preamble, *meng-shou* 盟首 ; the text of the covenant, *yen*; an oath, *shih*; and an invocation to the gods and spirits, *ming-shen*, to witness it.

In one case, the *tsai-shu* was "borne on the back" (Ai viii, 2) to the rendezvous of the ceremony, and judging from the length of some of the agreements, the document must in such cases have been both heavy and bulky. The preparation of this document was in the hands of the *chu* 祝 (family priest), the *t'ai-shih* 太史 (recorder), or the *hsiang* 相 (master of ceremonies) who attended to the rites.[7] The ritual acceptability of those involved in the carrying out of the rites was evidently important. So was regard for the magical property of the instruments used. On one occasion, the draft of a document drawn up but not used was ceremonially burned (Hsiang x, 8) and on another, sunk in the river (Ting xiii, 7). Such objects were "potent."

In the preamble, *meng-shou*, the contracting parties were named (Hsiang xxiii, 11). This gave rise to delicate problems of precedence in the order in which the names were recorded (Ch'eng iii, 15). In citing a precedent for a *meng* sworn by members of the Chou house, the rubric is given "those not bearing the family surname come last" (Yin xi, 1). In a dispute over precedence in 505 b.c. a previous document of 631 b.c. is cited which "can still be seen in the Chou archives" as a precedent for the order to be followed

---

[7] For *chu*, *t'ai-shih*, and *hsiang*, respectively, see Ai xxvi, *fu* ii; Chao i, *fu* vi, and Hsiang xxiii, 11; and Ai xvii, *fu* vii, and Ting ix, 3.

in recording the names of the participants (Ting IV, 2). A curious case occurs where a successor to the Headship of a Family is sworn, in which his predecessor is formally repudiated in a formula for which several previous examples are cited (Hsiang XXIII, 11).

Once written the text was sacrosanct. "A *meng* is an expression of good faith all round, and so it is determined upon in the mind, it is proffered up with gifts of jade and silk, the parties are bound by its terms and by the gods and spirits it is enforced, . . . once sworn, it cannot be altered" (Ai XII, 3). At the treaty of Hsi in 563 B.C. a request was made for an emendation of the text. "In this *meng* are binding words, exhibited before the gods and spirits," replies an objector; "if an amendment were possible, then the Major Powers could repudiate it" (Hsiang IX, 5). A text could be altered only if some ritual breach had occurred in the carrying out of the ceremony, thus nullifying the original, as happened in 623 B.C. (Wen III, 6).

The preamble and the main text were followed by the curse. The formula for the curse seems to have been a conventional one. Most citations in the *Tso* include one or more of the phrases given in the following curse used in the *meng* of 631 B.C.

> Should anyone abrogate this agreement, may the Gods and Spirits strike him dead, bring about the downfall of his peoples so that (his heirs) might not enjoy the government of the State. Down to the fourth generation, may none, old or young, survive.[8]

There is some reason to suppose that the curse was recited aloud.

> Yen-tzu looking up to Heaven sighed and said; "If I do not adhere to those loyal to the Lord of the Altars (i.e. to the ruler) then let it be as God on High directs." He then smeared his lips with the blood. (Hsiang XXV, 2)

In Ting VI, *fu* iii, we are told that the curse was proclaimed at "the Crossroads of the Five Fathers." This explains, I think, the phrase in Hsiang IX, 5, and Ting X, 3: *Yu ju tz'u meng* 有 如 此 盟 (Let it be as this *meng* directs). Underlying the curse is the thought expressed in Ai VI, 6, "It were better to die than to abrogate a *meng* in order to escape an enemy."

The deities who were thus adjured were the *ming-shen* — generic term for gods and spirits. In most citations in the *Tso* they are simply called *ming-shen*. But in the *meng* of 561 B.C. the gods and spirits are enumerated in detail.

> Should any depart from these instructions, may the Guardians of Sincere Affirmations and Sworn Agreements (two Heavenly functionaries), (the deities of) famous hills and

---

8 Hsi XXVIII, 5. See also Huan I, 5; Hsi XXVIII, 12; Ch'eng XII, 2; and Hsiang IX, 5.

streams, all who are gods, all to whom sacrifice is made, (the Spirits of the) Former Kings, of the Feudal Lords, of the ancestors of the seven clans and twelve city-state (rulers); (may these), the Gods and Spirits (i.e. *ming-shen*) strike him dead. (Hsiang xi, 5)

In this listing, almost the entire hierarchy of Heaven is invoked, with perhaps one significant exception to which we will return later. "*Meng*," according to a Lu statesman are "by gods and spirits enforced" (Ai xii, 3). To violate a *meng* is to incur the displeasure of the gods. To a prince who contemplated doing so, the advice is given: "To revoke a *meng* is inauspicious, to deceive a Major State is improper. It means certain defeat. Neither Gods nor men will assist you, — how could you win?" (Ch'eng i, 6). When the forces of the Paramountcy in the interests of the state of Lu, attacked the state of Ch'i in 554 b.c., a minister of Lu prayed to the Gods as follows:

Huan (i.e. Duke Ling of Ch'i), relying on the natural defenses of his State and trusting to his numerical strength, has set aside his old friendships (with other states) and repudiated the *meng* he has sworn (with them). Piao, who is your servent, is about to lead the forces of the Feudal Lords to punish him, while I, your servant, will support Piao If this expedition enjoys a successful outcome, may there be no impiety to the Gods. I will not presume to cross the river a second time. May you, the gods (of this river) adjudicate in this. (Hsiang xviii, 4)

At this, he dropped his offering to the gods — two sets of jades bound with red silk — into the river and crossed to the attack. In this instance, a party who had violated a *meng* was to be punished, but the gods are invoked before doing so, as a sort of disclaimer to any act of impiety.

As has been observed, careful note was made of the precise location at which a *meng* was sworn and of the day on which this took place. The location provided a means of identification — a sort of "short title"; thus when in the *Tso* reference is made to a particular *meng* it is described as "the *meng* of Ch'ing-ch'iu," "the *meng* of Ch'ien-t'u," etc. (Hsüan xiii, 2; Ting iv, 2). It is rare that a *meng* ceremony took place twice at the same location. Though we are not told so directly, the location chosen was evidently significant. There are several reasons for thinking this to be so. We find that the place-names given in the *Ch'un-ch'iu* for the sites of *meng* sworn between the states are rarely identifiable. Legge has frequently to observe "the exact location is obscure."[9] The remoteness or unfamiliarity of these place-names is also suggested by the variants for the characters used for them which occur in the

---

[9] See, for example, the notes on Ch'eng i, 5; xvii, 3; xviii, 15; Hsiang xv, 1; and Chao xi, 7, in James Legge, *The Chinese Classics*, vol. 5: *The Ch'un Ts'ew with the Tso Chuen* (2d ed., Hong Kong, 1960).

Ch'un-ch'iu, the *Tso*, and the *Kung-yang* and *Ku-liang* commentaries. There can be as many as three variants, while two are common.[10] This is not so when well-known towns, cities, and rivers are mentioned. In the place-names themselves we find words for "pool," "spring," "gulley," "valley," "mound," "marsh," "bridge," "river," but never (except in the circumstances to be described later) the names of familiar cities or towns. One gets the impression that some remote location was chosen in neutral ground, beyond the areas of jurisdiction of "the Altars of the Soil and Crops." This is borne out in the enumeration of the gods called upon to witness the swearing, in the *meng* previously referred to. The tutelary deities of the city are not mentioned. At a *meng* sworn between Lu and Ch'i at which Confucius acted as *hsiang* 相 , it was proposed to follow the rite with an entertainment. Confucius objected to this entertainment, saying, "Ritual vessels are not taken out of cities, musical instruments are not compatible with wild places" (Ting x, 3). In this instance evidently, the *meng* site was far removed from city, court, and temple, in some "wild place."

The significance of the choice of the site becomes even clearer when a *meng* is imposed under duress. This is called *ch'eng-hsia chih meng* 城下之盟 (*meng* imposed beneath the city wall). Such were considered humiliating in the extreme and tantamount to the most abject form of surrender. They constituted a denial for the vanquished of his "Lordship of the Altars of the Soil and Crops." After a protracted siege, an offer of terms to the besieged evokes the comment: "In this city of ours we are reduced to eating each other's children and using their bones for fuel, but even so, we would not consent to having a '*meng* imposed beneath the city-wall,' even if it meant the destruction of our entire state. Withdraw from the city thirty *li* and we will await your instructions" (Hsüan xv, 2). A peace-treaty was then sworn thirty *li* away. There are several instances recorded of *ch'eng-hsia chih meng* being imposed (Huan xii, *fu* i; Wen xv, 7). Another way of imposing a *meng* under duress is described in the words *ju meng* "to enter the city (and *there*) swear a *meng*." Like the *ch'eng-hsia chih meng* this similarly is a symbol of the surrender of local autonomy (Hsüan xii, 2, etc.). Thus a distinction was made between a *meng* sworn freely as between equals (*ch'i meng* 齊盟) and a *meng* sworn under duress (*yao meng* 要盟). The latter, sworn within the city, or beneath its walls, was a sign of submission. The former, sworn in neutral ground beyond the area of the participants' jurisdiction, was "freely" entered into.

---

10 See, for example, Wen xvi, 3; Chao xi, 6.

There is, however, another form of *meng*, the "private *meng*" (*szu meng* 私 盟) sworn between individuals, or members of the same clan, or ministers within the same state. Such oaths were family compacts, sworn between its members usually as compacts to place an heir on the throne, to recognize the "head of a family," to restore a minister to good standing, and the like. The place at which such oaths were sworn was in the Grand Temple (太 宮) or in a family temple, such as that of the Ch'en family or the Kung-sun Tuan family.[11]

The choice of location seems clearly to be (1) *neutral ground* for interstate relations freely negotiated, (2) *home ground* where the *meng* is made under duress and constitutes "a shame to the Altars," and (3) the *family temple*, where the pact is a matter of family or dynastic concern and thus a matter for the Spirits of the Ancestors.

At the *meng* between Lu and Ch'i at which Confucius acted as master of ceremonies, the Ch'i delegation brought armed soldiers. The presence of prisoners-of-war and of arms, Confucius protested, was improper at a *meng*: "As far as the gods are concerned, weapons are inauspicious, as far as virtue is concerned, they are contrary to justice, as far as men are concerned, they are a breach of ritual" (Ting x, 3). The impropriety of the presence of weapons at such rites is mentioned elsewhere. *Kung-yang* says that the *meng* sworn between Lu and Ch'i in 680 B.C. was made under the threat of a drawn sword, and observes that oaths sworn in these circumstances were not binding (Chuang xiii, 4). At the *meng* of 545 B.C. objection is taken to the "concealed weapons" of the Ch'u delegation (Hsiang xxvii, 5). This is not only a question of an implied threat or of duress, but of the "illomened" nature of weapons themselves, which, when not in use accompanied by the appropriate rites, were stored in the temples as "potent" objects. Punctilio in the rite and the observances of the tabus was an intrinsic part of the efficacy of the *meng* rite.

A *k'uei-meng* 匱 盟 was a *meng* at which some ritual aspect in its carrying out was deficient (Ch'eng ii, 10). On such occasions the "gods do not descend" and so the agreement could be held to be not binding. "The gods and spirits do not require adherence to an enforced *meng*. It is quite permissible to repudiate it" (Hsiang ix, 6).

Other ritual lapses mentioned are "to appear absent-minded while smearing the blood" (Yin vii, *fu* i); "to be remiss in ritual" (Wen iii, 6) (here given as the reason for swearing the *meng* anew); and "thrusting the

---

11 Hsüan iii, 9; Ch'eng xiii, *fu* i; Hsiang xxv, 2; xxx, 7; Ai xiv, 3; Chao i, *fu* vi.

other party's arm up to the elbow in the blood" when the rite required that the fingers only be dipped in the blood (Ting VIII, 10). It was improper to swear a *meng* with a perjured party. This is given as a reason for refusing to swear (Chao XXV, 8), and in Hsi VII, 4, the statement occurs: "In meetings of the Feudal Lords, the acts of virtue set forth, the punishments meted out the rites observed and the just decisions taken, are recorded in every State. When in these records standing is seen to have been accorded to one guilty of a crime, the *meng* will be disregarded."[12]

In summary, the *meng*, evidently a blood-brother pact in origin, became by extension a ritual form for binding Feudal Lords in unilateral agreements. From this it became the "joint-pact," the instrument by which the Feudal Lords allied themselves in the Paramountcy, and through which the Paramount Prince asserted his supremacy over them. In all forms the punctilio of a sacred rite was maintained, and the *meng* never lost its religious force and sanctions. Though more than two hundred instances of the *meng* rite being performed are described in the *Tso Chuan*, the religoius beliefs which underlie it are never questioned.

The Uses of the *Meng*

Perhaps the simplest, and possibly the earliest, use to which the blood-oath was put was the binding of a man by a woman to a recognition of any possible offspring which might result from an extramarital love affair. The *Tso* describes two such undertakings. In the first, a Duke of Lu, from a tower he had built, observed in the grounds of a house which it overlooked, the daughter of the house. He "followed her. She bolted the door against him, but he spoke of promising to make her his wife, whereupon she cut her arm (and with the blood) swore the Duke to an oath" (Chuang XXXII, 5). The Duke subsequently recognized the son which resulted from this liaison. In the second, "the daughter of a man of Ch'uan-ch'iu . . . ran after Tzu-hsi, followed by her companions. They (the daughter and Tzu-hsi) swore a *meng* at the Altar of Ch'ing-she. It said, 'If we have children, you will not abandon them,'" (Chao XI, *fu* i). Tzu-hsi duly recognized their offspring. In such cases, the kinship obligation inherent in the blood-oath is, I think, quite clear.

The blood-oath was used between a prince and a subject, particularly where a subject had rebelled and the prince wished to restore him to his

---

[12] The stigma of having a criminal ancestor "whose name is in the records of the states" is described in Wen XV, 3.

former allegiance. Thus a rebel general in Ch'i reverted to his former allegiance to the Marquis of Ch'i under the guarantee of a *meng* (Ch'eng XVII, *fu* iii), and the Duke of Wei attempted, by the offer of a *meng*, to restore a minister to allegiance, but without success (Hsiang XIV, 4).

Of a slightly different kind, is the compact sworn "of mutual good faith" by the princes of Cheng, generation by generation, with a merchant family in the state. The terms of this compact were as follows: "Your family will never rebel against us, and we, for our part, will never forcibly intervene in your business transactions. There will be no requests for gifts, or enforced exactions from you. You shall enjoy the profits of your trade and the possession of your valuables, without our taking cognizance of them" (Chao XVI, *fu* iii).

The blood-oath was fairly frequently used in the succession squabbles that arose on the death of a Feudal Lord. His sons, whether by lawful wives or by concubines, became the candidates of rival factions as successors to the throne. An aspirant to the throne might secure the allegiance of a powerful minister or of a faction by entering into a *meng* compact with them (Chuang XIV, *fu* i; Ch'eng X 3), or a powerful faction might secure the assistance of a minister for their candidate by swearing a *meng* with him (Huan XI, 6; Hsüan III, 9). The Hua family in Sung even succeeded in securing the succession for their nominee by swearing the reigning duke in a *meng* compact (Chao XX, *fu* iii).

The purpose of such oaths is clear from the following, sworn by a pretender to the throne of Wei, "If you can bring about my return to the State and my securing its government, you shall have the cap and carriage of the rank of a Great Officer and you will not be brought to account for the three capital offenses you have committed" (Ai XV, *fu* iii).

As will be seen, such agreements and undertakings, whether between parties to an irregular love affair, between a pretender and his patrons, or between a prince and a merchant, constituted contracts to engage in courses of action for which the legal precedents and authorities did not provide.

Four occasions are described in the *Tso*, when a *meng* ceremony was faked as evidence that treachery was contemplated. In the first case, a Crown Prince of Sung, hearing that a friend of his from Ch'u was passing through Sung, asked and received permission to go out and entertain his friend. A eunuch, not friendlily disposed to the Prince, asked permission of the Duke to follow him. The eunuch took with him "a sacrificial animal to use for the blood-smearing, and the document to be attached to it" and returned, offering them as proof that the Prince was plotting with the Ch'u envoy to rebel. "He is my son," said the Duke. "What does he want?" "He wants your speedy death," replied the eunuch. The Duke went out to see for himself and found the prearranged evidence for the *meng* allegedly sworn. The Prince was imprisoned, and there committed suicide. Afterwards the fraud was discovered (Hsiang xxvi, 6). In the second case, which happened ten years later, the Master of the Eunuchs in Sung, in collusion with a member of the Hua family, "framed" another member of the Hua family in a similar fashion (Chao vi, 5). In the third case, the Ch'in army, about to invest a city, during the night "dug a pit, put blood therein and added a document, and with this as 'proof' falsely alleged that Tzu-yi and Tzu-pien (allies of the beleaguered city) had sworn a blood-oath with them." This was taken to mean that Tzu-yi and Tzu-pien had gone over to the enemy, and so the city surrendered (Hsi xxv, 4). In the fourth case, a scheming minister wishing to implicate the Duke of Ts'ai "dug a pit, placed blood and a document in it, then falsely alleged that the Duke had covenanted with his two exiled brothers" in an attempt to incite the state against the Duke (Chao xiii, 3).

During the period of the oligarchies in the city-states, when power had passed from the city-state rulers to coalitions of the heads of powerful families, the heads of families began to use the *meng* to secure agreements among themselves. Thus Shu-sun Pao was established as head of the family by Chi-sun of Lu as the result of a *meng* (Ch'eng xvi, 15); and Tsang Hsieh was deposed as head of the Tsang family, the *meng* establishing his successor, specifically repudiating him (Hsiang xxiii, 11). In Tsin, Chih-po was sworn in as head of the Chao family at the instigation of Chao-meng and authorized to make the family sacrifices (Ting xiv, *fu* viii). The head of the Po-yu family of Cheng swore a *meng* with the Great Officers to guarantee the security of his family (Hsiang xxix, *fu* viii). In a *meng* sworn between the Ruler of Cheng and six Great Officers, a seventh "forcibly insisted on being included, and made the Grand Recorder include his name, and add the phrase 'the seven officers' " (Chao i, *fu* vi). Finally, when the Three Oligarchs of Lu (the *San Huan*) assumed command of the "Three Armies" they swore a *meng*, the imprecation of which was publicly proclaimed at the "Crossroad of the Five Fathers" (Hsiang xi, 1).

The *meng* thus far described are characterized as *szu meng*, "private compacts," and, particularly in matters of dynastic succession and clan succession, they took place in temples and shrines, presumably as being of concern to the ancestors.

But by far the preponderating number of *meng* recorded in the *Tso chuan* are those contracted between states. The most common are the friendship pacts, the battle alliances, pacts on the resumption of peace after battle, and the like negotiated between two rulers of two city-states. Some were of long standing. The blood-oath sworn between the Dukes of Lu and the Jung peoples was sworn by Duke Hui, renewed by his successor Duke Yin and by his successor Duke Huan in token of the hereditary friendship that existed between the state of Lu and the Jung (Yin II, 1 and 4; Huan II, 8). *Ku-liang* is the authority for the statement that the first occasion in which three states took part in a *meng* was in 714 B.C., which he calls a *ts'an meng* 參 盟 (tripartite agreement) (see Yin VIII, 6). It was *meng* of this kind that were sworn in "neutral ground," recorded in the state annals, and of which copies were kept in the state archives.

From 714 to 678 B.C., the "tripartite pact" gradually extended to larger coalitions of the Shantung Peninsular States in which the state of Ch'i played a leading role. The first "joint-pact" (同 盟) took place in 677 B.C. with Duke Huan of Ch'i presiding (Chuang XVI, 4). From this must date the beginning of the Paramountcy, for all the states at this meeting acknowledged the supremacy of Ch'i. At first the Paramountcy embraced only the Northeastern States, but in 655 B.C. the Paramount Princes engaged in a *meng* with the powerful state of Ch'u in the south (Hsi IV, 4), which, as with Ch'i earlier, had itself drawn together a number of states in the Yang-tzu valley into an alliance. The first direct affront by the Paramount Powers to the Son of Heaven came in 654 B.C. when they swore a *meng* with a prince of the royal house who aspired to succeed to the Chou throne contrary to the wishes of the king his father (Hsi V, 5). The prince was confirmed in a *meng* sworn by the Paramountcy in 651 B.C. (Hsi VIII, 1), and ascended the Chou throne as King Hsiang (650–618 B.C.). The king of Chou thus became the puppet of the Paramount Powers.

The hapless King Hsiang had proffered a *ming* to Huan of Ch'i relieving him of the necessity of "descending and doing obeisance" (Hsi IX, 4). Huan of Ch'i's successor in the Paramountcy, Wen of Tsin, secured a *ming* from King Hsiang in 631 B.C. which read, "The King says to his Uncle, with reverence carry out the King's Charge so as to bring peace to the States of the four quarters and expel the King's enemies" (Hsi XXVIII, 5). Thus the forms of legitimacy were extracted from a weak king.

Only Huan of Ch'i and Wen of Tsin obtained such a charge from the Son of Heaven. The convention, among the Warring States philosophers, of referring to "Five Paramount Princes" (*wu po* 五 霸) has little basis in reality. Even attempts to enumerate the five differ. A more realistic view of the Paramountcy, based on recorded instances of having acted as *meng-chu*

盟主 , would begin with the Paramountcy of Huan of Ch'i (from the *meng* of 677 B.C. to the *meng* of 644 B.C.), continue (with a slight interregnum from 640 to 638 B.C. when Sung made an abortive attempt to seize the Para- mountcy) with Wen of Tsin who — 戰而霸 "became Paramount Prince, as the consequence of a single battle" (Hsi XVII, 5). Wen of Tsin's Para- mountcy extended from the *meng* of 631 B.C. to the death of Wen in 627 B.C. Thereafter the Lordship of the Meng was held hereditarily by the state of Tsin until 528 B.C. when — at the *meng* of P'ing-ch'iu — the last meeting of the Paramountcy on any scale was held. The sole challenge to the Lord- ship of Tsin was from the state of Ch'u, which provided the Lordship once, in the Ch'i-Tsin interregnum in 632 B.C. (Hsi XXVII, 6); once, over the meeting of 597 B.C. (Hsüan XI, 2); and spasmodically, towards the decline of Tsin power from 545 B.C. onwards, when Tsin and Ch'u agreed to alternate as the "presider" at the *meng* (Hsiang XXVII, 5).

Thus, from the eighth to the sixth centuries B.C. China was governed, as it were, para-legally. The forms of legitimacy were recognized, but the realities of power were enacted through a legal fiction, the *meng*. This fiction developed from the *meng* as a personal contract, a blood-brother pact, to the *meng* as the instrument by which the "uncle of the King" — the Para- mount Prince — "reverently discharged the King's Charge, so as to bring peace to the States of the four quarters, and drove out all who were disaffected to the King," or in other words, exercised the powers of a sovereign.

This process was not without its effects. The period saw an ever increasing devolution of power. Beginning with the passing of power from the Son of Heaven to the Paramount Prince, power passed from the Feudal Lords themselves to the oligarchs in the city-states. It was the oligarchs, not the princes, who acted as the principals in the *meng* meetings toward the end of the Paramountcy. And finally, from the oligarchs, power passed to the tyrants, as happened when Yang-hu, the dictator of Lu, bound the Duke and the Oligarchy (the *San Huan*) by *meng* in allegiance to himself in 504–503 B.C. (Ting V, *fu* iii; VI, *fu* ii). In all of those transfers of power, the *meng* is the instrument — of the princes, of the oligarchs, and finally of the dictators. Thus, a legal fiction. once established, was turned upon its creators. *Real* power was exercised, without involving the ritual offense of using the ritual instruments of *legitimate* power.

Indexes

中　文　索　引

（先數筆劃，次依筆順、一丨口丶丿フ）

一　畫

（一）

一說，161，162*n*40
一枝花，104
一曰，161，162*n*40
一年漏將盡，123
一統志，182

二　畫

（一）

丁令威，60

（丿）

八歲偷照鏡，70
八公遊戲叢談，215
九江，62
九有，204*n*196
九域，204*n*196
九日，61
"九日"：李白 50，倪瓚 59
"九日宴集醉題郡樓象呈周殷二判官"
　（白居易），62
"九日龍山飲"，46
"九日齊山登高"（杜牧），63–64
"九日讀書山用陶詩露妻暄風息氣清天
　曠明爲韻賦十詩"第一首(元好問)，60
"九日藍田崔氏莊"（杜甫），61
"九日醉吟"（白居易），62
"九日五首"（杜甫），57–59

"九日曲江"（杜甫），61
"九日從宋公戲馬台集送孔令詩"（謝瞻，
　謝靈運），53–54
"九日閒居"，46–47
"九日登山"（李白），50，52

（フ）

又，176，204，205，207

三　畫

（丶）

亡老，201
之：毛詩大傳，詩，志 157，159，釋名，
　詩，志 163，166，天志 157*n*24，164，
　201，209*n*208，志功 164*n*45，切韻，廣
　韻"之部"部 178，178–179*n*92，寺，生，
　止 195–205，207–208，有之，部，時
　183*n*107，190，204*n*195，參看止，寺
之功，164*n*45

（一）

三季，14
三代世表，185
于省吾，170*n*69
土，198，265*n*27
土方，170，172，181 (map)，183*n*106
土地，242
大澤，24
"大宗師"，264
大唐三藏取經詩話，235

285

六　畫

（ 、 ）

江洪，126 (chart 1)
江淹，114, 126 (chart 1)
江州，62
沈約，113
沚（涭），194n157
汝南，45
宅殷，184
安仁，129
安國，112n9
衣，187

（ 一 ）

刑臣，192
寺：說文，詩 160，楊樹達 164，甲骨文 166, 167, 170, 172，圖片 169, 170, 173，金文 176, 177, 190，石鼓文 176, 189–190，陶文 176，楚繒 176，音讀 177–180，地望 179–189，地圖 181，初義 189–195，持(詩) 189, 190, 192–194，待 189, 190，侍 190–192，時 194，字源 195–208，射志 203–204，有之 204，手，足 205，峙 206, 207，參看寺人，詩，邿，志
寺人："巷伯" 154, 191, 192n48，"車鄰" 190，左傳 190，穀梁 190，經典釋文，侍人，說苑 191，毛傳，內小臣，高本漢 191–192，詩人 208，參看寺，詩，邿
寺（時）雨，190
寺人披，192
寺季鬲，177
寺季故公殷，177
寺伯鬲，177
寺人孟子，154, 191, 192n147
吉甫，153
老去悲秋強自寬，61
車遲國，231
"西京賦"，119
西梁女國，242
西遊記，229
西遊補，239
西山，129
西山（首陽山），7
西北有浮雲，144

（ 丨 ）

在昔曾遠遊，21
有，199
有之，204
有客常同止，25
有商，204
有夏，204
有苗，204
有周，204
有恨頭還白，62
有易（有扈），204
有任，204
有如此盟，274
有娀，204
成湯，185
成就，131

（ 丨 ）

同盟，272, 281
出，197, 198
出門復入門，56

（ 口 ）

"回中牡丹爲雨所敗" 第二首（李商隱），77
曲江，56, 61, 71
曲阜，183, 184
曲阿，21

（ ノ ）

先，196, 197
先秦，140 (chart 2)
朱公牼鐘，190, 206
朱爲弼，206
朱日光素冰，122
朱自清，166
仲蔚愛窮居，31
仲理（楊倫），24
仲偉，111
任城，180
任城縣，182
任昉，126 (chart 1)
"自喜"（李商隱），73
自笑不能孤九日，59
行止千萬端，14
"行軍九日思長安故園"（岑參），60
行帳適南下，60
竹葉，58

Inscriptions Index　古字索引

1. 止

〜 195, 196, 196n165, 198, 201, 207

〜 196

〜 196

〜 196

〜 196

〜 209n208

〜 196

〜 196, 196n165

〜 196

〜 196, 198

〜 198, 209n208

〜 196

〜 196

2. 出

〜 197

〜 197

3. 止 (之)

〜 195, 196, 196n165, 199

〜 195, 195n163

〜 195

〜 163, 195, 196n165

〜 〜 195

〜 〜 〜 195

〜 196n165

〜 196n165

〜 195

4. 祉 (之,有)

〜 163, 164, 169 (fig. 1), 171 (fig. 2), 172, 190n128, 195, 195n163, 196, 196n165, 197, 197n169, 198, 199, 199n176, 200, 200n176, 201, 203, 204, 204n195, 205, 207

300

English Index

Aaron, 231
Abel-Remusat, 261
Adam's Peak, 202
"Again to the Sung Sisters of Hua-yang Nunnery, Written on a Moonlit Night," 75
Ai, Duke (of Lu), 164. SEE ALSO *Tso chuan*
Altaic, 253
Altar: of the Soil and Crops, 276; location for *meng*, 277; of Ch'ing-she, 278
An-hsi, 56
"An Outing on Hsieh Brook," 27
An-yang, 181 (map), 183, 184, 185, 188, 189. SEE ALSO Yin
Analects. SEE *Lun-yü*
Anhui, 54
Annals of Spring and Autumn, 139, 157, 159, 179, 180, 275, 276
Apollinaire, 80
archery, 203, 206–207n203
Asia, Central, 56, 255
"At Tso's Estate in Lan-t'ien on the Ninth Day," 61
autumn, 31, 46, 48, 50, 53, 55, 56, 58, 59, 61, 63, 76, 97–98, 118, 123
Autumn Festival, 16

"Bamboo Leaves," 58
Bān Jyé-yẃ. SEE Pan Chieh-yü
Bàu Jàu. SEE Pao Chao
"Bearers' Songs," 23, 25
bi. SEE *pi*

Biographies of Good Officials (*Liang li chuan*), 113
Biographies of High-minded Men, 31
"Biography of the Gentlemen of the Five Willows," 27
Blue Maid (Ch'ing-nü), 75
bodhisattva, 226, 233
Bodhisattva Avalokitesvara (Bodhisattva Kuan Yin), 235, 241
Book of Changes (*I Ching*): "empty words" from, 8; Chung Hung's familiarity with, 112, 120; used by author Brooks, 148; explained in *Chuang-tzu*, 157; by Tung Chung-shu, 159; no word *shih* (poetry), 166; *ssu(-jen)*, 192n147; *chih* (blessing) and *yu* (protection) as oracle terms, 200; in rhyme or rhythm, 205
Book of History (*Book of Documents*, *Shu Ching*): *shih* (poetry) in "Yao tien," 152, 155; in "Chin t'eng," 153; explained in *Chuang-tzu*, 157; by Tung Chung-shu, 159; "Preface" to (on location of capital of Yin), 184; on Yin or Shang, 187; King P'an-keng of Shang, 203
Book of Music (*Yüeh*), 157, 159
Book of Poetry (*Shih Ching*): loved by T'ao Ch'ien, 13; "Great Preface" of Mao edition, 16, 117, 157-159, 161, 163, 205; T'ao Ch'ien reference to, 20, 28, 30, 36; proscribed during Burning of the Books, 38; poetry as intention, 135–136, 155–166; to locusts, 137; plantain gatherers

DATE DUE

APR 15 '71			
AUG 11 72			
GAYLORD			PRINTED IN U.S.A.